INTERVIEWING

Principles and Practices

SIXTEENTH EDITION

D0902151

INTERVIEWING

Principles and Practices

SIXTEENTH EDITION

Charles J. Stewart

Purdue University

INTERVIEWING

Some ancillaries, including electronic and print components, may not be available to customers outside the United States.

This book is printed on acid-free paper.

1 2 3 4 5 6 7 8 9 LCR 24 23 22 21

ISBN 978-1-265-75501-0 (bound edition)
MHID 1-265-75501-9 (bound edition)

Cover Image: *ESB Basic/Shutterstock*

mheducation.com/highered

To the memory of William "Bill" Cash, Jr., student,
co-author, and friend

Charles J. Stewart

Charles J. "Charlie" Stewart is the former Margaret Church Distinguished Professor of Communication at Purdue University where he taught from 1961 to 2009. He taught undergraduate courses in interviewing and persuasion and graduate courses in such areas as persuasion and social protest, apologetic rhetoric, and extremist rhetoric on the Internet. He received the Charles B. Murphy Award for Outstanding Undergraduate Teaching from Purdue University and the Donald H. Ecroyd Award for Outstanding Teaching in Higher Education from the National Communication Association. He was a Founding Fellow of the Purdue University Teaching Academy. He has written articles, chapters, and books on interviewing, persuasion, and social movements.

Charlie Stewart has been a consultant with organizations such as the Internal Revenue Service, the American Electric Power Company, Libby Foods, the Indiana University School of Dentistry, and the United Association of Plumbers and Pipefitters. He is currently a Court Appointed Special Advocate (CASA) for children.

BRIEF CONTENTS

Contents

CONTENTS

This sixteenth edition of *Interviewing: Principles and Practices* continues to focus on the fundamental principles applicable to all forms of interviewing and to seven specific types while incorporating the latest in research, interpersonal communication theory, the uses of technology and social media, the role of ethics, and EEO laws that affect employment and performance interviews. While including recent research findings and developments, the emphasis remains on developing the skills of both interviewers and interviewees. Ten chapters address diversity (age, gender, culture) in the United States and our involvement in the global village as they impact the interviews in which we take part.

A major goal was to make this edition more user-friendly by sharpening the writing style, eliminating redundancies, making definitions and explanations more precise, and employing different print types to emphasize critical words, terms, concepts, and principles. Several chapters were restructured to provide clarity and more logical progressions from point to point.

Changes in the Sixteenth Edition

- Chapter 1 includes a refined definition of interviewing by inserting the word "collaborative" and reads "An interview is an interactional, collaborative communicative process between two parties, at least one of whom has a predetermined and serious purpose, that includes the asking and answering of questions." This change emphasizes the importance of collaboration between interview parties and enables students to see the similarities and differences of interviewing from other types of interpersonal communication. There is a detailed discussion of how technology is impacting the nature of interviews.

- Chapter 2 includes an expanded treatment of the importance of self-disclosure in interviews and how self-disclosure impacts and is impacted by levels of communication, trust, self-esteem, and self-worth. Discussion of the nature and roles of verbal and nonverbal communication are expanded along with how our increasingly diverse society and interactions in the global village are affecting our use of each.

- Chapter 3 includes clearer explanations and illustrations of question types, the uses of questions as the tools of the trade, and a refined treatment of common question pitfalls that make it more difficult to perform interview tasks efficiently and effectively.

- Chapter 4 includes expanded explanations of interview guides and schedules, question sequences, rapport and orientation in openings, types of openings and closings, and the importance of making openings and closings dialogues rather than monologues.

- Chapter 5 is divided into two parts. Part 1 focuses on the information gathering interview and includes refined discussions of planning and structuring interviews, selecting interviewees, handling difficult interviewees and situations, conducting interviews, and taking part as the interviewee. Part 2 focuses on the deceptively difficult task of giving information in ways that will enable the interviewee to recall it accurately and completely over a period of time. It discusses how the interviewer can avoid overloading the interviewee with information, enhance verbal and nonverbal presentation, and to aid in recall of information. It also focuses on how the interviewee can prepare for the interview and improve listening skills to improve recall of important information.

- Chapter 6 includes refined discussions of qualitative and quantitative surveys, sampling techniques, incentives designed to increase participation, advantages and disadvantages of face-to-face (personal) interviews, and the telephone survey. Several factors receive expanded treatment, including the importance of time in surveys, the goal of conducting identical interviews over and over, and defining the target population for the survey.

- Chapter 7 includes revised and expanded discussions of searching for new talent (internships, career and job fairs, kiosks, and Web sites), reviewing EEO laws, understanding and adapting to the unique characteristics of the millennial generation, reviewing applicant materials prior to the interview, structuring interviews, asking on-the-job questions, and closing the interview effectively.

- Chapter 8 includes expanded treatment of developing and incorporating a personal brand; researching the field, positions and locations, organizations, current events, and the interview process; networking; using social media; creating appropriate resumes, curriculum vitae (CV), cover letters, and portfolios; replying to lawful and unlawful questions; and asking questions.

- Chapter 9 includes emphasis on conducting the performance review interview as a coaching opportunity, conforming to EEO laws, selecting an appropriate review model, establishing a relaxed and supportive climate, orienting the employee, and avoiding a "gunnysacking" approach in the performance problem interview in which the interviewer stores up grievances and then dumps them on an employee all at once. It identifies personal biases that may result in errors that affect employers' interactions with employees and influence their evaluation following performance review interviews. Errors include the halo effect, pitchfork, central tendency, length of service, loose rater, tight rater, and competitive rater.

- Chapter 10 includes new and revised materials on ethics and persuasion, the criteria essential for successful persuasive interviews, how to establish substantial similarity with the interviewee, the use of questions in persuasive interviews, how to anticipate and respond to objections, and how to be an active and critical interviewee.

- Chapter 11 includes revised treatments of the nature of the counseling interview; the role of lay counselors who are similar to counselees and open, caring, and good listeners; a code of ethics for the counseling interview; trust as the cornerstone of the counseling relationship; respect for and understanding of the interviewee's capabilities of making sound choices and decisions; the necessity to be culturally aware in today's global village; and maintaining relational boundaries.

- Chapter 12 includes emphasis on the roles we all play in health care interviews, the critical importance of relationship between health care provider and patient, the sharing control during the interview, the influences of culture and gender in health care interactions, ways to lessen the negative impact of long waiting periods, opening questions, reasons for patient resistance to disclosure during interviews, ways to lessen the loss of information during and after interviews, how collaboration can promote self-persuasion, compliance with recommendations, and closing interviews.

Chapter Pedagogy

Review questions at the end of each chapter are designed to help students recall and understand principles as they prepare for interviews and examinations. **Student activities** at the end of each chapter provide ideas for in- and out-of-class exercises, experiences, and information gathering. We have made many of these less complex and time-consuming. The **readings** at the end of each chapter will enable students and instructors to delve more deeply into topics, theories, and types of interviews. The glossary provides students with definitions of key words and concepts introduced throughout the text.

Intended Courses

This book is designed for courses in communication, journalism, business, supervision, education, political science, nursing, criminology, and social work. It is useful in workshops in various fields. This book is of value to beginning students as well as to seasoned veterans because the principles, research, and techniques are changing rapidly in many fields. Theory and research findings are addressed where applicable, but the primary concern is with principles and techniques that can be translated into immediate practice in and out of the classroom.

Ancillary Materials

The 16th edition of *Interviewing: Principles and Practices* is now available online with Connect, McGraw-Hill Education's integrated assignment and assessment platform. Connect also offers SmartBook for the new edition, which is the first adaptive reading experience proven to improve grades and help students study more effectively. All of the title's website and ancillary content is also available through Connect, including:

- A sample interview that illustrates the type of interview, situation, principles, practices, and mistakes parties make to challenge students to distinguish between effective and ineffective techniques, questions, and responses and know how to remedy them.

- An Instructor's Manual includes tips for teaching the interviewing course, course syllabuses, answers to exercises in textbook chapters, role playing cases, ice breaker interviews, cases for the skills building assignment, assignments and critique forms for skills building, informational, employment, persuasive, performance, counseling, and health care interviews, and a field project assignment.
- A full Test Bank of multiple choice questions that test students on central concepts and ideas in each chapter.
- Lecture Slides for instructor use in class.

Acknowledgments

We wish to express our gratitude to students at Purdue University and National-Louis University College of Management, and to past and present colleagues and clients for their inspiration, suggestions, exercises, theories, criticism, and encouragement. We thank Suzanne Collins, Mary Alice Baker, Vernon Miller, Kathleen Powell, Garold Markle, and Patrice Buzzanell for their resources, interest, and suggestions.

We are very grateful to the following reviewers for the many helpful comments and suggestions they provided us:

Merry Buchanan, University of Central Oklahoma

Rebecca Carlton, IU Southeast

Valerie B. Coles, University of Georgia

Stephanie Coopman, San Jose State University

Erin F. Doss, Indiana University Kokomo

Cheri Hampton-Farmer, The University of Findlay

Delia O'Steen, Texas Tech University

Christopher S. Perrello, Syracuse University

Cynthia A. Ridle, Western Illinois University

Sue Stewart, Texas State University

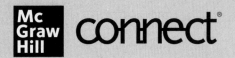

Instructors: Student Success Starts with You

Tools to enhance your unique voice

Want to build your own course? No problem. Prefer to use our turnkey, prebuilt course? Easy. Want to make changes throughout the semester? Sure. And you'll save time with Connect's auto-grading too.

65%
Less Time Grading

Study made personal

Incorporate adaptive study resources like SmartBook® 2.0 into your course and help your students be better prepared in less time. Learn more about the powerful personalized learning experience available in SmartBook 2.0 at **www.mheducation.com/highered/connect/smartbook**

Laptop: McGraw Hill; Woman/dog: George Doyle/Getty Images

Affordable solutions, added value

Make technology work for you with LMS integration for single sign-on access, mobile access to the digital textbook, and reports to quickly show you how each of your students is doing. And with our Inclusive Access program you can provide all these tools at a discount to your students. Ask your McGraw Hill representative for more information.

Padlock: Jobalou/Getty Images

Solutions for your challenges

A product isn't a solution. Real solutions are affordable, reliable, and come with training and ongoing support when you need it and how you want it. Visit **www .supportateverystep.com** for videos and resources both you and your students can use throughout the semester.

Checkmark: Jobalou/Getty Images

Students: Get Learning that Fits You

Effective tools for efficient studying

Connect is designed to make you more productive with simple, flexible, intuitive tools that maximize your study time and meet your individual learning needs. Get learning that works for you with Connect.

Study anytime, anywhere

Download the free ReadAnywhere app and access your online eBook or SmartBook 2.0 assignments when it's convenient, even if you're offline. And since the app automatically syncs with your eBook and SmartBook 2.0 assignments in Connect, all of your work is available every time you open it. Find out more at **www.mheducation.com/readanywhere**

> *"I really liked this app—it made it easy to study when you don't have your textbook in front of you."*
>
> - Jordan Cunningham, Eastern Washington University

Everything you need in one place

Your Connect course has everything you need—whether reading on your digital eBook or completing assignments for class, Connect makes it easy to get your work done.

Learning for everyone

McGraw Hill works directly with Accessibility Services Departments and faculty to meet the learning needs of all students. Please contact your Accessibility Services Office and ask them to email accessibility@mheducation.com, or visit **www.mheducation.com/about/accessibility** for more information.

CHAPTER 1

An Introduction to Interviewing

We designed this book to introduce you to the essential principles and practices of interviewing, the most common form of purposeful, planned, and serious communication. Rarely does a day go by that you are not involved in one or more interviews. They may be formal or informal, minimally or highly structured, simplistic or sophisticated, supportive or threatening, and momentary or lengthy. Common misconceptions are that interviewing is limited to what applicants do when seeking jobs, employers do when recruiting employees, and journalists do when getting information from politicians, accident victims, and athletes. Google searches of "interviewing" support these misconceptions. You may be reading this book and taking an interviewing course with the primary, dare we say sole, purpose of learning how best to start or change a career, and you will find this book helpful in fulfilling this goal and others of which you may be unaware. So, of all the human interactions you participate in each day, how do you know which are interviews? They share characteristics with brief encounters, social conversations, small groups, and presentations, but they differ significantly from each.

The objectives of this chapter are to identify the essential characteristics of interviews, distinguish interviews from other forms of communication, identify types of interviews, and examine the advantages and disadvantages of using technology when participating in a variety of interviews.

Interviewing Defined

Two Parties

> Dyadic means two distinct parties.

The interview is a dyadic—**two party**—process between an interviewer and interviewee. It typically involves two people such as a physician and a patient, a student and a professor, an employer and an applicant, a journalist and an accident victim, a counselor and a client. Many interviews, however, involve **more than two people** but **never more than two parties**. For instance, three members of a coaching staff may interview a college baseball recruit, a travel director may interview a husband and wife, or a homeowner may interview four students about leasing a home together. In each case, there are **two distinct parties**—an interviewer party and an interviewee party. If a single party is involved (three mechanics discussing how best to repair a truck) or more than two parties are involved (three students discussing their specific field projects with a professor), the interaction is not an interview.

■ *More than two people may be involved in an interview, but never more than two parties—an interviewer party and an interviewee party.*

Purpose and Structure

At least one party must arrive at an interview with a **predetermined** and **serious purpose**, a characteristic that distinguishes interviews from social conversations and chance meetings. Conversations and momentary meetings are rarely organized or planned in advance, and you would probably hesitate to participate in one that was. Interviews, on the other hand, always have a degree of planning and structure that may include searching for background information, preparing an opening, selecting topics, phrasing a list of questions, selecting a proposal, and preparing a closing. The predetermined purpose—to get or give information, to seek employment or recruit an employee, to counsel or be counseled, to persuade or be persuaded—determines the extent of planning and degree of structure. Chapter 4 introduces you to the principles of structuring interviews from opening to closing.

> Interviews are at least minimally structured.

Interactional, Collaborative Communication Process

Interviews are **interactional** and **collaborative** with both parties sharing and exchanging roles, responsibilities, feelings, beliefs, motives, and information. If one party does all of the talking and the other all of the listening, a lecture or presentation—not an interview—is occurring to an audience of one or a few. John Stewart writes that communication is a "continuous, complex, collaborative process of verbal and nonverbal meaning making."[1] This collaborative "meaning making" entails a **mutual** creation and sharing of messages that consist of words and nonverbal signs (raised voice, wink, smile, or hand gesture) that may express interest, compassion, understanding, belief, agreement, or their opposites. As an interactional, collaborative communication **process,** the interview is a dynamic, ongoing, ever-changing form of message sending and receiving. Once an interview commences, you cannot not communicate.[2] Even when you communicate poorly, you communicate something. Chapter 2 introduces you to the many interacting variables that make up interviews.

> Interactional means exchanging and sharing.

Questions

Questions play critical roles in every interview. They dominate survey, journalistic, and investigative interviews while sharing focus with information giving and getting in recruiting, counseling, and health care interviews. In other interviews such as persuasive, training, and performance review, questions play strategic roles in obtaining

> Questions play many roles in interviews.

and clarifying information, verifying impressions and assumptions, and provoking thoughts, feelings, and actions. Questions are literally the **tools of the interview trade** for gathering information and checking the accuracy of messages sent and received. Chapter 3 introduces you to the many types of questions and how and when to employ each.

We define the interview, then, as an **interactional, collaborative communication process involving two parties, at least one of whom has a predetermined and serious purpose, that includes the asking and answering of questions.** With this definition in mind, which of the following communication interactions is an interview and which is not?

Exercise #1—Explain Why Each of the Following Interactions Is or Is Not an Interview?

1. A police officer is questioning an eyewitness about a shooting at an elementary school?

2. Three students are preparing for an important examination by cross examining one another about class lectures.

3. An employer is talking to two students, one majoring in communication and one in industrial design, at a job fair on campus.

4. A therapist is talking to a child about possible sexual abuse.

5. A sales representative is explaining the features of a new SUV to a husband and wife who just purchased it.

6. Four members of a search committee are discussing the credentials of applicants they plan to interview during the day.

7. A member of a survey research firm is talking to a shopper in a mall about possible effects of higher tariffs on consumer goods made in China.

8. Co-workers Nichole and Ryan see one another at halftime during a football game and are talking about the first half when Nichole decides to ask Ryan about the results of a staff meeting she missed because of a medical appointment.

9. A student stops by a professor's office to discuss ideas he has about a field project assignment in her class.

10. A rugby player and his parents are talking to a specialist about treatment for a concussion.

Types of Interviews

There are many types of interviews, and they are typically identified according to situation and function. As you review the seven common types below and read this book, you will become increasingly aware that differing types of interviews require one or both parties not only to have a store of valuable information but also training, abilities, personality traits, and willingness to share this information that may be influenced by beliefs, attitudes, and feelings.

Information-Gathering Interviews

The primary purpose of the information-gathering interview is to obtain accurate, insightful, and useful information through the skilled use of questions created prior to the interview and ones created on the spot to probe into interviewee responses, attitudes, and feelings. Chapter 5 discusses the principles and practices of moderately structured interviews conducted by professionals such as journalists, law enforcement officers, and researchers and all of us in our everyday lives as students, professors, parents, travelers, and consumers. Chapter 6 discusses the principles and practices of highly structured interviews such as surveys and polls conducted by the media, political parties, market and consumer researchers, and organizations too numerous to mention.

Information-Giving Interviews

The primary purpose of the information-giving interview is to exchange information in interviews that involve training, orienting, coaching, instructing, and briefing. Although such interviews may appear simpler than many others—merely providing facts, data, reports, schedules, and opinions, they are often deceptively difficult in practice. Information-giving interviews are often loaded with detailed information, involve technical or philosophical concepts, and include specialized terminology. Recall when you showed up late for a meeting or on the wrong day because you forgot the time or day information. Chapter 5 discusses the principles, problems, and techniques of effective information-giving interviews that enable interviewees to understand and retain information adequately and accurately following the interaction.

Focus Group Interviews

The focus group interview usually consists of 6 to 10 similar but unrelated interviewees with a single interviewer and concentrates on a specific issue or concern such as customer or client perspectives about a new or developing idea, product, or service. The interviewer conducts the interview with a carefully crafted set of questions designed to generate interactions among the interviewees that produce a wide range of information, experiences, opinions, beliefs, attitudes, and understandings. Advocates of focus group interviews argue that they produce higher quality information and feedback than single-person interviews.[3] However, it is often difficult to arrange a meeting of 6 to 10 similar interviewees at the same time and place, each interviewee has less interacting time than in a single-person interview, and some interviewees may dominate a focus group interview.

Selection Interviews

The most common selection interview is the "employment interview" that occurs between a recruiter attempting to select the best qualified applicant to fill a position and an applicant attempting to convince the recruiter that he or she is the best qualified and best "fit" for this position with this organization. A second type of selection interview is the "placement interview" during which an employer or supervisor tries to determine the ideal placement for a staff member within an organization and an employee tries to convince the interviewer that he or she is the best fit for a position, sometimes not the same position the employer has in mind. The placement might be a promotion, reassignment, or new role in a restructured organization. Chapter 7 focuses on the recruiter in the employment interview, and Chapter 8 focuses on the applicant in the employment interview.

Performance Interviews

> **Performance review is essential for advancing the employee and organization.**

The performance interview, once called the appraisal interview, focuses on the review of an employee's skills, performance, abilities, and behaviors for the purpose of "coaching" the interviewee to continue that which is good, discontinue that which is bad, and set goals for future performance. The results of the interview may determine promotions, changes of positions, and increases in salary or, in some situations, termination of the interviewee's continuation with the organization. Chapter 9 focuses on models and principles of the performance review interview and the basics of the "performance problem interview," once called the disciplinary interview, in which the parties address a problem such as absences, failure to follow rules, insubordination, and simple theft. The goal is to resolve the problem through coaching while trying to avoid, when possible, disciplining or terminating the employee.

Persuasive Interviews

> **Persuasion attempts to alter or reinforce thinking, feeling, and/or acting.**

In persuasive interviews, one party attempts to alter or reinforce the ways the other party thinks, feels, and/or acts. While the sales situation comes readily to mind, you are involved in persuasive interviews on a daily basis. These range from informal interactions such as attempting to persuade your roommate to go to a comic-con with you, to formal interactions such as a defense attorney trying to persuade a prosecutor to drop some charges against a client and long-term, multi-interview efforts such as striving to convince a state legislator to support an immigration reform proposal. Chapter 10 focuses on the often-complex interactions in which the interviewer's goal is to change another's way of thinking, feeling, or acting.

Counseling Interviews

> **The counseling interview is a helping interview.**

The counseling interview occurs when an interviewer strives to assist an interviewee to gain insights into a personal or professional problem and discover ways of coping with this problem. Although trained therapists or counselors are required for serious psychological, physical, and personal issues, all of us act as "lay counselors" when we assume the roles of parents, teachers, supervisors, physicians, co-workers, team members, and friends. Chapter 12 focuses on the basic principles and practices of conducting and taking part in counseling interviews that address day-to-day problems encountered in life and the workplace and ways of dealing with them.

While this list of interview types identifies each with a specific goal such as information getting or information giving, a great many interviews entail several goals. During a typical selection interview, for instance, both parties give and get information and strive to persuade one another to offer or to accept an offer of employment. The recruiter might do a bit of career counseling. A journalist must persuade a person to take part in an interview and answer questions honestly and insightfully. A typical health care interview, the focus of Chapter 13, may involve information gathering, information giving, counseling, and persuasion.

Technology and Interviewing

Since the invention of the telephone by Alexander Graham Bell in 1876, technology has played ever-increasing roles in interviews of all types with interview parties no longer needing to be face-to-face but can be ear-to-ear, keyboard-to-keyboard, or screen-to-screen. Each new technology has brought about changes in how we communicate interpersonally, some good and some bad, and each requires interview parties to adapt in critical ways.

> Telephone interviews are convenient and inexpensive but lack the physical presence of parties.

The Telephone

Telephone interviews are now employed in nearly all types of situations and have become so commonplace that states and the federal government have passed "Don't Call" legislation to protect your privacy and sanity.[4] The popularity of telephone interviews is easy to understand because they save time, reduce expenses, and eliminate traveling. Interviewers can interact with interviewees in widespread geographical locations without leaving their home or office. The telephone is most effective in interviews when you want to ask brief, simple questions in a short time. Organizations risk alienating interviewees, however, when they call during dinnertime or late in the evening and want (often demand) several minutes of the interviewee's time. Political candidates, citizen action groups, and product sales representatives who employ the seemingly never-ending "robocalls" that dial your number over and over may antagonize you rather than motivate you to vote for a candidate, support a cause, or purchase a product.

Lack of **physical presence** of the parties is a significant limitation of the telephone interview. Hearing a voice is not the same as observing another's appearance, dress, manner, eye contact, facial expressions, gestures, and posture. Also missing are the physical surroundings that provide an atmosphere that contributes to effective interactions. The telephone limits the subtle cues interviewers use to indicate when it's time to switch roles, whether to continue with or end an answer, or when the closing is imminent or commencing. While some interviewees prefer the anonymity and relative safety of the telephone interview, others (particularly older ones) prefer face-to-face contacts and fear the growing number of telephone scams.[5] Interviewers reportedly prefer face-to-face interviews when they are lengthy, and this attitude may negatively affect interviewee responses.

fizkes/iStock/Getty Images

■ *The telephone is employed in nearly every type of interview.*

Interactive Video

Parties must focus attention on the interaction rather than the technology..

Video technologies such as Skype and videoconferences enable interview parties to interact visually and orally over long distances faster and with less expense than individual face-to-face interviews.[6] Advocates describe these as "virtual interviews" because they are "almost like being there in person." Video and sound are manipulated to provide the illusion of presence and eye contact in an effort to send the "right vibe." This illusion of reality can be costly if it requires a professional staff, high-quality technology to produce video and sound, mood lighting, and realistic sets to produce the illusion of reality. Some people find it difficult to interact freely and effectively with those on screens, and the absence of traditional cues that signal when a person has answered a question or made a point. The results are parties talking longer with fewer exchanges, and these problems are enhanced during videoconferences in which one or both parties consist of two or more people.

The pluses often cited for videoconferences and Skype such as taking more extensive notes, referring to notes, checking watches, and reading text messages may adversely affect interactions because of lack of attention and critical listening. Even with the best technology and manipulation of set and scenery, parties typically see only head or upper body shots of one another with little feeling of presence. Both parties must be aware of the importance of upper-body movement, gestures, eye contact, and facial expressions that are magnified on the screen when little else is visible to the other party. This may explain why a high percentage of suggestions for being effective in "virtual interviews" pertain to video production concerns and techniques.

E-Mail

E-mail lacks nonverbal cues critical in interviews.

With a cellphone or computer at your fingertips, you are able to communicate almost instantly with others around the world at any time of day or night by e-mail. E-mail is a highly convenient and inexpensive means of sending and receiving messages, but when does this sending and receiving become an interview and not what its name implies—mail? An interview is **interactive in real time**, so if two parties are sitting at their keyboards at the **same time** and are **asking and answering questions** without breaks in the interaction, an interview may be taking place. Otherwise, it is an electronic questionnaire little different from one being handed out or mailed to another party. Make an e-mail interview your last choice because you cannot see or hear the other party or experience the party's presence. Nonverbal elements critical to the interpersonal communication process are nonexistent. Participants in e-mail interviews experience difficulties in opening interviews, establishing rapport, determining emotional reactions, and translating verbal symbols and acronyms. While an e-mail interview may be fairer for a person who is **orally challenged**, it may be less fair to a **verbally challenged** person.

Webinars

The webinar is designed to train and educate large audiences with a presentational format.

A webinar is essentially what its name implies, a Web-based seminar (often educational in nature) in which professionals deliver presentations to large, multiparty audiences who view or listen to them.[7] It is becoming popular for conferences,

O N   T H E   W E B

Learn more about the growing uses of electronic interviews in a variety of settings. Search at least two databases under headings such as telephone interviews, conference calls, and video talk-back. Try search engines such as ComAbstracts (http://www .cios.org), Yahoo (http://www.yahoo.com), Infoseek (http://www.infoseek.com), and ERIC (http://www .indiana.edu/~eric_rec). In which interview settings are electronic interviews most common? What are the advantages and disadvantages of electronic interviews? How will new developments affect electronic interviews in the future? How will the growing use of electronic interviews affect the ways we conduct traditional face-to-face interviews?

training sessions, seminars, and workshops because presenters can display slides, stream video, talk with audience members in real time, ask and answer questions, edit what is on the screen, and record the entire presentation for later use. It may be an interview if it is a two-party, interpersonal communication process between professionals rather than a Web-based lecture, but it is designed primarily to reach large audiences located in diverse locations such as Boeing Aircraft facilities throughout the United States. Video chatting platforms such as Skype and Google Plus are better designed for interviews.

Summary

This chapter has defined the interview as an interactional, collaborative communication process between two parties, at least one of whom has a predetermined and serious purpose, that involves the asking and answering of questions. While this definition distinguishes it from brief encounters, social conversations, small group discussions, and presentations, it encompasses a wide range of human interactions in which you take part virtually every day. Since you take part in interviews so often, be careful of assuming that what you do often you do well. Many years of experience may not result in a high degree of skill but the repetition of mistakes from interview to interview for a lifetime. Interviewing is a learned skill, and this book is designed to introduce to the principles and practices of different types of interviews to start refining your roles as interviewer and interviewee by enabling you to prepare thoroughly and take part actively while recognizing possible mistakes before you make them. Practice makes perfect only if you know what you are practicing.

The initial step in developing and enhancing your interviewing skills is to understand the deceptively complex interviewing process and its many interacting variables. Chapter 2 does this by literally drawing you a picture of the process through the step-by-step creation of a summary model that contains all of the variables that interact during each interview.

Key Terms and Concepts

Beliefs
Collaborative
Conversation
Counseling
Dyadic
Electronic interviews
E-mail interviews
Exchanging
Feelings
Focus group interviews
Information-gathering
   interviews

Information-giving
   interviews
Interactional
Internet
Interpersonal
Meaning making
Motives
Parties
Performance review
Persuasion
Predetermined purpose
Process

Questions
Selection interview
Serious purpose
Skype
Structure
System
Technology
Telephone interview
Two-party process
Videoconference interview
Virtual interview
Webinar

Review Questions

1. What does the word dyadic mean?

2. How many parties are there in an interview?

3. If correspondents from three networks ask questions of opposing presidential candidates, explain why this is or is not an interview?

4. How does purpose set an interview apart from conversation?

5. How are interviews interactional in nature?

6. Explain how an interview is a collaborative process?

7. Why are questions called "the tools of the trade" in interviews?

8. What strategic roles do questions play during interviews?

9. What is a complete definition of an interview?

10. Explain why the following scenario is or is not an interview: two friends see each other after a concert and stop to get their reactions.

11. What is the primary purpose of the information-gathering interview?

12. Why is the "focus group" considered to be an interview?

13. Why are telephone interviews used so widely in our society?

14. What are the significant limitations of the telephone interview compared to the face-to-face interview?

15. How may the often-cited pluses of videoconference and Skype interviews adversely affect these interactions?

Student Activities

1. Keep a log of face-to-face interactions you have with others during a 48-hour period. Which matched all of the characteristics of this chapter's definition of interviewing? Which interactions you identified as "other-than-interviews" met most of the characteristics? Which characteristics seemed to set interviews apart most often from other interactions?

2. Arrange interviews with three different parties in which the purpose is identical such as purchasing a new cell phone, getting information about a location along the Gulf of Mexico for spring break, giving information about a new policy an organization just created, or seeking assistance with a class project. Conduct one interview face-to-face, one over the telephone, and one through interactive video. How did the medium appear to affect each interaction? Which medium did you prefer and why? Which medium seemed most effective and why?

3. Watch a number of interviews on television in which the setting and relationships of the parties vary. For instance, one might be a televised political interview between a candidate for Congress and a reporter from a friendly television network. Another might be an investigative interview in a parking lot or sidewalk between a reporter and a business owner who has been charged with unlawful sales practices. Another might be between two parties after a sporting event with a history of conflicts and ill feelings toward one another. How did these relationships and settings appear to affect the collaborative nature of the interview?

4. Take part in a face-to-face job fair and a virtual job fair. What did you like most and least about each? What did the traditional face-to-face interaction offer that the electronic interaction did not? What did the electronic interaction offer that the face-to-face interaction did not? How did your preparation differ for each? What roles did questions and answers play in each interaction?

Notes

1. John Stewart, ed., *Bridges Not Walls,* 11th ed. (New York: McGraw-Hill, 2012), p. 16.

2. Michael T. Motley, "Communication as Interaction: A Reply to Beach and Bavelas," *Western Journal of Speech Communication* 54 (Fall 1990), pp. 613–623.

3. Pierre-Nicolas Schwab, "Focus Groups vs. Interviews: Pro's and Con's," IntotheMinds, May 16, 2016, http://www.intotheminds.com/blog/en/focus-goups-vs-telephones-pros-cons, accessed February 29, 2020.

4. Emily S. Block and Laura Erskine, "Interviewing by Telephone: Specific Considerations, Opportunities, and Challenges," *International Journal of Qualitative Methods,* September 1, 2012, https://doi.org/10.1177/160940691201100409, accessed February 29, 2020.

5. Fred E. Jandt, *An Introduction to Intercultural Communication: Identities in a Global Community* (Thousand Oaks, CA: Sage Publications, 2016), p. 27.

6. Valeria Lo Iacono, Paul Symonds, and David H.K. Brown, "Skype as a Tool for Qualitative Research Interviews," *Sociological Research Online* 21(2) (2016), p. 12, https://www.socresonline.org.uk/21/2/12/html, accessed July 14, 2018; Peter Bright, "Microsoft Killing off the Old Skype Client, Adding Built-in Call Recording," July 16, 2018, https:/arstchnica.com/gadgets/2018/07/Microsoft-killing-off-the-old-skype-client-adding-built-in-call-recording, accessed February 29, 2020.

7. Elise Moreau, "What Is a Webinar?," https://www.lifewire.com/what-is-a-webinar-3486257?utm_term=how+does+webinar+work&utm+content=p1-main-1-title&utm_medium=sem&utm_sou, accessed July 14, 2018.

Resources

Anderson, Rob, and G. Michael Killenberg. *Interviewing: Speaking, Listening, and Learning for Professional Life*. New York: Oxford University Press, 2008.

DeJong, Peter. *Interviewing for Solutions*. Belmont, CA: Brooks/Cole, 2013.

Dykes, Fiona Ballantine, Traci Postings, Barry Kopp, and Anthony Crouch. *Counseling Skills and Training*. Thousand Oaks, CA: SAGE Publications, 2017.

Holstein, James A., and Jaber F. Gubrium, eds. *Inside Interviewing: New Lenses, New Concerns*. Thousand Oaks, CA: Sage, 2003.

Metzler, Ken. *Creative Interviewing: The Writer's Guide to Gathering Information by Asking Questions*. Boston, MA: Allyn and Bacon, 2010.

Parsons, Steven P. *Interviewing and Investigating: Essential Skills for the Legal Professional*. Frederick, MD: Wolters Kluwer Law & Business, 2019.

Stewart, John. *Bridges Not Walls: A Book about Interpersonal Communication*. New York: McGraw-Hill, 2012.

An Interactional, Collaborative Communication Process

> **An interview is more than questions and answers.**

This chapter develops step-by-step a general summary model of the interactional, collaborative communication process we call an interview. Perhaps a better word than model is puzzle because by the end of this chapter, we will have completed a picture of this process by identifying and connecting piece-by-piece all the variables that constitute an interview. It is a complex picture because each interview is a **deceptively complex process of interrelated and interacting variables.**

The objectives of this chapter are to develop a model (puzzle) that identifies, explains, and illustrates the intricate and often puzzling nature of the typical interview as completed in Figure 2.8. Understanding this process is an essential first step toward developing and improving your interviewing skills as interviewer and interviewee.

Two Parties in the Interview

> **Each party is a unique totality.**

The first pieces of our puzzle are the circles in Figure 2.1. that represent the two parties in interviews. Each party is a **totality** of culture, environment, education, training, and experiences; and is an **aggregate** of personality traits ranging from open to closed, trusting to suspicious, honest to dishonest, optimistic to pessimistic, patient to impatient, flexible to inflexible, and compassionate to indifferent. Motivation comes from a party's beliefs, attitudes, and values associated with ever-evolving needs, desires, interests, and expectations. In a very real sense, "the whole person speaks and the whole person listens."[1] Be aware that parties communicate both **intra-personally** (talking to themselves) and **inter-personally** (talking to others). What you say to yourself and how you say it influences the messages you send and receive and how you experience an interview.

> **Every interaction adds to a relational history.**

The circles overlap in Figure 2.1 to signify the **relational nature** of the interview process in which the parties interact **with** one another. Each has a stake in the outcome of the interview, and neither can **go it alone.** It must be a **collaborative** effort. Your relationship may commence with this interview or be another act within a **relational history** that dates from hours to weeks, months, or years. When you initiate a relationship during an interview, interactions may be brief or awkward because you do not know what to expect, how best to start the interaction, when to speak and listen, what information to share, and which beliefs and attitudes to reveal. Your feelings of uncertainty and anxiety are likely to be heightened when interviewing a party from a different culture.[2] Can the person speak and understand the English you speak? How may this party's nonverbal communication differ? How will your expectations differ? For instance, if you decide to study abroad, be aware that the relationship between students and professors differ markedly in different

Figure 2.1 *The interview parties*

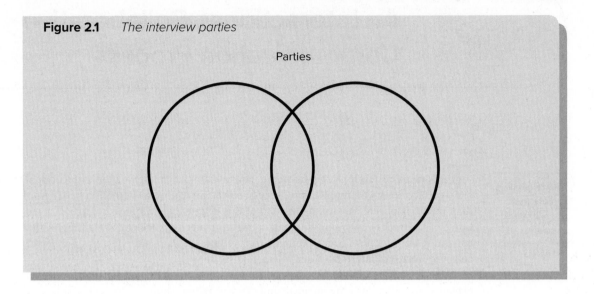

Parties

cultures. In some cultures, "all strangers are viewed as sources of potential relationships; in others, relationships develop only after long and careful scrutiny."[3] The stereotypes you have of age, gender, race, and ethnicity may have significant impact in zero relational-history interactions.[4] On the other hand, **established relationships** may significantly foster or impede the collaborative nature of an interview because of past interactions.

> Changing situations alter your relationships.

Relationships may be **intimate** (family member, close friend), **casual** (co-worker, fellow student), **functional** (therapist, attorney), **formal** (judge, surgeon), or **distant** (college president, senator). Relationships may change during the course of an interview, after several interviews, as situations vary and change, time passes, and you age, take on different roles, rise in the hierarchy of an organization, and have an abundance of experiences. For instance, you may have a formal relationship with a professor at the beginning of a semester, evolve to a more functional relationship during the semester and after several interactions, attain a casual relationship in social interactions after the class ends, and later develop an intimate relationship that lasts a lifetime. Each interaction affects how you communicate **who** you are and **what** you are to one another. Sarah Trenholm and Arthur Jensen write that it is essential to acquire **relational competence** so you know when and how to adapt to the roles you play in relationships and develop "workable rules and norms" appropriate for widely different situations.[5]

Relational Dimensions

Each relationship is multidimensional with five being critical: similarity, inclusion, affection, control, and trust.

Similarity

> Do not assume too much from too little.

You find it easiest to understand and communicate with others when you share important similarities such as gender, race, cultural norms and values, education, experiences, beliefs, interests, and expectations. These shared similarities enable you to establish

common ground with one another that is portrayed by the overlapping of the circles in Figure 2.1. Recognizing this perceived overlap prior to an interview enables you to initiate the interview on a positive note and expand upon it as an interview progresses to enhance the potential of a successful outcome.

On the other hand, perceived dissimilarities may make initiation of an interview difficult and impede interactions and development of a meaningful relationship. Do not **assume** that because the two of you look alike, sound alike, dress alike, and are alumni of the same university that you share significant similarities essential to the outcome of the interview.

Inclusion

Relationships are advanced and communication thrives when both parties are motivated to speak and listen, question and respond, and are open and straightforward. This happens when both parties have a **high desire** to be **included** in the interactional, collaborative communication process. The result is likely to be mutual satisfaction in the outcome. The opposite for either party will make the interview a waste of time and perhaps diminish a relationship beyond repair. Remember, it is not merely what you do or gain in an interview but **what you do with another**. It must be a **collaborative, joint effort** in which both parties want to take part and to make it work.

> Desire to be included is essential to motivation.

Affection

Affection is the extent to which parties like, admire, or respect one another, and your goal should be to cultivate interview relationships in which there is a marked degree of friendship and warmth. Such cultivation requires establishing a **we** rather than a **me-you** relationship, and results when both parties see interactions as pleasant, fair, and productive. Relationships suffer when signs of affection are inconsistent, ambivalent, or negative. For instance, interview parties might lower their loudness to express disliking or liking for one another. Clear signs of affection or liking occur when parties decrease talk time to show greater attentiveness or disaffection or disliking by disengaging from an interaction.[6] It is not unusual to come to an interview with an ambivalent or hostile attitude toward another party because of a **relational history** or what James Honeycutt calls **relational memory.** He writes that "even though relationships are in constant motion, relationship memory structures provide a perceptual anchor [so that] individuals can determine where they are in a relationship."[7]

> You communicate more openly with people you like.

Control

Collaboration and communication are increased when both parties **share control** and accept responsibility for successes and failures in an interview. The felt need to control interactions results from personality traits (narcissism being the extreme), the competitive spirit our society fosters, and organizational norms and policies. Hierarchies ever present in homes, schools, churches, governments, and corporations make **upward** and **downward** communication a part of your daily life and often make interactions problematic. Edward Hall writes that "People at the top pay attention to different things from those in the middle or bottom of the system."[8] John Stewart claims the concept of **nexting** is the "most important single communication skill" because each party should be asking "What can I help to happen next," rather than how can I control the nature and content of this interaction.[9]

> Sharing control heightens collaboration between parties.

Trust

We are introducing trust as the fifth relational dimension because the first four have direct bearings on the degree of trust each party has for one another prior to, during, and after an interview. Trust is vitally important in an interview because the outcome affects you personally–your income, your career, your purchase, your profit, your health, and your future. Trust comes from **mutual** honesty, sincerity, reliability, fairness, openness, and even-temper–in other words when you see interactions with one another as being **safe**. **Dialectical tensions** result from conflicts between "important but opposing needs or desires" and "between opposing" or contrasting "'voices,' each expressing a different or contrasting impulse."[10] As a result, you may become anxious and cautious during an interview and fearful about possible outcomes. The first casualty is level of **disclosure** because you hesitate to be direct and open or share information, beliefs, opinions, and attitudes. The risk to a relationship may be too great. Kory Floyd writes that dialectical tensions are a "normal part of any close, interdependent relationship, and they become problematic only when people fail to manage them properly."[11] A goal of this book is to help you manage these tensions in an increasingly polarized society.

> Trust is the key to openness and self-disclosure in interviews.

Culture and Relationships

Social, political, and work worlds are rapidly becoming global in nature, so it is critical not only that you understand how relationships are created and fostered in other countries and cultures but also how to adapt effectively and ethically to these differences during interviews. Here are how people in different countries establish and view relationships.

- Americans tend to create numerous, friendly, and informal relationships and discard them frequently.
- Arabs, like Americans, develop numerous relationships quickly but, unlike Americans, take advantage of relationships by asking for favors because they believe friends have a duty to help one another.
- Chinese develop strong, long-term relationships and believe they involve obligations.
- Australians make deeper and longer lasting commitments than do Americans.
- Mexicans develop trust slowly and sparingly in relationships and feel it must be earned and never betrayed.
- Germans develop relationships slowly because they see them as important, and using first names before a relationship is well-established is considered rude behavior.
- Japanese prefer not to interact with strangers, desire background information before establishing relationships, take their time in establishing relationships, and prefer to do business with persons they have known for years.

> Discover how relationships are created and sustained in other cultures.

The less you know about other cultures, the more likely you are to experience anxiety when initiating relationships. James Neuliep writes that "Communication with a stranger, particularly a person from a different culture, can be frightening and full of uncertainty. Uncertainly refers to the amount of predictability–that is, what you know about the person with whom you are interacting."[12] Martin, Nakayama, and Flores warn that "in intercultural conflict situations, when we are experiencing high anxieties with unfamiliar behavior (for example, accents, gestures, facial expressions) we may automatically withhold trust."[13] You may fear your words and actions will offend the other party or make you look ignorant.

Gender and Relationships

> Gender differences have evolved but not disappeared.

Although men and women are more similar than different in how they communicate and how they establish and refine relationships, research has revealed significant differences.[14] Men's talk tends to be directive and goal-oriented with statements that "tend to press compliance, agreement, or belief." Women's talk tends to be more polite and expressive, containing less intense words, qualifiers (perhaps, maybe), and disclaimers ("Maybe I'm wrong but . . ." "I may not fully understand the situation, but . . .").[15] Women use communication as a primary way of establishing relationships, while men communicate "to exert control, preserve independence, and enhance status."[16] Women give more praise and compliments and are reluctant to criticize directly in the workplace while men remain silent when a co-worker is doing something well and take criticism straight.[17] Women report "greater satisfaction with their interactions than do men.[18] On the other hand, researchers have found that "women are more likely to betray and be betrayed by other women." Men report they are more often betrayed by other men with whom they are competing.[19]

Interchanging Roles during Interviews

> The roles of interviewer and interviewee may alternate between parties from time to time during an interview.

Although the designated or presumed interviewer may dominate an interview, both parties must speak and listen, ask and answer questions, and give and get information. They may switch roles of interviewer and interviewee from time to time such as when an applicant asks questions in a selection interview or a customer decides to "bargain" with a sales representative. Neither party should expect the other to make an interview a success alone. John Stewart writes that "human communicators are always sending and receiving simultaneously. As a result, each communicator has the opportunity to change how things are going at any time in the process."[20] Small circles containing R/E and E/R are inserted into the party circles in Figure 2.2 to indicate the potential exchanging of roles by either party.

How often and to what extent the basic roles of interviewer and interviewee are interchanged during an interview may depend upon the type and purpose of the interview, which party initiated the interview and how, the status or expertise of the parties, the situation or context, and the atmosphere of the interaction such as open or closed, supportive or defensive, friendly or hostile, trusting or distrusting. One or more of these factors will determine which **approach** an interviewer assumes—**directive** or **nondirective.**

> A directive approach enables the interviewer to control all aspects of the interview.

Directive Approach

Use a **directive approach** when you want or need to exert considerable control over climate, formality, and pacing of the interview and design questions that seek closed and direct answers. Although the interviewee may have some latitude in replies and interactions, your goal is to control the process. The directive approach is employed most

Figure 2.2 *Sharing roles*

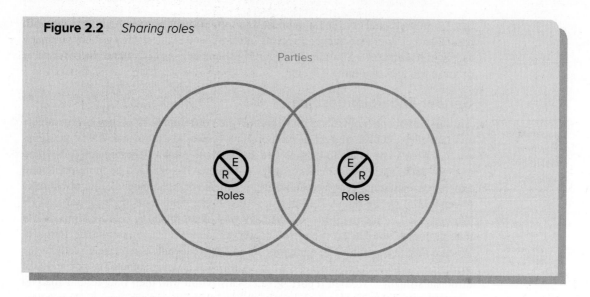

often in information-giving interviews, interrogations, surveys and polls, and persuasive interviews such as sales. It is easy to learn, takes less time, enables you to control interactions, and is easy to replicate from one interview to another. An interviewee may assume occasional control during the interview, but the interviewer dominates the process. The following interaction illustrates a directive interviewing approach:

1. **Interviewer:** Where were you when the accident happened?
2. **Interviewee:** I was right across the street by the Chocolate Shop. You see I . . .
3. **Interviewer:** And what time was that?
4. **Interviewee:** It was a few minutes past 4:00.
5. **Interviewer:** How do you recall this time?
6. **Interviewee:** I had just gotten off work at 4:00.
7. **Interviewee:** What did you see first?
8. **Interviewee:** Well, I stepped off the curb and heard the squealing of car tires. It was really loud, and I thought that . . .
9. **Interviewer:** What did you <u>see</u> first?
10. **Interviewee:** Oh, a SUV was heading toward a food truck by the microbrewery.

Nondirective Approach

> A nondirective approach enables the interviewee to reply freely and volunteer important information.

Select a **nondirective approach** when you want an interviewee to have considerable control over the amount and kinds of information to give, length of answers to open-ended questions, the interview climate, and formality of interactions. Your goal is to relinquish control of the process so the interviewee is free to contribute without direction and restraint. The nondirective approach is employed most often in counseling, health care, journalistic, oral history, and performance review interviews. It enables the interviewer to be more flexible and adaptable, enhances listening for insights, and encourages probing into answers. In addition, it communicates interest and trust in interviewees to provide and volunteer valuable information and insights and encourages them to continue talking, analyzing ideas and problems, and being self-reliant. The following illustrates a nondirective approach:

1. **Interviewer:** Tell me about the accident you witnessed this afternoon.

2. **Interviewee:** Well, I had just crossed the street by the Chocolate Shop. You see, I had just gotten off work at 4:00 p.m. from the University Shop where I work during the school year and stepped off the curb when I heard the squealing of car tires. It really startled me!

3. **Interviewer:** I understand. And then?

4. **Interviewee:** It was really loud, and I thought a couple of cars were going to hit one another right in front of me, maybe even hit me! That's when I saw a SUV heading straight for a food truck by the microbrewery where several people were seated at tables along the sidewalk. It was awful!

5. **Interviewer:** I can only imagine.

6. **Interviewee:** The SUV struck the food truck and then a couple of tables where people were drinking and talking. Bodies flew into the air, and the SUV proceeded to crash right through the front door and window. No one had a chance. It was all over in seconds, and then I heard terrible screaming.

7. **Interviewer:** Then what happened?

> **Neither approach is suitable for all interview situations.**

Be flexible in choosing a directive or nondirective approach so that you employ the one most appropriate for the interview you are planning. In some situations, organizational, societal, or cultural expectations may prescribe a particular approach or a combination of approaches. For example, a recruiter may start an interview with a highly nondirective approach to relax and get the applicant interacting, switch to a more directive approach when asking questions and giving information, change to a highly nondirective approach when inviting the applicant to ask questions, and close with a more directive approach.

Perceptions of Interviewer and Interviewee

> **Perceptions of self and other govern your interactions.**

The next piece of the interviewing process puzzle, shown in Figure 2.3, contains double-ended arrows labeled **perceptions**. They are pointed at both parties indicating that each party arrives with **perceptions** of self and **one another**. These perceptions are critical to the collaborative process and are frequently altered for good or ill as an interview progresses.

Perceptions of Self

Your self-concept or self-identity is a mental process by which you perceive and believe others perceive who you have been, are at this time, and are likely to be in the future. John Stewart writes that we "come to each encounter with an identifiable 'self,' built through past interactions, and *as we talk,* we adapt ourselves to fit the topic we're discussing and the people we are talking with, and we are changed by what happens to us as we communicate."[21]

Figure 2.3 *Perceptions of self and others*

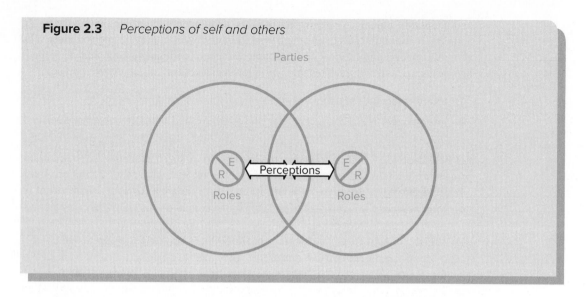

A self-fulfilling prophecy (positive or negative) may come true because you expect it to.

Self-esteem or **self-worth** is a critical element of your self-identify because you exert a great deal of mental and communicative energy trying to gain and sustain recognition and approval from family, peers, society, organizations, and professions because you have a "persistent and compelling" need to give an accounting of yourself.[22] When you **feel** respected or valued, you have high self-esteem and are likely to be more perceptive, confident, and willing to express unpopular ideas and opinions. When you **feel** disrespected or under-valued, you have low self-esteem and become self-critical, feel uncertain, and are hesitant to express unpopular ideas and opinions. Success in an interview may depend upon your ability or inability to convince yourself that you will be successful—a **self-fulfilling prophecy.**

Culture and Gender Differences

Know and understand the differences between individualist and collectivist cultures.

Positive self-identity and high self-esteem are fundamental elements in American and Western cultures that emphasize the value of the **individual's** image, esteem, worth, and achievements. This is not so in South American and Eastern cultures that emphasize the **group's** image, esteem, worth, and achievements. Success is attributed to the group, and claiming success in negotiations by an individual, for example, is considered egotistical, self-advancing, and disrespectful in China and other cultures.

Although high self-esteem is identified as a behavioral trait associated with individualism, striving to achieve it does not come easily in Western cultures, and failure rests primarily if not solely on the individual. Failure is not defused among a group or team like collectivist cultures.[23] You must understand and appreciate cultural differences when taking part in interviews to avoid communication problems and embarrassments.

Gender matters in self-identity because "gender roles are socially constructed ideas about how women and men should think and behave."[24] We expect men to be more assertive, in charge, and self-sufficient and women to be "feminine," submissive, and to show empathy and emotional expressiveness. Not all men and women act this way, of course, but we cannot ignore the impact of gender and self-identity on interviews.

Perceptions of the Other Party

> **Interactions may alter or reinforce your perceptions of the other party.**

Your perceptions of the other party may stem from previous interactions with or knowledge of the other party (including how others perceive this party) or commence as soon as you come into contact with the party and evolve as the interview progresses. Dress, physical appearance, size, attractiveness, gender, age, educational background, social or professional status, accomplishments, and reputation lead you to make judgments (some accurate and some erroneous) about this party prior to and during the interview. Many of your judgments will be culture based.[25] Strive to maintain an **open mind** so you are not held captive by **first impressions** and are able to modify judgments as the interview progresses, perhaps coming to perceive differences as assets rather than liabilities. A collaborative effort that seeks understanding and cooperation may overcome ambivalent or negative preconceptions.

Communication Interactions

The next piece of the interviewing puzzle consists of three double-pointed arrows that link the two parties in Figure 2.4. They symbolize verbal and nonverbal communication and levels of interaction that take place in interviews. Length of an arrow indicates the relationship of the parties and width indicates the frequency and depth of interactions. Think of interaction levels as metaphorical doors that are open to varying degrees.

Figure 2.4 *Communication interactions*

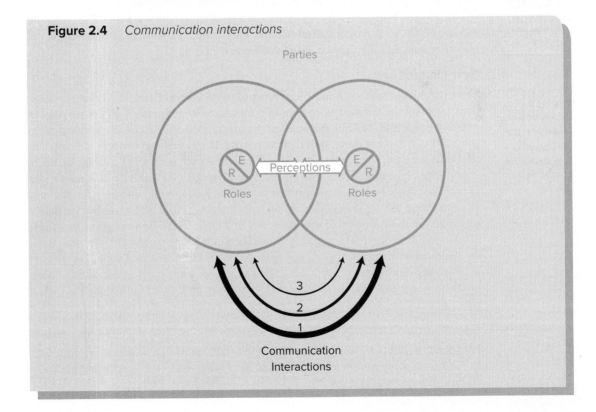

Communication
Interactions

Levels of Interactions and Self-Disclosure

Level 1 interactions are non-threatening and involve little risk.

Level 1 interactions are **safe and superficial** with the metaphorical door being slightly open. As an interviewer, you are likely to ask questions designed to prompt brief, simple, socially acceptable, and comfortable responses such as yes or no, facts (age, year in school, military experience, product you use), and ambiguous words and phrases such as "Fine," "Okay," "Not bad," and "Can't complain." They dominate many of your interactions, particularly when you have little or no **relational history** with another party. This is indicated by the length of the arrow. **Risk is low** for both parties because either can close the slightly open door quickly and safely at any time when feeling threatened. The degree of **self-disclosure** is minimal.

Level 2 interactions involve moderate risk-taking.

Level 2 interactions are **moderately safe** and **revealing** with the metaphorical door being half open. As an interviewer, you are likely to ask more open-ended and challenging questions into controversial and personal issues and probe into feelings, opinions, and information potentially harmful to the interviewee. Parties are willing to take some risks but want the freedom to close the door if they feel threatened. The width of the arrow indicates that Level 2 interactions are less common than Level 1, and the length of the arrow indicates that parties must have a positive relational history. The degree of **self-disclosure** is moderate.

Level 3 interactions are high in risk-taking and require a high level of trust.

Level 3 interactions are **high in risk-taking** with the metaphorical door being wide open. Avoidance of perceived threats in questions and answers is difficult. As an interviewer, you ask pointed questions and probe deeply into feelings, beliefs, attitudes, and information likely to be embarrassing or harmful to the interviewee or the interviewee's family, friends, associates, or organization. Level 3 interactions are the least common, and the parties must have **a well-established** and **trusting relationship** as the shortness of the arrow indicates. The degree of **self-disclosure** is maximum.

Self-Disclosure

Employ a variety of tactics to reduce risk and increase self-disclosure.

You will find it necessary in most interviews to move beyond Level 1 or Level 2 interactions to obtain the self-disclosure necessary for a successful interview. There are ways to reduce the risks involved and increase self-disclosure. Be keenly aware of the relationship you have with another party, including its history. If it is minimal or there is significant relational distance, begin with Level 1 interactions. As an interviewer, ask simple, open, nonthreatening questions. You may gradually build up to Level 2 and Level 3 interactions as a relationship develops. If your relationship is well-established and positive, you may move more rapidly to riskier questions. As an interviewee, begin with a safe level of disclosure until you feel comfortable with disclosing at a higher level. Be sensitive to the effects of what you disclose, to whom, and how on others not taking part in the interview. Insist on disclosing only what is relevant and appropriate for this interview. Disclose at the level at which the other party reciprocates.[26] Be cautious of what you disclose during online interactions because research indicates that you may have fewer inhibitions than when interacting face-to-face and make "hyper-personal" revelations you may regret.

Gender and Disclosure

Fred Jandt writes that "Women clearly exhibit patterns of behavior that are sufficient to distinguish women from men."[27] It is not surprising, then, that women and men may disclose differently during interviews.

Gender

> **Women disclose information and show feelings more freely than do men.**

Women tend to disclose more than men and are allowed to express emotions such as fear, sadness, and sympathy. Because women appear to be better listeners and more responsive than men, disclosure is often highest between woman-to-woman parties (perhaps because talk is at the very heart of women's relationships), about equal in woman-to-man parties, and lowest among man-to-man parties.

Culture and Disclosure

> **Culture may dictate what you disclose and to whom.**

Culture may determine what you disclose, when, to whom, and how. For example, people in the United States of European descent disclose on a wide range of topics including personal information. Japanese disclose more about their careers and less about their families. Asians disclose more to people with high expertise and ability to exhibit honest and positive attitudes than to those who like to talk and show emotions. People in high-context, collectivist cultures such as China are expected to work for the good of the group or team and both know and adhere to cultural norms. They disclose less than those in low-context, individualistic cultures such as the United States and Great Britain. Westerners strive to succeed as individuals and know less about their cultural norms, and this lack of familiarity with cultural norms makes them more flexible. Conflicts may result in interviews when you over-disclose, under-disclose, or disclose to a party from differing cultures. Be aware that perceived similarity, competence, involvement, and the need to take the relationship to a higher level may overcome cultural differences in self-disclosing.

While cultures vary, the notion of politeness—maintaining positive rather than negative face—is universal. According to **"politeness theory,"** all humans want to be appreciated and protected. Littlejohn writes,

> **Maintaining positive face is a universal motive.**

> *Positive face* is the desire to be appreciated and approved, to be liked and honored, and *positive politeness* is designed to meet these desires. Showing concern, complimenting, and using respectful forms of address are examples. *Negative face* is the desire to be free from imposition or intrusion, and *negative politeness* is designed to protect the other person when negative face needs are threatened. Acknowledging the imposition when making a request is a common example.[28]

Politeness is essential whenever you are involved in challenging, complaining, evaluating, disciplining, advising, and counseling situations. You may lose face and disclose less when the other party rejects an overture, insults you personally, disregards your status, reveals a personal weakness, forces you to sacrifice a cherished value or motive, or harm a valued relationship.[29] Guerrero, Andersen, and Afifi write that "people face a constant struggle between wanting to do whatever they want (which satisfies their negative face needs) and wanting to do what makes them look good to others (which satisfies their positive face needs)."[30] Severe "face threatening acts" include behavior that violates an important cultural, social, or professional rule; behavior that produces significant harm; and behavior for which the party is directly responsible. The desire to be polite—to avoid hurting or upsetting another and to show appreciation, understanding, or agreement—is one of the most common causes of deception.

Verbal Interactions

The **greatest single problem** with human communication may be **the assumption of it.** Too often we **assume** that if we share language—verbal (words) and nonverbal (signals)—we share meanings. Unfortunately, **words** are arbitrary and imperfect connections of letters and **signals** are arbitrary and imperfect physical actions to which we assign meanings to communicate in our daily lives. These imperfect symbols may cause misunderstanding, confusion, embarrassment, hurt feelings, and antagonism because they are not shared universally or locally as we assume. If you have lived most of your life in the United States and are asked what language you speak, you are likely to say "English." Then you might qualify it with "American English of course." Even this qualifier is inadequate because linguists have discovered that our American English "differs considerably from region to region, among ethnic and social groups, and by age and gender."[31] For example, they identify Appalachian English, Cajun English, California English, and Texas English. And if this were not confusing enough, it is virtually impossible to separate the **verbal** from the **nonverbal** in human interactions.[32] We will address them separately in this chapter for instructional purposes only.

On the one hand, we know there are thousands of words that we and others do **not use** or **understand** on daily basis, hence the need for printed and electronic dictionaries. On the other hand, we assume most English-speaking people understand common words. Journalism professor Michael Skube at Elon University made the same assumption until he started keeping track of words his students did not know.[33] His ever-growing list includes advocate, impetus, derelict, lucid, brevity, satire, afflicted, and novel. We too often assume that common words have **single meanings,** even when employed out of context. "Game," for instance, may refer to a wild animal, a sport, a prank, a computer or board game, or a person willing to try new adventures. "Ball" not only refers to a variety of objects used in sports, but any round sphere, a dance, a party, or having a good time as in "Have a ball." We assume words have **clear meanings** when many are **ambiguous**

such as a "large" high school, a "nice" apartment, an "affordable" education, and "simple" instructions. We rely on context when reading to understand words that **sound alike**, but most interviews are oral and provide less context for words such as sea and see, male and mail, plane and plain, sail and sale, there and their, and to, too, and two. **Jargon** is a specialized vocabulary used by groups or professions such as physicians, attorneys, engineers, accountants, and computer technicians. When those of us transitioned from typewriters to computers, we encountered a strange language that included bit, byte, megabyte, RAM, Rom, USB, WiFi, and the Web. **Slang** includes words and phrases used most often in informal situations and change as time passes. For instance, fast and powerful cars went from "keen" and "neat" in the 1940s and 1950s, to "hot," "cool," and "groovy" in the 1960s and 1970s, to "decent" and "mean" in the 1980s, to "outrageous" and "white hot" in the 1990s, to "awesome," to "hot," and "kickin'" in the twenty-first century. You may assume that words are neutral, but an interview party may apply negative or

positive **connotations** when labeling a running outfit as "inexpensive" or "cheap," a Jeep as "pre-owned" or "used," a computer as an "investment" or an "expense," a craft beer as "lite" or "diet," an economic crisis as a "downturn" or a "recession," and a hamburger as a "quarter-pounder" or a "four-ouncer." When Americans started substituting "woman" for "girl," "firefighter" for "fireman," and "police officer" for "policeman," it was not for so-called political correctness (or simply PC) but to address reality and to show respect in a society based on equality. The moral is: Choose words very carefully even if the other party in the interview appears to share your language and culture.

Gender and Verbal Communication

Men and women tend to use language differently. For example, men use power speech forms such as challenges, orders, leading questions, first-person pronouns such as I and me, and memorable phrases such as "Make my day," "Get a life," and "Read my lips." Women use powerless speech forms such as apologies, qualifiers, disclaimers, excuses, indirect questions, nonfluencies such as "Uh" and "Umm," and third-person pronouns such as we and us.[34] Our society expects men to use more intense language than women because it is considered masculine. When women use intense language, they are often seen as bitchy, pushy, or opinionated. While gender is important in how men and women use words, you must recognize that other factors also affect language choice including context of the interview, subject matter, status differences, and roles being played.

> **Gender differences may reveal power differences.**

Culture and Verbal Communication

North Americans tend to value precise, direct, explicit, and straightforward words, particularly in formal and professional encounters. They often start sentences with "I" because they live in an individualist society. Chinese, on the other hand, learn to minimize self-expression and are likely to start sentences with "we" or "our." Japanese tend to be implicit in words rather than explicit and to employ ambiguous words and qualifiers. Koreans try to avoid negative or no responses and imply disagreements to maintain group or team harmony. Arab-speaking people employ "sweet-talk" and accommodating language with elaborate metaphors and similes. Idioms such as "bought the farm," "get your feet wet," and "wild goose chase" are unique to North Americans and pose problems even for those who speak English. For instance, Wen-Shu Lee who was fluent in English and taking a graduate class in the United States was confused when a fellow student looked at her notes and commented, "That's Greek to me." When she replied that it was Chinese rather than Greek, the American student laughed, and then she realized the student had used a common idiom.[35] Common phrases vary among English-speaking nations. For instance, New Zealanders employ "Take away" for carry out, "Rubbish please" for trash, "Citizen Advice" for information, "thin milk" for skim milk, "Mind your head" for watch your head," "Road train" for a semi with one or more trailers, and "Overtaking lane" for passing lane.

> **Be sensitive to word use when interacting globally.**

Irving Lee observed many years ago that we tend to "talk past" rather than "to" one another.[36] You can reduce this tendency by choosing words carefully, expanding your vocabulary, being aware of common idioms, and learning the meanings of popular and professional jargon. Do not **assume** that the words you use everyday are understood and processed similarly by others different from you in gender, age, race, culture, or ethnic group.

> **You can avoid most language problems.**

Nonverbal Interactions

Nonverbal interactions are pervasive in the face-to-face, oral interview because the parties are close enough to interpret any behavioral act (or its absence) as a message sent even though the other party may at best be vaguely aware of sending one. The message may be intentional or unintentional, planned or spontaneous, accurate or inaccurate but, most important, a message is sent and detected. Nonverbal messages may complement or contradict, reinforce or weaken a verbal interaction without the sender knowing it. You may plan some nonverbal acts (what to wear, how to greet the other party, how to react to a message) while others come from experience, habit, or reflex.

Any behavioral act can and will send messages.

Researchers estimate that from 60 percent to 93 percent of communicative interactions are nonverbal in nature. More important than percentages, however, is the fact that numerous nonverbal behaviors, such as those identified and illustrated below, may overwhelm the verbal—the **how** overcomes the **what**.[37] For example, research subjects have indicated they believe nonverbal behaviors are more truthful than verbal messages when the two conflict. The power of nonverbal communication becomes evident as you review the sampling of messages behavioral acts send during an interview.

- **Eye contact** may show you are attentive, interested, and honest.
- **Face** may show understanding, agreement, and friendliness and reveal emotions and feelings.
- **Gestures** such as pointing may say "Sit here," waving may say "Hello," a V with two fingers may say peace or victory, a clenched fist may emphasize a point, an open palm turned upward may ask for something, thumbs up may signal everything is great or okay.
- **Touch** on the arm, hand, or shoulder may indicate relationship, show concern, or comfort.
- **Voice** tone, rate, and force may complement the verbal, call attention to important words (like underlining, italicizing, or highlighting in print), or indicate which party controls the interview.
- **Silence** may show attentiveness, express belief, encourage the other to continue speaking, or show respect.

Behavioral acts send positive and negative messages.

- **Head** nodding may say yes or express agreement while shaking the head may say no or express disagreement.
- **Movement** such as leaning forward may show interest and enthusiasm while leaning backward may indicate listening or desire for the party to continue.

We have illustrated each of these behavioral acts as sending positive messages, but each may send negative messages. For instance, eye contact or lack of it may convey dishonesty rather than honesty; touch may threaten rather than comfort; face may reveal frustration or anger rather than understanding or agreement; silence may show disbelief or skepticism as well as belief; and leaning forward may show defiance as well as interest; and a clenched fist may threaten or express strong disagreement rather than make a point.

A high level of attractiveness may be a handicap in some interviews.

Physical appearance and dress may indicate how you see yourself, the other party, the situation, and the importance of the interview. They may be important when initiating zero-history relationships and during the initial part of an interview. Research indicates that we are likely to respond more favorably toward attractive and well-dressed people and perceive them to be poised, outgoing, interesting, and sociable. Attractive

■ *Be aware of cultural differences in nonverbal communication.*

persons are neither too fat nor too thin, tall rather than short, shapely rather than unshapely, and pretty and handsome rather than plain or ugly. We may feel uncomfortable or intimidated by persons who are highly attractive, and very tall or large and perceive them as vane, egotistical, snobbish, or unsympathetic to person like us.[38] Since few interview parties match all of these social criteria, strive to eliminate these biases by keeping an open mind during interviews and while building relationships.

Verbal and Nonverbal Intertwined

It should be readily apparent by now why it is virtually impossible to separate the verbal from the nonverbal during interviews. The nonverbal **complements** the verbal when you call attention to and emphasize words through vocal emphasis and facial expressions. The nonverbal **reinforces** the verbal when you nod or shake your head or use a gesture such as a thumbs-up. The nonverbal **substitutes** for the verbal when you hold up fingers for numbers or extend your hand forward with fingers up for stop. Silence can show disagreement or disbelief more tactfully than words.

Gender and Nonverbal Interactions

Women are more adept at sending and receiving nonverbal messages.

When comparing women to men, research indicates that women are more skilled in sending and receiving nonverbal messages, have more expressive faces and employ more gestures, pause more during interactions, smile and laugh more, gaze more, and are less uncomfortable when eye contact is broken.[39] On the other hand, the low-pitched voices of men are interpreted as more credible and dynamic than the high-pitched voices of women.

Culture and Nonverbal Interactions

Many cultures use the same nonverbal acts to send and receive the same messages. People nod their heads in agreement, shake their heads in disagreement, give thumbs down for disapproval, shake fists in anger, and clap hands to show approval. There are significant differences, however. In the United States, African-Americans maintain eye contact more than European-Americans when speaking than when listening. They give more nonverbal feedback when listening than European-Americans. In general, African-Americans are more animated and personal, while European-Americans are more subdued. They avoid eye contact with superiors out of respect, a trait often misinterpreted by European-Americans who see lack of eye contact as a sign of disinterest, lack of confidence, or dishonesty. And African-Americans tend to touch more and stand closer together when communicating than do European-Americans.

Nonverbal Interactions in the Global Village

Residents of the global village share some nonverbal acts and messages, but identical acts may send different messages.[40]

- Americans are taught to look others in the eye when speaking while Africans are taught to avoid eye contact when listening to others.

- Americans value an honest "Look me in the eye" but this expresses a lack of respect for Asians.

- Americans widen their eyes to show wonder or surprise while Chinese do so to express anger, the French to express disbelief, and Hispanics to show lack of understanding.

- Americans are taught to smile in response to a smile while Israelites are not and Japanese are taught to mask negative feelings with smiles and laughter.

- Americans are taught to have little direct physical contact with others when communicating while those in Mediterranean and Latin countries are encouraged to have direct physical contact.

- Americans on a loudness scale of 1-to-10, with 10 being high, would be near the middle while Arabs would be near 10 and Europeans near 1.

- Arabs see loudness as a sign of strength and sincerity and softness of voice as a sign of weakness and deviousness while Americans and Europeans see Arabs as pushy and rude.

- Americans interpret a firm handshake as a sign of honesty and sincerity while French see it as rough or rude and Japanese see no meaning at all.

- Americans wave to say "Hello" while Algerians wave to say "Come here."

- Americans use a finger to the forehead to say "Smart" while Europeans may use it to say "Stupid."

- Americans use a thumb up to say "Way to go" while Iranians use it to say "Screw you."

- Americans use a circular motion with a finger around the ear to say "Crazy" while the Dutch use it to say "You have a telephone call."

- Americans use fingers in a circle to mean "Okay" while French use it to say "Zero" or "Worthless" and Brazilians use it as an obscene gesture more offensive than the American middle finger.

- Americans use thumbs-up to say "Okay" while it is an obscene gesture in Greece, Australia, and Nigeria.

Be cautious in the nonverbal acts you use when interviewing persons from different cultures and countries to avoid making disastrous mistakes.

Feedback

The next piece of the interviewing puzzle is a large double-ended arrow that links the tops of the party circles in Figure 2.5. It symbolizes the heavy stream of **feedback** that is immediate and pervasive in interviews and is essential when decoding what the other

Figure 2.5   *Feedback*

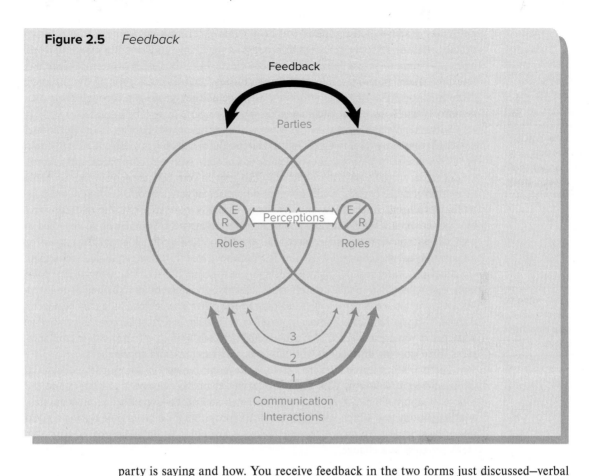

party is saying and how. You receive feedback in the two forms just discussed—verbal and nonverbal, so you must **observe** and **listen** to everything that is and is not taking place and being expressed aloud or merely implied. What is missing may be more crucial to the outcome of the interview than what is occurring between the interview parties.

Observed nonverbal acts are easy to misinterpret. For example, you may perceive that a person is fidgeting because your question is threatening when the person may be fidgeting because a chair is hard. A person may appear to be disinterested in what you are saying when the cause may be noise, interruptions, or lack of privacy. A person's lack of eye contact may be cultural or shyness rather than deceptiveness or mistrust.

Be cautious when interpreting nonverbal messages.

During the interview, does the other party select a power position and move closer or farther apart? Are there changes in tone or attentiveness? Are there changes in eye contact, voice, or posture? Is there more or less willingness to disclose information, feelings, and attitudes?

Hearing and listening are different processes and serve different purposes.

Listening

Skilled **listening** is essential to gathering information, detecting and deciphering clues, and to generating Level 2 and Level 3 responses. A common refrain is, "I hear you!" but **hearing** and **listening** are different processes. Hearing is the process of perceiving and making sense of the sounds you hear while listening (according to the International Listening Association) "is the process of receiving, constructing meaning from, and responding to spoken and/or nonverbal messages."[41] Burleson writes that "listeners interpret others' meanings, intentions, and motives," so it is not surprising that listeners often misinterpret or change another's message as they process it through their own system of beliefs, attitudes, and values.[42]

Listening like speaking is a learned and practiced skill.

Surveys indicate that few people listen well and this creates barriers in organizational positions from entry level to CEO. Active and insightful listening is a difficult skill to attain partly because our training and experiences as children, students, employees, and subordinates prepare us to be passive listeners. By this time in your education, you have probably taken one or more classes in speaking but no classes in listening or ones that address listening. As a result, interviewees may not listen carefully and perceptively to questions and interviewers do not listen carefully and perceptively to answers. You may be so absorbed in your role as interviewer or interviewee that you fail to listen to the other party's answers or information being exchanged. Listening is a collaborative effort that can build a strong link (relationship) with the other party by "listening to why they are and what they mean.[43] John

Learn when to select a specific listening approach.

Daly warns that, "No matter how effective, skilled, or competent an individual is in listening, unless he or she is perceived as listening by the other interactants, little may be accomplished."[44] If you want to become a more effective listener, you must become as satisfied as a listener as you are a talker. Listen actively and critically to both verbal and nonverbal messages while ignoring distractions, surroundings, interruptions, and appearances.

There are four approaches to listening: for comprehension, for empathy, for evaluation, and for resolution. Your task as interviewer or interviewee is to understand the roles each approach may play in giving, receiving, and processing information accurately and insightfully and which approach is most appropriate for a given time during a given interview situation. You must become skilled at switching listening approaches as interviews progress and change.

Listening for Comprehension

The goals of listening for comprehension are to receive, understand, and remember messages.

When you listen for comprehension, you strive to receive, understand, and remember nonverbal messages, words, content, instructions, and emotions as completely and accurately as possible during and following an interview. You are not to judge. This listening approach is most appropriate when you are gathering or giving information and during the initial interchanges in an interview when you are determining your role and how best to interact. Listen carefully, insightfully, and patiently to each question or answer. Focus on word choice, content, and intended or implied meanings as well as tone of voice, volume, and vocal emphasis for subtle meanings. Do not hesitate to ask questions to clarify and verify questions and answers as well as content or instructions.

Listening for Empathy

The goals of listening for empathy are to reassure, comfort, and show concern.

When you listen with empathy, you must communicate genuine concern, understanding, and involvement with the other party. Your goals may be to reassure, comfort, express warmth, and show sincere regard. You are showing the ability to "walk in another's shoes." Communicate empathy nonverbally through voice, facial expression, eye contact, leaning forward, and appropriate touch. Do not interrupt the other party.

Avoid criticisms and judgments. Reply tactfully and suggest options and guidelines rather than dictate rules, procedures, or solutions. Attempt as a listener is "to understand why the fellow communicator is responding as he/she responds."[45]

Listening for Evaluation

When listening for evaluation, avoid personal criticisms and judgments.

When you listen for evaluation, your intent is to criticize, judge, discriminate, or diagnose the content of interactions and how you hear and observe them. Employ this listening approach only after listening carefully to content and observing how it was communicated nonverbally. Ask questions for clarifications and explanations so you have a very clear picture of what you are evaluating. Avoid defensiveness when the other party challenges your criticisms and judgments. Instead, try to understand the nature and accuracy of the counter-criticisms and judgments before replying. Listening for evaluation must be collaborative in the best sense of the word. Be aware that critical assessments may diminish cooperation and level of disclosure as an interview progresses and do serious damage to the relationship you have with the other party, particularly when the other party is taken by surprise. Be sure the other party is fully apprised of your intent to listen for evaluation when arranging an interview.

Listening for Resolution

When listening for resolution, focus on resolving a problem rather than who gets the credit.

Listening for resolution, what John Stewart and Richard Johannesen call dialogic listening, focuses on **ours** rather than **mine** or **yours** with the belief that the agenda or means of resolving a problem or task supersedes the individual.[46] When you listen for resolution, encourage collaborative interactions, trust the other party's ability to make significant contributions to the task, paraphrase and add to the other party's replies and ideas for resolving a problem. Focus on the present rather than the past and on the interactions taking place at this time. Listening for resolution is most appropriate in problem-solving interviews in which the goal is a joint resolution, not an individual's success or achievement.

The Interview Situation

We are ready now for the final, interconnected, and all-encompassing pieces of the interview puzzle shown in Figure 2.6. The enveloping circle represents the **total situation** in which an interview takes place. The arrows that emerge from the top of the circle indicate that either party may **initiate** an interview. The arrows that point to the situation circle from the two parties indicate that **each party perceives** the situation from its own perspective. The imploding arrows that point from the situational circle to both parties indicate **situational variables** such as time and timing, location and setting, territoriality and proxemics, and seating. The circle to the right of the situational circle with arrows pointing to it represents **outside forces** that may suggest or dictate what happens and how during an interview.

Initiating the Interview

Whoever initiates an interview usually controls the interview.

Either party may initiate an interview and, at least at the outset, the party that initiates the interview takes on the role of interviewer, has a serious purpose, controls the agenda, and sets the tone for the interview. When and where an interview takes place may be a

Figure 2.6   *The interview situation*

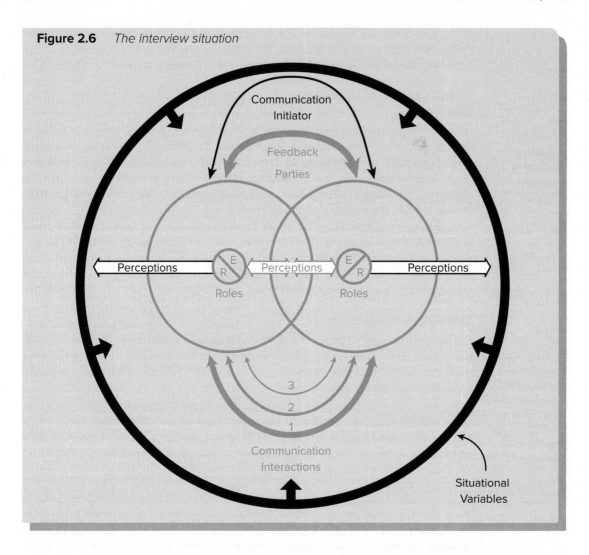

joint decision or determined by the nature of the interview. For instance, if you initiate
an interview with an academic counselor, you have a planned and serious purpose such
as discussing the courses you will take next semester, but the place is most likely to be
the counselor's office. This gives the counselor a degree of control over the situation.
Similar situations occur when you make an appointment with a physician to talk about a
painful elbow or visit a car dealer to shop for a new car. On the other hand, if the counselor, physician, or car dealer arranges an interview, roles and control are reversed. How
and when an interaction is initiated may determine the climate of the interview and the
degree to which one or both parties look forward to or dread the interaction. For example, you may enhance motivation and trust while reducing fear or defensiveness if you
contact the other party directly rather than through a third party, and explain carefully

your reason for wanting or needing an interview, the nature of the interview, the information or insights you want, and how you intend to use this information. Careful initiations that reduce questions and concerns are critical when, for instance, interviews are between teachers and students, supervisors and employees, investigative reporters and contacts, physicians and patients.

Perceptions

> How you perceive an interview situation may determine if you communicate beyond Level 1 to 2 or 3.

The arrows extending from each party to the situational circle indicate that each **perceives** the interview from his or her unique and yet similar perspective. One may see an interview as a routine event while the other sees the interview as a life-changing event; one may see it as a valuable experience while the other sees it as a waste of time; or one may see it as a threatening encounter while the other sees it as harmless. You experience these differences in common interactions. For instance, a recruiter may see an interview as a routine, daily event while an applicant may see it as a once-in-a-lifetime opportunity. A physician completing a routine physical examination wants it to be thorough, efficient, and effective while a patient may fear the results and want it to end quickly. A supervisor conducting a routine quarterly performance review may approach it as business as usual while the employee may see it as a threat to his or her financial life. You are more likely to attain or to communicate at Levels 2 and 3 when you perceive a situation to be familiar rather than unfamiliar, experienced rather than inexperienced, informal rather than formal, comfortable rather that uncomfortable, warm rather than cool, close rather than distant physically, socially, and psychologically, and private rather than public.

Time and Timing

> Not everyone views time as you do, so adapt to the party and situation.

Time is highly valued in the United States. You may have taken a college course in time management and have heard the expression, "Time is money." You are likely to expect people to be on time as you are, particularly when you have made an appointment with a specific time. You may wear a watch and carry a printed or electronic calendar with you throughout the day and check it often to be sure you are not late for an appointment. Clocks are everywhere in our society. Persons who are always late may irritate you to the point where you cease to interact with them, or give them a time that is 15 or 20 minutes earlier than needed so they will unknowingly arrive "on time." Physicians are notoriously late, so you may arrive at an appointment with work to do, a book to read, or messages to send from your phone so you do not "waste time." Other cultures do not hold time in such high esteem. In Great Britain, for instance, it is considered "correct" to be 5 to 15 minutes late, and in Italy a person may arrive two hours late and not understand why you are upset.

Be aware of the **amount of time** you have for an interview that either party may determine. A recruiter or an oral history interviewer may have an hour or more for an interview while a broadcast interviewer may have only a few minutes. Time limits determine what you can accomplish and in how much detail. As you will see in Chapter 5, a reporter at a press conference may have time for only a single question. Do not attempt to accomplish too much in too little time or violate the amount of time an interviewee has agreed to.

Timing can be
critical to the
success of an
interview.

Timing refers to the strategic selection of time and date for an interview to maximize the chances of achieving your purpose. Selecting the optimum time and date for an interview is tricky because each party may have differing notions of when it is best to communicate openly and effectively. For instance, you may be a morning person who is ready to go by 7:30 or 8:00 a.m. and considers the morning to be your most productive time of day. On the other hand, the other party may be an afternoon person who works best after a good lunch preceded by several cups of coffee, or an evening person who communicates best over dinner and well into the night. If you are arranging a dinner meeting in many European countries, plan for 8:00 p.m. or later rather than 5:00 p.m. as you might in the United States. You need to be open to exceptions determined by situation. A few years ago one of the author's students called his home at 3:30 a.m. the morning before a major examination, and he reacted strongly with, "Do you **know** what **time** it is?" The student replied, "I'm sorry to call so early, but I just learned that my brother was killed tonight in a car accident." The tone of the interaction changed abruptly from irritation to accommodation and understanding.

The legendary "cold calls" or "robo calls" interrupt meals, sleep, and important interactions so frequently that states and the Federal Government have passed "Don't call" legislation. Day of the week may be significant because Monday morning and Friday afternoon have traditionally been poor times for exchanging information and dealing with critical issues or problems. Holiday times such as Christmas, Rosh Hashanah, and Thanksgiving may be good times for some interview purposes and terrible times for others. Be aware of events that will precede or follow an interview. You would not want to be the third employee of the day to ask for a raise or ask for time off when a number of others have recently resigned or are on leave due to illness. Become as familiar as possible with a person and situation prior to arranging an interview.

Location and Setting

Location and
setting help to
create a climate
for free and open
interactions and
disclosure.

A popular saying in real estate, marketing, and business today is "It's all about location, location, location," and this saying often applies to interviews. For example, most medical interviews take place in medical facilities, academic interviews in professor's offices, journalistic interviews at the scenes of breaking news, recruiting interviews on-site, and legal interviews in attorney's offices. While an interview for auto insurance may take place in an insurance office, an interview for home or life insurance is likely to take place in a home with family present. An interview for business or agricultural insurance is likely to take place in the client's place of business such as a farm. The goal is to select a location most suitable for your interview to generate insightful interactions and disclosure. Seek a location when possible in which you feel safe and secure.

Regardless of location, make it as comfortable as possible for both parties. Select or create a moderate-sized room that is well-lighted, neither cold nor hot, is pleasantly painted, well ventilated, and has comfortable seating. You want the other party to feel at ease and, perhaps, familiar with the location. Some organizations have created settings that resemble living rooms, dining rooms, kitchens, and studies to make interview parties "feel at home" and ready to communicate because they often interact and address problems in such locations.

Decor may create an appropriate atmosphere and interview climate. Pay attention to colors and texture of painted walls, wall paper, carpeting, and curtains that enhance a warm and attractive atmosphere conducive to effective communication. Display academic degrees, awards, and professional licenses, to communicate professional credibility, achievements, and status within your field. Objects and decorations such as pictures, statues, and busts of famous leaders may communicate personal and organizational success, professionalism, recognition, and endorsements. Display models, pictures, or samples of state-of-the art products and services you offer. Personalize an area with family pictures, souvenirs from travels, and items you have made.

Noise in an interview is anything that interferes with the communication process, including background noise, doors opening and closing, music, others talking, objects being dropped, and traffic. The interview may be interrupted by a cell phone or a text message. People coming in and out of the room, walking by an open door, or asking for assistance are common distractions. Eliminate negative influences of noise by selecting locations free of background noise or taking simple precautions.

> Control noise to focus attention on the interaction.

Territoriality and Proximics

We are **territorial beings** to varying degrees, and our instinct to protect territory depends upon its nature, location, and perceived "ownership." Be aware of **whose turf** you will be on during an interview. You (and the other party as well) are likely to be most protective and defensive of **territory you actually own such** as a home, and you control this territory by determining who enters, where they go, and where they sit. You may be moderately protective of **assigned space** such as a room in a residence hall or office at work, and get upset if you find a visitor or your roommate sitting at your desk or on your bed without permission. You may be less protective of **public space** you have selected in a library, restaurant, or waiting room but stake out your territory strategically by arranging books, papers, backpack, and clothing to prevent others from moving in.

> Be keenly aware of how and when you might violate or intrude on another's territory.

You may resent others who invade your territory physically or with their eyes and voices. How have you reacted when another student walked into a professor's office while you were discussing a serious class issue with the professor, a visitor in your home placed a wet glass on top of an expensive table or book or sat in your favorite chair, a diner at a nearby table was obviously listening to what you were saying to a recruiter, or a colleague or stranger was laughing or speaking loudly while you were talking to a client? You might be less agitated and defensive if you know, like, and respect violators or know why a person appeared to violate your territory.

Proximics is the study of how you perceive and use occupational, social, and personal space. Be concerned about how the distance between interview parties might affect their comfort level and thus the degree or extent they are willing to communicate freely and openly. Trenholm and Jensen use the term "personal space" to describe an "imaginary bubble" around each of us that we consider to be "almost as private as the body itself."[47] Researchers have identified **intimate distance** as touching to 18 inches, **personal distance** as 1½ to 4 feet, and **social distance** as 4 to 12 feet. The optimum distance for most interviews is likely to be 2 to 4 feet or approximately an arm's length. You probably feel uncomfortable with persons who insist on talking "nose-to-nose" or "get in your face" and react by backing up, moving behind a chair or table, making your interactions as brief and safe as possible, or terminating the interview. The size of your imaginary bubble for interacting interpersonally depends upon the nature of your relationship with the other party and the

> We react negatively when others intrude into our personal space, our imaginary bubbles.

party's status. Your bubble is smaller when interacting with friends, close associates, and peers. High-status persons tend to stand closer to lower-status persons, while lower-status persons prefer greater distances when interacting with organizational superiors.

Age and gender may determine space preferences. For instance, persons of the same age tend to stand or sit closer together than those of mixed ages, particularly when the age difference is significant. The very old and very young tend to interact more closely for a variety of reasons including societal norms learned at an early age and communication context. All-male parties tend to sit or stand farther apart than all-female and mixed-gender parties who prefer intermediate distances. Females tend to interact more closely with either gender "as long as the conversations are neutral or friendly," but they assume greater distances if the conversation becomes threatening or alienating.[48]

Culture affects space preferences. North Americans prefer greater distances than do Latin Americans and those in the Middle East. Arabs of the same sex stand even closer than we do. Not surprisingly, Arabs and Latin Americans see North Americans as distant and cold, while we see them as intrusive. Northern Europeans prefer greater interpersonal distance than Southern Europeans. Studies reveal that Arabs, Latin Americans, and Southern Europeans are more likely to touch during interactions than Asians, Indians, Pakistanis, northern Europeans, and North Americans. India has elaborate rules about how closely members of each caste may stand or approach.[49]

Seating

Where you sit and on what you sit is often determined by status, gender, cultural norms, and relationship. A superior and a subordinate may sit across a desk from one another, arrangement A in Figure 2.7, with one sitting in a large leather swivel chair while the other sits on a simple chair. Two chairs at right angles near the corner of a desk or table, arrangement B, creates a less formal atmosphere and a greater feeling of equality between parties. Students often prefer this arrangement with college professors.

Remove physical obstacles and reduce the superior-subordinate atmosphere by placing chairs at opposite sides of a small coffee table or by omitting the table altogether, arrangements C and D. A circular table, arrangement E, is popular in counseling and interviews involving more than two people. It avoids a head-of-the-table position, allows participants to pass around materials, and provides a surface on which to write, review printed items, and place refreshments. Arrangement F is most suitable for a focus group.

Rob Daly/AGE Fotostock

■ *A corner seating arrangement is preferred by many interviewers and interviewees.*

Figure 2.7 *Seating arrangements*

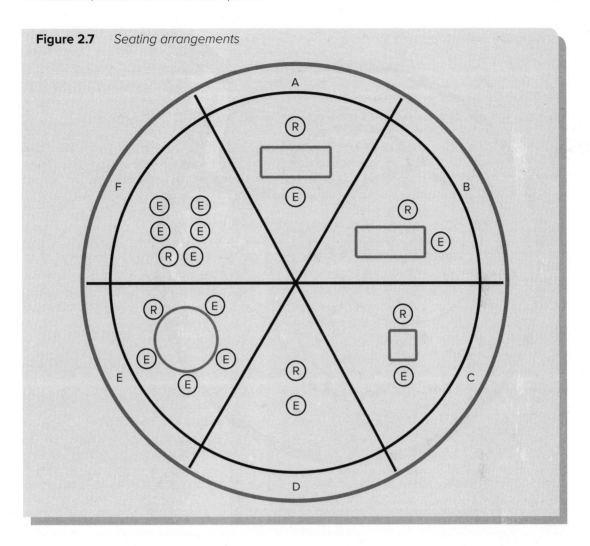

Outside Forces

Outside forces such as those identified in Figure 2.8 may suggest or dictate who takes part, when, and where; attitudes assumed; topics covered; structure followed; questions asked; and answers given. Organizational policies, union contracts, attorneys, pressures of a political campaign, Equal Employment Opportunity (EEO) laws, and competitors influence perceptions, levels of exchanges, self-disclosure, and interviewing approach. What may take place *following the interview*—a report you must submit, accounts in the media, possible grievances or lawsuits, reactions of peers—may make parties careful and wary or headstrong and hasty. You may feel pressure to relate that you "followed the rules," "drove a hard bargain," "got a deal," or told the other party "where to get off." Remember that the interview parties are seldom truly alone in the process.

> You are rarely alone with the other party.

Figure 2.8   *Outside forces*

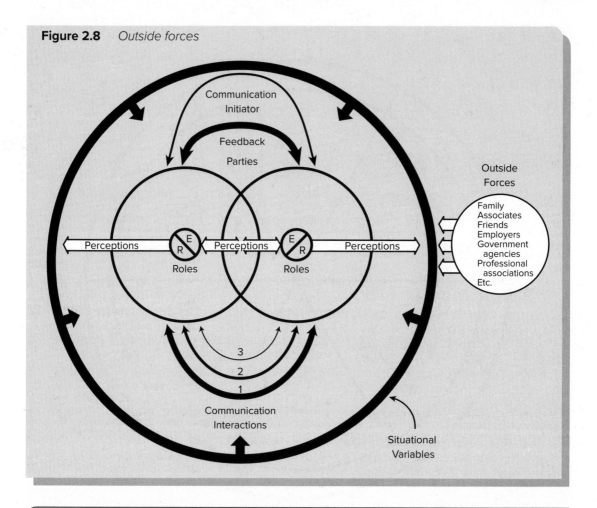

Summary

The completed **summary model** or **puzzle** of the interview shown in Figure 2.8 portrays all of the variables that make the interview an interactional, collaborative communication process. It looks very complicated because the interview is a very complex process of interrelated and interacting variables between two often unique and complex parties. Your understanding of this complicated process is a critical first step in developing and ever-improving your interviewing skills as both interviewer and interviewee.

Each interview involves two parties made up of complex individuals who may have prior relational histories or form a relationship as the interview progresses. In this collaborative process, the parties may exchange roles, maintain and alter perceptions of self, the other party, and the situation; exchange verbal and nonverbal messages; and disclose information, attitudes, opinions, and feelings at one or more levels from very safe and unrevealing to very open and highly revealing. Each party must listen appropriately for comprehension, empathy, evaluation, or resolution and realize that silence may be more effective than talking.

Each party must be flexible and adaptable in choosing which approach to take (directive, nondirective, or a combination) not only because each party is unique and each situation is different, but because each party is molded and affected by demographics such as age, gender, race, and culture. This chapter has tried to enhance your awareness of how demographics and culture affect self-esteem, disclosure, levels of communication, language, nonverbal communication, and territoriality. In the global village of the twenty-first century, be aware of how different people and different cultures interact.

Key Terms and Concepts

Age	Gender	Proximics
Appearance	Gestures	Relational distance
Assumptions	Global relationships	Relational history
Atmosphere	Head	Relational memory
Climate	Hearing	Risk
Collaborative	Idioms	Self-concept
Common ground	Initiating	Self Disclosure
Connotations	Interacting variables	Self-esteem
Context	Interview puzzle	Self-fulfilling prophecy
Control	Jargon	Self-identity
Culture	Levels of interactions	Silence
Décor	Listening	Situation
Defensive climate	Location	Slang
Dialectical tensions	Movement	Summary model
Dialogic listening	Noise	Supportive climate
Directive approach	Nondirective approach	Territoriality
Distance	Open-mind	Time
Downward communication	Outside forces	Timing
Eye contact	Perceptions	Verbal interactions
Face	Personal space	
Feedback	Politeness theory	

Student Activities

1. Interview four students on your campus: one from Central America, one from southern Europe, one from the Near East, and one from Asia. Ask them to identify and illustrate verbal and nonverbal communication problems they have encountered since coming to the United States. How have they managed to work through these problems?

2. Interview four students on your campus who come from different areas of the United States such as New England, the South, the Midwest, and southern California. Ask them to identify and illustrate verbal communication differences they have encountered since arriving on campus. What problems have these differences caused in interactions?

3. Research indicates measurable differences in communication between genders. Observe interactions between two males, two females, and a male and a female to see what differences if any you can detect in proximity, eye contact, gestures, body movements, and territoriality. What influence do you believe the prior relationships of the parties had on these nonverbal and situational factors?

4. Watch three different types of 10- to 15-minute interviews on ESPN, C-SPAN, 60-Minutes, or other programs. For example, one might be an interview with a coach prior to a major game, one might be an investigative interview after a school shooting, one might be an interview with the victim of a terrible accident, or one might be with a candidate for political office in the midst of a tough campaign. Which forms of listening did the participants use most often during each interview? How did the relationship between interviewer and interviewee appear to affect listening? How did the situation, including location, timing, territoriality, and proximics, affect the ability of parties to listen appropriately and insightfully?

Review Questions

1. What are the five dimensions of relationships?
2. How are relational history and relational memory similar and different?
3. Explain how upward and downward communication may affect interviews?
4. How might dialectical tensions affect an interview?
5. How does culture affect relationships?
6. Explain the difference between directive and nondirective approach to interviews?
7. What is self-concept or self-identity and why is it important in interviews?
8. Compare and contrast the three levels of interaction?
9. How do men and women differ in self-disclosure?
10. What may be the greatest single problem in human communication?
11. According to researchers, what percentage of communicative interactions is nonverbal in nature?
12. Compare and contrast listening for evaluation with listening for empathy.
13. What is the difference between time and timing in interviews?
14. Explain the notion of proximics and why it is relevant to interviews.
15. Explain the differences of intimate distance, personal distance, and social distance.

Notes

1. Robert S. Goyer, W. Charles Redding, and John T. Rickey, *Interviewing Principles and Techniques: A Project Text* (Dubuque, IA: Wm. C. Brown, 1968), p. 23.
2. James W. Neuliep, *Intercultural Communication: A Contextual Approach,* 6th ed. (Los Angeles, CA: Sage, 2015), pp. 331–332.
3. Judith N. Martin and Thomas K. Nakayama, *Intercultural Communication in Contexts* (New York: McGraw-Hill, 2007), p. 371.
4. Judith N. Martin and Thomas K. Nakayama, *Experiencing Intercultural Communication* (New York: McGraw-Hill, 2011), pp. 255–256.
5. Sarah Trenholm and Arthur Jensen, *Interpersonal Communication* (New York: Oxford University Press, 2013), pp. 38–39.

6. George B. Ray and Kory Floyd, "Nonverbal Expressions of Liking and Disliking in Initial Interaction: Encoding and Decoding Perspectives," *Southern Communication Journal* 71 (March 2006), p. 60.

7. Trenholm and Jensen (2013), p. 31.

8. Edward T. Hall, "Context and Meaning," in Larry A. Samovar and Richard E. Porter, eds., *Intercultural Communication: A Reader* (Belmont, CA: Wadsworth, 2000), p. 35.

9. John Stewart, ed., *Bridges Not Walls: A Book about Interpersonal Communication* (New York: McGraw-Hill, 2012), p. 317.

10. Kory Floyd, *Interpersonal Communication: The Whole Story* (New York: McGraw-Hill, 2011), p. 317; Trenholm and Jensen (2013), pp. 29, 276–277.

11. Floyd, p. 317.

12. Neuliep, p. 331.

13. Judith N. Martin, Thomas K. Nakayama, and Lisa A. Flores, *Intercultural Communication Experiences and Contexts* (New York: McGraw-Hill, 2004), p. 334.

14. Brant Burleson and Adrienne Kunkel, "Revisiting the Different Cultures Thesis: An Assessment of Sex Differences and Similarities in Supportive Communication," in K. Dindia and D. J. Canary, eds., *Sex Differences and Similarities in Communication* (Mahwah, NJ: Lawrence Erlbaum, 2006), pp. 137–159.

15. Trenholm and Jensen (2013), pp. 95–97.

16. John Stewart and Carole Logan, *Together: Communicating Interpersonally* (New York: McGraw-Hill, 1998), p. 84.

17. Trenholm and Jensen (2013), p. 315.

18. Stewart, p. 293.

19. Stewart, p. 334.

20. Stewart, p. 20.

21. Stewart, p. 26.

22. Trenholm and Jensen (2013), pp. 85 and 270.

23. Neuliep, p. 58.

24. Floyd, p. 77.

25. Fred E. Jandt, *An Introduction to Intercultural Communication: Identities in a Global Community,* 8th ed. (Los Angeles, CA: Sage, 2016), p. 44.

26. Stewart (2012), pp. 214–215; Trenholm and Jensen (2013), pp. 193–194; Floyd, pp. 98–99.

27. Jandt, pp. 270–271.

28. Stephen W. Littlejohn, *Theories of Human Communication* (Belmont, CA: Wadsworth, 1996), p. 262.

29. Raymond Cohen, *Negotiating Across Cultures: Communication Obstacles in International Diplomacy* (Washington, DC: Institute of Peace Press, 1997), as cited in Jandt, p. 51.

30. Laura K. Guerrero, Peter A. Andersen, and Walid A. Afifi, *Close Encounters in Relationships* (New York: McGraw-Hill, 2001), p. 46.

31. Neuliep, p. 271.

32. Mark L. Knapp, Judith A. Hall, and Terrence G. Hogan, *Nonverbal Communication in Human Action,* 8th ed. (Boston, MA: Wadsworth, 2014), p. 8.

33. Michael Skube, "Writing Off Reading," *Washington Post*, August 20, 2006, www.washingtonpost.com. Accessed August 30, 2006.

34. Guerrero, Andersen, and Afifi, pp. 297–298; Diana K. Ivy and Phil Backlund, *Exploring Gender Speak: Personal Effectiveness in Gender Communication* (New York: McGraw-Hill, 1994), pp. 163–165.

35. Wen-Shu Lee, "That's Greek to Me: Between a Rock and a Hard Place in Intercultural Encounters," in Larry A. Samovar and Richard E. Porter, eds., *Intercultural Communication: A Reader* (Belmont, CA: Wadsworth, 2000), pp. 217–219.

36. Irving J. Lee, *How to Talk with People* (New York: Harper & Row, 1952), pp. 11–26.

37. See for example Knapp, Hall, and Hogan, pp. 7–11.

38. Knapp, Hall, and Hogan, p. 155.

39. Knapp, Hall, and Hogan, p. 384.

40. Trenholm and Jensen (2013), pp. 331–333; Jandt, pp. 108–110 and 115; Neuliep, pp. 285–287; and Knapp, Hall, and Hogan, pp. 200–213.

41. Andrew D. Wolvin, ed., *Listening and Human Communication in the 21st Century* (Malden, MA: Blackwell Publishing, 2010), p. 9.

42. As cited in Wolvin, pp. 12–13.

43. Michael Purdy as cited in Wolvin, p. 17.

44. John Daly as cited in Wolvin, p. 15.

45. J. Walker as cited in Wolvin, p. 15

46. Stewart, pp. 192–194; Richard Johannesen (1971) as cited in Wolvin, p. 128.

47. Trenholm and Jensen (2013), p. 55.

48. Knapp, Hall, and Hogan, pp. 137–138.

49. Martin and Nakayama (2011), pp. 176–178; Jandt, p. 107; Knapp, Hall, and Hogan, p. 138.

Resources

Jandt, Fred E. *An Introduction to Intercultural Communication: Identities in a Global Community.* Los Angeles, CA: Sage, 2016.

Knapp, Mark L., Judith A. Hall, and Terrence G. Hogan. *Nonverbal Communication in Human Interaction.* Boston, MA: Wadsworth, 2014.

Stewart, John, ed. *Bridges Not Walls: A Book about Interpersonal Communication.* New York: McGraw-Hill, 2012.

Trenholm, Sarah, and Arthur Jensen. *Interpersonal Communication.* New York: Oxford University Press, 2013.

Wolvin, Andrew D., ed. *Listening and Human Communication in the 21st Century.* Malden, MA: Blackwell Publishing, 2010.

Questions and Their Uses

Technology editor Jamie McKenzie writes, "Questions may be the most powerful technology we have ever created" because "they allow us to control our lives and allow us to make sense of a confusing world" by leading "to insight and understanding."[1] Questions need not be complete sentences with question marks at the end. They are *words, phrases, statements, or nonverbal acts that invite answers or responses.*

It is difficult to imagine an interview of any type—investigative, journalistic, survey, employment, persuasive, counseling, or health care—without questions because questions are crucial to the interactional process. They are literally the "tools of the interview trade" much like golf clubs, screw drivers, wrenches, knives, and brushes. When you head out to play a round of golf, for example, you have a bag that contains a variety of clubs. You know when and how to use each club that has a specific purpose, unique characteristics, and name such as driver, 3 wood, 5 iron, putter, sand wedge, or pitching wedge. Likewise, each type of question has a name and unique characteristics that enable you to perform specific functions and tasks efficiently and effectively during interviews. Interviews may consist solely of questions and answers.

> A question is any verbal or non-verbal message that invokes an answer.

The objectives of this chapter are to name, define, and illustrate each type of question you may employ during interviews. You will learn when and how to use both basic and specialized types of questions while avoiding common question pitfalls. Let us begin with the two basic types of questions: open and closed.

Open and Closed Questions

Open and closed questions vary in the amount of information they solicit and degree of interviewer control. Answers range from single words to lengthy descriptions, narratives, and reports of statistical data. Control ranges from minimal for open-ended questions to maximum with closed questions.

> Open questions invite open answers.

Open Questions

Open questions vary in degree of openness and give respondents considerable freedom to determine the amount and kind of information to give.

Highly Open Questions

Highly open questions place virtually no restrictions on the interviewee.

- Describe the new baseball stadium being constructed on the south side of town.

Open questions let the respondent do the talking and allow the interviewer to listen and observe.

- Tell me about your new cell phone.
- What do you recall from your deployment in Afghanistan?

Moderately Open Questions

Moderately open questions are more restrictive but give respondents considerable latitude in answers.

- Describe the playing field in the new baseball stadium being constructed on the south side of town.
- Tell me about the new features of your new cell phone.
- Tell me about the most memorable event you experienced during your deployment in Afghanistan.

Advantages of Open Questions

> Interviewees can volunteer and elaborate.

Open questions show interest and trust in the respondent's ability to disclose important information. They encourage respondents to talk and to determine the type and amount of information to disclose. The lengthy answers open questions generate, reveal what respondents think is important and encourage them to provide details and descriptions you might not think to ask for. Answers disclose knowledge level, uncertainty, intensity of feelings, perceptions, and biases.

Disadvantages of Open Questions

> Interviewees can pick and choose, reveal and hide.

A single answer may consume a significant portion of interview time. On the one hand, respondents may give unimportant or irrelevant information, and on the other may withhold important information they feel is irrelevant or too obvious, sensitive, or dangerous. Keep respondents on track and maintain control by encouraging them to move on.

Closed Questions

Closed questions are narrowly focused and restrict the interviewee's freedom to determine the amount and kind of information to provide.

> Restricted questions lead to restricted answers.

Moderately Closed Questions

Moderately closed questions ask for specific, limited pieces of information, such as:

- Which New England states have you visited?
- What types of books do you read?
- What are your favorite ski resorts in Colorado?

Highly Closed Questions

Highly closed questions are restrictive, often asking respondents for a single piece of information.

- Where did you get your bachelor's degree?
- When did you attend the University of New Hampshire?
- What was your major area of study?

Bipolar Questions

Closed questions are **bipolar** when they limit respondents to two polar choices, sometimes polar opposites.

- Are you a Republican or a Democrat?
- Did you take the bi-pass or come through town?
- Did you cast your vote on election day or by absentee ballot?

Some bipolar questions ask for an evaluation or attitude.

- Do you like or dislike traffic circles?
- Do you approve or disapprove of raising tariffs on imported goods from Canada?
- Are you for or against restricting the sale of assault weapons?

A common bipolar question asks for a yes or a no response.

- Are you going to attend commencement?
- Do you have a passport?
- Have you replied to the health care survey?

Advantages of Closed Questions

Closed questions enable you to control the length of answers and guide respondents to specific information. They require little effort from either party and allow you to ask more questions, in more areas, in less time. Brief answers are easy to record and tabulate.

Disadvantages of Closed Questions

Answers to closed questions may contain little information, and may require you to ask several questions when one open question would do the job. They do not reveal why a person has a particular attitude, the person's degree of feeling or commitment, or why this person typically makes choices. Interviewers talk more than interviewees when asking closed questions, so less information is exchanged. Interviewees have no opportunity to volunteer or explain information and may select an answer or say yes or no with no knowledge about a topic.

Figure 3.1 illustrates the major advantages and disadvantages of open and closed questions. As you narrow a question, the amount of data decreases. As the amount of

Figure 3.1   *Question options*

Advantages and Disadvantages of Question Types	Type of Questions			
	Highly Open	Moderately Open	Moderately Closed	Highly Closed
Breadth and depth of potential information	10	7	4	1
Degree of precision, reproducibility, reliability	1	4	7	10
R's control over question and response	1	4	7	10
Interviewer skill required	10	7	4	1
Reliability of data	1	4	7	10
Economic use of time	1	4	7	10
Opportunity for E to reveal feelings and information	10	7	4	1
	10 High	7 Above average	4 Average	1 Low

data decreases, your control increases, less time and skill are required, and the degree of precision, reliability, and reproducibility increases. On the other hand, as you open up a question, the amount of data increases and interviewees may reveal knowledge level, understanding, reasons for feeling or acting, attitudes, and hidden motives.

Interviewers may include open and closed questions with varying degrees of constraint to get the information desired. For instance, an interviewer might follow up a bipolar question such as "Are you familiar with the new security master plan designed to prevent shootings in our classrooms?" with an open question such as "Tell me what you know about this security plan." An open question such as "Tell me about your river cruise on the Danube?" may precede or follow one or more closed questions such as "How many days did you spend in Vienna" and "What was the most memorable site on your river cruise?"

> **Combinations of open and closed questions may produce the best results.**

Primary and Probing Questions

Primary questions initiate topics or new areas within a topic and can stand alone when taken out of context.

- How did you train for the Chicago Marathon?
- Who influenced you most in choosing to major in biological sciences?
- Tell me about your experiences as a high school resource officer.

All examples of open and closed questions presented earlier are primary questions.

Probing questions, sometimes called follow-up questions, dig into responses to primary or probing questions for **more information** because they are superficial, incomplete, or require **clarification** because they are vague or suggestive. Unlike primary questions that can stand alone and make sense, probing questions make sense only when connected to another question or series of questions.

Types of Probing Questions

Nudging Probes

If an answer is incomplete or a respondent appears hesitant to continue, perhaps wanting to detect how much you want to know, use a **nudging probe** to encourage the person to continue talking. Nudging probes are simple and brief.

I see.	And?
Go on.	So?
Yes?	Unhuh?

Do not assume that all questions must be multiple word sentences with nouns and verbs. A lengthy probing question may stifle an exchange rather than encourage it to continue or inadvertently direct the respondent to a new area or subject. This is the opposite of what you want to happen.

Silent Probes

If an answer seems incomplete or a respondent appears to be hesitant to continue, substitute a nonverbal signal for a verbal one by using a **silent probe** such as eye contact, head nod, or gesture to encourage a person to continue. Silence can communicate continuing interest in or agreement with what is being said. On the other hand, it may communicate uncertainty, disbelief, or confusion more tactfully than words. An interaction might occur like this:

1. **Interviewer:** Tell me about the seminar you attended on employment interviewing.
2. **Interviewee:** Well, it lasted about an hour and included a lot of information on how to prepare for and take part in interviews.
3. **Interviewer:** (silence)
4. **Interviewee:** The speaker emphasized the need to brand yourself because you are basically trying to sell yourself to a recruiter and appear more attractive than other applicants.

Clearinghouse Probes

Do not assume
you have all of
the information
a respondent
has to offer.

A **clearinghouse probe** discovers whether a series of questions has uncovered everything of importance on a topic or issue by encouraging respondents to volunteer information you might not think to ask for and to fill in gaps your questions did not elicit. It literally clears out an area or topic, such as the following:

- Is there anything else you would like to add?
- What have I not covered that you think is important for me to know?
- Have you told me everything you can remember?

A **clearinghouse probing question** enables you to proceed to the next primary question or to closing the interview confident you have gotten all relevant and important information. It is virtually impossible to anticipate everything an interviewee might be willing or able to reveal.

Informational Probes

Dig deeper
into superficial,
vague, and
suggestive
answers.

Informational probing questions ask for additional information or explanation. If an answer is **superficial** or vague, ask a question such as:

- You say the proposed contract provides increases for health care, raises, and 401Ks. Tell me about these increases.
- You have listed several positions you have held in marketing. Tell me about your marketing responsibilities at Ford Motor Company.
- You say your position as ombudsman has enabled you to assist staff in resolving issues pertaining to duties, hours, overtime, and promotions. Explain your role in helping to resolve such issues.

If an answer is **ambiguous,** ask a question such as:

- Tell me about your "close relationship" with the mayor.
- You say you grew up in a "traditional" Midwestern family. How so?
- So you attended a "small" college. How many students were enrolled?

If an answer **suggests** a feeling or attitude, ask a question such as:

- You seem upset by the judge's decision.
- You appear to be somewhat fearful about your approaching graduation.
- Are you saying the school board is prejudiced against same-sex marriages?

Restate or
rephrase ques-
tions to refocus
responses that
are off target or
mistaken.

Restatement Probes

An interviewee may not answer a question **as asked.** Restate tactfully all or part of the original question, perhaps with vocal emphasis to focus attention on important words.

1. **Interviewer:** Why are you interested in this research position with Alcoa?

2. **Interviewee:** Well, I'm really interested in a position on the cutting edge of new developments in which I can play a major role on a research team.

3. **Interviewer:** I see. And why are you interested in **this position** with **Alcoa**?

If an interviewee **makes a mistake,** use a restatement probe that avoids embarrassing or judging the interviewee.

1. **Interviewer:** Which state park do you believe is the best for camping and hiking?

2. **Interviewee:** Clark State Forest is my favorite for camping and hiking.

3. **Interviewer:** And which state **park** do you like best for camping and hiking?

> **Has the respondent answered all of your questions?**

When an interviewee seems **hesitant** to answer, your question may be unclear or difficult to answer. Restate the question in a clearer, easier to answer wording.

1. **Interviewer:** You have been married for 25 years, what is your philosophy of marriage?

2. **Interviewee:** I'm not sure I have a marriage philosophy.

3. **Interviewer:** What do you believe are the ingredients of a happy, long-term marriage?

If your question has more than **two parts** or **options,** an interviewee may answer only one. Give the interviewee a moment to answer fully, then restate the part or option left unanswered.

1. **Interviewer:** When the cruise boat capsized in the storm, what did you think and do first?

2. **Interviewee:** My first thought was that it couldn't be happening. It was like a scene from a disaster movie.

3. **Interviewer:** What did you do first?

Reflective Probes

> **A reflective probe clarifies or verifies a specific answer.**

Interviewers ask **reflective probing questions** to **clarify** or **verify** answers to be sure they understand them as intended. When asking reflective probing questions, avoid words or nonverbal signals interviewees might perceive to be attempts to lead or trap them into giving answers you want to hear.

- That was your **net** income last year?
- Are you referring to New York **city** or New York **state**?
- You seem to be implying that **all** illegal immigrants are from Mexico.

Mirror Probes

> **Mirror probing questions reflect or summarize a series of answers.**

Interviewers ask **mirror probing questions** to **summarize** a **series of** answers to be sure they **understand** and **retain** information, instructions, elements of a proposal, prescribed regimens, and procedures as accurately and completely as possible. For instance, you might use a mirror question when interviewing a manager of an apartment complex.

1. **Interviewer:** Let me see if I have the basic information correct about your available two-bedroom apartments. Each has a living room, two bedrooms with two single beds in each, a kitchen with microwave, dishwasher, oven with broiler, a side-by-side refrigerator, a table with four chairs for meals, and a utility room with washer and dryer. Also, all utilities are covered in the monthly rental payment.

2. **Interviewee:** That's correct, but some units have a queen size bed instead of two singles.

Skillful Interviewing with Probing Questions

Be patient and be persistent.

Your skillful use of probing questions is essential to successful interviewing, the exception being survey interviews in which all questions and possible answers are prepared ahead of time. Otherwise, prepare primary questions with anticipated probing questions under each prior to an interview. Listen carefully during the interview to each response to determine if the answer is clear, accurate, and complete. If not, determine within seconds what is unsatisfactory and ask an appropriate probing question. Probing questions not only discover more relevant, accurate, and complete information but also heighten the other party's motivation because you are obviously interested and listening carefully. Do not leap in too quickly with a probing question while the interviewee is still replying meaningfully. Premature interruptions may prevent an interviewee from giving important information and insights and seriously damage the interactive process because you appear to be impatient and critical. Phrase probing questions carefully and be aware of your vocal emphasis on specific words. Stanley Payne illustrates how the meaning of a simple "Why" question can be altered by stressing different words.[2]

Why do you say that?

Why *do* you say that?

Why do *you* say that?

Why do you *say* that?

Why do you say *that?*

Be careful and tactful when probing into answers.

A "simple" why question may unintentionally communicate disapproval, disbelief, mistrust, and cause the other party to become defensive and reluctant to disclose openly. A poorly phrased probing question may alter the meaning of the primary question or bias the reply. Be tactful and not demanding.

Exercise #1—Supply the Probing Question

Supply an appropriate probing question for each of the following interactions. Be sure the question probes into the answer and is not a primary question introducing a new facet of the topic. Watch assumptions about answers, and phrase probing questions tactfully.

1. **Interviewer:** How much did that sailboat cost?

   Interviewee: A ton!

   Interviewer:

2. **Interviewer:** What did you do during your internship at ABC?

   Interviewee: I helped edit news stories and stuff like that?

   Interviewer:

3. **Interviewer:** Who did you vote for during the 2016 Presidential election?

   Interviewee: Mitt Romney.

   Interviewer:

4. **Interviewer:** What did you think of the President's commencement address?

   Interviewee: It was fairly typical.

   Interviewer:

5. **Interviewer:** I understand you think climate change is a hoax.

   Interviewee: Not completely.

   Interviewer:

6. **Interviewer:** What is your teaching philosophy?

   Interviewee: (silence)

   Interviewer:

7. **Interviewer:** Are you considering law school?

   Interviewee: Sort of.

   Interviewer:

8. **Interviewer:** Which candidate for Senator are you going to vote for?

   Interviewee: I don't know.

   Interviewer:

9. **Interviewer:** Why did you decide to major in English?

   Interviewee: I enjoy reading.

   Interviewer:

10. **Interviewer:** What do you think of the "Me Too" movement?

    Interviewee: It's out of control.

    Interviewer:

Neutral and Leading Questions

Neutral questions enable respondents to answer without direction or pressure from questioners. For example, in an open, neutral question, the interviewee determines the length, details, and nature of the answer. In a closed, neutral question, the interviewee may choose between equal choices. All questions discussed and illustrated so far have been neutral questions.

Leading questions indicate an interviewer's preferred answer.

The **leading question** may **intentionally** or **unintentionally** suggest the answer the interviewer expects or prefers, so the interviewee gives this answer because it is "easier or more tempting" to give that answer.[3] This **interviewer bias** may occur by the way a question is phrased, how a question is asked nonverbally, the interviewee's desire to please a person of authority, or a conspicuous symbol the interviewer is wearing such as a cross or star of David, a political button, or a police uniform. What may appear to be a bipolar question is actually a **unipolar question** because one option is made less acceptable than the other. Introductory phrases such as "According to the Constitution," "As we all know," or "All true conservatives (liberals) believe that" may lead respondents to give acceptable answers rather than express their true beliefs, attitudes, or feelings.

> Loaded questions may virtually dictate answers.

The **loaded question** virtually dictates the answer an interviewer wants to hear. It often includes extreme language such as name-calling, emotionally charged words, and expletives. The interviewer may send unmistakable nonverbal clues through voice, eye-contact, or gestures. Biased answer options give the interviewee little choice in how to respond. **Entrapment** occurs when an interviewer asks a no-win question such as the iconic "Are you still beating your wife" or "Are you still cheating on your taxes?" Interviewees cannot reply without admitting to an onerous or illegal act.

Regardless of their potential problems in interviews, leading questions are useful and often necessary question tools. Recruiters use them to see how applicants respond under stress. Sales representatives use leading questions to persuade customers to make decisions. Police officers ask leading and sometimes loaded questions to provoke suspects into revealing information and truths. Journalists ask leading questions to prod reluctant interviewees into responding. A counselor may use a loaded question such as "When was the last time you were drunk" to show that a range of answers is acceptable and none will shock the interviewer.

> Leading questions have legitimate functions.

Do not confuse neutral **reflective** and **mirror** questions with **leading** questions. Recall that reflective and mirror questions ask for clarification and verification for accurate understanding and information. If they lead an interviewee by accident to give an answer you appear to desire, they have failed to perform their designed task.

The questions below illustrate the differences between neutral and leading questions and distinguish leading from loaded questions.

Neutral Questions	Leading Questions
1. Have you ever smoked an electronic cigarette?	1. When did you last smoke an electronic cigarette?
2. How did this Alaska cruise compare with the last one?	2. Wasn't this Alaska cruise better than the last one?
3. Have you ever cheated on a final exam?	3. Have you stopped cheating on final examinations?
4. Do you want a diet Pepsi?	4. I assume you want a diet Pepsi?
5. Do you enjoy video games?	5. You enjoy video games, don't you?
6. What did you think of the CEOs presentation?	6. What did you think of the CEOs ridiculous presentation?
7. Are you a conservative or a liberal?	7. Are you a conservative or a Socialist?
8. How do you feel about daily workouts?	8. Do you hate daily workouts as much as I do?

9. Are you going to church today?

9. You're going to church today, aren't you?

10. How do you feel about gay marriages?

10. How do you feel about gay marriages that are destroying the very foundation of marriage?

Figure 3.2 compares types of questions available to interviewers and interviewees, including open and closed, primary and probing, and neutral and leading questions.

Exercise #2—Identification of Questions

Identify each of the following questions in four ways: (1) open or closed, (2) primary or probing, (3) neutral or leading, and (4) whether it is a special type of question tool: bipolar, loaded, nudging probe, clearinghouse probe, informational probe, restatement probe, reflective probe, or mirror probe.

1. And then?

2. Is there anything else I should know about the confrontation between the players and coaches yesterday?

3. You are concerned about your health, aren't you?

4. Okay, it sounds like our river cruise on the Rhine is all set. We fly from Indianapolis to JFK and then on to Zurich. You fly from Philadelphia to Frankfort and then to Zurich and land five minutes after we do. After a few days in Zurich and Lucerne, we travel to Basil where we board the AMA Dante on the 14th and head north through Switzerland, France, Germany, and the Netherlands to Amsterdam. From

Figure 3.2   *Types of questions*

	Neutral		Leading	
	Open	**Closed**	**Open**	**Closed**
Primary	How do you feel about the new tax law?	Do you approve or disapprove of the new tax law?	Most people favor the new tax law, how do you feel about it?	Do you favor the new tax law like most people I have talked to?
Probing	Why do you feel this way?	Is your approval moderate or strong?	If you favor the tax law, why did you initially oppose it?	I assume you favor the new tax law because you are in a top bracket?

there we fly to Detroit and on to Indianapolis while you fly non-stop to Philadelphia. Is this correct?

5. Are you saying the main reason you studied civil engineering was to work outdoors?

6. Tell me more about the backpacking portion of your vacation.

7. **Interviewer:** What did you think of the All Star game?

    Interviewer: The pre-game show was fantastic.

    Interviewer: And what about the game?

8. Did you vote in the last Presidential election?

9. What did you do in the Air Force?

10. Stopping in the middle of the Interstate was stupid, wasn't it?

Common Question Pitfalls

Interviewers and interviewees have a variety of question tools that enable them to gather information and insights into experiences, reactions, beliefs, attitudes, and feelings, but they must phrase each question carefully to avoid common **question pitfalls.** Each pitfall makes it more difficult to perform interview tasks efficiently and effectively.

The Unintentional Bipolar Question

The bipolar question is designed to elicit a yes or no answer or a choice among two poles. The problem arises when you **unintentionally** ask a bipolar question when you want a lengthy answer or when there are more than two choices from which a respondent may choose. Be aware of common phrases that initiate bipolar rather than open questions: *Do you, Did you, Are you, Have you, Will you, Can you, Would you, Is there, and Was it?* If you want an open-ended answer rather than a bipolar one, open your question with words and phrases such as: *What, Why, How, Explain,* and *Tell me about?*

The Yes (No) Question

> Predictable
> questions pro-
> duce predictable
> responses.

The yes (no) question pitfall occurs when you ask a question with only one obvious answer, a yes or a no. Too often a professor asks a student, "Do you want to fail this course?" or a physician asks a patient, "Do you want to have a heart attack?" Phrase each question carefully so you do not get the only answer you can expect.

The Tell Me Everything Question

The tell me everything question is the opposite of the unintentional bipolar question and the yes (no) question. This pitfall occurs when you ask an extremely open-ended question with no limits or guidelines. When you ask a question such as 'Tell me about your travels in eastern Europe." The interviewee may not know where to begin, what and how much to include, and when to end an answer. Narrow the focus of questions to enable the interviewee to answer succinctly and to the point.

How you ask a question may bias the answer you receive.

The Open-to-Closed Question

The open-to-closed pitfall occurs when you ask an open question and then switch it to a closed question, often bipolar, before the interviewee can reply. For instance, you may ask *"What did you do while you were in Paris?"* and then ask *"Did you go up the Eiffel Tower?"* before an interviewee can reply. The answer may be a yes or no and focus only on the Eiffel tower. You may lose a significant body of information even if you try to get back to your original question. Avoid this pitfall by preparing questions carefully in advance, thinking through each question before asking it, and allowing the interviewee to reply before rephrasing or narrowing the question.

> Ask an open question and then stop.

The Double-Barreled Question

> Ask one question at a time.

The double-barreled question pitfall occurs when you ask a question that actually poses two questions such as, *"Tell me about your internships at Microsoft and Intel"* or "Why did you choose Indiana State University for your bachelor's degree and the University of Illinois for your master's degree?" Interviewees may answer each embedded question superficially rather than give lengthy responses, answer only the question they can remember, or answer the preferred question. The result may be too little information on each or no answer to one unless you think to ask probing questions.

The Unintentional Leading Question

The unintentional leading question pitfall occurs when you ask a leading question without knowing it. The unintended influence may be verbal or nonverbal, and you may be unaware that an interviewee is giving an answer you seem to want to hear rather than what the person knows or believes or how the person feels or acts. Listen carefully to how you phrase and ask each question, and ask yourself "Did I do anything to provoke an inaccurate response?"

The Guessing Question

> Don't guess; ask!

The guessing question pitfall occurs when you try to **guess** information instead of **asking** for it. A string of guessing questions may fail to accomplish what a single open-ended or informational question can. For instance, instead of asking *"Did the tornado sound like a freight train?"* ask *"What did the tornado sound like?* Instead of asking *"Did you try to put out the fire? ask "What did you do when you saw the fire?*

SDI Productions/E+/Getty Images

The Curious Question

The curious question pitfall occurs when you ask for information you do not need. For example, are you merely **curious** about a person's age, marital status, income level, or religious beliefs that have nothing to do with the interview and its stated purpose. The interviewee has the right to say this information is none of your business or to ask the purpose of the question. If a question may **appear** to be irrelevant, explain why this information is relevant and necessary.

The Too High or Too Low Question

The too high or too low pitfall occurs when you fail to take into consideration the interviewee's levels of knowledge and expertise. Questions above these levels may cause embarrassment or resentment for appearing uninformed, ill-informed, uneducated, or unintelligent. Questions below these levels may be insulting. Know whether a respondent is a layperson, novice, or expert on a topic or issue and phrase your questions accordingly.

The Don't Ask, Don't Tell Question

Delve into inaccessible areas only when necessary.

The don't ask, don't tell pitfall occurs when you delve into information and emotions that interviewees may be incapable of addressing because of social, psychological, or situational constraints. For instance, we learn at an early age that it is more socially acceptable to be humble rather than boastful. So when we are asked to assess our beauty, intelligence, creativity, or bravery, we are most likely to pose an "Aw shucks" attitude or make a joke of our answer. We are told that there is an appropriate time and place for everything but that some areas are usually off limits or taboo such as sex, personal income, religious convictions, and certain illnesses. For instance, we find it easier to discuss physical rather than mental illnesses. Explain why a question is essential to ask, and delay "touchy" or "taboo" questions until you have established a comfortable climate and positive relationship. Phrase questions carefully to lessen social and psychological constraints and to avoid offending interviewees.

Gender and cultural differences may affect social and psychological *accessibility*. Research indicates that women disclose more information about themselves, use more psychological or emotional verbs, discuss their personal lives more in business interactions, have less difficulty expressing intimate feelings, talk more about other people's accomplishments and minimize their own, and appear to be more comfortable when hearing accolades about themselves.[4] Cultures also differ in readily accessible areas. Learn as much as you can about an interviewee prior to an interview to determine what can and cannot be asked and how it should be asked.

Avoid pitfalls by preparing and thinking.

Avoid common question pitfalls by planning questions prior to the interview so you do not have to create them on the spot in the give-and-take of the interaction. Think before asking a question, stop when you have asked a good open question instead of rephrasing it, use bipolar questions sparingly, avoid questions that are too open-ended, ask only necessary questions, ask for information at the interviewee's level, avoid complex questions, and be aware of the accessibility factor in questions and answers. Know the common question pitfalls well enough to catch yourself before tumbling into one.

O N   T H E   W E B

Browse an Internet site to locate a variety of question–answer interactions that vary in intensity from happy to sad, cooperative to uncooperative, friendly to hostile, and understanding to patronizing. Identify the different types of primary and probing questions in these interactions. Which question pitfalls can you identify? Which of these pitfalls were accidental and which purposeful? Use search engines such as the Knight Ridder Newspapers (http://www.kri .com), CNBC (http://www.cnbc.com), and CNN (http://cnn.com).

Exercise #3—What Are the Pitfalls in These Questions?

Each of the following questions illustrates one or more of the common question pitfalls: unintentional bipolar question, yes (no) question, tell me everything question, open-to-closed question, double-barreled question, unintentional leading question, guessing question, curious question, too high or too low question, and don't ask, don't tell question. Identify the pitfall(s) of each question and rephrase it to make it a good question. Avoid a new pitfall in your revised question.

1. Tell me about Japan.
2. Do you see yourself as a saint?
3. Do you approve or disapprove of legalizing marijuana?
4. (asked of an employee) Do you want to be fired?
5. Did you like the sermon this morning?
6. You believe in global warming, don't you?
7. Tell me about the classes you teach and your research.
8. What did you think when you first saw your home in ashes after the forest fire; was it "Why me?"
9. Did you study forestry so you could work outdoors?
10. Asked during a recruiting interview, "Are you planning to get married soon?"

Summary

You have a variety of question tools to choose from, and each tool has unique characteristics, capabilities, and pitfalls. Knowing which question to select and how to use it is essential for interviewing effectively and efficiently. Each question has three characteristics: (1) open or closed, (2) primary or probing, and (3) neutral or leading. Open questions are designed to discover large amounts of information, while closed questions are designed to gain specific bits of information. Primary questions open up topics and subtopics, while probing questions probe into answers for more information, explanations, clarifications, and verifications. Neutral questions give respondents freedom to answer as they wish, while leading questions nudge or shove respondents toward specific answers.

Phrasing questions is essential to get the information needed. If you phrase questions carefully and think before asking, you can avoid common question pitfalls such as curious; don't ask, don't tell; double-barreled; guessing; open-to-closed; tell me everything; too high, too low; unintentional bipolar; and unintentional leading.

Key Terms and Concepts

Bipolar question	Loaded question	Reflective probe
Clearinghouse probe	Mirror probe	Restatement probe
Closed question	Neutral question	Silent probe
Curious pitfall	Nudging probe	Tell me everything pitfall
Don't ask, don't tell pitfall	Open question	Too high, too low
Double-barreled pitfall	Open-to-closed pitfall	Unintentional bipolar
Guessing pitfall	Primary question	Unintentional leading
Informational probe	Probing question	Yes (no) pitfall
Leading question	Question pitfalls	

Review Questions

1. What is a question?
2. What are the advantages and disadvantages of open questions?
3. What are the advantages and disadvantages of closed questions?
4. Provide examples of the three types of bipolar questions.
5. What is a primary question?
6. What is a probing question?
7. How can you ask a silent probing question?
8. How does a nudging probe differ from an informational probing question?
9. What is the purpose of a clearinghouse probing question?
10. Compare and contrast a reflective probing question with a mirror probing question.
11. Compare and contrast a leading question with a loaded question.
12. Illustrate a yes (no) question pitfall.
13. Illustrate an open-to-closed question pitfall.
14. Compare and contrast a guessing question with a curious question pitfall.
15. When does a don't ask, don't tell question pitfall occur during an interview?

Student Activities

1. Watch an interview on C-SPAN or a program such as 60-Minutes that lasts at least 12 to 15 minutes. What was the ratio of open to closed primary questions? Which types of probing questions did the interviewer use? Which seemed most effective? Did you detect any leading questions and, if so, why do you believe the interviewer asked them? Did you find questions that did not match any of the types introduced in this chapter? If so, what made them different? What would you call them? What did you learn about types and uses of questions from this exercise?

2. Prepare two sets of 10 questions each, one with all neutral questions and one with four of the questions rephrased as leading questions. Conduct six interviews, three with all-neutral questions and three with the mixture of neutral and leading questions. Compare the answers you received and determine how types of questions may have influenced these answers. Why do you think some interviewees ignored the direction you provided in leading questions while others did not?

3. Create a list of closed questions, including bipolar questions, on a topic of importance in your state. Interview four people: a friend, a family member older than you, an acquaintance, and a stranger selected at random. Which ones gave you the shortest, least revealing answers? Which ones volunteered the most information regardless of question type? What does this tell you about using closed questions and the relationship between parties?

4. Listen to several interviews on television, including ones with politicians, company representatives, sports figures, and people who have experienced a crisis. Identify the question pitfalls exhibited in the questions asked and how they seemed to affect responses. Which were the most common pitfalls? Did you identify question pitfalls not covered in this chapter?

Notes

1. Joyce Kasman Valenza, "For the best answers, ask tough questions," *The Philadelphia Inquirer,* April 20, 2000, http://www.joycevalenza.com/questions.html, accessed September 26, 2006.

2. Stanley L. Payne, *The Art of Asking Questions* (Princeton, NJ: Princeton University Press, 1980), p. 204.

3. Robert L. Kahn and Charles F. Cannell, *The Dynamics of Interviewing* (New York: John Wiley, 1964), p. 205.

4. Kory Floyd, *Interpersonal Communication* (New York: McGraw-Hill, 2011), p. 99; Fred E. Jandt, *An Introduction to Intercultural Communication: Identities in a Global Community* (Los Angeles, CA: Sage, 2016), pp. 270–272.

Resources

Anderson, Rob, and G. Michael Killenberg. *Interviewing: Speaking, Listening, and Learning for Professional Life.* New York: Oxford University Press, 2008.

Devito, Joseph A. *Interviewing Guidebook.* Boston, MA: Pearson Education, 2010.

Payne, Stanley L. *The Art of Asking Questions.* Princeton, NJ: Princeton University Press, 1980.

Powell, Larry, and Jonathan H. Amsbary. *Interviewing: Situations and Contexts.* Boston, MA: Pearson Education, 2006.

Structuring the Interview

A s explained in Chapter 1, the interview is distinguishable from other interpersonal interactions because it is dyadic, has a predetermined and serious purpose, and entails both **planning** and a **degree of structure**. The extent of planning and structure depends upon interview type, other party, situation, length, and complexity.

The objectives of this chapter are to introduce you to the basic principles and structural techniques available to you when planning the opening, body, and closing of interviews and how to choose from among them for maximum effectiveness when interacting with specific persons in specific situations.

The Body of the Interview

When you start thinking about an upcoming interview, it is natural to begin mulling over questions you might ask. Make this period brief, and focus instead on your predetermined **purpose**. What exactly do you **need** to accomplish in **this interaction** with **this party** at **this time**? With this focus, start developing an **interview guide.**

Interview Guide

> An interview guide focuses on what you need from an interview.

An **interview guide** is a carefully structured outline of relevant topics and subtopics you need to address in the interview. Identify specific areas of inquiry to ensure adequate coverage of all relevant topics and issues. A guide does not include questions, but leads to the development of your questions, answers you record, impressions and insights you note, and what you recall when the interview is over.

Structural Sequences

An interview guide provides a clear and systematic outline for the interview you plan to conduct. Review five often-used outline sequences you have learned over the years.

> Sequences organize topics and impose structure on interviews.

A **topical sequence** follows natural divisions of a topic or issue. For example, if you are planning to interview pilots who fly hurricane hunter planes, you might include such topics as how they are trained, the planes they fly, where they are stationed, the potential dangers they encounter, what they see from the air, and the number of hours they are in the air for a typical weather mission. The traditional **journalist's guide** consisting of six key words—who, what, when, where, how, and why—is useful in many interview settings.

A **time sequence** treats topics or parts of topics in chronological order. For instance, in an interview with planner of the billion dollar campaign a local university recently ended after nearly a year of active fund raising, you might start with how the campaign was first envisioned and then proceed to how it was created, how it was initiated, which groups were targeted donners, how the campaign's progress was charted, how its progress was reported, and how it was concluded.

A **space sequence** arranges topics according to spatial divisions: left to right, top to bottom, north to south, or neighborhood to neighborhood. For example, when interviewing a leasing manager about an office in a recently renovated office building near the airport, you might begin with the reception area, and then proceed to offices, conference room, break room, kitchen, and parking facilities.

A **cause-to-effect sequence** explores causes and effects, but not necessarily in that order. For instance, if you know that a passenger plane landed in a lagoon short of the runway on a Caribbean island near Jamaica, you may focus primarily on possible causes of the accident (weather, pilot error, instrument failure, mechanical problem, or distraction such as someone flashing a laser into the cockpit). If you know the cause(s) of this crash landing, you may focus on the effects of the accident on the flight's passengers and crew (number of injuries and deaths), on vacationers in and near the lagoon (number of injuries and deaths), the lagoon (body of the aircraft, debris, oil and gas pollution), and economy of the island (cancelled flights, hotel reservations, tourist attractions).

> Select a sequence most suitable to your purpose.

A **problem-solution sequence** consists of a problem phase and a solution phase. For example, if you have become concerned about media reports of extremely overloaded animal shelters in your area, you might conduct interviews with directors of shelters and animal control agents to discover the extent of the problem and how it might be resolved.

Developing an Interview Guide

With your purpose firmly in mind, start creating an interview guide by identifying the major topics you want to cover in the interview. For instance, if you are a civil engineering student with a strong interest in flood control and want to study abroad for a semester, talk to professors familiar with your interests and study abroad opportunities and experiences. Your major topics may include the following:

> A guide ensures inclusion of all important topics and subtopics.

    I.   Countries with leading flood control programs

   II.   Universities that support these programs

  III.   Classroom and research opportunities

  IV.   Expenses

   V.   Cultures

  VI.   Research facilities

After you identify major topic areas, place subtopics under each.

    I.   Countries with leading flood control programs
        A.   The Netherlands
        B.   Austria
        C.   China
        D.   Egypt

II. Universities that support these programs
   A. Delft University of Technology
   B. Vienna University of Technology
   C. Tongji University
   D. Cairo University

III. Classroom and research facilities
   A. Courses and independent study
   B. Learning and support services
   C. Resources for learning
   D. Field experiences

IV. Expenses
   A. Food
   B. Housing
   C. Travel
   D. Academic

V. Cultures
   A. Language
   B. History
   C. Historical sites
   D. Arts and music

With major topics and subtopics in your guide, consider subtopics of subtopics. These might include language problems, cultural differences, and academic costs such as tuition, fees, insurance, and supplies. It may be difficult to know enough to list all important topics and subtopics prior to the interview. You may employ more than one sequence because of the nature of the topic.

Interview Schedules

A Nonscheduled Interview

> A nonscheduled interview is an interview guide.

If an interview will be brief such as determining date, time, and place of a meeting or a few biographical details, you might conduct the interview from a guide. This is called a **nonscheduled interview.** A nonscheduled interview conducted from an interview guide gives maximum freedom to probe into answers and adapt to the interviewee and situation as the interview progresses. It requires considerable skill, however, because there are no prepared questions and it may be difficult to maintain control during a freewheeling interaction.

A Moderately Scheduled Interview

> A moderate schedule lessens the need to create questions during the interview.

A **moderately scheduled interview** consists of all major questions with possible probing questions under each. The sentences and phrases in a guide become questions. The moderate schedule, like the nonscheduled interview, not only allows freedom to probe into answers and adapt to different interviewees and situations, but it also imposes a greater degree of structure, aids in recording answers, and is easier to conduct and replicate. It is unnecessary to phrase every question on the spot because they are thought out and carefully worded in advance. There are fewer pressures during the interview. Since interview parties tend to wander during unstructured interviews, listing questions makes it easier to keep on track and return to a structure when desired. Journalists, medical personnel, recruiters, lawyers, police officers, and insurance investigators, to name a few, use moderately scheduled interviews.

A Highly Scheduled Interview

Highly sched-
uled interviews
provide control
but no flexibility.

On paper a **highly scheduled interview** may look little different from a moderately scheduled interview, but they are very different in execution. Unlike a moderate schedule, all questions in a highly scheduled interview are asked exactly as they are worded on the schedule. There are no unplanned probing questions, word changes, or deviation from the schedule. Highly scheduled interviews are easy to replicate and conduct, take less time than nonscheduled and moderately scheduled interviews, and prevent parties from wandering into irrelevant areas or spending too much time on a topic. Flexibility and adaptation are not options, however. Probing questions must be planned. Researchers and survey takers use highly scheduled interviews.

A Highly Scheduled Standardized Interview

Highly scheduled
standardized
interviews
provide precision,
replicability, and
reliability.

The **highly scheduled standardized interview** is the most thoroughly planned and structured. It provides all questions the interviewer must ask and all answer options from which the interviewee must choose. There is no flexibility or adaptability. Interviewers are not allowed to rephrase or explain questions, change the order of questions, or ask probing questions. Interviewees are not allowed to ask for clarification or to explain, amplify, or qualify answers. The highly scheduled standardized interview is the easiest to conduct, record, and tabulate, so it is employed primarily by researchers and survey takers who need to replicate interviews conducted by many interviewers.

Combine
schedules to
satisfy multiple
needs.

Choose the schedule best suited to your needs, skills, type of information desired, and situation. One type of schedule does not fit all interview types and situations. A schedule appropriate for a survey would be a terrible schedule for an employment interview. Consider a strategic combination of schedules. For instance, use a nonscheduled approach when obtaining easily accessible information at the start of an interview and then switch to a moderately scheduled approach when carefully crafted questions are essential. When conducting a survey, employ a highly scheduled approach to ask open-ended questions and then switch to a highly scheduled standardized approach to obtain easily quantifiable information. Figure 4.1 reveals the advantages and disadvantages of each type of schedule and combinations.

Exercise #1—Interview Schedules

Which schedule or combination would be most appropriate for each of the situations below: nonscheduled, moderately scheduled, highly scheduled, highly scheduled standardized? Explain why you would select this schedule.

1. You missed an important school board meeting and are interviewing another parent who attended the meeting to learn what was discussed and what actions were taken.
2. You are conducting a survey among employees to discover their reactions to the benefits package recently proposed by a committee consisting of management and senior employees.

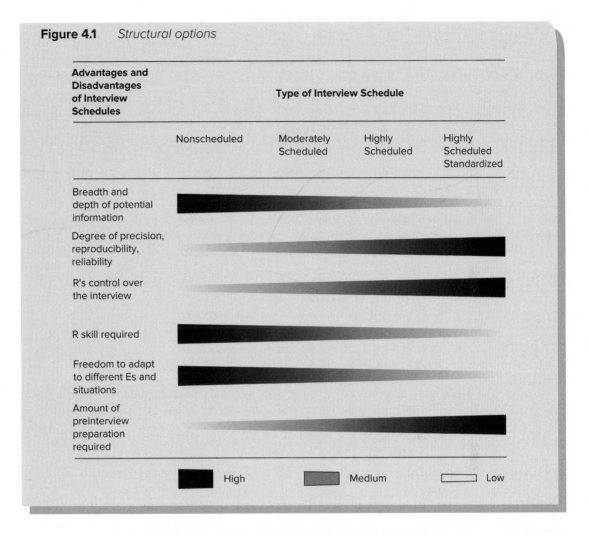

Figure 4.1   *Structural options*

Advantages and Disadvantages of Interview Schedules	Type of Interview Schedule			
	Nonscheduled	Moderately Scheduled	Highly Scheduled	Highly Scheduled Standardized
Breadth and depth of potential information	High			Low
Degree of precision, reproducibility, reliability	Low			High
R's control over the interview	Low			High
R skill required	High			Low
Freedom to adapt to different Es and situations	High			Low
Amount of preinterview preparation required	Low			High

High   Medium   Low

3. You are a journalist interviewing eye witnesses to a police action shooting to add important information to the officer's body cam.

4. You are a recruiter for WXYT conducting interviews with students at a job fair on campus. Your station has openings in sales, sports reporting, and photo journalism.

5. You own a franchise that operates motorized scooters and plan to locate a number of scooters throughout the downtown area of a medium-sized city with a university campus nearby. You are attempting to persuade the president of the city council to support your plan at the next city council meeting.

Question Sequences

Once an appropriate **interview schedule** or combination of schedules is determined, choose appropriate **question sequences**. There are six options: tunnel, funnel, inverted funnel, hourglass, diamond, and quintamensional design.

Figure 4.2   *The tunnel (string of beads) sequence*

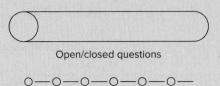

Open/closed questions

Tunnel Sequence

> A tunnel sequence works well with informal and simple interviews.

The **tunnel sequence,** or string of beads, is a comparable string of open or closed questions. See Figure 4.2. Each question may cover a specific topic, ask for a specific piece of information, or identify an attitude or feeling. A tunnel sequence looks like the following.

I've been told you ran the Chicago Marathon last year at the age of 54.

1. When did you decide to run a marathon?
2. Why did you choose the Chicago Marathon?
3. Where did you practice?
4. How often did you prepare for this marathon?
5. What was the toughest part of running 26.2 miles?

The tunnel sequence is common in polls, surveys, journalistic interviews, and medical interviews designed to elicit information, attitudes, reactions, and intentions. Answers to closed questions are easier to record and quantify.

Funnel Sequence

> A funnel sequence works best with motivated interviewees.

A **funnel sequence** begins with broad, open-ended questions and proceeds with more restricted questions. See Figure 4.3. The following is a funnel sequence.

I understand you served with Special Forces in Afghanistan.

1. Tell me about your experiences with Special Forces in Afghanistan.
2. What did you do on a typical day?
3. What were your impressions of Afghanistan's military units?
4. Which roles did your unit play most often?
5. How long were you on the ground in Afghanistan?

A funnel sequence is most appropriate when respondents are familiar with a topic, feel free to talk about it, want to express their feelings, and are motivated to reveal and explain attitudes. Open questions are easier to answer, pose less threat to respondents, and get people talking, so the funnel sequence is a good way to begin interviews. It lessens the chances of conditioning or biasing later responses. If you begin an interview with closed questions, you may signal that you want only brief answers. Open questions invite respondents to explain and qualify positions.

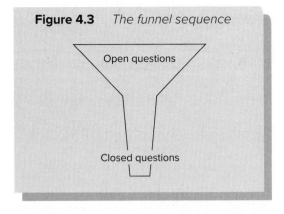

Figure 4.3 *The funnel sequence*

Open questions

Closed questions

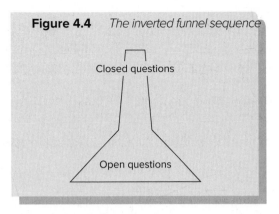

Figure 4.4 *The inverted funnel sequence*

Closed questions

Open questions

Inverted Funnel Sequence

> An inverted funnel sequence provides a warm-up time for reluctant interviewees.

The **inverted funnel sequence** begins with closed questions and proceeds toward open questions. It is most useful in motivating interviewees to respond or when interviewees are emotionally involved in an issue or situation and cannot readily reply to open questions. See Figure 4.4. The following is an inverted funnel sequence.

1. When did you first smell smoke in your condo?
2. Where did you see flames when you went into the hallway?
3. Who did you notify in the next few minutes?
4. What did you do until the fire trucks arrived?
5. What damage was done to the condo and the building?

The inverted funnel sequence is appropriate when interviewees feel they do not know enough about a topic or are hesitant. Closed questions serve as warm-ups and memory enhancers while open-ended ones might overwhelm a person or result in disorganized and confused answers. This sequence may end with a clearinghouse question.

Combination Sequences

A combination of sequences enables you to approach interview situations and interviewees with flexibility and adaptability. For example, the **hourglass sequence** begins with open questions, proceeds to closed questions, and concludes with open questions. This sequence allows you to narrow your focus before proceeding to broader concerns when the situation or topic warrants it. See Figure 4.5. A **diamond sequence** places funnel sequences top-to-top by beginning with closed questions, proceeding to open questions, and closing with closed questions. See Figure 4.6.

Quintamensional Design Sequence

George Gallup, the famous poll designer, developed the **quintamensional design sequence** to assess the intensity of opinions and attitudes. This five-step approach proceeds from

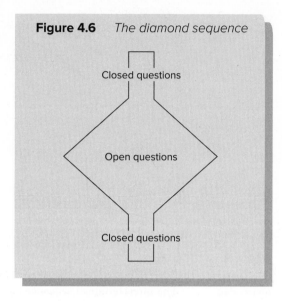

Figure 4.5 *The hourglass sequence*

Open questions

Closed questions

Open questions

Figure 4.6 *The diamond sequence*

Closed questions

Open questions

Closed questions

> **The quinta-mensional design assesses beliefs, attitudes, and feelings.**

an interviewee's awareness of the issue to attitudes uninfluenced by the interviewer, specific attitudes, reasons for these attitudes, and intensity of attitude. For example:

1. *Awareness:* What do you know about the DACA program?
2. *Uninfluenced attitudes:* How might the DACA program affect you?
3. *Specific attitude:* Do you approve or disapprove of the DACA program?
4. *Reason why:* Why do you feel this way about DACA?
5. *Intensity of attitude:* How strongly do you feel about DACA—strongly, very strongly, not something you will even change your mind on?

Opening the Interview

> **It takes two parties to launch an interview successfully.**

When you have determined a specific purpose and developed an appropriate structure for an interview that may include some or all of the questions to be asked, create an opening adapted to the purpose, parties, and situation. What you say and do or fail to say and do during the few seconds or minutes of the interaction are critical to your relationship with the interviewee and success of the interview. The **opening** sets the tone and mood of the interview and affects willingness and ability to go beyond Level 1 interactions. The tone may be serious or lighthearted, optimistic or pessimistic, professional or nonprofessional, formal or informal, threatening or nonthreatening, relaxed or tense. A poor opening may lead to a **defensive climate** with superficial, vague, and inaccurate responses.

The opening is critical to **motivating** both parties to participate willingly and to communicate freely and accurately. Motivation is a **mutual product** of interviewer and interviewee, so every opening must be a **dialogue,** not a **monologue.** Do it with the other party, not to the other party. Too often interviewees are given little opportunity to say anything beyond single-word responses to opening questions. Interrupting interviewees is common.

The Two-Step Process

The opening must establish rapport and orient the other party to encourage active participation and willingness to continue with the interview. Interview type, situation, relationship of the parties, and personal preferences determine what is included in the opening and how long it will last.

Rapport

> Do not overdo small talk or compliments.

Establishing **rapport** is a process of creating and sustaining a **genuine relationship** between interviewer and interviewee through enhancing feelings of **goodwill** and **trust.** If the relationship is long-standing and positive, consider a simple greeting, tasteful humor, and personal inquiries or references to families, mutual acquaintances, the weather, sports, or news events. Accompany each with nonverbal actions such as a firm handshake, good eye contact, a smile, and friendly voice. Determine what is appropriate by considering gender, local, national, and global customs and culture, organizational traditions and policies, status differences of the parties, formality and seriousness of the situation, and interview type. Avoid calling strangers, superiors, or high-status persons by their first names or nick names unless instructed to do so. Do not prolong the rapport stage or overdo "sweet talk" such as praise, congratulations, and admiration. Know when enough is enough and always be sincere.

Orientation

If the other party is **unfamiliar** with the purpose, length, and nature of the interview; how the information will be used; or why and how they were selected, address these during the opening. Do not **assume** the interviewee party understands what is going to take place during the interview and why. If uncertain, ask.

Interviewers often **assume** that when the other party **appears similar** to them in some ways—gender, age, ethnic background, culture, appearance, language, education—they are similar in ways critical to the purpose and success of the interview. LaRay Barna warns that "The aura of similarity is a serious stumbling block to successful intercultural communication. A look-alike facade is deceiving when representatives from contrasting cultures meet, each wearing Western dress, speaking English, and using similar greeting

James Hardy/PhotoAlto/SuperStock

■ *What you do and say in the opening seconds sets the tone for the remainder of the interview.*

rituals."[1] You may falsely assume that you share similar nonverbal codes, beliefs, attitudes, or values. "Unless there is overt reporting of assumptions made by each party, which seldom happens, there is no chance of comparing impressions and correcting misinterpretations."

Rapport and orientation are often intermixed to reduce **relational uncertainty.** By the end of the opening, both parties should be aware of the genuineness of the relationship, relevant similarities, desire to take part, and level of trust. Poor openings mislead and create problems as an interview progresses. Think about a situation in which you thought you were taking part in a political survey or discussing security concerns in your neighborhood only to discover that the interview was a disguised pitch for a political candidate or a security system for your apartment. The sample opening below illustrates the rapport and orientation steps for an interview taking place at the door of an apartment.

> **Do not assume too much or too little about the other party.**

1. **Interviewer:** Good evening. I'm Trent Goodnight and am working with other home owners in the area who are concerned about the heavy increase of traffic on our streets since the city made U.S. 33 a limited access throughway.

2. **Interviewee:** Hi Trent. I don't think I've seen you in the neighborhood before. Where do you live?

3. **Interviewer:** I don't think we've met though I've seen you walk your chocolate lab by my home occasionally. I live at the corner of Mapleleaf and Oak.

4. **Interviewee:** I know where that is. My name is Barbara Smelling, and my dog's name is Cinnamon. We have been getting a lot of contacts lately about various groups interested in our neighborhood claiming to have our best interests in mind and wanting donations.

5. **Interviewer:** I know what you mean. We have too. Several of us are interviewing residents with the sole purpose of gathering information on problems that concern them, examples of problems they have encountered, and what they would like to see done about them. I'll only need about 10 to 15 minutes of your time.

6. **Interviewee:** Okay. That sounds good, and my husband and I do have several concerns in addition to the traffic problem. For example, we hate traffic circles.

In some interview situations such as sales and surveys, you may have a carefully crafted opening from which you must not deviate because each interview must be as identical as possible. This is not the case with most interviews, however, and you should be as creative and adaptive as possible to each interviewee and situation. The "all occasions" opening may be an immediate turn off. **Verbal opening techniques** build rapport and inform the other party.

State Your Purpose

Explain **why** you are conducting the interview.

> **Adapt your opening to the interviewee and situation.**

Example: (A student to a student) I understand you have gone to Haiti on a number of mission trips, and I am planning to go there in March. I would like to talk to you about your experiences during your mission trips and what I should expect when visiting Haiti and working at a medical clinic in the mountains.

Summarize a Problem

Begin with a brief summary when an interviewee is unaware of a problem, vaguely aware of it, or unaware of details. The summary should **inform** the interviewee.

> **Example:** (Company representative to an owner) As you may have heard from news reports, we have discovered problems with the new automatic breaking system on our pickup trucks. There are times when it appears they have engaged unnecessarily and led to rear-end collisions or unexpected stops. I want to tell you about the recall that is going out to owners of the 300 Series.

Explain How a Problem Was Discovered

Explain *how* a problem was detected and perhaps *by whom* without placing the interviewee on the defensive.

> **Example:** (Personnel manager to an employee) I don't think you are aware of the efforts this past month by international hackers to obtain access to our employee files. We became aware of this when we did a routine check of all electronic data systems. We have managed to stop these efforts, but we need to inform you about what you can do to help us make your personal information safer.

Offer an Incentive or Reward

Offer an incentive to motivate an interviewee that is significant and appropriate for the situation.

> **Example:** (Manager on the telephone to a customer) Hi Margie. This is Nichole at the University Shop. We're calling a number of our frequent shoppers to get their opinions on our current brands, styles, and offerings and what they would like us to add to the University Shop. If you take part in our survey, you will receive a $20.00 gift certificate that you can apply to your next purchase.

Request Advice or Assistance

Make a request for assistance that is clear, precise, and appropriate for the interviewee.

> **Example:** (Student and counselor) I'm trying to develop a resume for a summer position with GE Aviation. Could you look over my draft and give me some suggestions?

Refer to the Interviewee's Position on an Issue

Be tactful, positive, and accurate when identifying the interviewee's position on an issue.

> **Example:** (Parent to principal) I understand you are opposed to using metal detectors on students as they enter the high school. Why is that?

Identify the Person Who Sent You

Identifying a person the interviewee knows and respects may create a positive connection and initiate a relationship. Be sure references have given you permission to use their names.

Example: (College student and a local resident) I'm doing a special project on the Great Depression for a history class. Professor Spencer in the history department suggested I talk with you because your family was in banking at that time.

Identify Your Organization

It may be important or necessary to identify the organization you represent to establish your identity and legitimacy. Be prepared for situations in which interviewees may have unfavorable attitudes toward your organization because of negative experiences or publicity.

Example: (A real estate agent and a prospect) Good evening. I'm Jill Adler, a real estate agent with Maple Leaf Reality.

Ask for a Specific Amount of Time

Request an amount of time necessary to achieve your purpose. Avoid the most misused and unrealistic request, "Got a second?"

Example: (Student to a professor) Hi Professor Chu. Do you have about 10 minutes to discuss my project idea for your class?

Ask an Open-Ended Question

Ask an easy to answer, open-ended question that is nonthreatening and starts the orientation stage of the opening.

Example: (A salesperson to a customer) What are you looking for in a truck?

Nonverbal Communication in Openings

How you say **what** you say is critically important when opening an interview. Nonverbal communication—voice, face, gestures, and appearance—is critical in creating a positive first impression that motivates the interviewee to respond and take part in the interview. The first few minutes of the interview reveal level of sincerity, trustworthiness, warmth, and interest.

Territoriality

We value our space (office, room, home, place at a table, the surrounding area when standing) and see intrusions as violations of social and organizational norms that dictate proper behavior. Always knock before entering a room, even when the door is open. Wait until the party signals verbally or nonverbally for you to enter and sit down. Never interrupt a conversation. Wait your turn. Women in our society continue to enjoy less territoriality than men. Judy Pearson writes that in the United States, "Few women have a particular and unviolated room in their homes while many men have man caves, studies, or work areas which are off limits to others. Similarly, it appears that more men than women have particular chairs reserved for their use."[2] Be aware of these outdated norms and practices but show equal respect to the space both men and women value and protect.

Touch

When shaking hands is appropriate for the relationship and the situation, give a firm handshake. Do not overdo handshaking with acquaintances and colleagues or during informal interviews. Recall that handshaking is a Western custom and degree of firmness may mean nothing in other cultures. Touching is appropriate only when parties have an established and close relationship and expect it. While the United States is not a touching society, do not be surprised if a party from Italy or Latin America touches you during an interview.

Reading Nonverbal Communication

> **Sex and culture regulate nonverbal communication in openings.**

Interpersonal communication theorists emphasize the importance of nonverbal clues. For instance, Trenholm and Jensen write, "People read a lot in our facial expressions. They infer some personality traits and attitudes, judge reactions to their own messages, regard facial expressions as verbal replacements, and, primarily, use them to determine our emotional state."[3] Beware of signaling catastrophe when an interview is routine, lack of concern when addressing an urgent problem, lack of empathy when an interviewee is encountering a critical issue, or closeness with a stranger. Regarding first impressions, Floyd notes that "the quality of a person's clothing is a relatively reliable visual cue to his or her socioeconomic status" and type or style of clothing may enable us, often quite accurately, to identify an interview party with a particular cultural or political group.[4] Stewart warns us, however, that we "tend to *notice* those behaviors [and possibly appearance and dress] that are consistent with the beliefs we have about another and ignore those that are inconsistent."[5]

The importance of nonverbal communication in openings is indisputable. The trick is to interpret the behavior accurately without underestimating or overestimating its importance in the process. Even people with similar backgrounds differ significantly in nonverbal behavior and the signals they send. For instance, men and women tend to communicate in different ways. Lillian Glass has catalogued 105 "talk differences" between American men and women in basic areas of communication: body language, facial language, speech and voice patterns, language content, and behavioral patterns. She has found that men touch others more often, tend to avoid eye contact and not look directly at the other person, sound more abrupt and less approachable, make direct accusations, and give fewer compliments.[6] Other research indicates that women are more skilled at "rapport talk" that establishes and strengthens relationships while men are more skilled at "report talk" that analyzes issues and resolves problems.

Exercise #2—Interview Openings

How satisfactory is each of the following openings? Consider the interviewing situation and type, the techniques used, and what is omitted. How might each be improved? Do not assume that each opening is unsatisfactory.

1. This is an interview between a recruiter for a software company and a senior in computer sciences.

   Interviewer: Hi Sally. Come in and have a seat. How's your last semester going?

   Interviewee: It's hectic.

   Interviewer: Well, let's get started.

2. This is an interview in the hallway near the U.S. Senate chamber between an ABC Capitol Hill correspondent and a senator. The senator is heading toward a hearing on climate control.

Interviewer: Senator Dickson (waving and shouting), what's your position on the Paris Climate Control Accord?

Interviewee: I'll wait until all of the facts are in.

Interviewer: Which facts are unknown?

3. This is an interview between a student and a professor concerning a recent reading assignment.

Interviewer: Professor Puchini, got a second?

Interviewee: Time's up! (laughing)

Interviewer: I'm sorry, do you have some time now?

4. This is an interview between an accident investigator and a person who claims to have seen a school bus accident.

Interviewer: Joe Smith? I'm an investigator for Sterling, Waters, and Zaire and would like to ask you a few questions.

Interviewee: Isn't that the law firm that has billboards all over the state and claims huge settlements?

Interviewer: Well, we do advertise widely and have been very successful.

5. This is an interview between a survey taker and a shopper at a mall.

Interviewer: Good morning. I would like to ask you a few questions about your experiences shopping here?

Interviewee: I'm in a hurry.

Interviewer: Do you shop here often?

Closing the Interview

A well-planned and executed closing may enhance the other party's perception of you, the importance of the role played in the interview, and attitudes toward future interactions. On the other hand, an abrupt or ill-planned closing may reduce your credibility and make the other party feel "used" or "taken advantage of."

> Take your time and be tactful in what you say and do in the closing.

It is natural to relax and let your guard down when the closing is approaching. Be attentive to everything you say and don't say, do and don't do during the final minutes of an interview. The other party will be listening and watching for signals that reveal interest, appreciation, and sincerity. Focus on this interaction, not on your next task or interview. Be sure the other party is aware the interview is ending.

We signal closings nonverbally before exchanging words. In their classic study of "leave-taking" in interpersonal interactions, Mark Knapp and his colleagues identified a variety of subtle and not so subtle actions that signal closure.[7] Interviewers may straighten up, lean forward, uncross legs, place hands on knees as if preparing to rise, look at a watch, pause briefly, or break eye contact. More obvious actions are standing up, moving away, or offering to shake hands. Whether subtle or not, nonverbal actions signal that one party wants to close the interview. As an interviewee, watch for signals to detect when a closing is commencing so you are not surprised or have an awkward ending. At the same time, be aware that a person may be checking a watch to see if there is adequate time for additional questions or information sharing, uncrossing legs to get more comfortable, or breaking eye contact to think of a new question. After noticing that students started into leave-taking mode when they glanced at their watches during interactions, the authors placed small clocks inconspicuously on their desks to avoid sending false messages.

Guidelines for Closing Interviews

First, make the closing a **dialogue** rather than a **monologue.** It takes two parties to produce a successful closing. As an interviewer, encourage interaction through verbal and nonverbal signals including silence. Do not interrupt the interviewee. A study of physicians, for instance, revealed that they did not permit patients to complete their closing comments 69 percent of the time.[8] As an interviewee, respond actively to questions, offer opinions and facts not mentioned, and express appreciation when appropriate.

Second, be sincere and honest in the closing. Make no promises or commitments you cannot or will not be able to keep.

Third, pace the interview to avoid rushing the closing. The **law of recency** suggests that people recall the last thing said or done, so being rushed or dismissed with an ill-chosen nonverbal action or phrase may jeopardize the effects of the interview, and future contacts with this party.

> Be careful of what you do and say.

Fourth, the other party will observe and interpret everything you say and do, and everything you don't say and don't do, until you are out of sight and sound. A slip of the lip or an inappropriate nonverbal act may negate all that you accomplished.

Fifth, lay the groundwork for future contacts. If an additional contact is planned (common in health care, employment, counseling, and sales interviews), explain what will happen next, where it will happen, when it will happen, and why it will happen. When necessary, make an appointment before leaving.

Sixth, don't introduce new topics or ideas or make inquiries when the interview has in fact or psychologically come to a close. A **false closing** occurs when verbal and nonverbal messages signal the interview is coming to a close only for you to open it back up. This may be awkward for both parties and such after-the-fact interactions are likely to add little to the interview.

■ *Remember that the interview is not completed until the interviewer and interviewee are out of sight and sound of one another.*

Seventh, avoid what Erving Goffman called **failed departures** that occur when you have brought an interview to a close and taken leave from the other party. Then a short time later you run into the party in the hall, parking lot, or restaurant.[9] The result may be awkward because both of you have said your good-byes and have nothing more to say. Practice situations to determine what you might say when this happens.

Closing Techniques

Be creative and imaginative when closing interviews. Adapt each closing to the interviewee and the situation. The following techniques may begin the closing process or complete the closing.

> Questions, intentions, and inquiries allow you to close effectively.

Use a Clearinghouse Question

A clearinghouse question enables you to determine if you have covered all topics, answered all questions, or resolved all concerns. The request must be a sincere effort to ferret out unaddressed questions, information, or areas of concern.

Have I answered all of your questions?

What have I not asked that you think is important for me to know?

Declare Completion of the Intended Purpose

State the task is completed. The word *well* often signals many closings so, when you hear it, you automatically assume that leave-taking is commencing and begin to wind things up. Is this what you want to happen?

Well, I believe that's all of the data I need at this time.

You have answered all of my questions.

> Show genuine interest in the other party.

Make Personal Inquiries

Personal inquiries are pleasant ways to end interviews and to enhance relationships. Be sincere and give the interviewee adequate time to reply.

Where are you traveling this summer?

How does your daughter like law school?

Make Professional Inquiries

Professional inquiries are more formal than personal ones, and must be sincere and express genuine interest.

How is your satellite office doing in Topeka?

What changes do you foresee in this year's corn crop?

> End the interview when most appropriate.

Signal That Time Is Up

Abide by the time limit agreed to in advance or during the opening, but be tactful and do not appear to be running an assembly line.

I see my time's up for today.

We are out of time for this broadcast segment.

Explain the Reason for the Closing

Explain why the interview must end.

I see you have another person waiting to talk to you.

I have a board meeting in five minutes.

Express Appreciation or Satisfaction

Express appreciation and satisfaction for what you have received—information, assistance, evaluation, a story, a sale, a position, a recruit, or time. Be sincere.

I really appreciate you making time for me on such a busy time.

Thanks for being so candid with me about the future of your baseball franchise.

Arrange for the Next Meeting

When another interview is needed, arrange it during the closing.

> **If another interview is necessary, arrange it before leaving.**

Your world travels are amazing. Could we continue talking about them next Wednesday at 3:00 p.m.?

I'm very interested in your sketches for our new laboratory. When would be a good time to meet again?

Be sincere when using such phrases as "Let's stay in touch," "I find your ideas very interesting and will let you know what we decide," and "Don't call us; we'll call you." The last one is a traditional "brush off" in our society that means never, but it may be interpreted as serious intent in other cultures. For instance, job applicants from other countries have been known to resign their positions in anticipation of imminent job offers by American firms that never came.

Summarize the Interview

A summary closing is common for informational, performance, counseling, and sales interviews. Repeat important information, stages, or agreements or verify accuracy and agreement.

> I'm glad we could get together this afternoon to resolve some of the misunderstandings you have about impending transfers to other locations in the east. We are still in the process of determining which positions are needed at our eastern facilities and which employees appear to be ideal for each of these positions. Obviously, we do not want to weaken our operations here. Rest assured that no decision will be made about a specific transfer without discussing it in detail first with an affected staff member. You will be contacted well in advance of any possible transfer.

> **Plan the closing as carefully as you do the opening.**

Consider which closing technique (or a combination) is most suitable to close this interaction with this party at this time. Focus on what your words and actions are **saying** to the other party at this critical time in the interview.

Your role in an interview and your relationship with the other party may require some techniques, rule out others, and determine who will initiate the closing and when. Closings often combine several verbal and nonverbal techniques.

Exercise #3—Interview Closings

How satisfactory is each of the following closings? Consider the interviewing situation and type, relationship, the techniques used, nonverbal communication, and what is omitted. How might each be improved? Do not assume each closing is unsatisfactory.

1. This is a market survey taking place in a shopping mall by a research organization hired by the owner of several shopping malls in the Midwest.

   Interviewer: Well, that's it.

   Interviewee: How will the results be used?

   Interviewer: I'm sorry, but I'm not free to answer that.

   Interviewee: Okay.

2. This is an interview between a journalist and a former member of the President's cabinet who resigned after the first year of the President's administration.

   Interviewer: Well (leaning forward), I certainly appreciate your openness and willingness to answer questions about your experiences and reasons for your resignation.

   Interviewee: Thank you for inviting me to tell my story.

   Interviewer: You're welcome. By the way, what are your plans now?

   Interviewee: I have a number of options I'm considering at present.

3. This is a recruiting interview for a chemist with a large pharmaceutical company.

   Interviewer: Your academic background certainly fits the position we have open.

   Interviewee: Thank you. I am really interested in this position with your company.

   Interviewer: I'm glad to hear that. Good luck with your search. We'll be in touch.

4. This is an interview between three college seniors who are shopping for a condo to share and a leasing agent for condos near campus.

   Interviewer: These condos are about what we're looking for, but we want to look at some others.

   Interviewee: Okay. Let me know if you have some questions.

   Interviewer: Thanks a lot.

ON THE WEB

This chapter has presented guidelines and techniques for developing effective openings and closings. Use the Internet to locate sample interviews on issues such as education, the economy, foreign affairs, and medicine. Critique the openings and closings used in these interviews. Two useful Internet resources for locating interviews are CNN (http://cnn.com) and C-SPAN (http://indycable.com/cabletv/comastindyupgrade/ch24.htm).

5. This is a performance review of Jack Rodgers conducted by his supervisor.

Interviewer: You're doing a good job Jack. Just keep an eye on the little things. How's your daughter doing in soccer?

Interviewee: She had knee surgery two weeks ago.

Interviewer: Bummer!

Summary

The opening sets the tone for the interview, orients the interviewee, and motivates both parties to communicate beyond Level 1. Select from among a variety of opening techniques the ones that are most appropriate for each interview. Take into consideration the atmosphere of the interview, your relationship with the interviewee, the purpose of the interview, topics or issues involved, and future interactions. Involve the interviewee as an active participant in a collaborative process.

Structure the interview by selecting and developing the most appropriate schedule. A nonscheduled interview is a guide that outlines the topics and subtopics you wish to cover organized into a sequence such as topical, time, space, cause-to-effect, and problem-solution. A moderately schedule interview transforms the guide into sequences of primary and probing questions. A highly scheduled interview includes all questions to be asked during an interview in the order in which they will be asked. A highly scheduled standardized interview includes all questions to be asked along with answer options from which the interviewee must select.

The closing brings the interview to an end. Select from among a variety of closing techniques the ones most appropriate for this interview and interviewee. You may summarize information received or given, verify agreements, and reiterate commitments. Be sincere and honest in all that you say and do while making no promises you cannot or will not be able to keep. Your future relationship is in the balance. When necessary, arrange future contacts.

Key Terms and Concepts

Accidental bias	Highly scheduled	Orientation
Built-in interviewer bias	standardized interview	Outline sequences
Cause-to-effect sequence	Hourglass sequence	Problem-solution sequence
Closing	Interview guide	Question sequences
Closing techniques	Interview schedules	Quintamensional design
Combination schedule	Inverted funnel sequence	sequence
Culture	Journalist's guide	Rapport
Defensive climate	Law of recency	Relational uncertainty
Diamond sequence	Moderately scheduled	Space sequence
Failed departures	interview	Territoriality
False closings	Nonscheduled interview	Time sequence
Funnel sequence	Nonverbal closing actions	Topical sequence
Highly scheduled	Nonverbal communication	Tunnel sequence
interview	Opening	Verbal opening techniques

Review Questions

1. What is an interview guide?

2. Compare and contrast a topical sequence with a space sequence.

3. What is the first thing you do when developing an interview guide?

4. Compare and contrast a moderately scheduled interview with a highly scheduled interview.

5. Compare and contrast built-in interviewer bias with accidental interviewer bias.

6. What are the advantages of a highly scheduled standardized interview?

7. Compare and contrast a tunnel with a funnel sequence.

8. What is a diamond sequence of questions?

9. Why did George Gallup create the quintamensional design question sequence?

10. An opening that leads to a defensive climate may produce what kinds of responses?

11. How can relational uncertainty be resolved through an opening?

12. Identify and explain three opening techniques that are designed to motivate an interviewee to participate in an interview.

13. Why should you be cautious when identifying a person who sent you to an interviewee?

14. How can an interviewer lessen the likelihood of violating an interviewee's territory?

15. Compare and contrast a "false closing" with a "failed departure."

Student Activities

1. Make an appointment to interview a college recruiter for a large law firm. As you prepare for this interview, begin by determining the purpose of your interview? With this purpose in mind, which sequence would you select when developing an interview guide? What topics and subtopics would you include? After completing your guide, which schedule would be most appropriate for this interview? Now prepare an opening by selecting from among the opening techniques that seem best for this interview and party. Finally, prepare a closing by selecting from among the closing techniques that seem best for this interview and party.

2. Watch a televised interview with a prominent political leader that lasts at least 15 minutes. Try to construct an interview guide from the topics discussed. With the guide outlined, determine which question schedule and sequences the interviewer employed. From your reconstruction of this interview, what was the interviewer's overall purpose? How well was this fulfilled? What recommendations would you make for this interviewer?

3. Watch a series of televised interviews with a variety of interviewees such as a physician, elected official, victim of a crime, author of a scholarly book, and an attorney. How did interviewers open each interview verbally and nonverbally? Which opening techniques did interviewers employ? Were the openings dialogues or monologues? How did the relationships between interviewers and interviewees appear to affect the nature of the openings? How did the topics or issues addressed appear to affect the openings?

4. Watch a series of televised interviews with a variety of interviewees such as a medical patient, candidate for a political office, perpetrator of a crime, author of a mystery novel, and a client of an attorney. How did interviewers close each interview verbally and nonverbally? Which closing techniques did interviewers employ? Were the closings dialogues or monologues? How did the relationships between interviewers and interviewees appear to affect the nature of the closings? How did the topics or issues addressed appear to affect the closings?

Notes

1. LaRay M. Barna, "Stumbling Blocks in Intercultural Communication," in Larry A. Samovar and Richard E. Porter, eds., *Intercultural Communication: A Reader* (Belmont, CA: Wadsworth, 1988), pp. 323–324.

2. Judy C. Pearson, *Communication in the Family* (New York: Harper & Row, 1989), p. 78.

3. Sarah Trenholm and Arthur Jensen, *Interpersonal Communication* (New York: Oxford University Press, 2013), p. 59.

4. Kory Floyd, *Interpersonal Communication: The Whole Story* (New York: McGraw-Hill, 2011), p. 188.

5. John Stewart, *Bridges Not Walls: A Book about Interpersonal Communication* (New York: McGraw-Hill, 2009), p. 186.

6. Lillian Glass, *He Says, She Says: Closing the Communication Gap between the Sexes* (New York: Putnam, 1993), pp. 45–59.

7. Mark L. Knapp, Roderick P. Hart, Gustav W. Friedrich, and Gary M. Shulman, "The Rhetoric of Goodbye: Verbal and Nonverbal Correlates of Human Leave-Taking," *Speech Monographs* 40 (1973), pp. 182–198; John Stewart, *Bridges Not Walls* (New York: McGraw-Hill, 2012), p. 153.

8. H. B. Beckman and R. M. Frankel, "The Effect of Physician Behavior on the Collection of Data," *Annals of Internal Medicine* (1984), pp. 692–696.

9. Erving Goffman, *Relations in Public* (New York: Basic Books, 1971), p. 88.

Resources

Anderson, Rob, and G. Michael Killenberg. *Interviewing: Speaking, Listening, and Learning for Professional Life*. New York: Oxford University Press, 2008.

Knapp, Mark L., Roderick P. Hart, Gustav W. Friedrich, and Gary M. Shulman. "The Rhetoric of Goodbye: Verbal and Nonverbal Correlates of Human Leave-Taking." *Speech Monographs* 40 (1973), pp. 182–198.

Krivonos, Paul D., and Mark L. Knapp. "Initiating Communication: What Do You Say When You Say Hello?" *Central States Speech Journal* 26 (1975), pp. 115–125.

Zunin, Leonard, and Natalie Zunin. *Contact: The First Four Minutes*. London: Random House, 1986.

CHAPTER 5

The Informational Interview

You encounter informational interviews nearly every day.

The **informational interview** is the most common form of interviewing because we take part in one or more nearly every day when gathering or giving instructions, recommendations, facts, data, observations, reactions, feelings, and attitudes. The purpose of the **information gathering interview** is to obtain relevant information as accurately and completely as possible in the least amount of time. The purpose of the **information giving interview** is to provide relevant information so it is understood, retained, and employed as accurately and completely as possible over time.

The informational interview is a staple of journalists and contacts, attorneys and clients, supervisors and staff members, health care professionals and patients, recruiters and applicants, professors and students, parents and children. Pulitzer-Prize winning journalist Eric Nalder writes that interviews are as varied as the conversations we have and the people we talk to.[1] They may be as brief as verifying or providing a date, time, and place of a meeting or as lengthy and formal as a journalist interviewing a state governor or a surgeon providing detailed instructions to a patient on what to do and not do during recovery.

Preparation is the key to success in gathering and giving information.

The objectives of this chapter are to introduce you to the fundamentals of information gathering and giving interviews that include how to prepare for and conduct interviews and how to perform the roles of interviewer and interviewee.

Part 1: The Information Gathering Interview

Asking for information sounds simple, but doing so effectively demands thorough preparation, skillful questioning, active listening, insightful observing, and persistent probing. Unfortunately, few of us, including professional interviewers, receive training in interviewing. Chip Scanlon, an author of books and articles on journalism, writes that "Journalists get little or no training in this vital aspect of their jobs. Most learn by trial and error."[2] The majority of us do the same. Effective information gathering interviewers combine skills in the basics of interviewing with personality traits such as curious, friendly, organized, patient, and persistent.

Preparing for the Interview

There are no simple formulas or short cuts in information gathering interviews because each is a process "that involves a series of decisions and actions designed to get the best possible information."[3] **Preparation** is essential when making these decisions and taking these actions because, to quote Benjamin Franklin, "By failing to prepare, you are preparing to fail."

ON THE WEB

Use the Internet to research your college or one that you might select as a graduate or professional school. Focus first on the college or university, then on the school or college within this larger structure, and finally on the department. What kinds of information are readily available? How up-to-date is the information? What kinds of information are not included that you would have to discover through interviews with faculty or students?

Frame Your Purpose

Your purpose should determine what you do and how.

Begin preparation by formulating a clear and precise **purpose** that indicates exactly why you are going to conduct this interview? It should direct everything you do from that moment until you close the interview. Focus on four questions:

1. What information do I **need**?
2. **Who** can best provide this information?
3. How **quickly** do I need this information?
4. How will I **use** this information?

Ken Metzler, a professor of journalism, writes that when you know exactly what you want in an interview, "You're halfway there."[4] Begin the second half by thoroughly researching the subject matter you wish to mine during the interview so you do not waste interview time asking for information you already have. Some journalists recommend that research time should be ten times the interview time.

Research the Subject Matter

Learn to use interview time wisely.

Research serves several functions for information gathering interviewers. First, it reveals what information is readily available in other sources. Do not spend valuable interview time asking for information you can obtain in Web sites, organizational reports and documents, newspaper files, social media, data bases, archives, and previous interviews.

Second, research reveals aspects of subject matter you might fail to consider such as seemingly unrelated facts or events or little-known interviewee contributions, experiences, insights, attitudes, and feelings. For instance, knowing that the interviewee's grandfather was accidently shot and paralyzed by his young son during a hunting trip, may explain a great deal about a person's feelings toward gun safety.

Have a healthy skepticism about what you discover, particularly on the Internet.

Third, research prevents you from basing questions on false assumptions and inaccurate information and data. Journalist Jaldeep Katwala warns, "Be sure of your facts. There's nothing worse than being told you are wrong by an interviewee—especially when it's live."[5] As you uncover information, beware of hidden agendas and prejudices that may have produced shoddy data through manipulation of results, biased interpretations, and unwarranted conclusions. According to an old saying, "Statistics don't lie, but liars make statistics." Most of us place great value on "eye-witness" accounts, but they are highly unreliable.[6] Check the recency of information and whether a source has changed

■ *Select interviewees with several criteria in mind.*

PA Images/Getty Images

positions on an issue since the statement was made or a recent study was reported?

Fourth, thorough research leads to insightful and thought-provoking questions that indicate you have done your homework. What you know, understand, and use correctly (professional jargon, technical terms, names, titles, and organization) enhances your credibility with the interviewee. Exhibiting that you cannot be fooled easily will motivate parties to answer questions openly, freely, and accurately.

> Let your research become obvious during the interview.

Do not **tell** an interviewee what you know; let your questions **reveal** what you know.

Fifth, research indicates the areas and subareas of the topic or issue from which you can develop an interview guide for this interview, with this party, at this time. In turn, the guide helps you formulate insightful, information-based questions that delve into information that is new, interesting, and relevant.

Select the Interviewee

> Select the interviewee with purpose and need in mind.

Your purpose and the information you need may dictate the person you will interview. For instance, if you need additional insights into the requirements and purposes of a research project for a psychology course, your psychology professor is the obvious choice. On the other hand, if you want to learn about topics or issues students have explored in the past and why, you will choose from among several students. If you want to discover why the police chief of your city has decided to run for the elected office of county sheriff, the police chief is the best interviewee. On the other hand, if you want to assess how the officers under the chief feel about the chief's decision, you need to select from among dozens or hundreds of officers.

When facing a situation in which you must select one or more interviewees, learn everything you can about each before choosing. Journalists Eugene Webb and Jerry Salancik recommend you know a "source well enough to be able to know when a distortion is occurring, from a facial expression that doesn't correspond to a certain reply."[7] Use the following criteria to select the best interviewee.

> Does this party have the level of information you need?

Knowledge level: Review each potential interviewee with your purpose and research as guides to discover the level and kind of information each may offer. For instance, if you are interested in studying the destructive and deadly wildfires in California, a climatologist can provide insights into how climate change appears to be a major cause of wildfires that have become so destructive. An investigator may address how wildfires have started. A firefighter can provide insights into what it is like fighting monster flames. An eye witness can give insights into what it was like trying to escape when surrounded by wildfires. A homeowner who has lost everything can give insights into what it is like when recovering from a total loss. A civil engineer can address how some houses and structures withstand fires better than others. Each of these potential interviewees has a unique level and type of knowledge. Which do you need for this interview at this time?

Do not assume a person in unavailable.

Availability: The best interviewee may be too busy to meet with you when needed or for the amount of time your interview requires. Be flexible when possible and consider two or more interviews instead of one in-depth interview. Distance may be a problem because of where the person lives, works, or will be located when needed. If so, consider the telephone, Skype, or a video conference. Never assume a person is unavailable. It costs nothing to ask, and there are instances about highly successful interviews with high-status, famous, or reluctant people simply because a person asked or was persistent in asking. You may be asking at just the right time.

Consider contacting a key informant.

Willingness: If an interviewee rejects your request, discover why. It may be too soon for a family to talk about the loss of a child in a school shooting, a father to Alzheimer's disease, or a home to foreclosure. An ideal source may not trust you personally, your position (as journalist, supervisor, police officer), your organization (political party, IRS, network), or your profession (journalism, health care, law)? Discover if a party has been "burned" in similar interviews and fears the worst. A person may see no advantage to participating in an interview with the risks involved. Try gentle persuasion, assurances, mild pressure, or references before abandoning a valuable interviewee. A "key informant" such as an aide, former associate, friend, or family member may assist you in securing an interview.[8] On the other hand, be cautious when a person appears to be too anxious to be interviewed. Is there a hidden motive or agenda you need to uncover and consider before proceeding with an interview?

A once reliable source may no longer be capable of assistance.

Competency: The best interviewee must be able to provide information accurately, freely, openly, and truthfully. A person may be prone to oversimplification or exaggeration or to biases and prejudices that compromise any information you receive. Age, mental health, or physical health may have impaired the person's memory or ability to communicate? An event may have been so traumatic that a person has psychologically suppressed details. Be highly skeptical of eye-witness accounts. Recognize that some people are excellent story tellers while others are not, and as copywriter Star Zagofky notes, "Some people are naturally talented at being interviewed and others aren't."[9]

Know Your Relationship with the Interviewee

Study your relationship with the selected interviewee by starting with the basics of relationships that include desire to take part in the interview, affection and respect, inclination toward control, and trust. In addition, consider the **status difference** between the parties that may offer advantages for one or the other or both.

When you are **subordinate** to the interviewee in status or superior role (learner or novice to expert, student to professor, associate to manager):

- The interviewer need not be superior in expertise.
- The interviewee may feel less threatened.
- The interviewee may feel freer to speak.
- The interviewee may desire to help.

When you are **superior** to the interviewee (expert to learner or novice, physician to nurse, or captain to lieutenant):

- The interviewer may control the interview.
- The interviewer may reward the interviewee.
- The interviewee may feel motivated to cooperate.
- The interviewee may feel honored to participate.

When you are **equal** to the interviewee (student to student, researcher to researcher, top correspondent with CEO):

- Rapport may be easier to establish.
- There may be fewer communication barriers.
- There may be fewer pressures.
- A high degree of empathy may exist.

Organizations give high-status-sounding titles to enhance their status as interviewer or interviewee: chief correspondent rather than reporter, vice president rather than director, department head rather than department chair, and executive rather than manager or supervisor.

Interviewees often prefer interviewers to be like them in important ways such as age, gender, race, culture, educational level, and experiences. A woman may feel more comfortable with a female physician when addressing health issues she feels only a woman can fully understand. Senior executives or partners with corporations, universities, or law firms may expect interviewers of equal status as a sign of respect for their status and with the ability to understand their positions and problems. Combat-experienced Vietnam veterans may believe that only an interviewer who experienced the terror in the jungles of Vietnam can truly understand them and their post-combat struggles.

Select the Best Possible Situation

Ideally, you should select the location of the interview, but it may not be your choice alone to make. A scholar may prefer a library, a U.S. Senator his or her office, a political candidate a rally, a physician a medical office. Regardless of who has the most say in choosing a situation, try to reach mutual agreement on a location that is beneficial to both parties.

Sarah Stuteville, journalist and multimedia specialist, recommends you strive for a location that is relevant to the information your interviewee has to offer because "you'll have much greater success ... not only because you'll gain a further sense of context" but "people are often more comfortable (and open) when they're in a familiar place or what feels like 'their territory'."[10] When the author agreed to take part in an oral history interview on the campus where he had spent his entire teaching career, the interviewer selected a comfortable conference room in the university archives surrounded by historical documents and artifacts. It was a perfect place for the interviewee to talk about his experiences and the interviewer to take notes and record the interview. Eric Nader writes that it is often essential to interview people "at the place where they are doing the thing that you are writing about" so you not only **hear** answers but **see** and get the **feel** of things.[11] When he was writing a book on oil tankers, a member of a crew told him he could not understand crews and life on oil tankers until he's been aboard in the Gulf of Alaska during the violent January seas "puking your guts out." Nalder took this advice and gained exceptional insights from his first-hand experiences.

Study the situation thoroughly.

While location is often critical to an interview, it is only one of several situational variables that may impact your interview positively or negatively. Proceed through a checklist of variables to prepare thoroughly for each interview and to avoid surprises.

_____	Timing of the interview	_____	Social space and distance
_____	Time for the interview	_____	Whose turf you will be on
_____	Perceptions	_____	Privacy
_____	Seating arrangement	_____	Noise and interruptions

Be prepared for surprises.

You may have seconds to ask a question during a press conference, a few minutes to gather travel information, or an hour or more for an in-depth interview. An interview may take place at the scene of a natural disaster, accident, shooting, or fire, so prepare yourself for horrific scenes of destruction, filthy conditions, human suffering, and threats to health and safety. No interview takes place in a vacuum, so always anticipate the unexpected. When the author was in the middle of an interview with a fire chief about new equipment, the alarm went off in the firehouse and the chief *jumped up and ran out the door. After waiting a few minutes, the chief returned,* reported it was a false alarm, and continued the interview. The more you are aware of situational variables the better able you will be to understand, manage, and adapt to them.

Structure the Interview

Review your research notes and select the materials that are both relevant and important to this interview with this interviewee. Develop an interview guide that outlines the major aspects of an issue or topic or consists of key words such as the traditional journalistic guide. The length and depth of an interview will determine how detailed your guide becomes.

Create flexible structural sequences and schedules.

Review the structural sequences in Chapter 4. A chronological sequence enables you to progress through stories and events that occur in time sequences. A logical sequence such as cause-to-effect and problem-to-solution is appropriate for interviews on issues and crises. A space sequence works well when interviewing about geographical areas, cities, college campuses, and production facilities. If your interview will be brief, a guide may be sufficient preparation.

Turn the guide into a moderately scheduled interview such as the following with **open-ended** questions that encourage the interviewee to elaborate on answers and allow you to listen, observe, and think of follow-up questions that probe for critical information and insights.

- *Who* was involved?
- *What* happened?
- *When* did it happen?
- *Where* did it happen?

- *How* did it happen?
- *Why* did it happen?

<table>
<tr><td>

A moderate schedule is ideal for most information gathering interviews.

</td><td>

A moderate schedule eliminates the necessity of phrasing each question carefully and precisely in the heat of the interview while providing the flexibility to modify, delete, or add questions as need or opportunity arises. You may discover aspects of an issue, insights, or surprises during an interview that warrant modifications or detours from your prepared schedule. Your schedule enables you to pick up where you left off without fear of getting off track. Thomas Berner recommends that if a question or area of inquiry comes to mind during an interview, jot it down in the margin of your schedule and come back to it when appropriate.[12] The freedom to adapt and improvise make a moderate schedule ideal for the informational interview.

</td></tr>
</table>

<table>
<tr><td>

Too many ground rules may produce an interview with little value.

</td><td>

Either or both parties may establish **ground rules** prior to an interview that will affect questions you ask and answers the interviewee gives. At the very least, both parties expect honesty, adhering to the stated purpose of the interview, and reasonable time to ask and answer questions. Common ground rules include areas that may be off limits, answers that are "off the record," and information that may and may not be attributed to the interviewee. As a rule, do not accept "retroactive off the record" requests after an interviewee has heard an answer replayed or following the interview. Excessive off the record demands may make an interviewee unacceptable.

</td></tr>
</table>

It is not uncommon for an interviewee to ask to see your questions prior to the interview. The interviewee may ask you to modify some questions while eliminating others. **As a general rule, don't do it.** If your questions follow the ground rules, there should be no justification in changing them. At the least, revealing questions in advance reduces the spontaneity of the interview. At the worst, an interviewee may prepare stock answers that are "safe" and reveal little valuable information.

Plan the Opening

<table>
<tr><td>

Craft your opening with several criteria in mind.

</td><td>

Prepare the opening carefully because the levels of trust and motivation are often established during the first few minutes of an interview. What is your relationship with this interviewee? If you are a stranger, identify yourself, your position, and your organization. What is your relationship and status with the interviewee? Do they warrant an informal opening and use of the interviewee's first name or nickname such as Dick for Richard or Maggie for Margaret? Review the opening techniques in Chapter 4, and select one or more that is appropriate for this **interview,** with this **interviewee,** in this **situation.** Explain carefully **what** information you need, **why** you need this information, and **how** you will use it. "Small talk" is traditional in many interviews, but it must seem natural rather than trite, mechanical, or forced. A busy interviewee who has granted you limited time for an interview may see small talk as a waste of valuable time. Use humor with caution. Make all compliments sincere.

</td></tr>
</table>

Conducting the Interview

The goal of the informational interview is to get in-depth and insightful information that only an interviewee can offer. It is essential, then, to get beyond superficial and safe Level 1 interactions to riskier and deeper Level 2 and Level 3 interactions.

Motivating Interviewees

Sarah Stuteville writes that a successful interview may depend "on a total stranger's cooperation and participation."[13] So, how do you motivate an interviewee, whether well-known or a stranger, to disclose beliefs, attitudes, feelings, and unknown facts? Above all, the interviewee must **trust** you to react with understanding and tact, maintain confidences, use the information fairly, and report answers accurately and completely. So how do you establish this trust?

There are six keys to motivating interviewees. **First,** be careful of everything you do and do not do, say and do not say, ask and do not ask during the interview. Interviewees size you up by the way you look, act, and sound. **Second,** explain your purpose carefully and do nothing that appears contrary to this purpose. **Third,** show respect for the interviewee and appreciation for the person's willingness to spend time with you and assist you in gathering information. **Fourth,** show sincere interest in and enthusiasm for the interviewee, topic, and answers by listening and paying attention to each answer you receive without being judgmental or revealing your own feelings. **Fifth,** maintain control of the interview without interrupting by looking for natural pauses to probe into answers or ask new primary questions. And **sixth,** make the interview a well-planned and professional conversation in which both parties speak and listen from time to time. Ken Metzler suggests replacing the word interview with conversation, talk, discussion, or chat to signify what it should be. These six keys are likely to open up the most difficult of interviewees. A report on interrogation interviews with insurgents in Iraq and Afghanistan noted that "the successful interrogators all had one thing in common in the way in which they approached their subjects. They were nice to them."[14]

> Motivation results from what you do and do not do during the interview.

Asking Questions

> Ask, listen, observe, and think.

Ask open-ended questions that encourage the interviewee to provide thorough answers while you listen to words and content and observe nonverbal behaviors. Be the listener rather than the talker in interviews. Ken Metzler claims "It's not the questions you ask that make for a successful interview but the attention you pay to the answers you receive." Questions are the tools of the trade in information gathering interviews, but interviewers often ask so many questions that they have little opportunity to listen, observe, or think. Excessive questioning usually results from asking closed questions that require three or four questions to obtain information one open-ended question would generate. Raymond and Moen write that interviewers earn an answer "by asking a substantial, interesting, and thought-provoking question."[15]

Be patient and persistent. Listen, observe, and think before asking a range of probing questions. Do not interrupt unless an interviewee's answer is off-target, evasive, or threatens to run on forever. **Remain silent** when an interviewee stops answering, and the interviewee is likely to provide more information because silence quickly becomes intolerable. For instance, if an interviewee replies to a tough question with a comment such as, "I don't want to talk about that," remain quiet for a few seconds. "You will be amazed at how many people are uncomfortable with silence and will rush to fill it with an explanation that moments ago they said they would not give."[16] Unfortunately, interviewers also find silence intolerable and may fill in every pause with a question. Practice patience until you are good at it.

Be an active
listener, not a
passive sponge.

Metzler writes that it's "seldom the first question that gets to the heart of the matter, it's the seventh, or maybe 16th question you didn't know you were going to ask but have chosen to ask because of your careful, thoughtful listening." **Silent** and **nudging probes** encourage interviewees to continue or to say something important about which you did not plan to ask. **Informational probes** detect cues in answers and get additional information or explanations. **Restatement probes** obtain direct answers. **Reflective** and **mirror questions** verify and clarify answers and check for accuracy and understanding. **Clearinghouse probes** make sure you have obtained everything of importance for your story or report. You cannot plan for every piece of information or insight an interviewee might have. Some journalists claim that "even if you go into an interview armed with a list of questions, the most important probably will be ones you ask in response to an answer." If an interviewee reveals unexpected information or an apparent secret, follow this lead with probing questions to see where it leads. Then go back to your schedule as planned until another lead pops up. Be flexible and understanding, particularly when dealing with sensitive or personal information, and back off when an interviewee becomes emotionally distraught or angry. Let the person cool down and ready to continue.

Persistent probing is essential in information gathering interviews, but you must know when to stop. An interviewee may become agitated, confused, or silent if you probe too far. This exchange occurred between an attorney and a physician[17]:

Know when
enough is
enough.

Attorney: Doctor, before you performed the autopsy, did you check for a pulse?

Physician: No.

Attorney: Did you check for blood pressure?

Physician: No.

Attorney: Did you check for breathing?

Physician: No.

Attorney: So, then it is possible that the patient was alive when you began the autopsy?

Physician: No.

Attorney: How can you be so sure, Doctor?

Physician: Because his brain was sitting on my desk in a jar.

Attorney: But could the patient have still been alive nevertheless?

Physician: It is possible that he could be alive practicing law somewhere.

Be persistent, even relentless, but know when enough probing is enough.

This lengthy exchange also illustrates the futility of asking one closed question after another when a single open-ended question would obtain the information needed.

Word every question carefully, especially probing questions you create on the spot with little or no time to think. Make each brief and to the point. Be so familiar with the common question pitfalls discussed in Chapter 3 that you catch yourself before stumbling into one.

- The unintentional bipolar question
- The yes (no) question

- The tell me everything question
- The open to closed question
- The double-barreled question
- The unintentional leading question
- The guessing game
- The curious question
- The too high or too low question
- The don't ask, don't tell question

Know when and
how to use a
question on the
pitfall list.

Occasionally, it is necessary to ask a question on the pitfall list for a specific purpose. For instance, you may ask an obvious question with a known answer as an "ice breaker" to relax an interviewee and get the person talking: "I see you are a junior in history at Miami University?" As a general rule, all of your questions should be neutral, but you might ask a leading question such as "Do you **really** believe that?" to provoke a response. Be cautious when asking leading questions of children. Adults can lead them easily because they "are very attuned to taking cues from adults and tailoring their answers based on the ways questions are worded."[18] Investigative interviewers of possible child abuse must be very cautious when interviewing children. You ask a double-barreled question at a press conference because you may be able to ask only one question. Ask a bipolar question if you need a yes or a no for the record.

Commonly used
questions may
gather little
information.

Phrase each question carefully to obtain the information you need, and beware of common questions that elicit little or no information. Ken Metzler instructs journalists to avoid the "How do you feel about that" question because "It's the most trite, overused question in American journalism and sources begin to hate it after time." Interviewees usually reply with brief answers such as "Okay," "Not bad," or "As good as might be expected" that reveal nothing. Metzler suggests substituting "What were you thinking about when ...?" for the "feel" question. Similar routine questions that produce little information are used during the greeting or opening: "How're you doing," "How's it going," and "How's your semester?"

Confusion can result even when you phrase questions carefully. For example, words common to you may lead to a strange and perhaps humorous response. This exchange took place between an attorney and a witness:

Attorney: Is your appearance here this morning pursuant to a deposition notice, which I sent to your attorney?
Witness: No, this is how I dress when I go to work.

Apparently commonplace professional jargon may lead to confusion. This exchange took place between a physician and a patient:

Physician: Have you ever had a history of cardiac arrest in your family?
Patient: We never had no trouble with the police.

Never embarrass an interviewee who gives a strange or humorous answer. Simply rephrase or explain what you meant. An interviewee may play a game with you when you are careless in word choice. This exchange took place between a reporter and a potential voter during a presidential election in New Hampshire:

Reporter: How are you going to vote on Tuesday?

Resident: How am I going to vote? Oh, the usual way. I'm going to take the form they hand me and put x's in the appropriate boxes (laughing).

Reporter: (pause) Who are you going to vote for on Tuesday?

Be particularly cautious when asking unplanned probing questions. An interviewee may get a laugh at your expense. This was an exchange between an attorney and a witness:

Attorney: Now Mrs. Johnson, how was your first marriage terminated?

Witness: By death.

Attorney: And by whose death was it terminated?

Witness: Take a guess.

Listen and **think** before probing. The attorney in the following example apparently did neither.

Attorney: She had three children, right?

Witness: Yes.

Attorney: How many were boys?

Witness: None.

Attorney: Were there any girls?

ColorBlind Images/Blend Images LLC

■ *Effective note-taking entails maintaining eye contact as much as possible.*

Note-Taking and Recording

Note-taking and electronic recording during interviews make it possible for you to recall and check figures, dates, names, times, details, and quotations more accurately than relying on memory. However, authorities disagree on the extent of note-taking and use of recording devices because the first may adversely affect the communication between interview parties and the second may be intrusive or threatening.

Note-Taking

Weigh carefully the pros and cons of note-taking when planning an interview.

Note-taking has advantages. It may focus your attention on what is being said and not said. It can indicate to the interviewee that you are interested in what you are learning and want to have a complete and accurate record for future use. This direct involvement enables the interviewee to see you are doing your job.[19] If your interview is carefully structured, your notes will be well organized for ease of locating information when writing your report or story.

Note-taking has drawbacks, however. When an interviewee speaks rapidly and provides detailed answers, you may find it difficult if not impossible to take notes precisely and accurately. You may also have difficulty maintaining nonverbal communication with the interviewee and listening while concentrating on note-taking. The result may be missed information and opportunities to formulate insightful probing questions. We have discovered that interviewees often become curious and anxious about what we are writing, sometimes to the point where they stop talking while we are writing or try to lean toward us or rearrange their chairs to see what we are writing or have recorded. Any semblance to an interpersonal conversation is lost.

Follow these guidelines while note-taking to maintain communication and record answers thoroughly and accurately.

Note-taking should not threaten the interviewee.

- Explain why note-taking is beneficial to both parties.
- Ask permission to take notes.
- Show your notes occasionally to the interviewee to reduce curiosity and anxiety, check for accuracy, and enable the interviewee to fill in gaps and volunteer information.
- Maintain eye contact by making note-taking as inconspicuous as possible.
- Use abbreviations or a personal shorthand similar to sending text messages.
- Write down only important information, key words, and the gist of some quotes.

Maintain communication while taking notes.

- Take notes selectively throughout the interview to avoid signaling that the interviewee just dropped a "bombshell" quote or causing the interviewee to become cautious.
- If an interviewee is answering too rapidly, ask the person tactfully to slow down, or to repeat an answer.
- Ask a stalling question such as "Tell me more about that" to give you time to get caught up.
- Immediately following the interview, fill in gaps, check for accuracy and objectivity, complete abbreviations, and translate your handwriting.
- Review your notes carefully to identify the points, information, and quotations that are best for your report.

Recording

Recording allows interviewers to listen and probe more effectively.

A recorder provides a complete and accurate record of *how, when,* and *what* an interviewee says. It enables you to relax, concentrate on what is being said and implied, and then create effective probing questions. You can hear or watch what was said and how it was said hours or days afterward.

Unfortunately, recorders can malfunction or prove tricky to use. Batteries can die. Our students have used recorders during lengthy interviews for class projects only to discover disks or memory sticks were blank when they tried to review them later. Some parties view recorders as intruders in interviewing situations and fear the permanent, undeniable records they produce. It takes time to transcribe and review lengthy recordings to locate facts, reactions, and ideal quotes.

Follow these guidelines when recording interviews.

> A recorder may add an intrusive element to the interview.

> Ask permission before using a recorder.

- Reduce mechanical difficulties by testing the recorder prior to the interview.

- Be familiar with the recorder and practice with it in a simulated interview setting.

- Research appropriate state laws before using a hidden recorder or recording interviews over the telephone. The law generally allows one party to record a second party (no third parties) without permission, but 12 states prohibit the recording of conversations without the consent of both parties, including California, Connecticut, Florida, Illinois, Maryland, Massachusetts, Michigan, Montana, Nevada, New Hampshire, Pennsylvania, and Washington. Twenty-four states have laws that pertain to the use of hidden cameras. An excellent source on legal aspects of interviewing is a guide published by the *Reporters Committee for Freedom of the Press* (http://www.rcip.org).

- Ask permission before recording an interview to avoid possible lawsuits and to establish goodwill.

- Reduce interviewee fears and objections by explaining why the recorder is advantageous to the interviewee, why you want or are required to use a recorder, how the recording will be used, and offering to turn off the recorder when desired.

- Instruct the interviewee ahead of time about wearing a microphone, looking at the lens of a camera instead of the light, limiting noise and interruptions, and speaking loud enough for the recorder.

Managing Difficult Situations

Three information gathering situations are difficult, unique in many ways, and necessitate changes in the ways both parties usually prepare for and participate when gathering information. These are the press conference, the broadcast interview, and the videoconference.

The Press Conference

The press conference is unique in that the **interviewee** has virtually total control of timing, place, length, ground rules, purpose, subject matter, who is allowed to participate and when, and whether questions are allowed. It may be called with little or no warning and minimal indication about what will be addressed. The interviewee determines whether the conference will commence with a prepared statement, presentation, or questions. Ground rules often identify topics or issues that are off limits to questions and whether names may be attached to quotations in reports or news items. You may be permitted to ask questions or address the interviewee only when the interviewee invites you to do so. Ground rules or protocol may enable the interviewee or a staff member to end the press conference without warning, perhaps to avoid or escape from an unwanted exchange.

> The interviewee has nearly total control of the situation and interview.

If you have little notice of a press conference and the issue(s) or topic(s) to be discussed, review your records and experiences and call contacts to discover what issue or topic might dominate this press conference. Often your purpose and the interviewee's purpose may be nearly identical with each trying to gather and give information of value to a larger audience of employees, members, voters, or the public. On other occasions, the interviewee's purpose and yours may be at polar opposites. The interviewee may want to use the press conference for self-promotion, promotion of a policy or product, public relations, free advertising, place a positive spin on an action or issue, or hide the truth. Your purpose may be to cut through the "smoke and mirrors" presentation and answers couched in vague generalities, allegations, unsupported claims, personal attacks, and non-facts presented as facts to get to the truth. The only control you may have is that the interviewee needs you or there would not be a press conference.

Prepare questions in advance even though some may be irrelevant, declared off limits, or asked by other interviewers called upon before you. Know your relationship with the interviewee. If the interviewee knows, likes, and trusts you, you may be chosen to ask the first question, more than one question later, or to ask the question that ends the press conference. If your relationship is negative, the interviewee might not call upon you, give you a superficial answer, or say "No comment" and recognize another participant. Worse, the interviewee may use you as a foil by purposely getting into a verbal sparring match in which to gain sympathy or paint you and the organization you represent as enemies out to get him or her.

Do not let the situation or the interviewee's status intimidate you. Journalist Tony Rogers writes, "It's your job to ask tough questions of the most powerful people in society."[20] The press conference may be a free-for-all with raised hands, interviewers jumping to their feet, and shouted questions. If you are recognized, ask your most important question first because it may be your only chance. Consider asking a double-barreled question to get two possible answers. Listen carefully to how the interviewee replies to other interviewer's questions not only for the information but also to formulate insightful probing questions that clarify or expand on answers.

The broadcast interview presents unique problems for both parties.

Visionhaus/Getty Images

The Broadcast Interview

The broadcast interview poses unique challenges to both parties. It may take place in a field, along a street, in a studio, or in a home. The places are endless, and interviewee and interviewer may be miles and time zones apart. The interview may be on a real or figurative stage in which both parties engage in "performing" for outside forces such as live audiences, viewers, and listeners that constitute "a three-way interaction."[21] This virtual third party may lead the interviewer or interviewee to adapt questions and answers

Become familiar with the setting to eliminate surprises and mistakes.

If you have little or no experience in conducting broadcast interviews or feel nervous about this experience, consider practicing in a situation that closely resembles the real thing. Become familiar with the **physical setting** including seating for both parties, lighting, sound, audio and video equipment, and **support staff** such as director, technicians, and camera operators. Pay attention to the **briefing** instructions that include program format, targeted audience, time limits, opening and closing signals, microphone use, and camera locations. If your interview will be "live," anything can happen from forgetting a question, and poor wording of a question, to a nonverbal reaction to an answer or probing question you regret. Keep verbal nudging probes such as "Uh huh," "Okay," and "I see" to a minimum. They clutter up the broadcast or the recording. Use head nods and smiles instead. There are no "do overs" during live broadcasts, and mistakes may be in full view or sound of an audience. Ask someone to debrief you after the practice session to determine what you did well and what you need to work on.

The "staging" of the broadcast interview is critical to its success. The interviewer or director determines the framing of shots—whether the interviewer or interviewee will face the camera left or right, eyelines (interviewee's eye level with the interviewer's), whether shots will be mid-shot or medium close-ups, and whether to select a sequence of shots. Other decisions involve lighting, props, background (not dark clothing on a dark backdrop, not an overly busy background), and limiting noise such as shuffling of papers, heating and cooling systems, bell towers, nearby interactions, and foot traffic. These decisions make the broadcast interview more complex than a simple face-to-face interview.

It takes two prepared parties to make the broadcast interview a success.

If the interviewee is inexperienced in broadcast interviews or the format for this interview, help the interviewee as you have been helped. It takes both parties to make the interview a success. Explain how best to wear a microphone and emphasize that the microphone will pick up everything the person says and every sound the person makes. Do speak loud enough to be heard easily. Tell the interviewee to look at you rather than the camera, staff, or audience. Emphasize that poor grammar, verbal fillers such as "uh" and "and uh" along with meaningless phrases such as "Know what I mean," "You know," and "Stuff like that" may be embarrassing and reduce the professional image of the interview.

Spontaneous questions generate spontaneous answers.

If time permits, try to relax the interviewee with some informal conversation before the broadcast starts. Open the interview with easy to answer open-ended questions to ease the interviewee into the meat of the interview. Realize that a "live interview may last no more than seconds or a few minutes and allows little time to ask challenging questions."[22] Regardless of the length and depth of the interview make it appear to be two persons conversing with you taking limited notes and maintaining eye contact. Your task is to get information, not give it, so ask questions rather than make statements or counterpoints. Make all of your questions relevant and neutral. Become so familiar with your planned questions that you can ask them from memory or a few small cards. This makes the interview look and sound spontaneous and professional. You want to avoid "dead air space" in which nothing appears to be happening while at the same time being tolerant of silence that encourages the interviewee to continue answering or thinking of an appropriate answer. Do not fill the space immediately with another question, perhaps one that introduces a new aspect of the topic, while the previous one remains in play.

Learn to tolerate and use silence.

Probe persistently for information you need while recognizing there is a major differ-ence between tenacity and incivility. Sparks recommends being aggressive with charm.[23] Show respect for interviewees even when you know they and their associates are likely to accuse you of bias, rudeness, or worse. Observe the interviewee carefully. If you notice signs of fatigue, excessive nervousness, increasing emotions, confusion, or anger, take a break or move to a less challenging and threatening line of questions.

Know how to handle intoler-ant comments and obsceni-ties if they occur during an interview.

While our current society may appear to be more prone to antisemitic, racist, sexist, and anti-LGBT remarks and attitudes, that does not mean we have become more toler-ant of them. If you know an interviewee has made such comments in other situations, emphasize that they will not be tolerated during your interview and how you will handle them. While society also seems more comfortable with profanities and obscene gestures, it is not yet ready to hear or see them in broadcast interviews where they expect a high degree of professionalism and restraint. Bleeping obscenities is now common, but there are limits to this practice. Some interview parties have used society's attitude toward obscenities to their advantage. For example, newsprint reporters, when being crowded out by cameras and microphones, have been known to shout obscenities to shut down their electronic counterparts and get closer to the action. A state legislator told the author that he would purposely insert profanities into answers to prevent interviewers from using them in broadcasts.

The Videoconference Interview

Videoconference interviews are becoming common and share many similarities with face-to-face interviews. There are obvious differences, however, so let us focus on what you need to know and do when taking part in videoconference interviews.

When planning for a videoconference interview, strive to eliminate or minimize dis-tractions. Choose a setting that is uncluttered and void of large patterns, designs, or colors such as red. Control the movement of others in the background. Turn off your cell phone. Dress appropriately for the situation while avoiding plaids, stripes, and white shirts or jackets. Clothing may range from professional business attire to casual. Select jewelry that does not make noise or catch light.

As the interview commences, avoid noises such as taping on the desk, moving papers, or playing with a ball point pen or other objects. These small noises may be loud and dis-tracting when transmitted electronically. Hesitate slightly before asking or answering ques-tions to handle the transmission delay in receiving audio and video. Look straight into the monitor or camera to appear to maintain eye contact with the other party. Focus attention on the other party. Avoid excessive or repetitive body motions or stiffness so you appear to be relaxed and enjoying the conversation. Speak naturally for a conversational interaction. The microphone will pick up your voice so you need not raise it. Let your voice and face show energy and enthusiasm. Smile. The other party will focus on your face because it is most visible on the screen.

Managing Difficult Interviewees

Information gathering interviewers often delve into personal and public tragedies and disasters and probe into causes and effects, reactions, attitudes, beliefs, and feelings. Be prepared to handle difficult situations with difficult interviewees.

Journalist Wendell Cochran warns, "If we aren't proficient at asking the right questions at the right time, we'll miss on accuracy, fall short on context, and stumble on fairness."[24]

Emotional Interviewees

> Silence is often better than words.

A respondent may burst into tears while trying to reply to a highly personal question, and the interviewer does not help the situation by commenting, "I know how you feel." There is no way you can feel as the interviewee feels even if you have had a similar experience such as death of a child, sexual assault, lung cancer, or military combat. The best advice is to remain silent until the interviewee regains composure and is ready to continue. You may use a sincere and tactful comment such as:

> No one can truly understand how you feel.
> It's okay to cry.
> Take your time.

If you have a close relationship with the interviewee, you may use a comforting gesture such as holding the person's hand, touching an arm, or placing an arm across the shoulders.

> Treat others as you would like to be treated.

Be sensitive to people who have experienced tragedies by not invading their privacy. How you broach a sensitive topic at a sensitive time is a serious ethical issue. Reporters are notorious for asking thoughtless questions such as, "How do you feel about your child's death?" or "Is the family devastated by this tragedy?" John and Denise Bittner suggest that you ask only direct and necessary questions. "Remember, people in crisis situations are under a great deal of stress," they write. "A prolonged interview won't provide additional information; it will only upset people."[25]

Managing Hostile Interviewees

> Discover why an interviewee is angry or hostile.

An interviewee may **appear** to be hostile because of too little sleep, a health issue, or a usual gruff manner. You may become a convenient outlet or scapegoat because the interviewee is angry, depressed, or frightened by circumstances beyond his or her control that have nothing to do with you or the subject of the interview. On the other hand, the interviewee may be hostile toward you as a person, your profession, or the organization you represent. The interviewee's hostility may have nothing to do with you personally but with the issue being addressed. For instance, the person may be strongly for or against gun control, and you just happen to be the interviewer. Try to discover tactfully if the apparent hostility is real and if so, its cause.

> You seem to be upset?
> You appear to be very angry.
> Why does this issue make you so angry?
> Would you like to talk about your concern?

There are many ways to avoid or reduce hostility. Do not invade the other's space, make unwarranted demands, or present a threatening physical presence or manner. Use neutral and open-ended questions. Substitute better-sounding words for antagonizing ones. Remain silent to permit the interviewee to offer full explanations or to blow off steam. Go to another topic if the current one is producing a hostile reaction.

Phillip Ault and Edwin Emery offer this simple rule: "Treat the average person with respect, and he [she] will do the same."[26]

Reticent Interviewees

An interviewee may be **disinclined to talk** because of a personality trait or experiences that have nothing to do with you or the subject matter of the interview, and there is little you can do to change this disposition in the few minutes you have. On the other hand, the person may be **consciously unwilling** to give lengthy, revealing answers because of your position (supervisor, superior, investigator) or your reputation. Bad interview experiences may make the interviewee reluctant to risk self-image or reputation in another interview. Reticence may result from the location of the interview in which others can see or hear what is taking place.

When interviewing reticent persons, use conversation starters such as asking about pictures, awards, or arrangement of furnishings in the room. Begin with easy-to-answer open-ended questions on nonthreatening topics. If open questions do not generate in-depth answers, use closed questions (an inverted question sequence) until the party is ready to talk. Use silent and nudging probes. Realize that no tactic can get some reticent people to talk openly and freely; they simply do not talk much.

Talkative Interviewees

> Controlling talkative persons may be more difficult than getting reticent ones to open up.

Unlike reticent interviewees, talkative interviewees may talk for long periods of time without seeming to take a breath. They give unending answers to open questions and lengthy answers to closed questions. Try to avoid awkward interruptions by using nonverbal signals such as leaning forward, nodding your head, stop note-taking, or glancing at your watch. Phone interviews pose problems because you have few nonverbal signals to halt answers. The best you may be able to do is use only targeted, closed questions with less verbal maneuverability and look for natural openings or slight pauses to insert a question such as:

> That's very interesting, now I was wondering . . .
> Speaking of fall break, let me ask you . . .
> I'm glad you mentioned that because . . .

Evasive Interviewees

Interviewees may attempt to evade questions that delve into feelings or embarrassing actions that may incriminate them in some way or force them to take a stand they wish to avoid. Respondents employ a variety of evasive strategies to dodge questions they do not wish to address, including attacking the interviewer with real or fake hostility, attacking the question, humor, ambiguous words, rambling answers that reveal nothing, questioning the meaning of a key word, answering only part of a question, diverting the question to another person or group, declining to answer, postponing an answer, substituting one question for another and answering it, or revolving a question onto the interviewer.

> Be persistent, be patient, and be polite.

There are a variety of ways to respond to an evasive interviewee. Be persistent and patient without being rude, angry, or replying in kind. Be pleasant and maintain a sense of humor. Use one or more of these strategies.

- Repeat your question.
- Rephrase your question.

- Go to another question and come back to this one.
- Use a leading question.
- Laugh and continue with your questions.
- Ask why a person will not or cannot answer a question.

Dishonest Interviewees

It takes more than a clue or two to determine honesty.

If you suspect an interviewee is being dishonest, listen and observe carefully for clues that support your suspicions. Strike a balance between being gullible and overly suspicious. **Verbal cues**, according to FBI agents Joe Navarro and John R. Schafer, include "text bridges" such as "I don't remember," "The next thing I knew," and "After that."[27] Stalling tactics include asking the interviewer to repeat or rephrase a question, including "It depends on what you mean by," "Where did you hear that," and "Could you be more specific?" Pat Stith writes that when an interviewee "says 'to be perfectly honest' or 'to be perfectly candid' the hair ought to stand up on the back of your neck. Almost always these phrases are followed by fibs."[28] Listen carefully to answers to determine if they match facts and discoveries from your research and interviews with others. Probe into answers for specifics and to discover if information and stories remain consistent.

Observe **nonverbal cues** and be aware that clever interviewees know how to **appear** to be honest by maintaining excellent eye contact and giving firm handshakes. Navarro and Schafer recommend looking for "clusters of behavior, which cumulatively reinforce deceptive behaviors unique to the person being interviewed." These behaviors may include fidgeting feet, increased eye contact, rapidly blinking eyes, leaning away, irregular breathing, folding arms or interlocking legs, and lack of gesturing or finger pointing. Be aware that these behaviors may be the result of nervousness or inexperience. That is why Navarro and Schafer emphasize "cluster."

Confused Interviewees

Interviewees may become confused because of a tense situation, unfamiliarity with a topic or issue, the way a question is phrased, technical jargon, uncommon words, or words with different meanings. An uncommon word led to confusion in the following exchange[29]:

Attorney: The truth of the matter is that you were not an unbiased, objective witness, Isn't it? You too were shot in the fracas.
Witness: No, sir. I was shot midway between the fracas and the naval.

A common word with multiple meanings led to confusion in this exchange:

Attorney: What gear were you in at the moment of impact?
Witness: Gucci sweats and Reeboks.

Handle confused interviewees with understanding in a way that does not embarrass them or lead to anger or reluctance to reveal important information in the exchanges that follow. Restate or reword a question tactfully or return to it later. Control nonverbal reactions. Observe how broadcast journalists react to strange, often humorous responses without exhibiting a smile or shock. They proceed to a carefully worded probing question or their next primary question as if nothing unusual or embarrassing has happened.

Dissimilar Interviewees

Gender and cultural characteristics are generalities that may not apply to a particular interviewee.

Our increasingly diverse society makes it likely that you will interview persons who are very different from you in age, gender, race, ethnicity, experiences, professions, political, religious, and social beliefs, and attitudes. It also means you will encounter and perhaps maintain stereotypes (usually negative) of a variety of hyphenated ethic groups such as Irish-Americans, Hispanic-Americans, African-Americans, Arab-Americans, and Native-Americans and expect them to interact, react, and respond in particular ways. When the author was interviewing funeral directors for a book on grief counseling, he was asked if he went to church. It was apparent that many of his interviewees believed that all college professors were atheists and were shocked to discover this was merely a stereotype.

Be aware of stereotypes and results of research, but strive to know each interviewee as an individual.

Treat each interviewee as a distinct human being who is different from you and do background research to see how you might adapt to each during an interview. Journalist Wendell Cochran asks, "How do you deal fairly with someone whose views are anathema to you?"[30] Adapt questions and structure to interviewees and be aware of gender and cultural differences that may influence how they respond to questions. Research indicates that African-Americans prefer indirect questions, consider extensive probing to be intrusive, and prefer frequent and equal turn-taking. Mexican-Americans rely more on emotion, intuition, and feeling than midwestern European-Americans. Persons of rural backgrounds value know-how, skills, practicality, simplicity, and self-sufficiency more than those of urban backgrounds. Contrary to common beliefs, men rather than women talk more and monopolize interactions, make direct statements (less beating around the bush), get to the point sooner, and answer with declarations. On the other hand, women tend to answer questions with questions and are less direct. Elderly interviewees may be less trusting because of experiences and perceived insecurity. If they live alone and with few social interactions, they may be very talkative during interviews.

Closing the Interview

Always express appreciation.

When you have asked your final question and gotten the information you need, bring the interview to a close without being abrupt. Make sure the interviewee is **an active participant in the closing.** Employ a clearinghouse probe such as "Is there anything else you would like to add?" or "What have I not asked that you think is important for me to know?" No matter how carefully prepared you are, you may miss information that is critical to your purpose. Express appreciation for the interviewee's assistance and willingness to help with your project. If the interviewee wishes to chat for a few minutes—perhaps talking about the interview, your project, or how you are doing in college or your profession, do so in a friendly, informal manner. Then bring the interview to a close.

Do not overstay your welcome.

If you have been allotted **a specific amount of time** for the interview, keep track of time during the interview so the interviewee need not worry that your interview is going to impinge on another commitment. If you have agreed to a 15-minute interview, end the interview within this time or start to close the interview with a minute or two to spare. The interviewee may grant you a few extra minutes when you signal that your time is nearly over or it is obvious you are approaching a closing. If the interviewee is reluctant to grant more time, close on a positive note and ask for another session.

An interviewee may relax and be less on guard when the interview appears to be ending and reveal important information, insights, and feelings, some of which may alter your understandings and impressions established during the body of the interview. Journalist Pat Stith writes that "some of the best stuff you're going to get will come in the last few minutes, when you're wrapping up the interview, packing your stuff, and getting ready to leave."[31] Observe and listen until both parties are out of sound and sight of one another.

Preparing the Report or Story

Prepare a story or report with your purpose front and center.

Begin preparing your **report** or **story** with a thorough review of the information you attained through research and the one or more interviews you conducted. Sift through the words, statements, facts, and opinions to identify what is most important to include in the limited space or time you may have to report your findings. Check information with other sources to be sure of the accuracy and completeness of information and any potential bias. As you recall interviews and listen to and observe recorded exchanges, look for nonverbal signals that may tell you more than the words spoken.

Now it is time to decide what to include and what not to include in your report or story. If the interview is a press conference, the information may include several topics and raise a variety of issues. You are likely to have far more information than you can use in a single report or story because of time or space limitations. Keep your purpose as a focal point. What is most important for readers or listeners to learn? These may include announcements, revelations, allegations, denials, facts, opinions, and intentions. Look for significant quotations, sound bites, and changes in labels such as accidental death to murder, explosion to terrorism, victim to victimizer, undocumented immigrant to illegal alien.

Be honest, accurate, and fair in reporting interview results.

Make sure questions and answers are reported in context, and preface them so readers and listeners have a clear understanding of each. Include proper qualifiers, and do not overstate or understate unfairly an interviewee's opinions, attitudes, intentions, and commitments. Arrange information in order of importance. Include quotations to enliven and support your story or report. Follow all ground rules and exclude "off the record" information, be careful of making assumptions, and check carefully all sources and reports.

Double-check everything you have written.

When you have prepared a draft of your report or story, begin a careful editing process in which you check for inaccuracies, excessive wording, spellings, grammar, redundancies, and necessary and unnecessary qualifiers. Beware of making your report a long series of quotations. If you are preparing a verbatim interview for publication or dissemination, determine if you should include unintentional errors, grammatical errors, mispronounced words, slang, expletives, vocalized pauses such as "uh" and "and uh," and fillers such as "and stuff like that." Some readers and listeners may enjoy a report with all of the warts showing, particularly if they dislike the interviewee, but the interviewee may be embarrassed and lose credibility and your relationship may be damaged beyond repair.

The Interviewee in the Interview

The interviewee is more than a warehouse of information.

The information gathering interview, like all interviews, is an **interactional, collaborative communication process.** When you play the role of interviewee, you are much more than a repository of information the interviewer needs. Take an active part from the start and be ready to take on the role of interviewer from time to time. **Preparation** is the key to playing your role successfully.

Use the opening to prepare for unplanned interviews.

Unfortunately, you may find yourself in interview situations in which you have little or no time to prepare ahead of time. You may receive a telephone call from a recruiter desiring information on an applicant you know personally or professionally; a student may walk into your office and want information about internships your students have; you may have witnessed a school bus accident and a police officer wants information on what you saw and heard. Discover who the interviewer is and who the person represents. Why does the person want to interview you and for what specific purpose? How will the information you provide be used and when? How long will the interview last? As you get answers to these questions, start thinking about the information you have and what you can and cannot tell the interviewer. Listen carefully to each question. Give yourself time to think and to weigh the possible ramifications of what you are about to say. You are under no obligation to answer every question an interviewer asks, but be tactful and amicable. When time allows, start preparing by doing your homework.

Do Your Homework

Review what you know and need to know prior to the interview.

If the interviewer has given a specific topic or identified an issue for the interview, review what you know and what is available to you that pertains to this topic or issue. Check relevant facts, opinions, research, current events, the history of this topic or issue, proposed solutions to a problem, pending judicial or organizational decisions, and relevant laws. Will you be speaking for yourself or as a representative of an organization? If an organization, check the organization's policies, positions, and involvement. Should you be representing the organization at this time, in this situation, with this interviewer on this topic or issue? You may need permission to take part and then follow prescribed organizational guidelines that may include ground rules.

Become familiar with the interviewer, including age, gender, ethnic group, education and training, special interests, and experiences. What are the interviewer's attitudes toward you, your organization, your profession, and the topic: friendly or hostile, trusting or suspicious, interested or disinterested. Some interviewers have little to no knowledge or expertise on a topic while others have engineering, management, economics, law, or science degrees or have developed a high level of expertise on topics such as energy, stem cell research, or foreign policy. What is the interviewer's reputation for fairness and honesty in questioning techniques. Observe the interviewer in action by watching the person reporting the news, reading reports of interviews, and reviewing story angles the person likes to take.

Understand Your Relationship with the Interviewer

What is your relational history? How similar are you? How willing and eager are each of you to take part? How much control will you have over the interview? Does each of

**How might
your relation-
ship impact the
interview?**

you perceive the other to be trustworthy, reliable, and safe? What problems may result from upward and downward communication because of status differences between you and the interviewer. For example, where does each of you fit into the hierarchy of this organization or the organizations you represent?

Study the Situation

Study the situation carefully. When will it take place? Is this a good time for you and your schedule? Does the timing pose concerns for you personally or the organization you represent? Where will the interview take place? Is this a neutral location or one more advantageous to you or to the interviewer? Is it a private or public setting? If it is a broadcast interview, become familiar with the media format and how you might help by providing visuals. Diana Pisciotta, an expert in strategic communication, warns that "An appearance on CNBC or an interview on NPR can help to make or break your company's reputation."[32] She suggests that if the interview is not "live," you should pretend it is because your interview might be picked up by the Internet or other media outlets. There is no substitute for practice, rehearsal, and role playing to prepare you for the broadcast interview. Dress for the camera; appear to be excited and engaged; be animated because body language enhances your voice, credibility, expertise, and authority; keep your eyes on the interviewer rather than the camera.

Set Ground Rules

**Ground rule
should be
necessary and
reasonable.**

Do you want to establish ground rules for time, length, place, privacy, and setting? Are there personal or organizational topics or issues that must be off limits? You may be unable to answer some questions because of pending litigation, current investigations, an IRS audit of tax returns, national security, or privacy laws. Be realistic in the ground rules you set. If all important topics or issues are off limits, there is no need for an interview, and this may be to your disadvantage.

Anticipate Questions

If you know the interviewer's purpose and have done your homework, you should anticipate many of the questions the interviewer will ask. Think through answers that will meet the interviewer's purpose and interests. What might be the most important information

**Be as prepared
to answer as
the interviewer
is prepared
to ask.**

to divulge or conceal? How should you qualify answers? What evidence can you provide for assertions and claims? How might you reply to questions you cannot answer because of lack of information, need for secrecy, protection of sources, legal consequences, or organizational policies and constraints?

In this age of litigation and media involvement in every issue, interviewees increasingly are undergoing training in how to handle questions. Prosecutors, attorneys, and aides prepare witnesses and clients (including presidents of the United States and CEOs) to answer questions in court, congressional hearings, board meetings, and press conferences. Seek help if you are facing a difficult encounter with a trained and experienced interviewer.

Responding to Questions

A good answer is concise, precise, carefully organized, clearly worded, logical, well supported, and to the point. Keep these guidelines in mind.

> Engage your brain before opening your mouth.

Listen and **think** carefully and insightfully to each question before replying. What is being asked and how? Do you understand the words and the ways they are being used? Misinterpreting a word can have serious repercussions for you and for others. Follow two pieces of advice when phrasing your answers: **keep it simple** and if you **are unsure** of what you about to say, **don't say it.** Never make up something to avoid looking uninformed or stupid because your answer will likely do what you fear the most.

Be patient. Respond only after you have heard a complete question and understand what the interviewer is asking. Do not interrupt the interviewer.

Focus on the question being asked at the moment, not on a question you have already answered. It is tempting and natural to replay in your mind answers to previous questions, particularly when you wish you had answered them differently. Those answers are history, and failure to focus on the current question may result in an answer that is incomplete or off point.

> Observe nonverbal behavior for what it might and might not reveal.

Observe the nonverbal signals that complement and substitute for verbal symbols and may reveal the interviewer's beliefs, attitudes, and feelings. Be cautious of reading too much into nonverbal actions, because it is easy to misread a person's eye contact, change in voice, and movements.

Judge a question's relevancy only after listening and answering to the best of your ability. A question may be one in a series leading up to a question that is right on target. An interviewer may be using an inverted funnel sequence that starts with closed questions and leads to more open questions.

Answering Questions Strategically

A good answer is concise, precise, carefully organized, clearly worded, logical, well supported, and to the point. There are many strategies for responding to questions.

- Avoid defensiveness or hostility.
    - Give answers, not speeches.
    - Give reasons and explanations rather than excuses.
    - Be polite and tactful in words and manner.
    - Use tasteful, appropriate humor.
    - Do not reply in kind to a hostile question.
- Share control of the interview.
    - Insist on adequate time to answer questions.
    - Do not allow the interviewer to "put words in your mouth."
    - Challenge the content of questions that contain unsupported assertions or inaccurate data or quotations.
    - If a question is multiple-choice, be sure the choices are fair and include all reasonable options.

—Ask interviewers to rephrase or repeat long, complicated, or unclear questions.

—Answer a question with a question.

—Search reflective and mirror questions for accuracy and completeness.

- Explain what you are doing and why.

—Preface a lengthy answer by explaining why it must be so.

—Preface an answer by explaining why a question is tough or tricky.

—Provide a substantial explanation why you must refuse to answer a question or simply say "No comment."

—Rephrase a question: "If what you're asking is . . ." or "You seem to be implying that . . ."

- Take advantage of question pitfalls.

—Reply to the portion of a double-barreled question you remember and can answer most effectively.

—Answer a bipolar question with a simple yes or no, when it suits you.

—Reply to the open or closed portion of an open-to-closed switch question that is to your advantage.

- Avoid common question traps.

—If a question is leading, such as "Don't you agree that . . . ," do not be led to the suggested answer.

—If a question is loaded, such as "Are you still cheating on your exams?," be aware that either a yes or a no will make you guilty.

—If an apparent bipolar question offers two disagreeable choices, such as "Did you go into medicine for the prestige or for the money," answer with a third option.

—Watch for the yes-no pitfall, such as "Do you want to die?" and answer or refuse to answer politely.

- Support your answers.

—Use stories and examples to illustrate points.

—Use analogies and metaphors to explain unknown or complicated things, procedures, and concepts.

—Organize long answers like mini-speeches with an introduction, body, and conclusion.

- Open your answers positively. The authors of *Journalistic Interviews: Theories of the Interview* offer these examples of interviewee responses[33]:

Negative	Positive
You failed to notice	May I point out
You neglected to mention	We can also consider x, y, z
You overlooked the fact	One additional fact to consider
You missed the point	From another perspective

Part 2: The Information Giving Interview

Giving informa-
tion appears
to be simple,
and that is the
problem.
You are involved in information giving interviews on a daily basis, and the process seems so simple that you seldom give it much thought. What is complicated about giving a few instructions, directions, dates, times, closing numbers on the stock exchange, or college football scores to another person? This apparent simplicity is deceptive, however. Research indicates that interviewees as highly motivated as health care patients forget 40 to 80 percent of medical information immediately and half of that information is remembered incorrectly.[34] Patients who remembered most were given only two items of information. In spite of problems that affect the amount and kinds of information interviewers give and interviewees hear, process, retain short-term and long-term, and follow as directed, there are ways both parties can enhance the effectiveness of information giving interviews.

Do not Overload the Interviewee

Lessen the risk
of overloading
by giving only
what is relevant
and essential.
Determine what information is absolutely relevant and essential for this interview, with this interviewee, at this time, and in this place. Weed out words, phrases, materials, examples, explanations, favorite anecdotes, or issues that are not essential. They may **interfere** with information you want the interviewee to recall completely and accurately. For instance, an interviewee may recall phrases or an anecdote rather than the critical information you are striving to communicate.

A study by Ley revealed how easy it is to **overload** a party's memory even when information is relevant and important. He discovered that within a few hours, 82 percent of medical patients could recall two items of information, but the percentage dropped to 36 percent for three or four items, 12 percent for five or six items, and 3 percent for seven or more.[35] This problem is exacerbated by rapid advances in information and communication technology that bombard us with information 24/7. It is becoming difficult to obtain and process what is useful.[36]

Know the Interviewee

What does the
interviewee
already know?
Become acquainted with the interviewee if you do not have a relational history. How well does this person process information? Some people have so-called "photographic memories" and can recall lengthy messages verbatim. Others have trouble remembering short messages within a few minutes. Does the interviewee have a **memory handicap** or an **attention deficit problem** that affects short- as well as long term-recall? Does the person get **distracted** easily by material considered unimportant or uninteresting? Does the person rely on **rote memorization** rather than attempting to understand information and how it might be applied to tasks?[37] What is the interviewee's level of knowledge, expertise, and experience. It may be unnecessary to include all of the information you have in mind because of the interviewee's familiarity with it. An interviewee may "tune out" what is already known and miss important new information. An interviewee's limited knowledge and experience may require you to elaborate on some information while defining key words and concepts.

Consider how
the inter-
viewee prefers
information.
Consider how a person prefers to receive or give information. For instance, one person may favor directions to a destination through **numbers** for streets, roads, highways, and exits while another prefers directions through **landmarks** such as a school, log cabin, big red barn, large oak tree, or river. A foster family directed the author to its

country home through numbers until he needed to know where to turn left off a major highway. Then it used landmarks including "a gray horse will be standing by a fence." Sure enough, the gray horse was standing by the fence when he approached the turning point. The more you know about a person the better able you are to select or organize relevant and important information in ways that will aid recall.

Enhance Verbal and Nonverbal Presentation

Structure can aid information recall and processing.

Structure enhances your verbal presentation. Start by reviewing the information you will give, give it, and then review what you gave as the interview closes. Generations of public speaking instructors have cited a country minister's explanation for his success as a preacher, "First, I tell 'em what I'm gonna to tell 'em; then I tell 'em; and then I tell 'em what I told 'em." This is sound advice for interviewers as well as preachers. Present information systematically and with signposts that make it easier to recall. Employ structure that is natural and logical to the interviewee. In a classic study of memory loss, Peterson and Peterson asked participants to memorize a three-letter sequence and then count backwards in sets of threes. Within 6 seconds of counting backwards, 50 percent of the original letters were lost; within 12 seconds, 85 percent were lost; and within 18 seconds, 100 percent were lost.[38]

Repetition and vocal emphasis can enhance information recall.

Repeat critical words and data strategically throughout the interview. Critical qualifiers such as not, maybe, probably, considering, unlikely, and theoretically are often the first to be forgotten or altered. Interviewees are more likely to recall words they encounter a number of times. Use concrete words and phrases and avoid meaningless slang such as "We made a ton of money in the fourth quarter." Employ **vocal emphasis** that amounts to **oral highlighting** and **pauses** to call attention to important words, phrases, names, numbers, and qualifiers to enhance importance and recall.

Be cautious when using jargon and acronyms.

Beware of professional jargon and acronyms with which the interviewee may be unfamiliar. Every profession and group have unique jargon and acronyms and often use them without hesitation when communicating with others who have no idea what they are talking about. When one of the authors became a Court Appointed Special Advocate for Children (CASA), represented Children in Need of Services (CHINS) in court, and became a witness and cross examiner during Termination of Parent Rights trials (TPRs), he found himself employing these acronyms and jargon with teachers, foster parents, employers, apartment managers, and others. Their puzzled expressions, if not questions, quickly revealed they had no idea what he was talking about.

Handouts may enhance the amount and accuracy of recalled information. It is estimated that about 33 percent of interviewees recall oral information while 70 percent recall information presented orally and in writing. Use **visual aids** such as models, objects, maps, pictures, and drawings to help interviewees apply, remember, and understand information.

Practice and encourage active listening.

The information giving interview like the information gathering interview is a collaborative process. The interviewer should encourage the interviewee to ask questions and answer them to the party's acknowledged satisfaction. Do not be in a hurry to move on or complete the interview as quickly as possible. Practice and encourage active listening. Ask an interviewee to repeat or to explain points, names, directions, facts, and instructions and fill in what is missing or correct what is misunderstood. Do not make this a quiz but an honest effort to check on memory and understanding of important information. When appropriate, encourage note-taking or electronic recording so an interviewee can verify and recall information later.

Process and Retain Information Effectively

Know how well you recall information over time.

Be an active interviewee in the information giving interview rather than a passive receptacle. Begin with an honest assessment of your abilities to recall information from interactions. In spite of data that indicates interviewees tend to forget much of what they receive, most exaggerate their memories and claim they recall information accurately and completely over time. How well do you really recall information in the short-term and long-term, particularly without notes or other visual aids? Studies indicate that "both types of memory can be extremely fragile over their respective timescales."[39] Other research on memory and recall indicates that we tend to recall what we hear early or late in interactions and forget the middle. What is your tendency?

Focus on what is being said and not on "noise" or the past.

Prepare yourself to focus attention during the interview and enhance later recall by learning what will take place during an interview and what is expected of you during and afterward. How might your relational history with this interviewer affect your ability to focus on the content you are receiving? How might the physical setting and "noise" affect the communication that takes place? Is a report you have been preparing, an unpleasant interaction that just ended, or exciting/disturbing professional, social, or family news dominating your thinking? Try to have some "down-time" prior to the interview to clear your head so you can focus fully on **this interaction** and its content.

Do not overestimate what you know.

As the interview commences, listen carefully to how the interviewer explains the purpose and content of the interview, your role as interviewee, and what is expected of you following the interview. If you are an experienced veteran in a position and the interview begins with materials you know well such as policies, rules, procedures, and examples, do not dismiss it too quickly as unimportant, irrelevant, or uninteresting. You may miss or fail to recall nuggets of information that are new or important to you personally, the organization, or people with whom you deal such as students, clients, customers, and staff. At the very least, the information may serve as a refresher. Your attitude is critical when receiving information.

Be an active, collaborative listener.

Be an **active listener** by listening carefully, insightfully, and patiently to words, content, and intended as well as implied meanings. Pay attention to voice, volume, and vocal emphasis and their changes. All of these provide **context** for words, phrases, names, and data so you can understand and recall accurately what is being said. For instance, if an interviewer says a person is into "shipping," the context surrounding it should tell you whether the interviewer means dispersing goods to customers through the mail or managing ships on the ocean? If a person says an applicant worked for Ford, does this mean the applicant worked for Ford Motor Company that manufactures cars and trucks or the Ford company that manufactures food processing machinery. Ask the interviewer to repeat specifics, offer explanations, or summarize portions of information. Take careful but limited notes, perhaps using a sort of shorthand, to focus attention during the interview and to aid in accurate and complete recall later.

Summary

You are involved in informational interviews nearly every day when you gather or give instructions, recommendations, facts, opinions, observations, data, reactions, feelings, and attitudes. The purposes of these interviews are to **obtain** relevant and important information as accurately and completely as possible, or to **provide** important information so it is understood, retained, and used or passed along to others accurately and completely. Unfortunately, the frequency of informational interactions often leads us to assume the processes are simple and pose few problems.

Information gathering and information giving interviews require careful planning, analysis, flexibility, and the skills necessary to perform the roles of interviewer and interviewee effectively. This chapter has provided guidelines for structuring and conducting these interviews. Both parties must know how and when to share control, speak and listen, observe what is taking place, concentrate on the information being shared, and adapt to one another and the situation as the interview progresses.

Key Terms and Concepts

Broadcast interview	Ground rules	Press conference
Confused interviewees	Hostile interviewees	Research
Dishonesty	Icebreaker questions	Reticent interviewees
Dissimilar interviewees	Information overload	Status difference
Emotional interviewees	Key informants	Strategic answers
Evasive interviewees	Metaphorical questions	Talkative interviewees
False assumptions	Off the record	Videoconference

Review Questions

1. What are the personality traits of a skilled information gathering interviewer?
2. Ken Metzler writes that when you know exactly what you want in an interview, "You're halfway there." What does the interviewer do in the second half of preparation?
3. How reliable are "eye-witness" accounts of events?
4. What are the four criteria for selecting the best interviewee?
5. What are the advantages of being in a subordinate status to the interviewee?
6. Aside from location, what are four other important situation variables?
7. What six key words constitute the journalist's interview guide?
8. What are four key ways to motivate interviewees?
9. Persistent probing is essential in information gathering interviews, but why is it important to know when to stop?

10. What are the advantages of note-taking during interviews?

11. How might you manage a hostile interviewee?

12. What guidelines would you give to the interviewer in the information giving interview?

13. Why is information "overload" a significant problem in information giving interviews?

14. How can the interviewer enhance the information giving interview through verbal and nonverbal presentation?

15. How can the interviewee in the information giving interview improve memory and recall of information after the interview?

Student Activities

1. The plight of the Dreamers, children brought into the United States as children by parents who entered illegally, has been in the news a great deal during the last several years. Research this issue carefully, create a moderately scheduled interview, and select a Dreamer who meets the criteria discussed in this chapter is willing to be interviewed for a minimum of 15 minutes. Learn everything you can about this interviewee, analyze the relationship you have with this person, and select an appropriate location and setting. Write a critique of your interview while it is fresh in mind. How successful were you in getting the information you wanted? Which questions worked best? What information and insights did your probing questions elicit from the interviewee? How effective were you at maintaining focus on critical areas of information? What would you do differently if you were doing the interview over again?

2. Select an interviewee to whom you must give extensive information about how to use a new computer program, how to find a location some distance away, how to sail a small boat, or how to cook a meal. The interviewee must have little to none of the information you will give. Follow the guidelines in this chapter for exchanging information effectively. Arrange to have the interviewee send to you from memory alone the information retained from the interview at three intervals: an hour later, 24 hours later, and 48 hours later. How accurate was the information retained at each level? What might you have done to enhance this retention?

3. Select a 20- to 30-minute interview from C-SPAN. Study it carefully to see if you can detect an interview guide of planned major points and sub-points. How were these points turned into questions during the interview? How effectively did the interviewer employ probing questions when needed? How well did the interviewer avoid common question pitfalls? Which techniques did the interviewer use in the opening, and which did the interviewer use in the closing? How did the interviewer involve the interviewee in the opening and closing?

4. Interview a newspaper journalist and a broadcast journalist about their interviewing experiences and techniques. How does the nature of the medium affect interviewers and interviewees? How does the medium affect interview structure, questioning techniques, and note-taking? What advice do they give about note-taking and recording interviews? How do the end products differ? What constraints does each medium place on interviewers?

5. Record a televised press conference in which one person is answering questions from several interviewers. How is this situation similar to and different from one-on-one interviews? What stated or implied rules governed this interview? What skills are required of interviewers and interviewee? How did the interviewee recognize interviewers? What answering strategies did the interviewee use? What questioning strategies did interviewers use?

6. A growing number of interviewers are turning to the Internet to conduct probing interviews. Develop a moderately scheduled 20-minute interview on a topic that will require fairly lengthy answers and then conduct one face-to-face interview and one employing Skype. Identify the advantages and disadvantages of each with respect to relationship building, communication interactions, depth of answers, self-disclosure, probing questions, spontaneity, and ability or inability to observe and hear the interviewee's answers.

Notes

1. Eric Nalder, *Newspaper Interviewing Techniques,* Regional Reporters Association meeting at the National Press Club, March 28, 1994, The C-SPAN Networks (West Lafayette, IN: Public Affairs Video Archives, 1994).

2. Bob Steele, "Interviewing: The Ignored Skill," http://www.poynter.org/column .asp?id=36&aid=37661, accessed September 25, 2006.; Chip Scanlan, "How Journalists Can Become Better Interviewers," March 3, 2013, https://www .poynter.org/news/how-journalists-can-become-better-interviewers, accessed June 21, 2018.

3. Steele.

4. Ken Metzler, "Tips for Interviewing," http://darkwing.uoregon.edu/~sponder/cj641 /interview.htm, accessed September 26, 2006.

5. Jaldeep Katwala, "20 Interviewing Tips for Journalists," http://www.mediahelpingme-dia.org/training-resources/journalism-basics/475-20-interviewing-tips-for-journalists, accessed May 7, 2012.

6. Hal Arkowitz and Scott O. Lillenfeld, "Why Science Tell Us Not to Rely on Eyewitness Accounts," *Scientific American,* www.scientificamerican.com/article/do-the-eyes-have -it, accessed September 8, 2015.

7. Eugene C. Webb and Jerry R. Salancik, "The Interview or the Only Wheel in Town," *Journalism Monographs* 2 (1966), p. 18.

8. Raymond L. Gorden, *Interviewing: Strategy, Techniques, and Tactics* (Homewood, IL: Dorsey Press, 1980), p. 235.

9. David Sparks, "30 Tips on How to Interview like a Journalist," http://www.sparkminute .com/2011/11/07/30-tips-on-how-to-interview-like-a-journalist, accessed May 11, 2012.

10. Sara Stuteville, "13 Simple Journalist Techniques for Effective Interviews," http:// matadorenetwork.com/bnt/13-simple-journalist-techniques-for-effective-interviews, accessed May 7, 2012.

11. Nalder.

12. R. Thomas Berner, *The Process of Writing News* (Boston, MA: Allyn and Bacon, 1992), p. 123.

13. Stuteville.

14. Stephen Budiansky, "Truth Extraction," *The Atlantic Monthly,* June 2005, 32.

15. Eric Steven Raymond and Rick Moen, "How to Ask Questions the Smart Way," http://www.catb.org/~esr/faqs/smart-questions.html, accessed September 26, 2006.

16. "Interviewing Tactics and Techniques," http://schoolvideonews.com/Broadcast-Journalism-Tactics-and-Techniques, accessed January 1, 2019.

17. Originally cited in The Point of View, a publication of the Alameda District Attorney's Office.

18. "Leading Questions," http://www.mediacollege.com/journalism/interviews/leading-questions.html, accessed October 4, 2006.

19. William Zinsser, *On Writing Well* (New York: Harper Perennial, 1994), p. 70.

20. Tony Rogers, "Tips for Taking Good Notes," http://journalism.about.com/od/reporting/a/notetaking.htm?p=1, accessed May 21, 2012.

21. "Interview Structure," http://www.mediacollege.com/video/interviews/structure.html, accessed October 4, 2006.

22. Fred Fedler, John R. Bender, Lucinda Davenport, and Paul E. Kostyu, *Reporting for the Media* (Fort Worth, TX: Harcourt Brace, 1997), p. 227.

23. Bill Marimow, "Delicate Art of the Interview: Civility vs. Tenacity," http://www.npr.org/templates/story/story/php?storyId=6438613, accessed May 23, 2012.

24. Reporter and editor Wendell Cochran in Steele.

25. John R. Bittner and Denise A. Bittner, *Radio Journalism* (Englewood Cliffs, NJ: Prentice Hall, 1977), p. 53.

26. Phillip H. Alt and Edwin Emery, *Reporting the News* (New York: Dodd, Mead, & Co., 1959), p. 125.

27. Joe Navarro and John R. Schafer, "Detecting Deception," *FBI Law Enforcement Bulletin,* July 2001, pp. 9–13, accessed on the Internet, July 20, 2009.

28. Pat Stith, *Getting Good Stories: Interviewing with Finesse* (ProQuest Research Library, April 24, 2004), p. 2.

29. "62 Of The Most Hilarious Things That Court Reporters Have Ever Recorded To Be Said In Court," https://www.boredpanda.com/funny-court-reports-disorder-in-court/?, accessed December 12, 2018.

30. Steele.

31. Pat Stith, *Getting Good Stories: Interviewing with Finesse* (ProQuest Research Library, April 24, 2004), p. 2.

32. Diana Pisciotta, "How to Prepare for a Broadcast Interview," http://www.inc.com/guides/2010/05/preparing-for-the-broadcast-interview.html, accessed May 21, 2012.

33. "EE's Perspective," http://www.uwgb.edu/clampitp/interviewing/interviewing %20Lectures/Journalistic%20Interviewsppt, accessed October 4, 2006.

34. Roy P.C. Kessels, "Patients' Memory for Medical Information," *Journal of the Royal Society of Medicine* 19.

35. P. Ley, *Communicating with Patients: Improving Communication, Satisfaction and Compliance* (New York: Croom, 1988).

36. Angela Edmunds and Anne Morris, "The Problem of information overload in business organizations: A review of the Literature," *International Journal of Information Management* 20 (February 2000), pp. 17–28.

37. Glenda Thorne, "What Are Some Problems Students Have with Memory," January 1, 2003, https://www. Problems with Working Memory, accessed October 1, 2018.

38. L.R. Peterson and M.J Peterson, "Short-term Retention of Individual Verbal Items," *Journal of Experimental Psychology* 58 (1959), pp. 193–198.

39. "How Quickly We Forget: The Transience of Memory," PsyBlog, https://www. Spring. org.uk/2008/01/how=quickly-we-forget-transience-of.php, accessed October 1, 2018; D.L. Schacter, "The Seven Sins of Memory. Insights from Psychology and Cognitive Neuroscience," *American Psychologist* 54 (1999), pp. 182–203.

Resources

Adams, Sally, Wynford Hicks, and Harriett Gilbert. *Interviewing for Journalists.* Florence, KY: Routledge, 2008.

Lee-Potter, Emma. *Interviewing for Journalists.* London: Routledge, 2017.

Metzler, Ken. *Creative Interviewing: The Writer's Guide to Gathering Information by Asking Questions.* Boston, MA: Allyn and Bacon, 1997.

Rich, Carole. *Writing and Reporting News: A Coaching Method.* Belmont, CA: Thomson /Wadsworth, 2012.

Synge, Dan. The Survival Guide to Journalism. New York: McGraw-Hill, 2010.

6

The Survey Interview

If you feel like you are being bombarded with survey requests, it's because you are. The author decided to keep track of survey requests received during a 48-hour period and came up with this list: a customer service satisfaction survey from a car dealership, a current issues survey from a State Senator, an Amazon purchase survey, a survey from a health care provider after a six-month checkup, an Arby's online survey request after ordering lunch, a neighborhood needs survey, and a "Where Are They Now" survey from an alma mater. The frequency of surveys has escalated significantly since the advent of the Internet and cell phones. Research indicates that adults in the United States are being asked to take part in surveys 7 billion times a year.[1] Before you become irate, remember that many groups to which you belong, your employer, and you as a student, teacher, physician, politician, or business owner may conduct surveys for a variety of purposes because they are a versatile, efficient, and a generalizable means of gathering important information and insights.

> **Surveys literally reach out and touch everyone.**

The objectives of this chapter are to provide guidelines for preparing and conducting, evaluating results, and determining when and how to participate as an informed and responsible respondent. Chapter 5 focused on information gathering interviews that are **flexible, adaptable,** and **moderately scheduled.** This chapter focuses on survey interviews (face-to-face and ear-to-ear) that are **reliable** (assurance that the same kinds of information are collected in repeated interviews) and **replicable** (the duplication of interviews from respondent to respondent), **highly scheduled,** and **standardized.**

> **Reliability and replicability are essential for survey interviews.**

Purpose and Research

Begin preparing your survey interview by determining a **precise purpose** that identifies the information you **need, how** you will **use** it, and **when.** If you plan to explore issues, behaviors, perspectives, and motivations in depth, you will conduct a **qualitative survey** in which you will report findings in **narrative form.** If you need to discover frequencies of behaviors, degrees of feelings, consensus of attitudes or opinions and offer predictions or make strategic decisions, you will conduct a **quantitative survey** in which you will report findings in numbers and percentages.

> **Time may determine your purpose and research.**

Time is often a major factor in determining your purpose and the amount and kinds of research you must conduct. For instance, if you want to determine the level of satisfaction for service in your car dealership, you want interviews to be brief and to the point and the research is simple: names and telephone numbers of customers, the types of

ON THE WEB

service performed, and when. Questions are likely to focus on satisfaction when making an appointment, registering at the dealership, the waiting area, promptness of service, explanation of what was done, and results. The same is true for surveys pertaining to crises, accidents, results of severe storms, and Presidential speeches that must take place and be reported literally overnight. On the other hand, you may have weeks or months to prepare for and conduct survey interviews that are lengthy and cover several issues. Research may be lengthy and varied. A **cross-sectional survey** measures feelings, attitudes, and thoughts during a narrow time span after an event, political debate, or disaster. A **longitudinal survey** measures trends or changes in feelings, attitudes, and thoughts at various intervals over time such as weeks, months, or years.

> Do not waste time and energy discovering what you already know.

When you have established a clear and precise purpose, investigate the topic or issue thoroughly, including its past, present, and future. Review previous surveys, coverage on the Internet and in newspapers, published research, books, archives, and interviews. Talk to people who have experience with or who have studied the topic or issue. Become familiar with important terminology and technical concepts. Your research determines the complexities of the topic or issue and distinguishes areas of major concern from those of little or no concern.

Structuring the Interview

Create a highly structured interview starting with an interview guide.

Interview Guide and Schedule

An interview guide is essential for survey interviews because it identifies the topics and subtopics you will cover and primary and probing questions you will ask. Review carefully the suggestions for creating interview guides in Chapter 4.

> A detailed guide is easily transformed into a scheduled format.

Begin your **interview guide** by listing major areas. For example, if you are going to survey parents of high school age children on a proposed Career Academy for students throughout the county that would expand student trade skills to prepare them for the workforce, major topics might include need, curriculum, qualified teachers, location, cost, funding, and transportation of students. If you plan to conduct a **qualitative survey,** develop a highly scheduled interview that includes open-ended questions, planned probes, and the possibility of unplanned probes that depend upon interviewee responses. The flexibility in questioning enables you to adapt and probe. The traditional interview guide (who, what, when, where, how, and why) is adaptable to qualitative surveys, but requires a more detailed guide and schedule to ensure complete coverage of a topic or issue.

> **Standardization is essential for surveys.**

If you plan to conduct a **quantitative survey,** your questions must elicit answers that are easy to record, tabulate, and analyze. The flexibility and adaptability of the qualitative survey may lead to difficulties in coding and tabulation of results.

The Opening

With the proliferation of surveys in recent years and many so-called surveys not being surveys at all but clever sales, political messages, or frauds, "there has been a markedly negative shift in attitudes toward public opinion researchers and polls across several dimensions" since the mid-1990s.[2] Craft your opening with care to avoid knee-jerk reactions from potential respondents. Although "each interview is unique, like a small work of art . . . with its own ebb and flow . . . , a mini-drama that involves real lives in real time,"[3] each respondent must go through an identical interview. A typical opening includes a greeting, name of the interviewer, the organization conducting the survey, subject matter of the interview, purpose, amount of time the survey will take, and assurance of confidentiality. Encourage interviewers to state the opening verbatim without reading it or sounding stilted. You may allow skilled interviewers to modify openings as long as each opening includes all of the elements you have stipulated. The following is a standardized opening for a survey and includes a qualifier question.

> Good afternoon. I'm _____. The Department of Natural Resources has hired my firm to conduct a survey of Indiana residents who have purchased a hunting license during the past five years to determine how it can promote interest in hunting among the younger Indiana population. As you may know, there has been a steady decline in hunting permits during the past ten years. This survey takes only 10 minutes and your answers will be strictly confidential. (GO TO THE FIRST QUESTION.)
>
> **1.** How frequently do you go hunting in Indiana? (*If the answer is less than one time a year, place an x by answer 1.1 and terminate the interview. If the answer is 1 or more times a year, go to Q.2.*)
> 1.1 _____ less than one time a year
> 1.2 _____ 1–2 times a year
> 1.3 _____ 3–4 times a year
> 1.4 _____ 5–6 times a year

> **Avoid icebreaker questions and small talk in surveys.**

This opening identifies the interviewer and organization and states a general purpose, need, and length of the interview. The interviewee is not asked to respond. The interviewer moves smoothly and quickly from orientation to the first question without giving the respondent an opportunity to refuse to take part. The first question determines the interviewee's qualifications. Respondents must hunt in Indiana at least one time a year. The schedule provides instructions for the interviewer to follow and has precoded the question for ease of tabulating results.

An opening may not identify the group that is paying for it (a political candidate, a pharmaceutical company, special interest group, for instance) or the specific purpose (to determine which strategies to employ during a political, advertising, or lobbying campaign) because such information might influence how interviewees respond. When a newspaper such as the *New York Times* or the *Washington Post*, a cable or television network such as CBS or CNN, or a well-known polling group such as Harris or Gallup conducts a survey, the organization's name is used to enhance the prestige of the poll and the interviewer and motivate respondents to cooperate. Interviewers may have to show identification badges or letters that introduce them and establish their legitimacy as survey takers.

Small incentives reduce rejections.

The quality of survey results depends on response rates, so creators of surveys have increasingly focused on incentives ranging from simple assurances to prepaid monetary offers as high as $40 per interview. Incentives come during the opening minutes of the interview to motivate a contact to take part. The higher the financial incentive the greater the likelihood of participation; even token incentives may improve response rates.[4] Non-monetary incentives include emphasizing how interviewees might benefit personally from the study, stressing the civic obligation to help others and to be active citizens, and assuring privacy and confidentiality. Some survey researchers are concerned that emphasis on incentives may persuade some persons to take part to the detriment of the survey.[5]

The Closing

Make the closing brief and express appreciation for the time and assistance with the survey. For example:

> That's all the questions I have. Thank you very much for your help.

If the survey organization wants a respondent's telephone number to verify that a valid interview took place, the closing might be:

> That's all the questions I have. May I have your telephone number so my supervisor can check to see if this interview was conducted in the prescribed manner? (gets the number) Thank you very much for your help.

If an interviewee is very reluctant or refuses to provide a telephone number or e-mail address, consider moving on to another question if you have been given the authority to do so. Try to avoid damaging the rapport and goodwill created during the interview.

If you can provide respondents with results of a survey, a common practice in research interviews, the closing might be:

> That's all the questions I have. Thank you for your help, and if you'll give me your e-mail address, I'll be sure that you receive a copy of the results of this study. (gets the address) Thanks again for your help.

Interviewees may prefer anonymity.

Respondents may be curious about a survey or interested in the topic and want to discuss it. This can be a good relationship builder and motivator for taking part in future surveys, but do so only if time permits, the interviewee will have no opportunity to talk to future interviewees, and the survey organization has no objections.

Survey Questions

Phrase each question carefully because you cannot rephrase, explain, or expand on questions during interviews without risking your ability to replicate interviews, an essential element of surveys. In quantitative surveys, all question phrasing and strategic decisions are made in the planning stage; none on the spot. In qualitative surveys, all primary questions and most probing questions are planned ahead of time.

Phrasing Questions

An interviewer may not alter the wording of any question.

All interviewees must hear the same questions asked in the same words and manner. The slightest change in wording, vocal emphasis on a word, or facial expression may generate a different answer. This is critical in survey interviews because you must strive for replicability to achieve reliability. For example, in a religious survey, interviewers asked one set of respondents, "Is it okay to smoke while praying?" Over 90 percent responded "No." When they asked another set of respondents, "Is it okay to pray while smoking?" over 90 percent replied "Yes." Although these questions appear to be the same, respondents interpreted them differently. The first sounded sacrilegious, lighting up while praying. The second sounded like a good practice, maybe even necessary. Recall the discussion of *why questions* in Chapter 3 that illustrated how emphasis may change the focus and meaning of questions.

A single word may alter significantly how people respond to a question, and alter the results of a survey. Researchers asked the following question to one group of respondents:

"Do you think the United States should allow public speeches against democracy?"

The results were "should allow" 21 percent and "should not allow" 62 percent. Then these researchers substituted a single word and asked respondents:

"Do you think the United States should forbid public speeches against democracy?"

The results were "should not forbid" 39 percent and "should forbid" 46 percent.[6] Respondents viewed the word "forbid" as stronger and more dangerous than "not allow"—perhaps un-American—even though the effect of the governmental policy would be the same.

Precise wording is critical in survey questions.

Be certain each question is unambiguous, relevant, appropriate to the interviewee's knowledge level, neutral, and socially and psychologically accessible. Survey researchers compared efforts to measure attitudes and beliefs in interviews that employed indirect, ambiguous questions such as "Some people think that" and "Other people think" with ones that employed direct, clear questions such as "How do you think that?" They discovered validity was higher when using direct questions with response options and it took less time to ask and answer.[7] Avoid ambiguous words and phrases such as a lot, often, sometimes, much, large school, and small city. The increasing diversity of survey populations necessitates care when employing acronyms, abbreviations, colloquialisms, jargon, euphemisms, and slang.

Phrase questions positively rather than negatively because negative questions may be misleading and confusing. Jack Edwards and Marie Thomas note that "a negative answer to a negatively worded statement may not be equivalent to the positive answer to a positively worded statement."[8] Even the explanation sounds confusing. They give this example: "Disagreeing with the statement 'My work is not meaningful' does not necessarily mean that the same individual would have agreed with the statement 'My work is meaningful.'" Forcing a respondent to disagree with a negative statement can be confusing. Think of the difficulties you have had with negatively phrased multiple-choice questions in examinations. Respondents may fail to hear the word "not" or qualifiers in a question.

Sample Question Development

Questions may evolve as you develop a survey schedule. Here is how a question on a proposed law mandating that all motorcyclists wear helmets might change.

> How do you feel about the proposed law mandating that all motorcyclists wear helmets?

The word **feel** is likely to elicit a wide range of answers ranging from angry, furious, resentful, steamed, disgusted, betrayed, bitter, ticked off, and sad to happy, pleased, glad, relieved, delighted, excited, and satisfied. How would you code these words when it comes time to write up the results of this question? And what would you do with answers such as "I have mixed feelings," "I don't really care," and "I think it's probably a good idea." The word **mandating** may bias results because it sounds tyrannical or unconstitutional to some respondents. How would you handle an interviewee who decides to lecture you on motorcycle safety or the fundamental rights of cyclists?

> When developing questions, ask how you will code answers.

Try a second version that closes up the question, changes feel to no feelings as a third option, and eliminates mandating that may invite instant negative reactions.

> Are you for, against, or have no feelings about the proposed law that would require motorcyclists to wear helmets?
>
> _____ for
> _____ against
> _____ no feelings

This version eliminates the potential bias of the first while resolving potential recording problems, but it may be too closed. Interviewees may not be simply for or against the law or believe there should be exceptions or qualifications. Intensity of feelings is not accounted for.

Develop a third version such as the following:

> **2.** Do you strongly agree, agree, disagree, or strongly disagree with the proposed law requiring motorcyclists to wear helmets?
> 2.1 _____ strongly agree
> 2.2 _____ agree
> 2.3 _____ disagree
> 2.4 _____ strongly disagree
> 2.5 _____ undecided (*Do not provide unless requested.*)
> 2.6 _____ Why? _____
> (Ask only of respondents choosing strongly agree or strongly disagree.)

Build in
secondary ques-
tions for reasons,
knowledge
level, and
qualifiers.

This version assesses intensity of feelings, is easy to record and code, leaves undecided as an unstated option, provides instructions for interviewers, and includes a built-in secondary "*Why*" question to discover reasons for strong approval or strong disapproval. Those with moderate responses tend not to have ready explanations for agreeing or disagreeing, approving or disapproving, liking or disliking. They just have that general feeling.

Work with each question until it is worded to obtain the information needed. Careful phrasing avoids interviewer bias, confusion, and inaccurate results. Later we will address the pretesting of surveys to detect problems with questions.

Probing Questions

Probing ques-
tions must be
planned and
repeated from
interview to
interview.

A fundamental goal of every survey is to conduct identical interviews over and over regardless of who is conducting them. Probing questions are planned carefully in advance because off-the-cuff probing by interviewers tends to elicit widely different answers. If some interviewers probe more often than others, the amount and kind of information will vary greatly from interview to interview. Interviewers must record all probing questions asked and answers received carefully, clearly, and accurately for later tabulation and analysis. This is nearly impossible to accomplish when questions vary from interview to interview. In addition, interviewer bias is more likely to occur when interviewers phrase questions differently and send differing nonverbal signals that suggest preferred answers. Some interviewees will give you the information they think you want to hear. The result of free-wheeling probing is data that is impossible to tabulate and analyze with any degree of confidence.

Question Strategies

Five question strategies enable interviewers to assess knowledge level, honesty, and consistency; reduce undecided answers; prevent order bias; and incorporate probing questions.

Filter Strategy

The **filter strategy** enables you to filter out those who have no information from those who claim to do so and then to discover the extent and accuracy of the information a respondent claims to have. An interviewee may say yes to your first question to avoid the appearance of being uninformed or misinformed.

> **Interviewer:** Are you familiar with the possible effects the new tax laws may have on charitable giving?
>
> **Interviewee:** Yes I am.
>
> **Interviewer:** What are these possible effects as you understand them?

Don't take "yes"
as the final
answer.

If an interviewee says no, go to the next question. If the interviewee says yes, ask the interviewee to reveal the extent and accuracy of knowledge. The follow-up question may reveal confusion or misinformation. Interviewees may say yes to bipolar questions when they have no idea what the interviewer is talking about to avoid appearing uninformed.

Repeat Strategy

The **repeat strategy** enables you to determine if an interviewee is consistent in responses on a topic, particularly a controversial one. You may ask the same question several minutes apart or disguise the question by rephrasing it slightly and compare answers for consistency.

6. Do you use cell phone apps to spy on your children when they are away from home?
6.1_____Yes
6.2_____No

14. Do you use cell phone apps to monitor your children when they are away from home?
14.1_____Yes
14.2_____No

Another example of a repeat strategy is to go from a moderately closed to a highly closed question.

11. How often during a typical week do you eat at a restaurant?
_____

> **Repeat questions must be essentially the same to determine consistency in answers.**

20. I am going to read a list of how often during a typical week you eat at a restaurant.
Stop me when I read the frequency that reflects your eating habits.
20.1_____less than once a week
20.2_____1–2 times a week
20.3_____3–4 times a week
20.4_____5–6 times a week
20.5_____7 or more times a week

Do not make the repetition too obvious or similar and be sure the rewording does not change the intent of the initial question.

Leaning Question Strategy

Respondents may be reluctant to take stands or reveal intentions. If so, employ a *leaning* question, not to be confused with a *leading* question, to reduce the number of "undecided" and "don't know" answers. The following is a typical **leaning question strategy.**

9a. Do you plan to vote for or against the reappointment of Judge Carter?
(*if undecided, ask question 9b.*)
_____ for
_____ against
_____ undecided

9b. Which way are you leaning today?
_____ for
_____ against
_____ undecided

The "undecided" option remains in question 9b because an interviewee may be truly undecided. A variation of the leaning question is, "Well, if you had to vote today, how would you vote?" "Undecided" and "don't know" options may invite large percentages of these answers, but some sources recommend that you always include "don't know" or "not applicable" answer options in questions, unless all interviewees will have a definite answer, to reduce interviewee frustration, and to provide the most honest and accurate answers.[9]

Shuffle Strategy

The order of answer options may affect interviewee responses. Research indicates that last choices in questions tend to get negative or superficial evaluations because interviewees get tired or bored. Interviewees may select an option because it is the first mentioned or the last heard. The **shuffle strategy** varies the order of answer options from one interview to the next to prevent **order bias.** The method of rotation is explained when training interviewers. Notice the built-in instructions in the following example:

> Now, I'm going to read you a list of the five leading tourist destinations in the United States. I want you to tell me if you have a highly favorable, favorable, neutral, unfavorable, or highly unfavorable attitude toward each. (*Rotate the order of the tourist destinations from interview to interview. Encircle answers received.*)

	Highly Favorable	Favorable	Neutral	Unfavorable	Highly Unfavorable
New York	5	4	3	2	1
Las Vegas	5	4	3	2	1
San Francisco	5	4	3	2	1
Miami	5	4	3	2	1
Orlando	5	4	3	2	1

Potential order bias has resulted in strange events in political, persuasive, and advertising surveys. A political candidate in Indiana changed his name legally so it would begin with A. This placed him at the top of the ballot on election day, the belief being that voters select the top names in lists of candidates. He lost, but his and similar actions have led states to shuffle names on ballots.

Chain or Contingency Strategy

The **chain or contingency strategy** enables the survey interviewer to include preplanned probing questions in highly scheduled and highly standardized formats. You can probe into answers while maintaining control and replicating interviews from one respondent to the next. Notice the built-in instructions and precoding for ease of recording answers and tabulating data.

All probing
questions in
surveys are
included in the
schedule.

1a. During the past month, have you received any free samples of toothpaste?
(PLACE AN X BY THE ANSWER RECEIVED.)

Yes _____ 1—ASK Q. 1b.

No _____ 2—ASK Q. 2a.

1b. Which toothpaste did you receive?

Colgate _____ 1

Crest _____ 2

Sensodyne _____ 3

Aquafresh _____ 4

Arm and

Hammer _____ 5

1c. (ASK ONLY IF AQUAFRESH IS NOT MENTIONED IN Q. 1b; OTHERWISE SKIP
TO Q. 1d.)

Did you receive a free sample of Aquafresh?

Yes _____ 1—ASK Q. 1d.

No _____ 2—SKIP to Q. 2a.

1d. Did you use the free sample of Aquafresh?

Yes _____ 1—SKIP to Q. 2a.

No _____ 2—ASK Q. 1e.

1e. Why didn't you use the free sample of Aquafresh?

_____ _____ _____

_____ _____ _____

Question Scales

A variety of scale questions enables you to delve more deeply into topics and feelings
than bipolar questions and to record and tabulate data more easily.

Interval Scales

Likert scales
provide a range
of feelings,
attitudes, or
opinions.

Interval scales provide distances between measures. For example, **evaluative interval
scales** (often called **Likert scales**) ask respondents to make judgments about persons,
places, things, or ideas. The scale may range from five to nine answer options (five is
most common) with opposite poles such as "strongly like . . . strongly dislike," "strongly
agree . . . strongly disagree," or "very important . . . not important at all." Here is an
evaluative interval scale:

Do you strongly agree, agree, have no opinion, disagree, or strongly disagree with
the state's plans to allow private companies to log selectively in its virgin forests?

5 Strongly agree _____

4 Agree _____

3 Neutral _____

2 Disagree _____

1 Strongly disagree _____

<table>
<tr><td>

Provide aids for interviewee recall of answer options.

</td><td>

You may provide respondents with cards (color-coded to tell them apart) for complex questions or ones with several choices or options. A card eliminates the faulty-recall problem respondents experience. They need not recall from memory all of the options for evaluating, rating, or ranking people, places, products, or proposals. Here is an example:

</td></tr>
</table>

> Please use the phrases on this card to tell me how the television coverage of recent terrorist acts in Paris and London have affected your interest in studying abroad.
>
> 5 Increases my interest a lot   _____
> 4 Increases my interest a little _____
> 3 Will not affect my interest   _____
> 2 Decreases my interest a little _____
> 1 Decreases my interest a lot   _____

<table>
<tr><td>

Frequency scales deal with number of times.

</td><td>

Frequency interval scales ask respondents to select a number that most accurately reflects how often they do something or use something. For example:

</td></tr>
</table>

> How frequently do you eat pasta?
>
> More than once a week _____
> Once each week   _____
> Every other week   _____
> Once or twice a month _____
> Less than once a month _____
> Rarely   _____

<table>
<tr><td>

Numerical scales deal with ranges.

</td><td>

Numerical interval scales ask respondents to select a range or level that accurately reflects their age, income, educational level, or rank in an organization. For example:

</td></tr>
</table>

> I am going to read several income ranges. Stop me when I read the one that applies to your household income.
>
> Less than $20,000   _____
> $20,000 to $34,999   _____
> $35,000 to $49,999   _____
> $50,000 to $74,999   _____
> $75,000 to $99,999   _____
> $100,000 to $149,999 _____
> $150,000 to $199,000 _____
> $200,000 or more   _____

Nominal Scales

<table>
<tr><td>

Nominal scales deal with naming and selecting.

</td><td>

Nominal scales provide mutually exclusive variables and ask respondents to name the most appropriate variable. These are self-reports and do *not* ask respondents to rate or rank choices or to pick a choice along an evaluative, numerical, or frequency continuum. Choices may be in any order. For example:

</td></tr>
</table>

> Do you consider yourself to be a:
>
> Democrat   _____

Republican   _____
Libertarian   _____
Independent   _____
Other   _____

When you last ate dinner in a restaurant, did your entree consist of:

Beef   _____
Pork   _____
Lamb   _____
Poultry   _____
Fish   _____
Other _____ (PLEASE WRITE NAME.)

In nominal questions, the options are mutually exclusive and include those from which most respondents are most likely to choose. "Other" is included because a respondent may have an uncommon or unexpected choice.

Ordinal Scales

Ordinal scales ask for ratings or rankings.

Ordinal questions ask respondents to rate or rank the options in their *implied* or *stated* relationship to one another. They do not name the most applicable option as in interval and nominal scales.

The following is a **rating ordinal scale:**

You have traveled to several European countries with our agency during the past five years. Please rate your experiences in each of the following applicable countries as excellent, above average, average, below average, or poor.

France	Ex.	Abv. Av.	Av.	Bel. Av.	Poor	N/A
Germany	Ex.	Abv. Av.	Av.	Bel. Av.	Poor	N/A
The Netherlands	Ex.	Abv. Av.	Av.	Bel. Av.	Poor	N/A
Switzerland	Ex.	Abv. Av.	Av.	Bel. Av.	Poor	N/A
Austria	Ex.	Abv. Av.	Av.	Bel. Av.	Poor	N/A
Czech Republic	Ex.	Abv. Av.	Av.	Bel. Av.	Poor	N/A
Hungary	Ex.	Abv. Av.	Av.	Bel. Av.	Poor	N/A

This rating scale generates six responses, including not applicable for a country not visited. The following is a **ranking ordinal scale:**

On this card are the names of five national news programs. Rank order them in terms of accuracy and dependability with 1 being highest and 5 being lowest.

	Rank
ABC WorldNews	_____
CBS Evening News	_____
CNN Newsroom	_____

Fox Report   _____

NBC Nightly News   _____

The following ordinal question asks respondents to select from among options and rank them in order.

> On this card are several reasons offered for constructing a rapid transit system from the northern part of the county to downtown. Pick the three you think are most important and rank order them in importance to you.
>
> _____ Safety
>
> _____ Shorten travel time
>
> _____ Reduce congestion in the center city
>
> _____ Convenience
>
> _____ Enhance commercial activity in the center city
>
> _____ Reduce pollution

Bogardus Social Distance Scale

Bogardus scales measure effect of relational distances.

The **Bogardus Social Distance Scale** determines how people feel about social relationships and distances from them. You want to know if a person's attitude or feeling changes as an issue comes closer to home. This scale usually moves progressively from remote to close relationships and distances to detect changes as proximity narrows. For example, you might use the following Bogardus Social Distance Scale to determine how interviewees feel about needle exchanges created to reduce diseases such as HIV/AIDS and hepatitis by those who use drugs.

> **1.** Do you favor creating needle exchanges for drug users in the United States?   _____ Yes _____ No
>
> **2.** Do you favor creating needle exchanges for drug users in your state?   _____ Yes _____ No
>
> **3.** Do you favor creating needle exchanges for drug users in your county?   _____ Yes _____ No
>
> **4.** Do you favor creating needle exchanges for drug users in your city?   _____ Yes _____ No
>
> **5.** Do you favor creating needle exchanges for drug users in your neighborhood?   _____ Yes _____ No

Respondents may be safely distant from the attitude or feeling they are expressing about a product, issue, action, or person. The Bogardus Social Distance Scale brings an issue ever closer to home so it is no longer something impersonal or one that affects others "over there."

Minimize guessing in surveys.

Survey designers employ a variety of scale questions to obtain results beyond Level 1 disclosures and reduce the percentage of respondents who try to "out psyche" interviewers by trying to pick "normal" answers in nominal and ordinal questions and safe middle options in interval scales. To avoid embarrassment, a respondent might pick an option that stands out such as the second in a list that includes 10 percent, 15 percent, 20 percent, and 30 percent. Respondents who first agree that a certain activity would make most people uneasy are less likely then to admit ever engaging in that activity and may attempt to change the subject.

> **Anticipate confusion in scale questions.**

Phrase scale questions carefully to lessen game playing, guessing, and confusion. Listen and observe reactions during pretesting interviews to detect patterns of responses, levels of interviewee comprehension, and hesitancy in responding. Lengthy scales, complicated rating or ranking procedures, and lengthy explanations may confuse respondents, perhaps without either party realizing it.

Question Sequences

> **Question sequences complement question strategies.**

The tunnel sequence is useful when no strategic lineup of questions is needed. Gallup's quintamensional design sequence, or a variation of it, is appropriate when exploring intensity of attitudes and opinions. Funnel, inverted funnel, hourglass, and diamond sequences include open-ended questions, so answers may be difficult to record, code, and tabulate. They are appropriate for qualitative surveys because the wealth of information interviewers obtain from open questions is worth the problems involved. You may choose a funnel sequence by starting with general questions and then move to more specific questions.

Selecting Interviewees

Interviewees are your sole source of information in surveys. Select them carefully because a meticulously designed schedule of questions is useless if interviewers talk to the wrong people.

Defining the Population

Initiate the selection of interviewees by defining the **target population** you wish to study. It may be small and homogeneous such as members of a college football team or as large and diverse as all registered voters in Milwaukee. You may be interested in a subset of a large target population such as all registered voters in Milwaukee from age 21 to 35. Your target population consists, then, of all qualified persons about whom you wish to draw conclusions.

If your target population is small such as the 20 deputies in a county sheriff's department, you may interview all of them. Many surveys deal with populations that far exceed your finances and time such as all 25,000 undergraduate students at a major research university. Dozens of carefully trained interviewers could not contact, let alone interview, all of these students, so you select a **sample** of them and extend your findings to all of them.

Digital Vision/Alamy Stock Photo

■ *The first step in selecting interviewees is to define the population or target group you wish to study.*

Sampling

The fundamental principle is that a sample must accurately represent the population under study. Watermelon sellers practice this principle when they carefully cut a triangular plug from a watermelon. This plug is intended to represent the entire watermelon.

Each potential respondent from a defined population must have an equal chance of being interviewed. Determine the probability that each person might be selected by deciding upon an acceptable **margin of error.** The precision of a survey is the "degree of similarity between sample results and the results from a 100 percent count obtained in an identical manner."[10] Most surveys attain a 95 percent **level of confidence,** the mathematical probability that 95 out of 100 interviewees would give results within 5 percentage points (margin of error) either way of the figures you would have obtained if you had interviewed the entire targeted population. Survey results reported in the media routinely state a survey margin of error of 4 percent. This means that if 35 percent of respondents approve of the way Congress is doing its job, the real figure might be as low as 31 percent or as high as 39 percent.

A tolerable margin of error depends on the use of survey results. If you want to predict the outcome of an election or the effects of a new medical treatment, you must strive for a small margin of error, 3 percent or less. If you are conducting a survey to determine how residents of Kentucky feel about logging in state forests, a higher margin of error is acceptable, 4 or 5 percent.

> A sample is a miniature version of the whole.

Determine **sample size** by the size of the population and the acceptable margin of error. Some survey organizations produce accurate national surveys with a margin of error in the 3 percent range from a sample of 1500. Standard formulas reveal that as a population increases in size, the percentage of the population necessary for a sample declines rapidly. In other words, you must interview a larger percentage of 5000 people than of 50,000 people to attain equally accurate results. Formulas also reveal that you must increase greatly the size of a sample to reduce the margin of error from 5 percent to 4 percent to 3 percent. The small reduction in the margin of error may not be worth the added cost of conducting significantly more interviews.

> A sample is the actual number of persons interviewed.

CheckMarket and Creative Research Systems offer sample size calculators that enable you to determine sample size. For instance, if your preferred margin of error is 5 percent at a confidence level of 95 percent, you would need to conduct the following number of interviews within different sample sizes to reach this level.[11]

Population Size	Sample Size
100	80
500	217
1,000	278
5,000	357
10,000	370
50,000	381
100,000	383

Sampling Techniques

Size of sample is important, but how you select the sample is of utmost importance to the validity of a survey. There are two general types of sampling, **probability** and **non-probability.** In probability sampling, you know that each member of your population has a certain chance of being interviewed. In non-probability sampling, you do not. There are five common methods of probability sampling, the most accurate method of sampling.

Random Sampling

> Random sampling is like "drawing names from a hat."

Random sampling is a simple method of selecting a representative sampling. For example, if you have a complete roster of all persons in a population, place all names in a container, mix them thoroughly, and draw out one name at a time until you have the sample needed.

Table of Random Numbers

A complicated random sampling method is to assign a number to each potential respondent and create or purchase a **table of random numbers.** With eyes closed, place a finger on a number and read a combination up, down, across to left or right, or diagonally. Select this number as part of the sample or decide to read the last digit of the number touched (46) and the first digit of the numeral to the right (29) and thus contact respondent number 62. Repeat this process until you have the sample you need.

Skip Interval or Random Digit

> In skip interval you select every *n*th name from a list.

In a **skip interval** or **random digit sampling,** you may choose every 10th number in a telephone book, every fifth name in a roster of clients, or every other person who walks into a supermarket. The Random Digital Dialing system now in wide use for conducting surveys randomly generates telephone numbers in target area-code and prefix areas, gives every telephone number in the area an equal chance of being called, and ensures anonymity because no interviewee names are used.[12] This sampling technique may have built-in flaws. For instance, a growing percentage of the population has unlisted phone numbers or relies on cell phones. On the other hand, a growing number of households have more than one telephone number, and this increases the probability that a particular household may be contacted more than once. A voter, customer, or membership roster might be outdated. Time of day, day of the week, and location may determine the types of persons available for interviews.

Stratified Random Sample

> A stratified sample most closely represents the whole.

If a population has clearly definable groups (males and females; ages; education levels; income levels; and diverse cultural groups), employ a **stratified random sampling method.** This method enables you to include a minimum number of respondents from each group, typically the percentage of the group in the target population. For instance, if you wanted to survey the attitudes of Ohio residents about the importance of education attainment, your target population might consist of 10 percent less than high school, 33 percent high school graduate, 20 percent some college,

9 percent associate's degree, 17 percent bachelor's degree, and 12 percent graduate or professional degree.[13]

Sample Point

A sample point represents a geographical area (a square block or mile, for instance) that contains specific types of persons (students, grain farmers, or retired persons, for instance). Instructions may tell interviewers to skip corner houses (corner houses are often more expensive) and then try every other house on the outside of the four-block area until they have obtained two interviews with males and two with females. The U.S. Department of Agriculture uses aerial photographs of farm areas and crops to determine which farmers to interview to determine the amounts of various crops planted and possible yields of these crops each year. From this sample, the USDA conducts 35,000 personal interviews.[14] The **sample point** or **block sample** gives the survey designer control over selection of interviewees without resorting to lists of names, random digits, or telephone numbers.

> **A sample point is usually a geographical area.**

There are two common methods of non-probability sampling, the least accurate forms of sampling. Survey interviewers employ them because they are convenient and inexpensive.

Self-Selection

The most inaccurate sampling method is **self-selection** in which people voluntarily call in to radio and television talk shows and newscasts or reply on the Internet or to mailed surveys. Who is most likely to reply to surveys by ABC News or Fox News, Sean Hannity or Howard Stern? Bias is rampant in self-selection samples because those who are very angry, most opposed to legislation, or most committed to a political figure are far more likely than anyone else to volunteer. It is easy to predict the outcome of self-selected surveys that deal with issues such as abortion, gun control, immigration, and higher taxes.

Convenience

> **Self-selection and convenience sampling are prone to high levels of selection bias.**

Convenience sampling is common because it is easy, cheap, and quick. Interviewers merely stop students walking on campus, shoppers walking through a mall, or people strolling down a street. There is no target population, only convenience for the interviewer who pays no attention to gender, race, ethnic group, age, income, or education. Anyone who will stop is a viable subject. This sampling has little credibility because of selection bias and no distinction among a diverse population.

Selecting and Training Interviewers

Creating a survey instrument and developing a careful sample of interviewees are critical, and so is selecting interviewers and training them to conduct the interviews properly.

Number Needed

If you plan to conduct brief interviews with a small target population, a single interviewer may be sufficient. You will need several interviewers if your interviews are lengthy, the sample is large, time allotted for completing the survey is short, and interviewees are scattered over a large geographical area. Lengthy and difficult interviewing assignments may result in interviewer fatigue that reduces motivation and attention, particularly in latter parts of interviews and the survey assignment.

> **Consider possible Interviewer fatigue with lengthy assignments.**

Qualifications

> **Interviewers must follow the rules.**

A highly scheduled, standardized interview does not require interviewers to be experts on a topic or skilled in phrasing questions and probing into answers. It does require a person who can learn and follow guidelines, read the questions verbatim and effectively, and record answers quickly and accurately. If you are using a highly scheduled interview format that requires skillful probing into answers, interviewers must be able to think on their feet, adapt to different interviewees, handle unanticipated interviewee objections and concerns, and react effectively and calmly to strange answers. Professionally trained interviewers are more efficient and produce more accurate results. One study revealed that "experienced interviewers obtain higher rates of acquiescent reports than do inexperienced interviewers, even after accounting for potential differences in interviewer and respondent characteristics."[15]

Personal Characteristics

> **Personality and attitude of the interviewer are critical in surveys.**

Older interviewers with a non-threatening demeanor and optimistic outlook have higher response rates and greater cooperation in surveys, regardless of their interviewing experiences, than do younger interviewers. Age appears to enhance credibility and self-confidence while optimism motivates interviewees to cooperate. On the other hand, personality and attitude of interviewers appear to be most important in shaping interviewee attitude toward surveys.

Interviewee Skepticism

> **Interviewees are increasingly wary of surveys.**

Nearly one-third of respondents believe that answering survey questions will neither benefit them nor influence decisions, that there are too many surveys, that surveys are too long, and that interviewers ask too many personal questions. Some 36 percent of respondents in one study said they had been asked to take part in "false surveys," sales or political campaign interviews disguised as informational surveys. The authors of a report on how the Gallup Organization conducts public opinion polls note that "The public's questions indicate a healthy dose of skepticism about polling. Their questions, however, are usually accompanied by a strong and sincere desire to find out what's going on under Gallup's hood."[16] Make every effort to establish a positive relationship with the respondent. Critical dimensions are warmth, involvement, dominance, and trust.

Similarity of Interviewer and Interviewee

Similarity of interviewer and interviewee is a critical dimensional element in determining the willingness of a person to participate in an interview. If you *look like me* and *sound like me,* I am more likely to cooperate and to answer appropriately and honestly. An in-group relationship such as senior citizen to senior citizen, black to black, Hispanic-American to Hispanic-American may avoid cultural and communication barriers and enhance trust. You are most likely to be perceived as safe, able to understand, and sympathetic if you speak the interviewee's language, including dialects and regional differences.

Training Interviewers

Provide carefully written instructions to all interviewers regardless of their experience because each survey has unique features and purposes. Face-to-face training sessions that include simulated interviews are highly recommended. The following are typical instructions.

Preparing for the Interview

> **Guard against interviewer bias.**

Study the question schedule and answer options thoroughly so you can ask rather than read questions and record answers quickly and accurately. Dress appropriately, and be neat and well groomed. Do not wear buttons or insignia that identify you with a particular group or position on the issue that might bias responses. Choose an appropriate time of week and day.

Conducting the Interview

Be friendly, businesslike, and interested in the topic. Speak clearly, at a good pace, and loudly enough to be heard easily. Maintain eye contact and don't be afraid to smile. Ask all questions clearly, without hesitation, and neutrally. Adopt an informal speaking manner that avoids the appearance of reading or reciting openings, questions, and closings.

Opening the Interview

Motivate the interviewee from the moment the interview commences. State your name, identify your organization, and present your credentials if appropriate. Explain the purpose, length, nature, and importance of the study; then move to your first question without appearing to pressure the interviewee to take part.

Asking Questions

> **Do not alter a question or answer option.**

Ask all questions, including answer options, exactly as worded. You may repeat a question but not rephrase it or define words. Do not change the order of questions or answer options unless instructed to do so. If you are doing a qualitative study, probe carefully into answers to obtain insightful and thorough answers free of ambiguities and vague references.

Receiving and Recording Answers

> **Maintain a pleasant "poker face" throughout.**

Give respondents adequate time to reply, and then record answers as prescribed in your training and on the schedule. Write or print answers carefully. Remain neutral at all times, reacting neither positively nor negatively to responses.

Closing the Interview

When you have obtained the answer to the last question, thank the interviewee for cooperating and excuse yourself without being abrupt. Be polite and sensitive, making it clear that the interviewee has been most helpful. Do not discuss the survey with the interviewee.

Conducting Survey Interviews

With preparation completed, it's time to **pretest the interview** with a sample of the targeted audience to detect potential problems with questions and answer options.

Pretesting the Interview

The best plans on paper may not work during real interviews. Try out the opening, questions, recording answers, and closing.

> **Lack of pretesting invites disaster.**

Leave nothing to chance. For instance, in a political poll conducted by one of my classes, students deleted the question "What do you like or dislike about your major?" because it took too much time, generated little useful data, and posed a coding nightmare because of diverse replies. When interviewees were handed a list of political candidates during another project and asked, "What do you like or dislike about . . . ?" many became embarrassed or gave vague answers because they did not know some of the candidates. This question was replaced with a Likert scale from "strongly like" to "strongly dislike," including a "don't know" option, and interviewers probed into reasons for liking or disliking only for candidates ranked in the extreme positions on the scale. Respondents tended to be informed about candidates they strongly liked or strongly disliked. In a survey of mudslinging during political campaigns, the author discovered that scale questions tended to confuse elderly respondents, so he added special explanations to complex questions.

> **Review every aspect of the interview to eliminate problems prior to the survey.**

Ask these questions after pretests. Did interviewees appear to understand why you were conducting this survey and its potential value to them? Did interviewees understand each question? Did interviewees reply to each question with little hesitation or complaint? Did each question elicit the information desired? Was recording of answers easy and efficient? Was the survey length appropriate without indications of interviewee fatigue? If the answer to any of these post-test questions is "No," determine why and make necessary changes, including deleting questions. **Interviewee fatigue** may be detectable late in lengthy interviews when attention and motivation decline, and respondents start choosing more "Don't know" answer options, giving shorter or half-hearted answers, fidgeting noticeably, or glancing at watches.[17] When pretesting is complete, you are ready to conduct the survey.

Interviewing Face-to-Face

Interviewing face-to-face has a number of advantages over other means of conducting surveys.[18] The "personal interview" attains a better response rate because of the presence of the interviewer and the naturalness of the interaction. Interviewees are able to see, feel, touch, experience, and taste products. The interviewer can establish credibility through physical appearance, dress, eye contact, voice, and credentials. Personal interviews enable interviewers to identify interviewees who are part of the target population (particularly those who tend to be "marginalized" in our society) and interview them in specific locations and at specific times. The interviewer can control the interview by keeping the interviewee focused on track until the completion of the interview. Respondents are more willing to take part in long interviews and provide lengthy answers, and this enables interviewers to ask more questions and focus on in-depth attitudes and information. Personal interviews may reveal respondent attitudes and reactions detectable only through nonverbal cues such as voice, facial expressions, eye contact, gestures, and posture.

Disadvantages of the personal interview include expense, time consumption, and the need for large numbers of thoroughly trained interviewers. Answers are recorded in writing and may be time-consuming to record completely and accurately. It may be impossible to conduct personal interviews in the time allotted to conduct and report the survey or to conduct interviews over a wide geographical area.

Interviewing by Telephone

Telephone interviews may be less expensive in money but costly in results.

Because personal survey interviews are expensive and time-consuming and societal changes make it difficult to predict when and where interviewees will be available, organizations have turned increasingly to telephone (ear-to-ear) interviews, particularly since the advent of random-digit-dialing (RDD). Telephone interviews are less expensive, can be conducted quickly over a wide geographical area, and provide faster results when speed is critical.[19] There may be less interviewer bias because of the greater uniformity in manner and delivery and no effect from dress, appearance, mannerisms, facial expressions, and eye contact. Interviewers do not face the potential dangers of venturing into dangerous neighborhoods or residences, particularly at night. Interviewees provide fewer socially acceptable answers because they may feel safer by maintaining anonymity when providing controversial answers or personal information.

Advances in technology have aided and hindered telephone interviews.

The telephone survey interview has disadvantages. Respondents are reluctant to stay on the telephone for longer than 10 to 15 minutes, and this means the interview schedule must be shorter with fewer open-ended and probing questions that may consume several minutes each. People are using call identifiers to filter out unwanted calls, particularly ones from unknown numbers. As fewer persons have landlines in their homes, perhaps only 1 in 10, and are relying on cell phones, it is becoming increasingly difficult to contact them. The widespread use of RDD and the shrinking portion of the population relying on landlines are making the telephone survey more expensive and "unattractive for most general population surveys."[20] There is the real possibility that while an interviewer is speaking to a respondent over a landline, the respondent is multitasking on a cell phone. When a person answers the phone, the interviewer may have difficulty determining if this person is part of the target population. While the

A growing number of interviewers are turning to the telephone for easier and less expensive means of conducting surveys and polls.

fizkes/iStock/Getty Images

telephone provides anonymity, people are increasingly reluctant in the age of "identity theft" to divulge personal information or to answer sensitive questions from persons they cannot see and whose credentials are invisible. Because of the problems with telephone surveys, sources predict that the telephone-only survey will decline considerably while the telephone in combination with other types of data collection will increase.[21]

Opening the Telephone Interview

Most refusals in telephone surveys occur prior to the first substantive question: one-third in the opening seconds, one-third during the orientation, and one-third at the point of listing household members. Speaking skills (pitch, vocal variety, loudness, rate, and distinct enunciation), particularly during the opening, are more important than content. One study concluded, "Respondents react to cues communicated by the interviewer's voice and may grant or refuse an interview on that basis."[22] Telephone interviewers must establish trust through vocal and verbal analogs to the personal appearance, credentials, and survey materials that enhance trust in face-to-face interviews.

How to Use the Telephone

The literature on survey interviewing contains important advice for would-be telephone interviewers. These guidelines are equally relevant to personal interviews.

- *Do not give a person a reason or opportunity to hang up.* Develop an informal but professional style that is courteous (not demanding) and friendly (not defensive). Get the interviewee involved as quickly as possible in answering questions because active involvement motivates people to take part and cooperate.

- *Listen carefully and actively.* Give undivided attention to what the interviewee is saying by not drinking, eating, sorting papers, or playing with objects on your desk. Do not communicate nonverbally with others in the room, and say nothing you do not want the interviewee to hear even if you believe you have the mouthpiece covered. Explain any pauses or long silences of more than a few seconds or signal you are listening with cues such as "Uh huh," "Yes," "Okay."

> Do nothing but ask and listen during telephone interviews.

- *Use your voice effectively.* Talk directly into the mouthpiece. Speak loudly, slowly, clearly, and distinctly because the interviewee relies solely on your voice. State each answer option distinctly with vocal emphasis on important words and pause between each option to aid in comprehension and recall.

- *Use a computer-assisted telephone interview system* that enables you to dial random numbers quickly and to compile results within minutes of completing interviews.

Interviewing through the Internet

Survey interviews are increasingly taking place through the Internet—e-mail, Web pages, and computer direct. They are substantially less expensive and faster than either personal or telephone interviews. A survey posted on a popular Web site may generate thousands of responses within hours. Internet surveys can target large populations over great distances. A major problem of survey interviews—interviewees giving socially acceptable answers—is lessened because of the anonymity and perceived safety of the Internet interview. A significant concern in personal and telephone interviews, interviewer bias, is not a problem in Internet surveys. Respondents give more honest answers to sensitive topics. Unlike paper-and-pencil surveys, and some personal and telephone surveys, interviewees tend to provide more detail in answers to open-ended questions, perhaps because it is easy and quick to type lengthy answers on a keyboard and they can reply when it suits them.

On the other hand, the critical nonverbal communication that aids personal and telephone interviews is lost when using the Internet. Response rates may suffer because it is more difficult to establish the credibility of the survey or to distinguish the survey interview from a slick telemarketer sales interview. While the Internet gives respondents time to think through answers, it may lose the spontaneity of interactions in face-to-face and telephone interviews; they are essentially electronic bulletin boards. However, "real-time chat" software can ensure spontaneity. It's nearly impossible to probe into answers or employ question strategies such as shuffle, leaning, and repeat. Evidence indicates that completion rates are lower for lengthy surveys because respondents grow tired and log off.

It is difficult to target populations in wide-ranging, Internet surveys because you may not know who in a family, corporation, school, or state replied to your survey. Your sample, and thus your results, may be highly questionable. Those who feel most strongly about an issue, usually with negative attitudes, may overwhelm the results in self-selected Internet surveys. This has led researchers Chris Mann and Fiona Stewart to warn, "There is no doubt that the unrepresentativeness of current Internet access remains the greatest problem for data collection on-line."[23]

Coding, Tabulation, and Analysis

After all interviews are completed, the final phase of the survey begins with coding, tabulation, and analysis of the information received.

Coding and Tabulation

Begin the final phase of the survey by **coding** all answers that were not precoded, usually for open-ended questions. For example, if question 9 is "You say you are strongly opposed to making recreational use of marijuana legal in your state. Why do you feel this way?" it will receive a wide variety of answers. If it is coded #9, each response can be coded 9 plus 1, 2, 3, 4, 5, etc. such as the following:

9-1 It would lead to stronger drugs such as heroin and cocaine.

9-2 It will increase drug addiction in this state.

9-3 It will lead to the legalization of other drugs.

9-4 It will attract drug users and dealers from states where marijuana is illegal.

9-5 It will greatly increase deadly vehicle accidents.

9-6 It will cause students to drop out of school.

9-7 It will cause more crime, not less crime.

Record answers to open-ended questions with great care.

Answers to open-ended questions may require analysis and structuring before developing a coding system. For example, in a study of voter perception of mudslinging in political campaigns, the interviewer asked, "What three or four words would you use to describe a politician who uses mudslinging as a tactic?" Answers included more than 100 different words, but analysis revealed that most words tended to fit into five categories: untrustworthy, incompetent, unlikable, insecure, and immature. A sixth category, "other," received words that did not fit into the five categories. All words were placed into one of these six categories and coded from one to six.

Analysis

Analysis is making sense of your data.

After all answers are coded and the results tabulated, begin the **analysis** phase. This task can be overwhelming. The author surveyed 354 clergy from 32 Protestant, Catholic, and Jewish groups to assess their interview training during college and seminary and since entering the ministry. The 48 questions in the survey times 354 respondents provided 16,992 bits of information.

How can the survey interviewer handle massive amounts of information generated in most surveys? Charles Redding offered several helpful suggestions.[24]

- *Be selective.* Ask "What findings are likely to be most useful?" and "What will I do with this information once I get it?" If you have no idea, do not ask for it.

- *Capitalize on the potential of data.* Subject data to comparative breakdowns to discover differences between demographic subgroups.

- *Dig for the gold.* What is the really important stuff hidden within raw data and simple tabulations? For instance, in polls of registered voter attitudes, interviewers often discover that female respondents favor a candidate far less than male respondents and that Americans who have recently become citizens are likely to have very different views toward immigration than third or fourth generation Americans.

- *Look for what is missing.* What you do not find may be more important than what you do find. What information did you not obtain?

Know the limitations of your survey.

Ask questions such as these when analyzing your survey data. What conclusions can I draw and with what certainty? For which segment of a target population can I generalize? What are the constraints imposed by the sample, schedule of questions, the interviewing process, and the interviewers? Why did people respond in specific ways to specific questions? What unexpected events or changes have occurred since the completion of the survey that might make this survey dated or suspect? What should be done with the "undecided" and "don't know" answers or blanks on survey forms?

Be careful in using survey results.

Consider subjecting data to a statistical analysis designed to test reliability and significance of data. Research methodologists (see resources) provide detailed guidelines for conducting sophisticated statistical analyses.

When the analysis of data is complete, determine if the purpose and objectives of your survey are achieved. If so, what are the best means of reporting the results?

The Respondent in Survey Interviews

The ever-growing number of surveys conducted throughout the world each day ensures your involvement in these highly structured interviews. They are rarely compulsory, so you are free to "just say no," but when you do, you may forfeit an opportunity to influence important decisions that affect you, your family, your field of work, and your community. Do not walk away, close the door, hang up the phone, or hit the delete button too hastily, but approach each survey request cautiously and with a healthy skepticism.

The Opening

> **Understand what a survey is all about before participating.**

Become thoroughly oriented before starting to answer questions. Observe, listen, and question. Discover the interviewer's identity, the name of the organization sponsoring the survey, the purpose of the survey, why and how you were selected, the length of the survey, the confidentiality of your answers, and how the information you give will be used.[25] If the interviewer does not provide important information, ask for it. When the author was visiting his daughter and her family in Vancouver, Washington, more than 2000 miles from home, a market researcher approached him in a shopping mall. The researcher explained who she was, what she was doing, and why she was doing it. She did not state that he had to be a local resident. When asked if it made any difference that he was visiting from the Midwest, the interviewer said she wanted only those who regularly visited the mall. The interview ended.

Determine if the interview is a survey or a slick persuasive interview under the guise of a survey. Is it a nonpartisan political survey being conducted by a nationally known and reputable polling organization or part of a political campaign for a specific candidate or party? When the author responded to the doorbell at his home, a college-age person announced that she was conducting a survey of families with children as a part of summer internship. A few questions revealed that she was selling child-oriented magazines for a summer job, not an internship sponsored by her college as implied in her opening.

The Question Phase

> **Listen perceptively.**

Listen carefully to each question and answer options in interval, nominal, and ordinal questions. If a question or option is difficult to recall, ask the interviewer to repeat the question slowly. If a question is unclear, explain why and ask for clarification. Do not try to guess what a question is going to be from the interviewer's first words. You might guess wrong and become confused, give a stupid answer, or needlessly force the interviewer to restate a perfectly clear question.

> **Think before answering.**

Think through each answer, then respond clearly and precisely. Give the answer that best represents your beliefs, attitudes, or actions. Do not permit interviewer bias to lead you toward an answer you think the interviewer wants to hear or how other respondents have answered.

You can refuse to answer poorly constructed or leading questions or give data that seem irrelevant or an invasion of privacy. For instance, an interviewer recently asked the authors "Do you favor boutique solutions to our energy needs such as wind farms or environmentally friendly nuclear power plants that can supply electricity to major industries and cities?" The word "boutique" revealed the bias and agenda of the interviewer. Demand tactful, sensitive, and polite treatment from interviewers. Insist on adequate time to answer questions. If you have agreed to a 10-minute interview and the interview is still going strong at the 10-minute mark, remind the interviewer of the agreement and proceed to close the interview unless only a few more seconds are required. Survey interviews can be fun, interesting, and informative if both parties treat one another fairly.

Summary

The survey interview is the most meticulously planned and executed of interviews. Planning begins with determining a clearly defined purpose and conducting research. The purpose of the survey interview is to establish a solid base of fact from which to draw conclusions, make interpretations, and determine future courses of action. Only then does the survey creator structure the interview and develop questions with appropriate strategies, scales, sequences, coding, and recording methods. Selecting interviewees involves delineating a target population to survey and choosing a sample of this population that represents the whole. The creator of the survey chooses sampling methods, determines the size of the sample, and plans for an acceptable margin of error. Each choice has advantages and disadvantages because there is no one correct way to handle all surveys.

Survey respondents must determine the nature of the survey and its purposes before deciding whether to take part. If the decision is to participate, respondents have a responsibility to listen carefully to each question and answer it accurately. Be sure you understand each question and its answer options. Demand enough time to think through answers. Feel free to refuse to answer obviously leading or poorly phrased questions that require biased answers or choosing among options that do not include how you feel and what you prefer.

Key Terms and Concepts

Bogardus Social Distance Scale
Chain or contingency strategy
Convenience sample
Cross-sectional survey
Evaluative interval scale
Face-to-face interview
Filter strategy
Frequency interval scale
Internet interview
Interval scale
Leaning question strategy
Level of confidence
Likert scale

Longitudinal survey
Margin of error
Marginalized respondent
Nominal scale
Non-probability sampling
Numerical interval scale
Order bias
Ordinal scale
Personal interview
Population
Probability sampling
Qualitative survey
Quantitative survey
Precision journalism
Random digital dialing

Random sampling
Ranking ordinal scale
Rating ordinal scale
Reliability
Repeat strategy
Replicability
Sample point
Sampling principles
Self-selection
Shuffle strategy
Skip interval scale
Stratified random sample
Table of random numbers

Review Questions

1. How are qualitative and quantitative surveys fundamentally different?
2. Compare and contrast a cross-sectional survey from a longitudinal survey.
3. What information does a typical opening of a survey interview include?
4. Describe a typical closing for a survey interview.
5. Why is phrasing of questions so critical in survey interviews?
6. Why is training of survey interviewers so vital to successful surveys?
7. When should a survey include repeat strategy questions?
8. How does a leaning question differ from a leading question?
9. How are interval scale questions and evaluative interval scale questions similar and different?
10. How are frequency interview scale questions and numerical scale questions similar and different?
11. Describe the purpose and nature of Bogardus Social Distance Scale questions.
12. How can you determine sample size necessary for a survey?
13. What is a stratified random sample?
14. Why is a self-selection sampling method so inaccurate?
15. What are the advantages and disadvantages of personal or face-to-face interviews?

Student Activities

1. For instance, Volunteer as an interviewer for a survey a cereal manufacturer is conducting to determine which of its current offerings might be eliminated and what cereals should replace them. What is the target population of this survey? How will you locate and qualify interviewees? How will you motivate them to take part? What types of questions are included in the survey? If there are open questions, how are you instructed to record answers? How do you close each interview?

2. Try a simple interviewer bias experiment. Conduct 10 short opinion interviews on a current issue, using an identical question schedule for all interviews. During five of them, wear a conspicuous T-shirt, button, or badge that identifies membership in or support of an organization that supports one side of the issue: a Republican elephant, or Democratic donkey, a crucifix or a Star of David, an organization's logo or a product slogan. Compare results to see if and how your identification with an organization on one side of the issue affected respondent willingness to participate in an interview, answers they gave to identical questions, questions they asked or objections they raised, and stated desire to see results.

3. Obtain a number of market survey schedules used in face-to-face, telephone, and Internet surveys. Compare and contrast these schedules. How are the openings similar and different? How are schedules and sequences similar and different? How

are question strategies and question scales similar and different? How are closings similar and different? What surprises did you discover in your comparisons?

4. Interview a person who has created or conducted surveys for clients such as politicians, universities, and manufacturers. Cover such topics as determining the purpose, conducting research, selecting the target population, determining the sampling method, arriving at an acceptable margin of error, creating and pretesting the interview schedule, selecting and training interviewers, and deciding upon the method: face-to-face interviews, telephone interviews, Internet interviews.

Notes

1. Jeffrey Henning, "Survey Nation: 7 Billion Survey Invites a Year," http://blog.vovici /blog/bid/51106/Survey-Nation-7-Billion-Survey-Invites-a-Year, accessed June 4, 2012.

2. Jibum Kim, Carl Gerschenson, Patrick Glaser, and Tom W. Smith, "Trends—Trends in Surveys on Surveys," *Public Opinion Quarterly* 75 (Spring 2011), pp. 165–191.

3. http://www.socialresearchmethods.net/kb/interview.htm, accessed September 29, 2006.

4. Morgan M. Millar and Don A. Dillman, "Improving Response to Web and Mixed-Mode Surveys," *Public Opinion Quarterly* 75 (Summer 2011), pp. 249–269; Jens Bonke and Peter Fallesen, "The Impact of Incentives and Interview Methods on Response Quantity and Quality in Diary- and Booklet-based Surveys," *Survey Research Methods* 4 (2010), pp. 91–101.

5. Eleanor Singer and Cong Ye, "The Use and Effects of Incentives in Surveys," *The ANNALS of the American Academy of Political and Social Sciences* 645 (January 2013), pp. 112–141.

6. Stanley L. Payne, *The Art of Asking Questions* (Princeton, NJ: Princeton University Press, 1980), p. 57.

7. David Yeager and Jon Krosnick, "Does Mentioning 'Some People' and 'Other People' in an Opinion Question Improve Measurement Quality?" *Public Opinion Quarterly* 76 (Spring 2012), pp. 131–141.

8. Jack E. Edwards and Marie D. Thomas, "The Organizational Survey Process," *American Behavioral Scientist* 36 (1993), pp. 425–426.

9. Alexander Debronte, "Pitfalls of 'Don't Know/No Opinion' Answer Options in Surveys," https://checkmarket.com/2014/01, accessed February 11, 2015.

10. W. Charles Redding, *How to Conduct a Readership Survey: A Guide for Organizational Editors and Communication Managers* (Chicago, IL: Lawrence Ragan Communications, 1982), pp. 27–28.

11. Gert Van Dessel, "How to Determine Population and Survey Sample Size," https:www .checkmarket.com, accessed February 13, 2013.

12. Pew Research Center, "Random Digit Dialing—Our Standard Method," www.people -press.org, accessed February 11, 2015.

13. "Educational attainment distributions in Ohio in 2017, Ohio," accessed March 4, 2019.

14. "USDA—National Agricultural Statistics Service—Surveys—June Area," https://www.nass.usda.gov/Surveys/Guide_to_NASS_Surveys/June_Area, accessed March 2, 2019.

15. Eleanor Singer, Martin R. Frankel, and Marc B. Glassman, "The Effect of Interviewer Characteristics and Expectations on Response," *Public Opinion Quarterly* 47 (1983), pp. 68–83.

16. "Evaluation Tools for Racial Equity: Tip Sheets," http://www.Evaluationtoolsforracialequity.org/, accessed September 29, 2006.

17. Paul J. Lavrakas, "Respondent Fatigue," *Encyclopedia of Survey Research Methods* (2008), http://methods.sagepub.com/reference/encyclopedia-of-survey-research-methods/n480.xml, accessed February 25, 2019.

18. Susan E. Wyse, "Advantages and Disadvantages of Face-to-Face Data Collection," http:www.snapsurveys.com/blog/author/swyse/, accessed October 15, 2014.

19. Sara Mae Sincero, "Telephone Survey," https://Explorable.com.telephonesurvey, accessed December 12, 2015.

20. "The Future of U.S. General Population Telephone Survey Research," American Association for Public Opinion Research, https://www.aapor/Education-Resources-Reports/The-Future-Of-U-S-General-Population-Telephone-Sur.aspx, accessed February 28, 2019.

21. "The Future of U.S. General Population Telephone Survey Research."

22. Joe Hopper, "How to Conduct a Telephone Survey for Gold Standard Research," http://www.verstaresearch.com/blog/how-to-conduct-a-telephone-survey-for-gold-standard-research, accessed 26 June 2012.

23. Chris Mann and Fiona Stewart, "Internet Interviewing," in *Inside Interviewing: New Lenses, New Concerns,* James A. Holstein and Jaber F Gubrium, eds. (Thousand Oaks, CA: Sage, 2003), p. 243.

24. Redding, pp. 119–123.

25. "Participating in a Survey," catalyst.harvard.edu/SocialBehavioralResearch.pdf.

Resources

Conrad, Frederick G., and Michael F. Schober, eds. *Envisioning the Survey Interview of the Future.* San Francisco, CA: Wiley-Interscience, 2007.

Fink, Arlene. *How to Conduct Surveys: A Step-by-Step Guide.* Thousand Oaks, CA: Sage, 2012.

Gwartney, Patricia A. *The Telephone Interviewer's Handbook.* San Francisco, CA: Jossey-Bass, 2007.

Holstein, James A., and Jaber F. Gubrium, eds. *Inside Interviewing: New Lenses, New Concerns.* Newbury Park, CA: Sage, 2003.

Meyer, Philip. *Precision Journalism.* Lanham, MD: Rowman & Littlefield, 2002.

Scheuren, Fritz. *What Is a Survey?* Alexandria, VA: American Statistical Association, 2004.

The Recruiting Interview

Recruiting outstanding employees is critical to every organization's future. As Tom Peters writes, "talent rules" because talent of employees largely determines the success or failure of every organization.[1] **Locating** this talent is the easy part while **recruiting** them for your organization is often a competitive, difficult, time-consuming, and expensive process.

Recruiting outstanding employees is an elaborate courtship process that includes a variety of contacts with each recruit, the most important of which is the selection interview. Resumes, portfolios, cover letters, letters of recommendation, and transcripts provide you with valuable information, but only the interview enables you to meet recruits face-to-face during which you can observe appearance, demeanor, body language, behavior, and personality and probe into experiences, skills, abilities, attitudes, and honesty. In the author's 48 years of experience recruiting applicants for positions ranging from clerical staff to vice president, he never ceased to be amazed at how different **paper applicants** were from **live applicants**. The interview enables you to put all of the pieces together to decide if an applicant is an ideal **FIT** for **this position** with **this organization's culture.**[2]

> Interacting face-to-face with an applicant gives insights no paper applicant can provide.

The majority of you reading this chapter are undoubtedly looking toward Chapter 8 because you are thinking about or are actively involved in seeking a position and starting or changing a career. After all, isn't the recruiting interview something that HR personnel or senior staff members conduct? HR is usually involved in the hiring process. However, when the process reaches the interview stage, whether an initial contact at a career fair, professional conference, or university career center or a visit to the organization for a series of decision-making interviews, multiple staff members with expertise and experiences in the area of the opening conduct the interviews, evaluate applicants, and make hiring recommendations. Many of our students have returned to campus within months of graduation to help recruit talent for their organizations because applicants can identify more readily with alums who are recent, successful applicants. By learning and applying the principles addressed in this chapter, you will become a more effective applicant because you will gain insights into what recruiters are seeking in applicants and how they strive to discover them and become an effective recruiter for future employers.

The objectives of this chapter are to introduce you to the fundamental principles of successful employee recruiting. These include locating high-quality applicants, preparing for the recruiting process, obtaining and reviewing information on applicants, structuring interviews, conducting interviews, and evaluating interviews. Learning and applying these principles will make you a valuable asset to your organization while enhancing the quality of your future colleagues.

Preparing the Recruiting Effort

Thorough planning and preparation are essential for every recruiting effort, and it should start by ensuring that all employees involved in the hiring process understand their responsibilities in helping to prevent discrimination of any type.[3] Be sure they are familiar with all applicable federal and state EEO (equal employment opportunity) laws and executive orders.[4] Some state laws are more stringent than federal laws.

Reviewing EEO Laws

> Unintentional violations of EEO laws are violations.

EEO laws can be traced back to the Civil Rights Act of 1866, but most became law in the 1960s.[5] The EEOC (Equal Employment Opportunity Commission) oversees compliance with these laws. Review them carefully so you understand their relevance to every element of the recruiting process. Be aware that the EEOC and courts are not concerned about **intent** to violate laws but with **effect,** and organizations are held liable if unlawful information is attained, maintained, or used in any way even if they did not seek it.

- The Equal Pay Act of 1963 requires equal pay for men and women performing work that involves similar skill, effort, responsibility, and working conditions.
- The Civil Rights Act of 1964, particularly Title VII, prohibits the selection of employees based on race, color, gender, religion, or national origin, and requires employers to discover discriminatory practices and eliminate them.
- The Age Discrimination in Employment Act of 1967 prohibits employers of 25 or more persons from discriminating against persons because of age.
- The Rehabilitation Act of 1973 (Sections 501 and 505) orders federal contractors to hire persons with disabilities, including alcoholism, asthma, rheumatoid arthritis, and epilepsy.
- The Pregnancy Discrimination Act of 1978 prohibits discrimination of women because of pregnancy alone and protects job security during maternity leaves.
- The Civil Rights Act of 1991 (often referred to as the 1992 Civil Rights Act) caps compensation and punitive damages for employers, provides for jury trial, and created a commission to investigate the "glass ceiling" for minorities and women and reward organizations that advance opportunities for minorities and women.
- The Americans with Disabilities Act of 1990 (effective July 25, 1992), Title I and Title V, prohibits discrimination against persons with physical and mental impairments that substantially limit or restrict the condition, manner, or duration under which they can perform one or more life activities and requires reasonable accommodation by employers.

Morsa Images/DigitalVision/Getty Images

Review EEO laws carefully.

Following these
laws enables
you to avoid
stereotypes and
assumptions
about applicants.

Everything you do, ask, and say during the selection process must pertain to **bona fide occupational qualifications (BFOQs),** qualifications that are essential for performing a specific job. BFOQs **include** education, training, licenses and certificates, work experiences, skills, communication abilities, relevant convictions for felonies, physical attributes, and personality traits. BFOQs **exclude** gender, gender identity, age, race, ethnic group, religion, marital status, pregnancy, parental status, sexual orientation, physical appearance, disabilities, citizenship, national origin, language spoken in the home, veteran status, military records, military discharge, and arrest records. These laws pertain to **every communication** you have **with** or **about** a potential employee.

EEO laws pertain to most employers, including labor unions and employment agencies, with at least 15 employees, 20 in age discrimination cases.[6] There are exceptions to these laws, but you must be able to prove that they are essential BFOQs. For instance, appearance or gender may be a BFOQ for a modeling position, religion for a pastoral position, age for performing specific tasks (serving alcoholic beverages, driving a bus, operating dangerous equipment), physical abilities such as eye sight and manual dexterity for pilots, physical strength for construction workers, legal status to work in the United States, and Spanish language skills for working with Spanish speaking clients. These guidelines will enable you to avoid EEO violations, "turning off" applicants, and lawsuits.

Employers must
be able to prove
exceptions to
EEO laws.

1. Meet the test of **job relatedness** by making certain that all selection criteria are BFOQs.
2. Ask questions that are aimed specifically at BFOQs.
3. Focus questions on what applicants can do rather than on what they cannot do.
4. Standardize interviews so recruiters ask essentially the same questions of all applicants.
5. Be cautious when probing into answers because EEO violations often occur in these on-the-spot questions.
6. If applicants begin to volunteer unlawful information, steer them tactfully back to job-related areas.
7. Be cautious during unguarded and informal small talk prior to the interview, in the opening and closing minutes of interviews, when the formal interview is over, and you are escorting the applicant to another location.
8. Do not write or doodle on application forms or resumes that might be seen as a discriminatory code.

It is not difficult
to avoid violat-
ing EEO laws.

Exercise #1—Testing Your Knowledge of EEO Laws

Test your knowledge of EEO laws and selection interviews by rating each question below as *lawful* (can be asked), *depends* (may be asked under certain circumstances), or *unlawful* (cannot be asked). Explain why it is lawful, unlawful, or depends.

	Lawful	Unlawful	Depends
1. Which religious holidays do you observe?			
2. How did you become so fluent in Arabic?			
3. Do you have a significant other?			

4. How fast can you go in that motorized chair?

5. Do you go by Richard or Dick?

6. Have you even been arrested?

7. Would you have a problem working in Brazil?

8. Which preprofessional organizations do you belong to?

9. Where are you from?

10. Do you drink?

11. I see you served in Afghanistan. Which type of discharge did you receive?

12. Are you a U.S. citizen?

13. Which software programs have you used?

14. Do you have children?

15. Would you say you are a conservative or a liberal?

Three recent issues have arisen in EEO laws: domestic partners, same-sex marriages, and hearing disabilities. If an applicant starts to give you any information that is not a BFOQ, reply tactfully such as, "We hire persons based on how well they are qualified and can do the job, not on personal preferences or disabilities." Your organization must be prepared to make suitable arrangements for applicants with disabilities that affect hearing, eye sight, seating, mobility, and reaching the location of the interview.

Developing an Applicant Profile

With EEO laws in mind, conduct a thorough analysis to develop a **competency-based applicant profile** for each position for which you are recruiting. This profile typically includes specific skills, abilities, education, training, experiences, knowledge levels, personal characteristics, and interpersonal relationships that enable a person to fulfill a position with a high degree of success. Measure all applicants against this profile to ensure that recruiting efforts meet EEO laws, are as objective as possible, encourage all interviewers to cover the same topics and traits, and eliminate the **birds of a feather syndrome** in which recruiters favor applicants who are most like themselves—traditionally this has favored white, male applicants.

Many organizations are employing a **behavior-based** selection process to ensure that each interviewer asks questions that match each applicant with the applicant profile. Behavior-based interviewing rests on two interrelated principles: past behavior in specific job-related situations is the best predictor of future behavior and past performance is the best predictor of future performance. Interviewers ask interviewees to describe situations in which they have exhibited specific skills and abilities.[7] A National Institutes of Health publication states that the behavior-based interview technique "seeks to uncover how a potential employee actually did behave in a given situation; not on how he or she might behave in the future."[8] The behavior-based technique begins with a needs and position analysis to determine which behaviors are essential for performing a particular position. Behaviors might include:[9]

advises	facilitates	remains current
applies	implements	solves problems
builds	influences	understands
conducts	investigates	utilizes
consults	leads	
communicates	monitors	
develops	recommends	
establishes	researches	

Other organizations have modified this approach into a **trait-based** or **talent-based** system in which specific traits or talents rather than behaviors are identified in a position analysis. For instance, traits might include:

ambitious	fair	people-oriented
achiever	initiative	reliable
assertive	listens	responsible
competitive	motivated	responsive
dependable	open-minded	self-confident
		trustworthy

Does a profile discriminate against non-dominant applicants?

Check each profile behavior or trait carefully. Is each essential for job performance? Is leadership necessary for an entry-level position? Can you measure the behavior or trait? Are you expecting recruiters to act as psychologists? Will some targeted behaviors or traits adversely affect your organization's diversity efforts and discriminate unintentionally? For example, traits such as competitiveness, aggressiveness, direct eye contact, forcefulness, and oral communication skills may run counter to the upbringing and culture of many nondominant groups.[10] Traits and behaviors being sought must be position-related—BFOQs—and clearly defined so that all interviewers are looking for the same ones.

After developing an applicant profile, write a clear description that "encapsulates requirements for a given position." Karen O'Keefe writes, "Ultimately, the job description is the inspiration for any subsequent interview so defining the position up front will make finding the right person for the job much easier."[11] Being underprepared is the biggest mistake you can make.

Understanding Today's Applicants

How and why are applicants apparently changing?

In 1992, the appearance of john Gray's book *Men Are from Mars, and Women Are from Venus* started a national discussion, with a lot of head nodding, about the differences between men and women, particularly in the workplace. As time went on, however, research revealed that men and women are more alike than different in their desires. Their experiences, career paths open to them, and stage of work-lives rather than gender appeared to indicate fundamental differences. Today, a similar discussion is taking place, but this time generational differences between baby boomers and millennials dominate the discussion, once again with lots of head nodding.

The millennial generation will soon be the largest segment of the working population, and they appear to have very different desires and expectations as applicants than generations that preceded them. It is critical that recruiters recognize and adapt to these desires and expectations while also recognizing that they would probably share them if they were starting their work-lives in today's society with similar experiences, paths open to them, and electronic marvels at their fingertips. Your **organization's Web site** may be critical in searches because applicants review them to see if your organization is attractive and a good fit. They may decide not to pursue a position because they see your site as poorly done. Make it easy to read, interesting, updated, professional, and sophisticated.

> Today's applicants are different because they live and work in a different world.

What Do Millennial Applicants Seek in a Position and Career?

Millennials top interests do not include money but do include flexible schedules and work locations, a collaborative work environment and culture, mentoring, career development opportunities and tuition assistance for graduate work that will enable them to continue learning and growing personally and professionally, and opportunities to make a difference not only within the organization but in the world. They are more comfortable with and used to diversity in society and the workplace, and national and geographical boundaries are of less concern because many have traveled, studied, or worked abroad. They are more interested in the reputation of an organization than its brand name. Millennial applicants do not expect to remain with one organization or one career for long periods of time.[12]

Millennial applicants place strong emphasis on the communication that takes place and their attraction to the interviewer's behavior. They assume the interviewer's behavior strongly indicates what they might expect from the organization. They want the interviewer to be friendly, attentive, sensitive, sincere, warm, honest, enthusiastic, and genuinely interested in them. Applicants prefer interviewers to be young and relatively new employees rather than veterans of the organization because they do not want sales pitches but opportunities to connect with interviewers and their interests, desires, and motivations. Applicants of nondominant groups (women, minority races and ethnic groups, and those from lower economic classes) prefer interviewers to be more like them, but they may become confused and angry if they feel scrutinized by "one of their own."[13]

> The recruiter is the organization in the applicant's eyes.

Millennials want recruiters to ask them open-ended, job-related questions that allow them to express themselves and elaborate in answers. They do not want to be interrupted or subjected to a strict schedule of questions that are read to them. Millennials seek extensive information about positions and organizations prior to interviews so, during interviews, they want detailed information about what is unavailable in other sources. They are interested in what recruiters like about their positions and organizations, but do not want them to spend too much time talking about themselves and their careers. Millennials want the focus to be on them and their career interests. They are turned off by pressure tactics.

> Today's applicants are information-driven.

Where to Locate Talented Applicants

Commence your search for talent by reviewing your professional and social contacts and checking your files of persons who have gotten your attention at conferences and in publications. Visit college career centers and attend career fairs on campuses and at professional meetings. Review the records of college students who have served or are

> Strive to make personal contacts with potential employees.

serving as interns or in cooperative programs with your organization. You and others are likely to have had opportunities to observe and assess them in action to determine if they might be good fits for specific positions within your organization.

Career or **job fairs** can be fertile ground for contacting high-quality applicants that fit the positions you have open—**if** you select **appropriate fairs.** Most fairs attract **entry level** applicants, and many are targeted to specific majors or careers such as those in liberal arts, education, engineering, biology, management, or health sciences. If you are looking for experienced or senior staff, fairs are not for you. Be sure the fair warrants the number of staff you are sending and has a good reputation for attracting significant numbers of quality applicants.[14] When you take an active part in career and job fairs, set up booths with exhibits that are both attractive and professional in appearance, and have promotional materials such as brochures, pamphlets, newsletters, photos of locations and award-winning employees, and well-known or new products. Handouts such as mugs, mouse pads, book bags, and pens attract participants and get your name around the fair. Staff your booth with employees who have excellent interpersonal skills, enjoy meeting young people, and experience with on-the-spot interviews. Be honest if you are not currently hiring. Contact fairgoers who appear to be good fits for your positions and organization.

> **Recruit at job fairs that attract applicants you are seeking.**

A **staffing firm** (often called placement agencies, employment agencies, or head hunters) may help you locate experienced applicants and conduct initial screening interviews. Select a firm carefully by its success rates and suitability for your organization and positions. The American Staffing Association offers guidelines for choosing the best staffing firm for your needs, but you should also rely on your first impressions and how the firm selects its recruiters.[15]

Kiosks are common sights in department stores, pharmacies, and restaurants. They enable firms to establish and update applicant databases on an hourly basis and complete reviews in a timely basis. They may not be appropriate for your organization and the positions you wish to fill.

> **Do not overlook resume databases and Internet resources.**

There are numerous **resume databases** and **Internet sources,** some free and some fee-based. Select ones that are suitable for the positions you have open and your organization. Resume databases include Flexjobs, Jobspider, Behance, and Eresumex.[16] Most professional organizations have Web sites, and they may list and describe job openings. These include colleges and universities, religious organizations, senior citizen organizations, political parties, and special interest groups. Key Internet sources include the following:

- CareerBuilder.com
- Kennedy's The Directory of Executive and Professional Recruiters
- Monster Jobs
- Monster.com
- Wall Street Journal Careers

Many organizations are striving to diversify their workforces through advertisements in the **media.** Joyce Gioia recommends advertising in the ethnic media (such as alternate language newspapers, magazines, Web sites, radio, television, and movie theaters) that attract a highly diverse clientele. She claims that recruiting employees from diverse ethnic groups "holds opportunities for companies beyond their wildest dreams."[17] Some organizations publish job openings in **social media**, but not every applicant has access to social media. This may result in attracting a non-representative applicant pool, so do not rely too heavily on this one source.

Obtaining and Reviewing Information on Applicants

Do a thorough search for all relevant information pertaining to each applicant prior to the interview by reviewing the application form, resume, letters of recommendation, objective tests, and social networking Web sites. This is your initial opportunity to determine how well this person fits the position you have open and your organization's unique culture. Your review will reveal areas to probe into during the interview, perhaps comparing oral and written answers to similar questions. Fredric Jablin and Vernon Miller discovered that employers who review applicant credentials thoroughly ask more questions, a wider variety of questions, and probe more into answers to determine the fit.[18]

Application Forms

Make application forms compatible with BFOQs.

Create application forms that comply with EEO laws and ask for information relevant to the position or positions you have open. Include open questions similar to ones you will ask during interviews, and provide adequate space for thorough answers. When reviewing completed application forms, look for what is and is not included with fit always in mind. If an applicant includes information that might violate an EEO law, delete it before anyone involved in the selection process sees it.

Cover Letters

What sets this applicant apart from others?

The cover letter is often the applicants' first opportunity to create a favorable impression and your first opportunity to determine if the applicant is a good fit for a specific position with your organization. Read the letter with these questions in mind. Has the applicant expended the effort to identify the name and address of the person in your organization who is in charge of this search? Does the applicant tailor the letter to this position starting with career (rather than job) goals and interests and proceeding to qualifications and experiences that make him or her an ideal candidate? Is the person clearly a "doer" with activities and achievements beyond courses and grades while in school and minimal duties in work experiences? What sets this applicant apart from others? Is this person sincerely interested in **this position** with **your organization**? Is the letter professionally written with good choice of words and grammar and free of spelling and punctuation errors and typos? Susan Heathfield, a human resources specialist, admits that she may be "an old fuddy-duddy," but claims that such errors "are indicative of what you can expect from the candidate as an employee. Looking for careless, sloppy, or unconcerned? I doubt it. Your evidence is sitting before you on your desk or on your computer screen."[19]

Resumes

Applicants often do not match their resumes.

When an applicant's resume arrives at your organization, have a person not involved in the selection process delete any information that may violate EEO laws. If you keep this information, even though you did not ask for it, you can be held liable for possible

fizkes/iStock/Getty Images

■ *Review the applicant's credentials prior to the interview so you can devote full attention to the applicant during the interview.*

discrimination. Then have each person involved in the recruiting effort review the resume **prior to the interview.** Reading it for the first time during the interview shows lack of preparation and interest and is a major turnoff for quality applicants.

Start reviewing a resume with the career objective if one is included. How well does it match the applicant profile for the position the applicant is seeking? If this is a good match, move to education, training, and experiences to see if they complement the career objective stated in the resume and cover letter and fit the applicant profile. Does the applicant appear to be over qualified or under qualified for this position? Look for gaps in dates and missing details concerning education, training, employment, and relevant experiences. As with the cover letter, look at word choice, grammatical errors, misspellings, punctuation errors, typos, and errors in dates. Does the applicant value details and proof writings?

Lying is a growing problem in job searches, particularly with cover letters, application forms, and resumes. Eighty-five percent of employers in 2017 reported they had caught applicants cheating, up from 66 percent five years earlier. Recent statistics indicate that 50 percent of all applicants lie to get the job they seek, and as many as 70 percent say they would "fib," "fudge," or "fake" a little here and there to get the job they want.[20]

Be aware of common fudges and fakes on resumes so you can detect them quickly. On the one hand, they are willing to enhance, inflate, stretch, mask, or exaggerate their education (including degrees they do not have), experiences, skills, job titles, employment dates, salaries and responsibilities on previous jobs, achievements, military decorations, and medals. On the other hand, they may omit or conceal information they perceive to be detrimental to their chances of landing a position. Do your homework. Be skeptical of claims that appear too good to be true, and be suspicious of missing information.[21]

Consider a scanner if you attract hundreds of applicants.

If you are hiring several new staff or your postings will receive a large volume of resumes, consider applicant tracking software programs that will scan resumes quickly and efficiently and identify applicants best suited to your opening and organization. They can also store a large volume of resumes if you need to scan the pool again.[22] Scanning software sorts applicants based on key words, skills, interests, and experiences. You need to load these carefully to minimize losing excellent applicants. For instance, if candidates use the word personnel or purchasing instead of human resources or procurement management, they will be eliminated from the pool. The same is true if they use abbreviations that do not match those in the system, headers the system doesn't recognize, spaces between the letters of their names for graphical purposes that cannot be accurately parsed out, and font sizes and typefaces the software finds less readable. Idenitfy guidelines in your advertisements and recruiting literature to prepare scannable resumes so all candidates are on a level playing field.

Letters of Recommendation and References

Letters of recommendation and lists of references have a long history in recruiting employees, but evidence indicates they add little more validity than GPAs or GRE scores in predicting future success. Applicants select references carefully to be sure they will provide positive reviews, so it is not surprising that only about 7 percent provide average or below average ratings, particularly when applicants do not waive their right to see references.[23] At the least, references do not want applicants to get angry at them and, at the most, they may fear law suits for defamation of character. These fears have resulted in former employers providing little more than dates when applicants worked for them. Be cautious in reading "between the lines" for what is and is not included in letters because differences may be due to the writers' styles and what they think is important to report rather than the applicant's background.

Fears of lawsuits are hampering reference checks.

As you review letters of recommendation or information from references, look for important pieces of information about an applicant and who is willing to serve as a reference. If you ask applicants for letters of recommendation or contact references, ask for specific behaviors, experiences, contributions, and personality traits that address key elements of the applicant profile. Before contacting references, check your organization's policy about doing so. Some organizations require you to obtain permission from applicants.

Who writes a letter of recommendation may be most important.

Standardized Tests

Standardized preemployment tests have become an integral part of the employment selection process in many organizations, and they are most effective when combined with carefully structured behavior-based or trait-based interviews. Organizations use them to screen a large pool of applicants to select the best ones to interview. Unless your organization has the time, money, and staff with sophisticated test-development skills, select commercially available tests that are job-related or tailored, reliable from applicant to applicant, validated on a cross-section of the population, and meet EEOC guidelines to avoid charges of discrimination.[24] Four common types of tests are aptitude, personality, basic skills, and honesty/integrity.[25]

All tests must meet EEOC guidelines to avoid discrimination.

Aptitude tests measure a potential employee's ability to think critically, solve problems, process new information and concepts, and learn new skills.

Personality tests measure personality types and traits along with people skills that indicate interpersonal communication and relations, behavioral traits, attitudes, ability to handle stress, emotional adjustment, motivation, and openness to change. Assessing these traits may help employers determine applicant fit with a position and an organization. The Myers-Briggs Indicator has been a popular personality test in businesses for decades.

Few tests are able to identify or assess common sense.

Basic skills tests measure mathematics, measurement, reading, spelling, verbal, and communication skills that appear to be declining when they are more important than ever. Only computer skills are increasing, particularly among younger applicants. Many skills come from experiences, education, and careers and are essential when employees work as individuals or teams and are required to deal with problems and write up the results and recommendations.

Honesty tests are intrusive but are here to stay.

Honesty/integrity tests are designed to measure an applicant's propensity to lie, steal, cheat, and commit fraud and to use drugs, be tardy or absent, waste time, and commit safety violations. They have become common in the employment process because organizations are encountering serious problems resulting from dishonest and deceitful employees. Be cautious when using honesty and integrity tests. What messages are you sending to future employees? Are you inviting applicants to provide answers they believe you want to hear or read? Studies of the American Psychological Association suggest they may identify persons with a *high propensity* for stealing but not those in the *moderate* to *low* ranges. Others suggest they may rule out large percentages of perfectly honest applicants while eliminating a small number of undesirable applicants.[26]

Integrity Interviews

> Persistent probing may reveal the truthfulness of responses.

The primary purpose of the integrity interview (face-to-face interaction) is to assess an applicant's standards of trustworthiness and honesty.[27] They come in two formats. The first consists of highly structured interviews that focus on ethics and integrity by probing into previous work experiences related directly to the available position. The second is used when applicants have little previous work experience, and interviewers ask situational questions that focus on dimensions of ethical and honest behavior. Donna Pawlowski and John Hollwitz developed a structured situational interview "based on the assumption that intentions predict behavior."[28] Interviewers ask interviewees to reply to hypothetical scenarios and employ a 5-point scale with the agreed upon definition of the dimensions such as relationship manipulation, interpersonal deception (lying),

> Motivate applicants to give honest answers.

security violation (revealing trade secrets), and sexual harassment (telling dirty jokes, displaying nude pictures, flirting). Truthful applicants tend to acknowledge the probability of employee theft, reply without hesitation, reject leniency toward dishonesty, and expect reliable results from interviews. Interviewers report a phenomenon called "outguessing" in which applicants freely admit to unethical, dishonest activities because they believe that "everyone does it." Interviewers must persuade applicants of the importance of being honest by asking work-related questions and offering incentives. Studies have revealed that 75 percent of applicants admit to lying on applications, 41 percent admit to abuse of sick leave, 32 percent admit to illegal drug use, and 28 percent to having been fired or forced to resign.[29]

ON THE WEB

Integrity interviews are becoming more common during the selection process as employers attempt to assess the integrity of potential employees in an age when honesty often seems the exception rather than the norm. Many employers and researchers are raising serious questions about the accuracy and value of honesty tests in the employment selection setting. Search the Internet for discussions of the uses and concerns raised by written and oral honesty tests. These sources should get you started on your search: Infoseek (http://www.infoseek.com), PsycInfo (http://www.psycinfo.com), The Monster Board (http://www.monster.com/), CareerBuilder (http://www.careerbuilder.com/), and PsychLit (http://www.psychlit.com/).

Social Media

Many organizations have stopped accessing applicant's social media accounts because of the legal risk. Information readily available on these sites may lead to EEOC violations and charges of discrimination. For instance, photographs may reveal age, gender, race, disabilities, and ethnicity while content may divulge religious and political beliefs, marital and parental status, health issues, and sexual orientation.[30] Your organization may lessen the risks involved by asking an applicant's permission in advance to search Web sites or if the applicant "has any online presence they would like for you to check out."[31]

Organizations that access social media **following interviews** are more confident they will be within the laws because they have already seen the applicants in person. Social media may tell you a great deal about how well applicants would fit into your positions (including motivations, work habits, attitudes, and future plans) and the culture of your organization (including badmouthing former employers, racist or ethnic rants, and photos of scantily clad dress and excessive alcoholic consumption). Jonathan Segal writes, it is "said there are only two times when a person is perfect: at birth and at the job interview."[32] Recruiters use a variety of methods to distinguish the real from the make-believe applicant.

Conducting the Interview

Once your position announcements have attracted a number of qualified applicants and you have had an opportunity to review information on each, it is time to schedule interviews with ones who appear to be the best fits for the position and organization.

The Atmosphere and Setting

Conduct recruiting interviews in an environment that is conducive to revealing and sharing information, feelings, attitudes, and motivations. An ideal environment is comfortable, private, quiet, and free of interruptions of any kind. Close doors and windows and turn off phones, computers, and beepers. Select a seating arrangement that maximizes interpersonal communication. Unfortunately, you will encounter circumstances in which you have little or no control over the environment. The author has interviewed applicants in hallways, on staircases, in hotel lobbies, rooms, restaurants, and bars, on benches at outdoor job fairs, and in ballrooms during open houses. Make the best of each situation. Interested applicants will understand and do their best to make a good impression.

Make every interview your top priority of the moment because the interview determines your organization's future and the applicant's career. Patricia Buhler reminds us that "The interview is a two-way street. While the interviewer is screening applicants for fit with the organization and position, the applicant is 'interviewing' the company for fit as well. The interview, then, should also be viewed as a public relations tool." She warns, "Bad publicity travels quickly."[33] Applicants see you as your organization and are more likely to accept a job offer if they perceive you to be a good representative of your organization. You want applicants to be open and honest with you, so you must be open and honest with them. Provide a supportive climate. Give accurate descriptions of the position and the organization, including its culture and expectations of employees. Practice a **conscious transparency** in which you promote a dialogue by exchanging information, explaining the purpose of questions, and answering the applicant's questions.

Interview Formats

The **traditional format** consists of a recruiter and an applicant asking and answering questions and providing information. It is often called a "personal interview." During a "plant" or "site" visit, several staff, department, or team members conduct traditional interviews with each asking somewhat similar questions, giving information, and then answering questions. It is not unusual for two or more recruiters to meet with an applicant at the same time, particularly during lunch or dinner.

> Select an interview format that works best for your search.

In a **chain format,** each recruiter has a specific assignment. For instance, one may conduct a traditional interview to get a general impression of how the applicant fits the position and organization. A second may probe into education and training relevant to the position. A third may probe into specific job skills and experiences. A fourth may probe into the applicant's technical knowledge. The chain format enables each recruiter to probe more deeply into specific areas. The findings are later shared to get a complete, detailed picture of the applicant.

A **panel format** is a variation of the chain format in which each member of the panel focuses on specific concerns or issues.

A major advantage of the panel is that each member hears the same questions and answers and may bring a variety of expertise and cultural diversity to the table. It reduces the common problem of single interviewers interpreting differently or claiming to have received different answers in their one-on-one contacts.

In a **seminar format,** one or more recruiters interview a number of applicants at the same time and in the same place. Although it is less common than other formats, it has some advantages. It takes less time than single interviews, enables an organization to see several applicants replying and reacting to the same questions at the same time, and may provide valuable insights into how applicants might work with one another as a team. If conducted with skill, applicants will not see the interview as a competition but an opportunity to build upon others' comments while revealing their qualifications and experiences. If you are looking for leaders, this may be the best format.

Opening the Interview

The opening few minutes of the interview create the all-important **first impression** of you and your organization and sets the tone for the remainder of the interview. As far as most applicants are concerned, **you are the organization.** Make applicants an active part of the process from the start.

Rapport

> Make the interview a professional conversation.

Greet each applicant by name in a warm, friendly, and professional manner. Smile, maintain eye contact, and give a firm but not crushing handshake. Introduce yourself by name, your position with the organization, and the role you are playing in the recruiting process. Do not ask the applicant to address you by first name or nickname because applicants rarely feel comfortable doing so at this stage of your relationship. Most interviewers engage applicants in a bit of small talk to get them relaxed, but avoid trite comments about the weather or the applicant's travel. Focus on what you have in common with the applicant such as home town, college, travel experiences, hobbies, or relationships. Listen more than talk to get the applicant involved from the start. Be aware that prolonged small talk may heighten the suspense of what happens next and raise the applicant's anxiety.

> Do not delay the inevitable.

Meaningful rapport building is particularly important in cross-cultural interviews that are becoming ever more common in our global community. Build a relationship "that is based on trust, understanding, and acceptance" from the first moments of the interview, and bear in mind "that speaking the same language does not mean sharing the same culture."[34]

Orientation

Take the suspense out of the interview by briefly explaining how it will proceed in enough detail so the applicant knows what to expect and when. Traditionally, this means asking the applicant questions, giving information, and then answering the applicant's questions. If you use a different format, explain this to the applicant. Tell the applicant if you are willing to answer questions at any time or prefer to wait until it is the applicant's turn. If this interaction is the first of a series of interviews during an on-site visit or plant trip, provide the applicant with an agenda that explains the who, what, when, and where of the process.

The Opening Question

Begin the interview with an open-ended, easy-to-answer question on a specific topic with which the applicant is familiar such as the following:

- What do you know about us?
- Why did you apply for this position?
- What are your short-range career goals?
- Which college courses have prepared you most for this position?
- What do you like best in your current position?
- What was the most valuable experience during your semester in Prague?

> Ask an open-ended question but not too open.

An open question not only gets the applicant talking and the recruiter listening and observing but it relaxes and prepares the applicant for tough questions to come. Do not make the question too open-ended such as the frequently asked, "Tell me about yourself." Where should the applicant begin: growing up, grade school, high school, college? What should the applicant talk about: personal traits, family life, achievements, experiences, hobbies, community involvement? When should the applicant stop? Rather than relax the applicant, a highly open question can be very stressful. Avoid any question that might put the applicant on the spot and lead to a poor answer that creates a negative impression of the applicant in the opening minutes of the interview.

The Body of the Interview

> Highly structured interviews are more reliable but less flexible and adaptable.

Not many years ago recruiters relied upon what might best be described as "seat of the pants" or "off the top the head" interviewing in which they asked a mixture of traditional questions and whatever came to mind. The nature of the position and culture of the organization played little part in their questions and interpretation of answers. There was no coordination among recruiters seeking employees to fill specific positions within the same organization.

Some organizations went to the opposite extreme by creating **highly structured interviews** to achieve a high degree of reliability and validity in the selection process and avoid violating of EEO laws.[35] All recruiters interviewing applicants for a specific position asked identical questions in the same order, agreed upon acceptable answers, and evaluated all applicants on a common rating scale. There were no probing questions because they might compromise the tightly controlled process. The goal was to determine the best fit for this position with this organization, and highly structured interviews improved reliability and validity.

Some organizations have created **behavior-based**, highly structured interviews in which all primary and probing questions are prepared ahead of time and asked of each applicant without variation. Interviewers rate each applicant's responses on behaviorally defined dimensions such as a five-point scale according to the degree to which they exhibit or give information about one or more behaviors: 5 = strongly present and 1 = minimally present.

Rating	Behavior	Question
_____	Initiative	Give me an example of when you have resolved conflicts between employees.
_____	Energy	How many times have you done this?
_____	General intelligence	What was the outcome?
_____	Decisiveness	How did you feel about the results you got?
_____	Adaptability	When faced with intransigence, what did you do?

In this example, the interviewer listens to the applicant's answer to a primary question and then asks a pre-planned probing question.

While highly structured interviews have achieved higher reliability and validity and adherence to EEO laws than non-structured interviews, they lack the spontaneity desired in interpersonal interactions in which applicants volunteer job-related information and reveal how well they might fit into the culture of your organization. Interviewers are relegated to question readers and rating checkers and cannot use their interviewing skills to gain insights into answers. Applicants soon become familiar with questions organizations ask and recite carefully phrased answers for each. Lack of on-the-spot probing questions makes it difficult to check for accuracy and truthfulness—to distinguish the real from the make-believe applicant in interviews. Organizations and interviewers cannot anticipate with confidence how applicants will answer primary questions, so there is no way to pre-plan all probing questions for each. Highly structured interviews with rating scales for responses are most appropriate for positions that require specific skills for which there can be little or no deviation. A great many positions are not reducible to such clear-cut basics and expectations and standardized scales.

I recommend **moderately structured interviews** that have a significant degree of structure but allow skillful interviewers the freedom to do their jobs. The process begins by developing a detailed **interview guide** that includes the information essential for selecting and evaluating the candidates for a specific position and organization. Experienced interviewers then create moderate schedules of primary and probing questions that may differ from one interviewer to another but zero in on essential information. Applicants are less able to come to an interview with pre-planned answers to questions they have learned to expect. Interviewers probe skillfully, often with multiple questions, to gain insights into answers and applicants, determine the accuracy and honesty of answers, and gauge fit for the position and organization.

THINK before
asking probing
questions.

Asking Questions

Ask open-ended, neutral, job-related questions that conform to all EEO laws. Open-ended questions encourage applicants to elaborate when answering and enable you to listen and observe and to formulate insightful probing questions.

Common Question Pitfalls

Be Guard
against pitfalls
in primary
and probing
questions.

You will often find it necessary during interviews to rephrase or create probing questions when answers seem incomplete, superficial, vague, suggestive, or irrelevant; you notice unusual nonverbal behaviors; or you discover unexpected areas to explore. When you ask spontaneous questions, however, you are susceptible to committing the common question pitfalls identified and illustrated in Chapters 3 and 5. There are three pitfalls in addition to these that are particularly relevant in the employment interview.

1. *The evaluative response:* The interviewer expresses judgmental feelings about an answer that may bias or skew the next response.

    I'm sure you regret that decision.
    Hmm, that was a mistake, wasn't it?
    Was that the *only reason* for leaving RGM Manufacturing?

2. *The EEO violation:* The interviewer asks an unlawful question.

    How active are you in your synagogue?
    How did you lose the finger on your left hand?
    What are your plans after your husband completes his medical degree?

3. *The resume or application form question:* The interviewer asks a question that is already answered on the resume or application form.

    Where did you study abroad?
    What are your career goals?
    I see you got your degree from Miami. Which one?

Traditional Questions

The following **traditional recruiter questions** avoid pitfalls and gather important job-related information.

- Interest in the organization

    What attracts you most to our company?
    What do you know about the history of our company?
    Which of our products interests you the most?

- Work-related (general)

    Which of your work experiences has prepared you most for this position?
    What did you like best about your last position?
    What were the most important things you learned during your internship with
        Williams & Williams?

- Work-related (specific)

  What strategy do you use most when motivating people?

  What type of supervision do you find most helpful?

  How do you feel about compensation based in part on your division's performance?

- Teams and teamwork

  What does the word "teamwork" mean to you?

  When you are leading a team, what criteria do you use when assigning tasks?

  How do you check on progress of tasks you have assigned team members?

- Education and training

  Tell me about the computer programs you have studied.

  How has your major in organizational communication prepared you for this position?

  If you were starting your college education over again, what would you do differently?

- Career paths and goals

  If you join us in June, where would you like to be in five years?

  How do you feel your career has gone since graduation three years ago?

  How do you think a position in sales will prepare you for future advancement in our organization?

- Performance

  What do you believe are the most important performance criteria for a broadcast reporter?

  All of us have pluses and minuses in our performance? What are some of your performance pluses?

  How do you evaluate your own performance?

- Salary and benefits

  What are your salary expectations?

  Which fringe benefits are most important to you?

  How would you rank salary among the criteria you are using to choose a position?

- Career field

  What do you think is the greatest challenge facing the auto industry today?

  What do you believe will be the next major breakthrough in solar energy?

  How do you feel about OSHA's requirements in the construction industry?

The trend is toward on-the-job questions.

On-the-Job Questions

A significant trend in recruiting interviews during the past several years has been an emphasis on **behavioral questions** that assess how applicants have performed or will perform in work-related situations.[36] Such **on-the-job** questions counter the predictable results of traditional questions for which applicants have carefully prepared answers and impression management tactics applicants are increasingly employing such as self-promotion (designed "to evoke attributions of competence") and ingratiation (designed "to evoke interpersonal liking and attraction"). Studies have shown such tactics are "positively related to interviewer evaluations."[37]

Behavior-based questions ask applicants about past experiences in which they have had to deal with situations closely related to the position they are seeking.

> Tell me about a stressful situation at work and how you handled it.
>
> Tell me about an idea you developed and implemented successfully primarily through your efforts.
>
> How did you handle a very difficult relationship with a team member?
>
> How did you resolve a particularly difficult disagreement with a supervisor?
>
> Describe a time when you managed to sell an unpopular management decision to fellow workers.
>
> Describe a setback you experienced in a class, sport, or job and how you handled it successfully.

In **critical incident** questions, recruiters choose incidents or problems that **are occurring** or **have occurred** within their organizations and ask applicants how they would handle or would have handled the incident or problem.

> We are experiencing a growing problem with absenteeism in the 4-12 shift. How would you recommend we deal with this problem?
>
> Like many big-box stores in sporting goods, we are losing sales to online operations. What would you suggest we do?
>
> Last year there was growing strife between our union and non-union personnel. If you had been with us, what solution would you have recommended?

In **hypothetical questions,** recruiters create highly realistic, job-related questions applicants may face during their careers and ask them to explain in detail how they would handle each.

> If an employee came to you with a complaint about sexual harassment, what would you do?
>
> If you suspect a worker is stealing electronic components from the company, how would you handle this?
>
> If a member of your team appears to be reporting data that is not supported by the research generated by other members of the team, what steps would you take?

In a **case approach**, recruiters craft realistic job-related situations that may take minutes or hours to resolve. Some develop simulations that may require role-playing and involve a number of people, including personnel from the organization and more than one applicant. Situations and simulations may address personal issues, working relationships, production problems, safety issues, or customer complaints. A case approach may be the most realistic on-the-job format, but it is time-consuming.

Distinguishing the Real from the Make-believe in Answers

Applicants are under considerable pressure during employment interviews to make the best possible impressions because their futures literally depend upon the outcomes of

13. How should a recruiter determine the type and amount of information to give an applicant?

14. How are closings likely to be different in screening and determinant interviews?

15. What five questions are critical in your postinterview evaluation of an applicant?"

Student Activities

1. Many recruiters believe that incentive is critical to a good hire. Contact your campus career center and ask permission to pose two questions to a dozen recruiters: What questions do you ask that pertain to incentive? How do you assess incentive from applicant credentials, applicant answers, and applicant questions?

2. Contact a number of recruiters from different career fields and ask them to discuss the pluses and minuses of hiring recent college graduates. Probe for specifics and illustrations (without names). What changes have they seen in recent college graduates compared to 10 years ago?

3. Contact a number of recruiters to see how many employ a behavior-, trait-, or talent-based approach to recruiting new employees. If they do not use or have abandoned one of these approaches, what are their reasons for doing so? What differences can you detect among the three approaches? How do recruiters using one or more of these approaches detect dishonest answers?

4. Do a Web-based search of sources on EEO laws and regulations and the recommendations these sources make to recruiters to ask lawful questions and to applicants for recognizing and replying to unlawful questions. What changes have affected employment interviews during the past five years? What are the most controversial and often violated EEO laws and regulations? Which state laws tend to be more stringent than federal laws?

Notes

1. Tom Peters, *Re-Imagine: Business Excellence in a Disruptive Age* (London: Dorling Kindersley, 2003), pp. 18 and 81.

2. George N. Root III, "Importance of Personal Interviews in a Selection Process." Updated September 26, 2017, https://bizfluent.com.info-8467501-importance-personal-interviews-selection-process.html, accessed March 8, 2019; Society for Human Resource Management, "Interviewing Candidates for Employment," https://www.shrn.org/resourcesandtools/tools-and-samples/toolkits/pages/interviewingcandidatesforemployment.aspx, accessed March 8, 2019; Gaurav Akrani, "Importance of Interview for Employers and Job Seekers," July 12, 2011, http://kalyan-city.blogspot.com/2011/07/importance-of-interview-for-employers.html?m=1, accessed March 8, 2019.

3. "Making an Employment Decision," *U.S. Equal Employment Opportunity Commission,* https://www.eeoc.gov/employers/smallbusiness/checklists/recruiting_hiring_promoting.cfm, accessed March 9, 2019.

4. "Prohibited Employment Policies and Practices," *U.S. Equal Employment Opportunity Commission*, https://www1.eeoc.gov//laws/practices/index.cfm?renderforprint+1, accessed March 9, 2019.

5. "Federal Laws Prohibiting Job Discrimination Questions and Answers," http://www.hum.wa.gov/FAQ/FAQEEO.html, accessed July 12, 2012.

6. "Overview," U.S. Employment Opportunity Commission, https://www.eeoc.gov/eeoc, accessed March 10, 2019.

7. Bill Roberts, "Make Better Hires with Behavioral Assessments," Society for Human Resource Management, https://www.shrm.org/hr-today/news/hr-magazine/pages/0414-predictive-analysis-hirinbg-aspx, accessed March 11, 2019.

8. "Behavior Interview Guide," National Institutes of Health, Equal Employment Opportunity Specialist, GS – 260," hr.od.gov/hrguidance/employment/interview/...260-intrerview.do..., accessed July 12, 2012.

9. "Behavioral Hiring Assessments," www.selectivehiring.com/behavioral-hiring-assessments, accessed March 11, 2019.

10. Patrice M. Buzzanell, "Employment Interviewing Research: Ways We Can Study Underrepresented Group Members' Experiences as Applicants," *Journal of Business Communication* 39 (2002), pp. 257–275; Patrice M. Buzzanell and Rebecca J. Meisenbach, "Gendered Performance and Communication in the Employment Interview," in *Gender and Communication at Work,* Mary Barrett and Marilyn J. Davidson, eds. (Hampshire, England: Ashgate Publishing, 2006), pp. 19–37.

11. Karen O'Keefe, "Five Secrets to Successful Interviewing and Hiring," http://www.writingassist.com, accessed September 14, 2006.

12. Adam Miller, "3 things millennials want in a career (hint: it's not more money)," fortune.com/2015/03/261/-3-things-millennials-want-in-a-career-hint-it's-not-more-money; Rob Asghar, "What Millennials Want In The Workplace (And Why You Should Start Giving It to Them)," www.forbes.com/sites/robasghar/2014/01/13/what-millennials-want-in-the-workplace-and-why-you-should-start-giving -it-to-them; Carol Phillips and Judy Hopelain, Summer 2015, "What Do Millennials Want in a Job? *Insights for Making Talent Brands Millennial-Relevant,*" www.slideshare.net/CarolPhillips/What-Do-Millennials-Want-in-a-Job. David Sturt and Todd Nordstrom, "Generational Differences: When They Matter, and When They Don't," August 16, 2016, https://www.forbes.com.sites/davidsturt/2016/08/16/generational-differences-when-they-matter-and-when -they-dont/#4874fa9d692d, accessed March 12, 2019.

13. Patrice M. Buzzanell, "Tensions and Burdens in Employment Interviewing Processes: Perspectives of Nondominant Group Applicants," *Journal of Business Communication* 36 (1999), pp. 134–162.

14. Matt Krumrie, "Should You Recruit at Job Fairs?," https://www.ziprecruiter.com/blog/should-you-recruit-at-job-fairs, accessed on March 13, 2019.

15. "Tips on choosing a Staffing Firm," http://www.american staffing.net, accessed December 19, 2015.

16. Heather O'Neill, "9 Free Resume Databases for Employers: Search for Quality Candidates," May 10, 2017, https://www.mightyrecruiter.com/blog/9-free-resume-databases-for-employers-search-for-quality-candidates, accessed March 13, 2019.

17. Joyce Gioia, "Special Report: Changing the Face(s) in Your Recruiting Efforts," Workforce Stability Institute, http://www.employee.org/article_changing_the_face.html, accessed September 14, 2006.

18. Fredric M. Jablin and Vernon D. Miller, "Interviewer and Applicant Questioning Behavior in Employment Interviews," *Management Communication Quarterly* 4 (1990), pp. 51–86.

19. Susan M. Heathfield, "5 Resume Red Flags for Employers," http://humanresources.about.com/od/hire-employees/tp/resume-red-flags-for-employers.html, accessed July 13, 2012; M. Susan Heathfield, "5 More Resume Red Flags for Employers," http://human resources.about.com/od/hire-employees/tp/five-more-resume-red-flags.html, accessed July 13, 2012.

20. Resume Falsification Statistics," www.statisticbrain.com/resume-falsification-statistics, accessed December 30, 2015. Monica Torres, "Nearly Half of Us Are Lying on Our Resumes, Survey Finds," https://www.theladders.com/career-advice/nearly half-of-us-are-lying-on-our-resumes-survey-finds, accessed March 14, 2019.

21. J.T. O'Donnell, "85 Percent of Job Applicants Lie on Resumes: Here's How to Spot a Dishonest Candidate," INC, https://www.com/jt-odonnell.staggering-85-of-job-applicants-lying-on-resumes-html, accessed March 14, 20119; Megan Elliott, "Lying on Your Resume? Here's How You Will Get Caught," November 19, 2018, https://www.glassdoor.com/blog/lying-on-your-resume, accessed March 14, 2019.

22. "Top Applicant Tracking Software Products," www.capterra.com/applicant-tracking-software, accessed December 30, 2015. Jon Shields, "8 Things You Need to Know About Applicant Tracking Systems," August 30, 2018, https://www.jobscan.co/blog/8-things-you-need-to-know-about-applicant-ytacking-systems, accessed March 15, 2019.

23. Michael G. Aamodt, "Are Letters of Recommendation Worth the Effort?," *Psychology Today,* Posted February 22, 2012.

24. "Screening by Means of Pre-Employment Testing," Society for Human Resource Management, September 10, 2018, https://www.shrm.org/resourcesandtools/tools-and-samples/toolkits/pages/screeningbymeansofpreemploymenttesting-aspx, accessed March 18, 2019.

25. "What Are Pre-Employment Tests?," https://www.criteriacorp.com/resources/defnitive_guide_what_are_preemployment_tests.php, accessed March 18, 2019.

26. Wayne J. Camara, "Employee Honesty Testing: Traps and Opportunities," *Boardroom Reports,* December 15, 1991; David J. Cherrington and J. Owen Charrington," "The Reliability and Validity of Honesty Testing," www.creativeorgdesign.com, accessed December 31, 2015.

27. Robert Osborne, "Integrity Interviewing," *The Risk Management Blog,* July 29, 2014, https://blog.lowersrisk.com/integrity-interviewing, accessed March 19, 2019.

28. Donna R. Pawlowski and John Hollwitz, "Work Values, Cognitive Strategies, and Applicant Reactions in a Structured Pre-Employment Interview for Ethical Integrity," *The Journal of Business Communication* 37 (2000), pp. 58–75.

29. Osborne, "Integrity Interviewing."

30. Jonathan A. Segal, "LEGAL TRENDS Social Media Use in Hiring: Assessing the risks," Society for Human Resource Management, https://www.shrm.org/hr-today/news/hr-magazine/pages/0914-social-media-hiring.aspx; Taryn Barnes, "Screening Applicants Via Social Media Yea or Nay," https://www.applicantpro.com/articles/screening-applicants-via-social-media-yea-nay, accessed March 19, 2019.

31. Brian Libby, "How to Conduct a Job Interview," http://www.cbsnews.com/8301-505125_162-5105294/how-to-conduct-a-job-interview, accessed July 9, 2012.

32. Segal, "LEGAL TRENDS Social Media Use in Hiring," p. 2.

33. Buhler.

34. Choon-Hwa Lim, Richard Winter, and Christopher C.A. Chan, "Cross-Cultural Interviewing in the Hiring Process: Challenges and Strategies," *The Career Development Quarterly* 54 (March 2006), p. 267.

35. "Structured Interviews: A Practical Guide," U.S. Office of Personnel Management, September 2008.

36. "A Guide to Conducting Behavioral Interviews with Early Career Job Candidates," Society for Human Resource Management, 2016.

37. Aleksander P. J. Ellis, Bradley J. West, Ann Marie Ryan, and Richard P. DeShon, "The Use of Impression Management Tactics in Structured Interviews: A Function of Question Type," *Journal of Applied Psychology* 87 (2002), pp. 1200–1208.

38. Jim Kennedy, "What to Do When Job Applicants Tell . . . Tales of Invented Lives," *Training*, October 1999, pp. 110–114.

Resources

Davidson, Marilyn J. and Mary Barrett. *Gender and Communication at Work*. London: Gower Publishing, 2012.

Knight, Rebecca. How to Conduct an Effective Job Interview. *Harvard Business Review*, January 23, 2015.

Lynn, Adele. *The EQ Interview*. New York: AMACOM, 2008.

Powell, Larry, and Jonathan H. Amsbary. *Interviewing: Situations and Contexts*. Boston, MA: Pearson Education, 2005.

Yeung, Rob. *Successful Interviewing and Recruitment*. London, England: Kogan Page, 2008.

CHAPTER 8

The Employment Interview

The ideal position you are seeking is out there, but competition may be stiff and employers may have many qualified applicants from which to choose. There are no simple formulas, foolproof answers, magic acts, or shortcuts to success, only hard work. As Lois Einhorn has written, "Getting a job is a job in itself."[1] Approach each search systematically and analytically, recognizing that each will be unique in important ways.

The objectives of this chapter are to prepare you for the stages inherent in the search process. Start by developing a personal brand after an insightful and thorough self-analysis and then proceed to doing preliminary research, conducting the job search, studying prospective employers, presenting yourself to the employer, creating a favorable first impression, answering questions, asking questions, closing the interview, evaluating the interview, and dealing with offers and rejections. Begin by developing a personal brand.

Developing a Personal Brand

> You must market yourself.

It may sound crass to address the employment interview as a sales interview, but that is precisely what it is. **You** are the **product** you are **selling** and the recruiter's organization is the **buyer.** You cannot sell your product unless you know precisely **what** you are selling, to **whom,** and **why.** Recruiters want to discover through your credentials and interviews **who** you are, **what** you have **done,** what you are **most interested** in doing, and **contributions** you can make if hired. Create a **personal brand** that convinces an organization **you** are the **best fit** for the position they seek to fill and their organizational needs, plans, and culture.

Conducting a Self-Analysis

> You can't sell you to me if you don't know you.

The first step is to conduct a thorough self-analysis to discover exactly who you are and what you want in a position. Start with a checklist such as the following to probe deeply and honestly into your personality traits, strengths and weaknesses, accomplishments and failures, likes and dislikes, desires and needs. Your self-analysis may be painful at times, but your personal and professional futures depend upon it.

- What are my *personality traits?*

  _____ Able to work under pressure   _____ Flexible

  _____ Adaptive   _____ Motivated

  _____ Agreeable   _____ Open to criticism

  _____ Assertive   _____ Open-minded

  _____ Conscientious   _____ Willing to take risks

- How *trustworthy* am I?

  _____ Dependable   _____ Loyal

  _____ Disciplined   _____ Reliable

  _____ Ethical   _____ Self-controlled

  _____ Even tempered   _____ Sincere

  _____ Fair   _____ Tolerant

  _____ Honest

- What are my *intellectual* strengths and weaknesses?

  _____ Analytic   _____ Organized

  _____ Creative   _____ Planner

  _____ Critical thinking   _____ Open to learning

  _____ Intelligent   _____ Rational

> Be totally honest with yourself.

- What are my *communicative* strengths and weaknesses?

  _____ Interpersonal   _____ With diverse people

  _____ Public   _____ With peers

  _____ Listening   _____ With subordinates

  _____ Written communication   _____ With superiors

- What are my *accomplishments* and *failures?*

  _____ Academic   _____ Professional

  _____ Extracurricular   _____ Work

  _____ Goals set and met   _____ Social

- What are my *professional* strengths and weaknesses?

  _____ Experiences   _____ Informal education

  _____ Formal education   _____ Training

- What are the strengths and weaknesses of my *skill set?*

  _____ Leadership   _____ Teamwork

  _____ Computers   _____ Social media

  _____ Foreign languages   _____ Technology

  _____ Problem solving

- What are my *professional* interests?

  _____ Advancement   _____ Long-range goals

  _____ Growth   _____ Short-range goals

- Do I have a *realistic perception* of my field?

  _____ Areas of specialization   _____ Essential education/training

  _____ Challenges   _____ Essential experiences

  _____ Current problems/changes   _____ Future problems

  _____ Developments   _____ History

  _____ Employment opportunities   _____ Trends

- What do I **want in a position?**

  _____ Authority   _____ Responsibility

  _____ Benefits   _____ Salary

  _____ Contact with people   _____ Security

  _____ Decision making   _____ Type of work

  _____ Independence   _____ Variety

  _____ Prestige

- What are my *most valued needs?*

  _____ Feeling of success/accomplishment   _____ Possessions

  _____ Free time   _____ Recognition

  _____ Geographical location   _____ Recreational opportunities

  _____ Home and family   _____ Respect

  _____ Income

Creating a Personal Brand

Once you have completed your self-analysis, create a personal brand that **sets you apart** from other applicants and makes you **attractive** to prospective employers.[2] Your brand should emphasize your talents, expertise, accomplishments, experiences, education, and training that makes you **unique** when compared to the dozens or hundreds of other applicants and graduates seeking similar positions or the position you are targeting. What makes you **special?** Your brand should express and demonstrate a passion for your career and this position. Dwell on your strengths, qualities, experiences, education, and skill sets that give you an edge. Identify long-range and short-range career goals that fit this organization and position. Show a genuine interest in the people and world around you.

> Your brand reveals what makes you unique.

Create a branding statement—an attractive catch phrase—rather than merely stating a career goal.[3] Make it concise, no more than two sentences long. It is easier for an applicant with years in the field and clear professional accomplishments to develop a simple but attention-getting statement. It is more difficult for applicants who are completing or have just completed a college degree or specialized training that is nearly identical throughout the country. Focus on what sets you apart. Merely claiming that you are

> You must be what you claim to be.

highly motivated, enthusiastic, dynamic, and trustworthy means little unless you can back the claims with experiences, activities, and achievements. For instance, were you on an award-winning marketing team? Did you study abroad in a country in which the organization is active and speak the language fluently? Did you have unique internships in your field? Did you volunteer at a crisis center, read with children at a local school, or raise money to help victims of a tornado? Did you earn a certificate in entrepreneurship and innovation from your university? Check the Internet for sample branding statements, and use your network to get suggestions. Ultimately, the statement must be adapted to you and employers you want to attract. Are you comfortable with it? If you feel superlatives come across as being boastful or egotistical rather than a good fit, exclude them. Remember, interviewers ultimately determine if your claims and words match your record. Your statement must not lead interviewers to expect more than your record warrants.

Doing Research

Research the field in which you are interested and qualified, positions available and locations, current events, and the interview process. A great many interview questions focus on these areas, and thorough research prepares you for the diverse interviews you will encounter and sets you apart from other applicants.

Your Field

> What excites you about this field?

Learn everything you can about the past, present, and future of your field. How have products and services changed? How have some organizations survived and adapted to revolutionary changes as a result of new technologies, demands of ever-changing generations, and the global economy while others have failed? Contact persons who have witnessed these changes and have insights into the future. Recruiters expect you to know why you are interested in a specific field and to have a positive attitude toward this field. Which career opportunities are available and interest you most in your chosen field? Published and Internet resources on fields ranging from acting and advertising to visual arts and writing can be highly informative. These include: *Careers.org, CareerOne-Stop, Campus Explorer, AOL. Jobs, Peterson's Job Opportunities, Occupational Outlook Handbook, WetFeet.com, and Vault.com.*

Positions and Locations

> Have a realistic conception of what working in your field entails.

Discover the types of positions available in your field. How are positions changing now and likely to change in the future? What are the typical hourly or annual salaries and how are they affected by size of organization and location? Which positions require advanced degrees, specialized training, or prior experience? Which organizations help employees with the cost of additional degrees and training? Do you have an insightful and mature understanding of everyday lives and typical workdays in various positions? How qualified are you for positions of interest? Have you taken advantage of internships, cooperatives, study abroad, volunteer activities, part-time positions, observational visits, or shadowing members of the profession to gain unique insights into the work world you wish to join?

> How important is location in your life?

Discover where positions are located. Do you have preferences such as close to family, in the south, in large or small cities, in areas with mountains or beaches, or near top quality graduate programs in your field? If you are interested in working in other countries, what positions might be available in locations you desire or where English is the official language or very common in day-to-day encounters? Realize that you might have to go where the jobs are and adjust. It is common for people to take positions reluctantly with plans to move within a few years only to remain in this location for decades, often because they have come to love the organization, area, or city.

Current Events

> Know what is happening in the world around you.

Be aware of what is going on in the world, not just on your campus or in your city but in the country and beyond. Recruiters expect mature applicants to keep themselves informed and to develop intelligent, rational positions on important issues such as immigration, climate change, abortion, voting rights, safety in schools and the workplace, and vaccinations. Be informed of trends, changes, developments, accidents, research findings, and mergers that are affecting your chosen field, career path, and organizations you find attractive. If you are interested in working in another country, be aware of the country's relations with the United States, cultural differences, policies affecting noncitizen workers, and cost of living. To keep abreast of current events, read a good newspaper such as *The New York Times* or *The Wall Street Journal* and a good news magazine such as *Time, Business Week,* or *Fortune.* Watch network news programs on NBC, CBS, and ABC or cable networks such as CNN, FOX, and CNBC. Be conscious of potential bias of coverage in some political, social, cultural, and religious coverage of issues, events, organizations, and persons.

The Interview Process

> Expect different insights in answers to your questions.

Learn everything you can about typical interview practices and expectations in your field so you can adapt to these while lessening the impact of surprises and avoiding mistakes. Start by reviewing Chapter 7 on the recruiting interview. Talk to recent graduates or peers in your field who have been through the recruiting process recently and professors who are actively involved and have connections with employers. These along with the Internet and social media will provide insights into questions such as What is the best way to prepare for interviews? How important is appearance? What types of questions are interviewers likely to ask? What answers are interviewers looking for? What kinds of information do interviewers provide? What questions should I ask and avoid? How do so-called "plant trips" differ from screening interviews on campus or at job fairs? You will receive a wide variety of answers because interviewers, even from the same organization, have differing techniques and strategies and disagree on which answers are best. Students often asked the author to bring a recruiter to class to "show how it's done," and he replied that he could fill up the classroom with recruiters and there would still be differences in opinions and practices. Be suspicious of sources who claim to offer "winning answers" to frequently asked questions or simple formulas for success.

Research into the interviewing process will produce surprising results. For instance, some studies reveal that 50 percent of "speech acts" during interviews are declarative statements rather than questions and answers. Most interviewers have had no training in conducting job interviews, and a significant number do not give applicants an opportunity to ask questions. Interviewers are increasingly viewing the interview as a "work sample" and employ behavioral and trait-based, critical incident, and hypothetical questions to determine if applicants can do the job, will do the job, and will fit into their organization. A quick check of the Internet reveals there is not a shortage of jobs in the United States but a growing shortage of qualified applicants.[4]

Conducting the Search

Begin your search for a position by employing every available resource to locate openings that match your interests and qualifications.

Networking

> Networking is often the key to finding the position you want.

Do not overlook one of the oldest and most effective resources for finding the position you desire—**networking.** Surveys estimate that from 70 to 85 percent of open positions are filled through networking.[5] Networking is forming connections with people who know you, will attest to your qualifications, and connect you with people who do not know you but can help in your job search. Personal interactions and relationships continue to surpass written and electronic contacts and enable you to access the estimated 80 percent of jobs that are never listed but are filled internally and through networking.

So how do you go about networking? Start by creating a **networking tree** with you as the trunk and **major limbs** that include people you know well: relatives, friends, neighbors, professors, co-workers, and people from your past such as former employers, supervisors, and roommates. **Smaller limbs** include acquaintances from schools, the military, volunteer activities, churches, temples, and synagogues, social groups, professional organizations, fitness centers, and sports. **Branches** include persons you do not know personally such as relatives, friends, and associates of your personal contacts, a former roommate's spouse or parent, a physician's neighbor, or a friend's employer or supervisor. Make note of each contact's telephone number, mailing address, and e-mail address so you can contact them early and often.

> Use, maintain, update, and keep your network informed.

Contact each source in your network tree personally and explain your situation by focusing on your career choice, specific type or types of positions in which you are most interested, preferred locations, qualifications, and experiences that make you a particularly strong candidate. Do not merely tell a contact you are interested in sales, the media, marketing, or construction. Be as precise as possible so the person can match you with a specific position.

If a contact in your network has no leads for you, ask for names who might know of relevant opportunities. As your search progresses, add persons to your network tree while pruning those who have not provided assistance or contacts. When you get a lead, write down the lead's full name, position, organization, and telephone numbers under the contact's name so you know who suggested the lead and ask if you can use the contact's name. The *who* may be a major factor in a lead's interest in helping you.

Use your network not only to seek advice in locating open positions but also the best ways to contact sources, gather information about sources, and discover how sources might help in your job search. Ask for advice on how to construct, modify, and adapt your resumes and cover letters to specific positions and organizations. Seek tips on how best to prepare for interviews in your field. Keep in touch with your contacts. Let them know what you are doing, interviews you will have and have had, and progress you are making. Prepare them for contacts they may be getting from potential employers. Inform your network when you receive an offer, reject an offer, or accept an offer. Always send thank you notes for any assistance you receive.

Web Sites, Classified Ads, and Newsletters

Overlook no source.

Every organization has a Web site, and each is likely to include a section on careers and positions they wish to fill. Identify organizations for which you would like to work to see if you are a good fit. Check classified ads in local, regional, and national newspapers. These ads attract candidates and satisfy the EEOC test of making openings known to all who might be interested and qualified. Join professional organizations to show you are a professional and to keep abreast of what is happening in your field. Take advantage of newsletters organizations send out in print and online. Some have job listings in your field.

Social Media

Use social media professionally because employers may be looking.

Use social media such as LinkedIn, Facebook, and Twitter to create and post profiles and keep your network apprised of your search progress, reconnect with people from your past, reach out to people who do not know you personally but may help you, and become visible to potential employers.[6] You can post professional headlines such as "media consultant," "online teacher," and "construction manager" on LinkedIn or take part in career field chat rooms on twitter to broadcast your areas of expertise that attract potential employers, result in contacts, and lead to interviews. Expand and enhance your online presence by creating your own Web site, blog, video postings, and media updates to advertise your brand and enable employers to find you.

Barbara Stefani, owner of Career Savers, writes that "over 90 percent of recruiters perform Internet searches on candidates before making a hiring decision, and over half of employers solidify their decision to hire based on a strong online presence."[7] On one hand, social media can demonstrate your social media capabilities, skills, professionalism, values, maturity, and good judgment. On the other hand, more than 50 percent of employers report they have found content on social media that led them to reject applicants, some after making initial offers. Remember the brand you have crafted so carefully. Be as careful with punctuation, grammar, spelling, word selection, and content in social media as you are in cover letters and resumes. Never use profanity; brag about drinking excessively, breaking the law, or having sexual exploits; or post pictures that show you posing in a sexually explicit manner, acting goofy, or looking "wasted" at a party.

ON THE WEB

Select a position you will be interested in when you complete your education or training. Search at least three Internet resources to discover the availability of such positions, geographical areas in which they are located, organizations that are seeking to fill them, and the nature of the positions being offered. Check resources such as Job Hunt (http://www.job-hunt.org), CareerBuilder Center (http://www.careerbuilder.com), and MonsterTrak (http://www.monstertrak.com). After collecting this information, develop a list of interview questions to which you would need answers before making a decision to accept one of these positions.

Career Centers and Employment Agencies

Colleges and universities operate career centers that are available to their students and alumni. Use your center to determine which careers are best suited to your interests, education, and experiences and review its wealth of materials about organizations and guidelines for doing online research. Counselors can help you develop resumes appropriate for your career interests and qualifications and assist you in writing effective cover letters. Your center may provide contacts for interviews, many of which will take place on your campus, to eliminate travel expenses and time. If you are an alumnus interested in changing positions or careers, trained counselors at your career center can help you determine future directions.

> Your campus center is a goldmine.

Employment or placement agencies, often referred to as head hunters, can help you locate positions and arrange interviews. Some agencies specialize in career fields such as health care, teaching, management, communication, engineering, and government positions.[8] When you sign up with an agency, it "becomes your advocate and 'represents you'—a relationship that starts whenever you apply for a job through" it and by "listing and submitting your resume."[9] An employment agency may perform tasks similar to those provided in college career centers with one important exception. As "head hunters," they actively seek positions for you and arrange interviews, sometimes even conducting them.

> If it sounds too good to be true, it probably is.

Percentage agencies will place you for a fee, often a percentage of your first year's salary, payable upon assuming a position they helped you obtain. Most agencies advertise **fee-paid positions,** which means an organization has retained them on a fee basis to locate quality applicants. You pay nothing. If you use a percentage agency, expect to pay a registration fee to process your credentials. Most agencies are ethical, but be cautious. If they want a great deal of money in advance to process your resume or make claims of placing nearly all of their applicants in high-paying positions, go elsewhere. Beware of agencies that want to produce expensive videotapes and other expensive credentials.

The Career/Job Fair

> Know how to make the most of job fairs.

Attend career or job fairs held on your campus, local malls, or civic centers because they bring a variety of employers to one convenient location. If there are no job fairs in your area, Web sites will help you locate ones around the country, including virtual job fairs you can attend online. Fairs give you opportunities to network, meet representatives personally, and have face-to-face interviews. Some fairs are specialized according to industry (aircraft, construction, electronics), field of study (engineering, agriculture, liberal arts, medicine), government agency (FBI, Homeland Security, foreign service, transportation), or specific groups (veterans, disabled, recently laid off due to plant closings). Be prepared for professional encounters by knowing your strong points, career goals, where you would like to be in five years, what you are looking for in a position, and who you would like to talk to. Dress professionally if you expect to have interviews or in your better student attire if merely browsing. Be attractive and neat. Always have copies of your resume(s) with you.

Scout the terrain when you arrive to see who is there and with whom you most want to interact. Are representatives setting up interviews as well as handing out information and answering questions? Gather printed materials, listen, and observe interactions as you walk about or wait your turn to talk to a representative. For which positions are you most qualified? Does an organization have positions open or is it attending for public relations purposes and future openings?

When you come face-to-face with a representative who may also be a recruiter, be aware that this person is sizing you up just as you are sizing up the organization and its representative. Appearance, friendliness, communication skills, and professionalism are top priority for both parties. Stay calm but also show enthusiasm and assertiveness. The worst question you can ask is, "What are you hiring for?" and the worst answer you can give to a counter-question such as "What are **you** looking for?" is "A job." This may seem cute, but it is an immediate turnoff.

■ *Appearance, friendliness, and communication skills are keys to successful contacts.*

Vince Talotta/Toronto Star/Getty Images

Knocking on Doors

Do not hesitate to knock on doors. Organizations are always on the lookout for talent but may not have a specific position open at the moment. When a door opens, state clearly the nature of the position you are seeking and how you are uniquely qualified and capable of contributing immediately to this organization's needs, plans, products, or services. It may be unable to offer you a position at this time, but it might keep you in mind for when it can. The person you are talking to may identify openings in your field or recommend you to a friend. This person becomes part of your network. Be persistent. Nearly every employer has a story about a person who kept coming to the office time after time until finally the employer, impressed with the person's persistence and qualifications, created an opening to use this person's tenacity and abilities.

> Knocking on doors works.

Doing Your Homework

At this stage, your search moves into high gear with direct contacts with prospective employers and arranging interviews. Do your homework that focuses on each position with each organization.

The Position

> Are you a good fit for this position?

Learn everything you can about the position for which you are interviewing. Review the job description word-for-word to determine how well you **fit** specified requirements, including education, training, experiences, skills, responsibilities, advancement possibilities, required travel, location, commuting time, and starting date. You need not be a **perfect fit,** but you must be close enough for serious consideration. If the description lists three to five years of experience and you have a little over a year with an outstanding record, try for it. If you have a two-year degree in software engineering technology and the job listing specifies a bachelor's degree in software engineering, check it further. On the other hand, if the job description specifies a degree in finance and your degree is in history, do not waste your or the recruiter's time. If you have no intention of moving to Phoenix from Virginia because of geographic preference or family connections, do not pursue it further unless, perhaps, the organization has current or planned locations on the east coast. If you cannot imagine yourself doing this job on a daily basis, look elsewhere. A thorough understanding of the position also prepares you to answer and ask questions more effectively during interviews.

The Organization

Learn everything you can about the organization that has this opening. A common question is "What do you know about us?" A poor answer may end your chance of further consideration because it shows little interest in the organization or willingness to do your homework. Virtually every organization has a Web site that contains a wealth of information. For example, if you are interviewing for a position with Subaru of North America, click on its official global site to learn about its history, parent organization, location, models, new developments, commitment to quality and the environment, news and events, awards, standing in its field, people, community activities, mission, values, and vision.

> Are you a good fit for this organization's activities, mission, and culture?

For information not available on Web sites or to verify what is posted on an official Web site, contact current and former employees, people who have used the organizations products or services, clients, professors, friends, and relatives. They may be good sources on what day-to-day life is like in the automotive industry in general and Subaru in particular. Check the Internet, newspapers, trade journals, and your campus library for resources such as *American Business Disc, Dun's Electronic Business Directory, Hoovers: Your Fastest Path to Business Information, Standard and Poor's Corporate Records, and Thomas Register of American Manufacturers.*

The Recruiter

You may become aware of the personal identity of the recruiter who will be interviewing you. Many recruiters have come to your campus for years while others routinely conduct interviews in their positions as department or division heads, leader of recruiting teams, and reputation for selecting outstanding employees. It helps to know and understand the person with whom you will interact face-to-face. Learn everything you can about the person's position with the organization and professional background, memberships, and accomplishments.

> Knowing the recruiter may tell what to expect in an interview and how best to prepare.

Information on the recruiter may be available in social media. Talk to friends and acquaintances, alumni of your college, professors, associates, and career center personnel who can provide insights into the recruiter as a person and interviewer. Does the interviewer have a sense of humor, relaxed or formal manner, structured or flexible approach, understanding or judgmental personality? What about questioning techniques such as behavior or trait-based questions, occasional leading or loaded questions, and simple role-playing activities? What kinds of information does the interviewer provide, and does the interviewer reserve adequate time for you to ask questions? If you know, for instance, that an interviewer prefers crisp, to-the-point answers, avoid rambling, lengthy answers, or fishing expeditions.

Presenting Yourself to the Employer

Now you are ready to present yourself to the recruiter and organization, and the first significant contact is the submission of credentials, including resume, cover letter, and portfolio. Be sure each is flawless, matches your branding, and is carefully adapted to the employer's needs and desires.

Resume

Developing the **perfect resume** commands so much attention that you may come to believe it has magical powers to launch and advance your career. The resume's primary purpose, however, is to assist you in getting an initial interview that may lead to additional interviews and eventually an offer of employment. Notice the "perfect resume" is singular, but you will almost certainly need several versions of your resume to match different positions with different organizations. Customize your resume to match the specifics of each job announcement and the nature of the organization posting it.

Your resume is your *silent sales representative* and may be the first opportunity a prospective employer has to *see* you. Most recruiters will spend only seconds scanning the resume you send them, so it must gain and sustain a positive impression, one that will motivate them to read further. Think like the recruiter. If your resume was sent to you, would you read further and consider inviting you for an interview?

Segments of Resumes

> Make it easy for interviewers to locate you.

Countless Web sites and publications claim to offer "award-winning resumes" or "the perfect resume." Richard Bolles, author of the famous book entitled *What Color Is Your Parachute?,* updated annually, claims he collects such resumes and shows them to his employer friends. Inevitably they declare that each award-winning and perfect resume would never get a job for anyone.[10] With such diverse preferences in mind, we will offer guidelines that fit most hiring situations while emphasizing the necessity of developing **targeted resumes** for specific openings at specific organizations.

Contact Information: Place your *full name* at the top center of the page in larger font than the remainder of the resume and in bold print. Avoid nicknames. Provide one or two mailing addresses with ZIP codes and the e-mail address you access most often. Provide a landline telephone number and a cell phone number with area codes. Make it easy for a recruiter to reach you quickly. Do not place silly, immature material on your answering machine. If you provide a campus telephone number, place a date when it may no longer be operable. List a business telephone number only if it is appropriate for prospective employers to use.

> Make your career focus other-directed.

Since recruiters typically spend only seconds scanning your resume, stating your career objective (sometimes referred to as your profile, professional background, or simply as objective) is an ideal place to catch and maintain the recruiter's attention. Employ the branding you have refined and focus your objective on what the **employer wants,** not what you want. Make it other-directed rather than self-directed. Make your objective brief with key words included in the announcements for this position.

Avoid "puffery," words that sound impressive and mean nothing and clichés such as "I'm a team player," "I have great communication skills," "I'm a problem solver," "I am highly motivated," and "I give 110 percent." Puffery and clichés will send your resume to the rejection pile. The remainder of your resume must live up to your claims and branding in your career focus.

> Your educational record is most important for your first position.

Education and Training: If you are in the process of completing your education and training or recently did so and your work experiences are minimal or unrelated to the position, your educational record should come next. Indicate specifically how your education and training are *a fit* for the position you are seeking in this organization. List your degrees or training **in reverse chronological order** so the employer can detect quickly what you are *doing* *now* or have recently completed. List degree, diploma, certificate or license, date of graduation or completion, school, location of the school if it shares the same name with others (such as Loyola University in Chicago, Baltimore, and New Orleans and Indiana University in Indiana and Pennsylvania) or has multiple campuses. If you are short on experiences, provide a **selective** list of courses that are **relevant** to the opening. Do not use abbreviations for courses, majors, or degrees because a recruiter may not know if Eng. refers to English or engineering. List your grade point average (GPA) if it is a B or better, and indicate the numerical system used at your college, for example: 3.35 (4.0 scale) or 3.35/4.0.

Job-Related Experiences: The next resume segment presents your experiences relevant to this position with this organization. If you are young and just completing your education and training, you may have had limited work or salaried positions in your field, but you should have relevant experiences you can showcase. These may be co-op programs through your university, internships (paid and unpaid), research or teaching assistantships, and volunteer activities. If for instance you are seeking a position in building construction, having experience in building a Habitat for Humanity home or a program to rehabilitate homes for the poor and elderly can be impressive. Recruiters tend to rate leadership roles in student organizations and volunteer community service as very important or above average in importance. Show you are a **doer** by highlighting such leadership roles in your resume.

Activities: The next section after experiences, lists activities and organizational memberships, including college, professional, and community activities and groups. Be selective and continually update your resumes. High school activities are excluded for college graduates, and college organizations and activities are excluded once you have an established record in your career. Employers are interested in *doers* rather than *joiners,* so a long list of organizations minus leadership roles may give a negative impression. Include honorary organizations, professional, and pre-professional organizations in your field (such as the Public Relations Student Society of America). Provide brief descriptions of any organization likely to be unfamiliar to an employer.

Volunteer Experiences: If you have significant volunteer experiences that may not be directly related to a position but reveal important information about you, list them as a segment in your resume. Employers are becoming increasingly interested in applicants who have shown interest in community involvement and are likely to become involved in their communities if hired.

Do not list references because employers know you will provide references if needed. Exclude personal information (ethnicity, age, marital status, parental status, health or disabilities, height, and weight), a photo, and political, religious, and ethnic memberships and activities that may pose EEOC problems for employers. You do not break laws if you do so, but you are providing information that is not a bona fide occupational qualification (BFOQ).

Types of Resumes

There are basically two types of resumes, chronological and functional. If you are developing a **chronological format,** the most common resume, list your experiences (including internships, co-op arrangements, assistantships, unpaid positions, organizational activities) in *reverse* chronological order so the employer can see quickly what you have done most recently. See Figure 8.1 for a sample of chronological resume. List organization,

> Emphasize your job-related experiences.

> Recruiters look for leaders.

> Provide relevant information.

Figure 8.1   *Chronological resume*

Nancy A. Williams
1214 Oak Drive
Decatur, IL 62521
(217)226-3499/(217)413-2679
nawilliams@hotmail.com

Objective: A position as a family case manager with a child services agency that would allow me to use my skills and experiences to work effectively with families and children in need of services.

Education: **University of Illinois at Urbana-Champaign**
Bachelor of Science in Social Work, May 2020
Minor in Social Psychology
GPA: 3.25/4.0 overall and 3.6/4.0 in major

Experience: Court Appointed Special Advocate for children (CASA)
September 2018 to June 2020
Champaign County, Illinois

- Acted as Educational Surrogate Parent for children.
- Worked with DCS Family Case Managers.
- Counseled parents on following court orders.
- Consulted with school and psychological counselors.
- Wrote reports for Juvenile Court hearings.

Volunteer at the Crisis Center for Women
June 2017 to August 2018
Urbana, Illinois

- Registered women who came to the shelter.
- Coordinated activities for the children.
- Assisted in maintaining security.

Volunteer at Bar Q Ranch
Summers 2013, 2014, 2015
Paris, Illinois

- Worked with special needs children.
- Assisted with orientation sessions.
- Guided children in riding activities.

Activities: Secretary/Treasurer of the Social Work Student Association
2018-2019

title of your position or positions, dates, and what you did in each position. Emphasize the skills and experiences most relevant for this opening. Recruiters are most interested in applicant achievements and accomplishments. A chronological resume is easy to write and organize, emphasizes relevant experiences and skills, and is easy for employers to scan quickly.

If you are developing a **functional format,** most appropriate for creative positions and those in which writing is important, place your experiences under headings that highlight your qualifications for the position (see Figure 8.2). Typical headings are management, sales, advertising, training, counseling, team building, organizational development, recruiting, finance, teaching, administration, supervision, project manager, and marketing. Include a variety of experiences from different positions, internships, and organizations under each heading. This is important when you have had few paying positions or ones directly related to the opening. Your outside activities indicate motivation, communication skills, ability to work with people, work ethic, ability to lead, and that you are not a narrow specialist.

Select the
resume format
best suited
to you.

A functional format focuses attention on relevant skills to match the ideal applicant profile. It does not repeat the same skills and experiences under different positions, so it can be tighter and shorter. Some employers do not like functional resumes because they often do not identify dates for education, training, and work experiences, so they cannot detect gaps in employment.

You are not confined to chronological and functional resume formats. If neither seems ideal for you, consider blending the two so the end result presents a clearer and more effective picture of you to potential employers.

Guidelines for Resumes

Regardless of the resume type you select, follow these guidelines to make them precise, informative, and persuasive.

Dishonesty is a
candidate killer.

Be absolutely honest in every detail. In recent studies, 85 percent of employers reported they had caught applicants lying on their resumes and nearly 50 percent of employees said they knew someone who had lied on a resume. One CEO referred to lying as an "epidemic."[11] Some of the most common lies applicants include on resumes pertain to experiences, colleges attended, coursework, graduation indexes, degrees, technical abilities, foreign language fluency, awards, employment dates, employment duties and positions, volunteer work, and reasons for leaving positions. Employers check credentials, access social media, and contact references, so it is not that difficult to catch liars. For instance, do dates and details match, do experiences sound too good to be true, do job titles appear unrealistic for the applicant's age and background? If you make it to an interview, the employer may use behavioral questions to delve into your experiences and assess language fluency and computer skills. Career sources warn applicants that getting caught lying may be "career sabotage" because it trashes your chance of getting hired and damages your reputation.[12]

Select every
claim and
phrase as if
your career
depended
upon it.

Select every word carefully. Choose words and phrases carefully because each may have positive or negative consequences with employers. They may see the following as meaningless puffery: gives 110 percent, has a proven track record, is hardworking,

Figure 8.2 *Functional resume*

Steven C. Akerman

1914 Lakeland Avenue
Kent, OH 44243
(330)327-1212/(330)147-1324
scakerman@gmail.com

Objective: A position as a public relations and fundraising manager with a liberal arts college that would allow me to employ my inter-personal, writing, and speaking skills to work effectively with faculty, staff, students, and alumni.

Education: Kent State University
Bachelor of Science in Public Relations, December 2020
Minor in Journalism
GPA 3.00/4.00 overall and 3.4/4.0 in major

Experience: **Writing**
- Reports for public relations clients
- Drafts of speeches for fundraising events and reports
- Press releases

Communicating
- With supervisors
- With Team members
- With clients
- With the public

Organizing
- Developing teams
- Special events
- Fundraising campaigns

Managing
- Campaigns
- Crisis situations
- Budgets

Activities: Vice-President of the Public Relations Student Society of America goal-oriented, well-organized, responsible, and ambitious.[13] Employers prefer action verbs such as the following that you can substantiate to show you are a **doer.**

administered	facilitated	oversaw
advised	fashioned	performed
arbitrated	formulated	persuaded
arranged	founded	planned
built	generated	recommended
budgeted	improved	reconfigured
coached	increased	researched
consulted	instructed	sold
counseled	led	solved
created	maintained	supervised
designed	managed	tested
directed	modified	trained
edited	negotiated	updated
eliminated	operated	wrote
evaluated	organized	

When inserting these action verbs into your resume, you must be able to back them up with examples and facts or they become meaningless puffery.

Proofread and then proofread again. Check every word for correct spelling, every phrase and sentence for correct grammar, and every comma, semicolon, colon, period, and question mark for correctness. A serious misspelling, grammatical error, or typo may result in your resume being filed in a wastebasket. Do not rely on spellcheck to bail you out because if a word is spelled correctly, spellcheck will ignore it. Here are a few legendary mistakes recruiters have encountered.[14]

Double or triple check every detail for correctness.

"My last employer fried me for no reason."

"I am looking for my big brake."

"Studied public rations."

"Earned a diploma from a repudiated college."

"Bare me in mind for in-depth research projects."

"Ruining an eight-person team."

"I am very interested in the newspaper add for the accounting position."

"Deetail-oriented."

Make your resume easy to review.

Design appearance and layout with care. Print your resume on white, off-white, light gray, or light beige bond paper. Pay attention to how the resume is blocked so it looks neat, attractive, organized, carefully planned, and uncrowded. Employers like white space on resumes, so indent sections carefully, double-space parts, and leave at least one-inch margins all around. Center your name at the top in bold letters so it stands out. Use different printer fonts so headings guide the reader through important information about you. Employers prefer resumes with bullets that separate and call attention to important information because this helps them scan the resume more efficiently. If you provide two addresses, place one on each side under your name. If you provide one address, place it in the center or on the right side away from staples and paper clips.

Employers prefer a single-page resume. However, a two-page or longer resume is acceptable if it is necessary to provide valuable information, experiences, and insights. Do not try to adhere to the one-page rule by using a tiny font or narrow margins to fit everything onto a single page. Employers prefer a less crowded two-page resume. If you develop a two-page resume, print it front to back on one sheet of paper because a second page may get misplaced or ripped off when your resume is taken from a file or briefcase. Signal with a page number or notation that there is more on the back. Repeat your name at the top on the left and a page number on the top right.

Be professional in everything you say and do in the resume. Control your urges to use script resume fonts or to employ several font sizes and styles. Keep color and graphics to a minimum unless you are applying for a position that places a high value on creativity such as advertising, video production, and graphic design. In the sometimes zany world of resumes, the author has encountered pictures of university mascots, pets, and cute kittens in the top corners. One applicant printed his name in two inch high letters to get our attention and be remembered. He was remembered but not in the way he had hoped. An applicant to a law firm in Atlanta recently produced a resume in a font so fancy that it was virtually impossible to read.

> **Control your urge to be "creative" or "different."**

The Electronically Scanned Resume

Some organizations are employing resume scanning software to save time and money if they will receive dozens or hundreds of applications for a position. Follow these basic rules for mechanics and wording of a scanned resume.[15]

Mechanics are of critical importance because the scanner must be able to **read** your resume. Use black ink and only one side of 8½ inch white paper. Do not staple. Margins should be at least 1.5 inches on both sides, and characters should be 75 or fewer per line. Do not use boxes or columns. Employ size 11 to 14 fonts because the scanner may not read smaller print. Most recommended typefaces are Times Roman Numeral, Arial, and Times New Roman. Avoid fancy fonts. Use little punctuation because punctuation may confuse a scanner. You may use bold face or all capital letters. Avoid bullets (solid or hollow), italics, underlining, graphics, or spaces between the letters of your name.

> **Key words are critical in electronically scanned resumes.**

Key words are important because they will help in determining whether an employer will arrange an interview or discard your resume. Include words pertinent to the job posting so the scanner is able to locate what the employer has programmed it to look for. Have a clearly identifiable objective or profile linked to the description of the position you are seeking because employers may scan objectives to sort resumes for different positions. Joyce Lain Kennedy, an authority on the electronic job search, recommends, "The more keyword marketing points you present about yourself, the more likely you are to be plucked from an electronic resume database now, in six months, or a year from now."[16] The Purdue Online Writing Lab recommends replacing action verbs with nouns that are easier to scan. For example, change manufacturing to manufacturing supervisor, design to design assistant, production to production manager, and injection molding to injection molding inspector.[17] Be sure your resume contains up-to-date terms, labels, and names the scanner is programmed to detect. The following are examples of correct and incorrect terms for scannable resumes:

Yes	No
human resources	personnel
administrative assistant	secretary
sales associate	sales clerk
information systems	data processing
environmental services	housekeeping
accountant	bookkeeper
facilities engineering	maintenance
inside sales	customer relations
meteorologist	weatherman
server	waiter

Terms and labels are critical in scannable resume:

Organizations may ask for your resume to be sent electronically to save time and to create electronic files. Be sure your software system will send your resume in an attractive format. Instructors and students at some universities have reported that organizations have requested all applicant files be sent on CD-ROMs. Paper files are unacceptable. Unless told to do otherwise, include a cover letter that clearly identifies the position you are applying for and stresses how you are a good fit. Always bring a copy of your cover letter and resume to the interview.

Online Resumes

A growing number of organizations have created online sites for posting resumes. These sites make it easy for you to apply for a wide variety of positions with organizations worldwide. Be cautious. The ease of posting your resume online may make you easy prey for unscrupulous Web searchers pretending to be employers to take your money. Heather Galler of Carnegie-Mellon University has created a computer program called "identity Angel" that searches online job boards for the "holy trinity" of information thieves love to attain: name, address, and Social Security number. When locating sources asking for such information, it sends a warning to potential targets of thieves and frauds.[18]

Use online services with caution.

Galler offers several suggestions. Read the privacy policy carefully to determine how long your resume will be active and how you can delete it. Be sure there is a privacy policy. If not, look elsewhere. Be aware of fake recruiters, particularly if they ask for a driver's license or other personal information under the pretense of needing this for background checks. Ask recruiters for references and check to see if they are members of local or national recruiter's associations. Set up an alternative e-mail address, use a cell phone, and provide a P.O. box as your address for job hunting. Do not provide additional information to check your online listing because thieves may use spyware to attain even more personal information about you.

The Curriculum Vitae (CV)

The curriculum vitae or CV is common in other countries, but in the United States it is used most often for positions in colleges and universities, science, medical fields, and research. It literally means a presentation of your professional life and is much longer than a resume, two or three pages or longer if you have been in your field for a number of years. It is far more detailed than a resume and does not start with a branding statement or career objective.[19] Instead, it may state your specific teaching or career interests. Your cover letter makes a case for your qualifications and interest in the specific position for which you are applying. Your CV is likely to include headings such as the following:

Education (degrees)

Academic/Research appointments

Fellowships

Professional certificates/licenses

Grants

Awards

Professional publications

Professional presentations/papers/lectures

Professional memberships and affiliations

You present detailed lists under each heading without comment. The employer is likely to be familiar with the content, so you seldom need to explain the nature or significance of specific items. Be certain everything is accurate, up-to-date, and without spelling or typing errors.

The Portfolio

Your portfolio shows you in action.

Portfolios are essential if you are in fields such as photography, advertising, public relations, art and design, journalism, architecture, teaching, and professional writing. Your **portfolio** should be a small yet varied collection of your best work. Organize your portfolio thematically and make it visually attractive. Provide excellent copies of your work—not faded, soiled, marked-up, graded, or wrinkled samples. Employers focus on how well you write, design, photograph, edit, and create, and the well-designed and presented portfolio is the best means of exhibiting this. If you are going into broadcasting, your portfolio must include an audio or videorecording of selections that illustrate your best oral and video work. Quality, not quantity, sells.

Some colleges and universities are encouraging or requiring students to create electronic portfolios that include a wide variety of materials in an attractive, compact, and highly usable package. In addition to revealing what you have done and can do, the e-portfolio demonstrates your ability to apply new technologies.

The Cover Letter

> The all-purpose form letter is rarely taken seriously.

Your cover letter may be the first contact you have with an employer, so be positive and to the point. The fundamental purposes of your cover letter are *to gain this employer's attention* and *to entice this employer* to read your resume. The first purpose requires you to make a good impression by revealing a positive attitude, pleasant personality, motivation, and enthusiasm. The second purpose requires you to include highlights of your education, training, and experiences that show you are interested in and qualified for a specific position in the employer's organization. Never send a resume without attaching a cover letter.[20]

> Design and target letters to specific positions and organizations.

Mechanics of the Cover Letter: Make your letter brief, usually three or four paragraphs in length, and never more than one page. See Figure 8.3. Provide margins of 1.5 inches left and right and adjust top and bottom margins to balance your letter on the page. If you have difficulty placing all information you feel is absolutely necessary to include on a single page, adjust the margins to keep the letter to one page. Use simple to read fonts of 10 to 12 points. Ask another person to read your cover letter. If the person mentions the font, change it. Your letter must be neat, printed on white bond paper, and professional with no typos, grammatical errors, punctuation errors, or misspellings. One of the author's former journalism students applied for an editing position with the Cincinnati *Enquirer* and misspelled Cincinnati in the cover letter. The student did not get the job, but the editor did send an irate letter, along with the student's original letter, to the student's academic department head.

> Show interest and enthusiasm or do not apply.

Content of the Cover Letter: Tailor each letter to the position and organization. Form letters impress no one. Address your letter to a specific person involved in the hiring process, and spell this person's name correctly. Be careful when you address the person as Mr. or Ms. For instance, first names such as Jordan, Chris, and Justice may be a man or woman. Letters addressed "To Whom It May Concern" or "Dear Sirs" don't get positive responses. Organize your letter into three paragraphs. In the *first* paragraph, tell the employer why you are writing, in which position you are interested, and why this position with this organization appeals to you. Reveal how you discovered this opening and that you have researched both position and organization. In the *second* paragraph, explain briefly how your education, training, and experiences—your qualifications—make you an ideal fit for this position, with this organization, at this time. *Be persuasive!* You may refer to your resume, but do not insert large portions of it in the cover letter. Let your cover letter and resume do the jobs they are designed for. In the *third* paragraph, restate your enthusiasm for the position and ask for an interview opportunity. Indicate when and where you will be available for an interview. Mention enclosures and offer to send additional information if needed. Express appreciation for the employer's consideration.

Figure 8.3   *Cover letter*

1214 Oak Drive
Decatur, IL 62251
May 15, 2020

Ms. Mary Kay O'Bannon, Director
Department of Children and Family Services
401 Industrial Ave.
Effingham, IL 62401

Dear Ms. O'Bannon:

I am applying for the position of Family Case Manager posted on the Department of Children and Family Services Web site on May 13, 2020. I am very excited about this position because it matches my career goal, education, and experiences.

I will graduate from the University of Illinois at Urbana-Champaign on May 18 with a Bachelor Social Work Degree. In my position as a CASA volunteer in Macon County since 2018, I have worked closely with Family Case Managers in a number of cases involving Children in Need of Services. I have observed their work with parents and children and come to appreciate their critical roles in maintaining families when possible and seeing that children are placed in safe and loving environments when the family option is no longer viable. I believe my experiences as a CASA, a volunteer in the Crisis Center for women, and as a horse therapist for children with special needs makes me uniquely qualified for the position you have open in the Department of Children and Family Services.

I look forward to the opportunity to meet with you and discuss my interests and background. Enclosed is a copy of my resume that provides additional details about my qualifications and experiences. You may contact me at either of the telephone numbers listed on my resume or my e-mail at nawilliams @hotmail.com. I am available for an interview at your convenience.

Sincerely,

Nancy A. Williams

Enclosure: resume

Creating a Favorable First Impression

Creating a favorable first impression is critical to the success of every interview, and this occurs during the first few seconds or minutes. Sources agree the first impression is likely to result in the recruiter looking for input that supports this initial impression. If it is positive, the recruiter is likely to have a higher regard for you as the interview progresses, reveal important job information, try to sell the position and organization, and spend less time seeking information. There are many ingredients in creating this favorable impression.

Attitudes

Be interested in this interview and show it.

Be sincerely interested in taking part in the interview and show it. Enthusiasm is contagious. On the other hand, if you have little interest in the position or organization, are interviewing merely for the experience, or have not been able to find a position that you really want, you are likely to find it difficult to get "fired up." Authentic enthusiasm is difficult to fake and, if you succeed, what have you accomplished?

Avoid self-fulfilling prophecies.

Strive to communicate positive attitudes about yourself including your qualifications, relationships, current and past employers, and future. Never badmouth a school or former employer. Be confident. If you feel you are not going to do well during an interview, you probably will not. Be thoroughly prepared to take an active part in the interview and be fully informed about the position and organization. Be **professional** and **ethical** in everything you say and do during the interview.

Dress and Appearance

Dress and appearance are critical elements in making a favorable first impression. Your clothes and accessories should support the strong image you want to make, an image that shows confidence, attentiveness to details, and understanding of what is appropriate dress and appearance for a formal business setting in your field. Our society has become increasingly informal in its dress, and so have many organizations and career fields. As a result, it has become increasingly difficult to determine what is appropriate dress for an employment interview. If you have any doubt about what is or is not appropriate, contact professors and counselors in your career center or someone within the organization and ask discretely how you should dress. Organizations and career fields may have their own unique cultures, environments, and modes of dress, but permitting casual dress for work does not necessarily apply to formal employment interviews. These fields

Wavebreakmedia Ltd/Getty Images

■ *Creating a favorable first impression is vital in the employment interview.*

are most likely to prefer **formal dress:** finance, government, human resources, banking, sales, hospitality, broadcasting (on camera), and law. These fields are most likely to prefer **informal or casual dress:** public relations, advertising, graphic design, technology, broadcasting (off camera), manufacturing, and trades. Some fields such as health care, science, engineering, and agriculture have so many career tracks that it is nearly impossible to place them in either list. Being overdressed is better than being underdressed. Always think **competence** rather than **fashion.**

> Dress appropriately for the field, organization, and position.

Your appearance will affect both you and the employer. "When you look good, you feel good and when you feel good you are more likely to articulate intelligent and well thought out answers to questions."[21] A casual or sloppy appearance may end your chance of further consideration. You need not spend a fortune on interview dress, but purchase well-fitting clothing that will maintain a press and is wrinkle free. Be neat, clean, and lint free. Polish your shoes. Check for missing buttons or unremoved tags. Brush your teeth, clean your hands and fingernails, comb your hair, shave or trim facial hair, take a breath mint, and use cologne sparingly. Consider covering up tattoos if they might be a turnoff for recruiters. A professional appearance also applies to jewelry, watches, pens, and briefcases.

> Neatness costs little and may pay big dividends.

Your goal should be to have your dress and appearance play a strong **supporting role,** one that generates positive attention and approval at the start of the interview. Then you want the recruiter to focus attention on your interpersonal skills, answers, and questions that indicate you are prepared and well-qualified for this position with this organization. If the recruiter remembers you because of the way you looked, you are probably in trouble.

Advice for Men

If you know your field prefers formal business attire for interviews, wear a two-piece dark suit (blue, gray, black) with a white or pastel solid shirt and a contrasting but not "wild" tie. Wear conservative, professional apparel to the interview, even if the interviewer may be dressed informally. Wear a long-sleeved shirt even during the summer. Do not wear a turtleneck shirt. Wear leather, laced business shoes with leather soles, preferably black or cordovan, and not clunky looking. Your belt should match your shoes.

> Be on the conservative side in dress and appearance.

Try the sit-down test to check for fit. Almost anyone can wear clothes that are a bit too tight when standing, but sitting down quickly reveals if the jacket, waistband, seat, or collar is too tight or the shirt gaps at the waist. Insert one finger into the collar of your shirt. If the collar is too tight, you need a larger shirt; if it is too loose, you need a smaller shirt to avoid the sloppy look of a drooping collar.

Wear dark socks that complement your suit and cover at least half a calf so when you sit down and cross your legs, no skin is visible. Tie size and design depend upon what is in style, but it is always safe to wear a wide stripe, small polka dot, or conservative pattern that is blue, red, gray, or burgundy.

> Coordinate colors carefully.

Choose clothing that is appropriate for your body shape: regular, thin or slender, heavy or muscular, and tall or short. A heavy, muscular male for instance, should choose dark shades with small pinstripes. A thin or slender male may wear a greater variety of clothing, and some plaids might add size and depth to the physical appearance.

> When in doubt, ask for help.

A sport coat or blazer may be too casual except for informal gatherings or dinners associated with the selection process. Your hair should be trimmed and neatly combed or brushed. Facial hair is generally accepted (if neat and trimmed), but know your industries preferences. Professional and conservative also applies to watches, ballpoint pens, briefcases, earrings, tattoos, and cologne. It is wise to play it safe and seek every advantage.

Advice for Women

> Appearance should not call attention to itself.

Makeup, hairstyle, and clothing are personal decisions that reveal a great deal about your personality—who you are, your self-concept, and what you think of others. Take them seriously. No makeup is probably too little, but if makeup calls attention to itself, it is too much. Recruiters suggest small (not dangling) earrings with one per ear, one ring per hand, and no noisy bracelets. Coloring is essential, and a cosmetic counselor can help determine what is professionally appropriate for you. Keep perfume to an absolute minimum or use none at all. You do not want to be recalled for your smell.

> Provocative clothing can end your candidacy.

If you know your field prefers formal business attire for interviews, wear a tailored two-piece suit with skirt or slacks and in navy, black, dark gray, or brown. Skirt length should be to the bottom of the knees when standing and cover your thighs when seated. If you must tug at your skirt when you sit down, it is too short. Avoid skirts with long slits. Select a tailored, conservative blouse that matches your suit while avoiding "see through" blouses or ones with plunging necklines. Wear clear or plain styled stockings appropriate for your outfit. Low, closed-toe, and comfortable pumps are more appropriate than high heels. Carry a simple handbag and a professional-looking briefcase.

Nonverbal Communication

Nonverbal communication (voice, eye contact, gestures, and posture) are important ingredients in every interview. Scott Reeves reports a typical example in which an applicant looked very strong on paper but "offered a deadfish handshake, slouched and fidgeted in his chair, failed to make eye contact with the interviewer and mumbled responses to basic questions." He was not hired.[22] Interviewers react more favorably toward applicants and rate them higher if they smile, have expressive facial expressions, maintain eye contact, and have clear, forceful voices. Technology plays important roles in the employment process, but recruiters prefer to interview applicants face-to-face because they prefer "high touch" to "high tech" when selecting people who will join and influence the futures of their organizations. They want to see, hear, and observe you in action.

> Good communication skills are important in all positions.

You communicate dynamism and energy through the way you shake hands, sit, walk, stand, gesture, and move your body. Appear to be calm and relaxed, but sharp and in control. Avoid nervous gestures, fidgets, movements, and playing with pens or objects on the interviewer's desk. Respond crisply and confidently with no sign of arrogance. When replying to questions, maintain eye contact with the recruiter. If there are two or more recruiters in the room, glance at the others when answering a question but focus primarily on the questioner, particularly as you complete your answer.

Speak in a normal conversational tone with vocal variety that exhibits confidence and interpersonal skills. Interviewers prefer standard accents. If English is your second language or you have an accent developed since birth, work on your accent and pronunciation so interviewers can understand you clearly and effectively.

Do not hesitate to pause before answering difficult questions, but frequent pauses may make you appear hesitant, unprepared, or "slow." Interviewers interpret pauses of one second or less as signs of ambition, self-confidence, organization, and intelligence.

Interview Etiquette

Arrive at the interview a few minutes before the scheduled time. If you arrive late, the recruiter is likely to assume the interview is of little importance to you and, if hired, you are likely to arrive late for work. Avoid arriving too early. The recruiter may have other work to do and does not want to assign staff to entertain you until your scheduled time. Discard chewing gum before arriving, turn off you cell phone and keep it out of sight, and do not have a cup of coffee or bottle of water in hand. Shake hands, if and when the recruiter offers to do so, in a firm but not crushing manner. Smile. Introduce yourself formally with no nick names. Place your briefcase and other belongings on the floor and nothing personal on the recruiter's desk or table. Avoid the temptation to play with or rearrange items on the interviewer's desk. Sit down when the recruiter indicates you should, and then sit up straight but not stiff with your feet on the floor. If the recruiter asks if you would like a glass of water, take it. Let the recruiter take the lead with small talk during the opening and questions as the interview progresses. Do not interrupt the recruiter.

> **Be on time and ready to interact.**

When interviewing over a meal, give your full attention to the interaction because this is a continuation of the interview, not a time until the interview resumes. **Mind your manners!** Do not check your watch, peruse your resume or organizational literature, or check your cell phone for messages. Be aware that the recruiter may be testing you to see how you might act in the future when dining with clients or upper management. Using proper etiquette during meals can make or break your interview experience. Wait until others have become seated before you sit down or until asked to do so. Never start eating until everyone at the table has been served. Know how to place your napkin in your lap, how and when to use silverware properly, how to pass food to others, and how to eat soup. Do not place your elbows on the table. Order an alcoholic drink only if the recruiter invites you to do so, and then drink **one slowly** throughout the meal. If you do not drink alcoholic beverages, simply decline the offer tactfully. Let the recruiter initiate business. Say thank you at the end of the meal.

> **Learn and practice proper etiquette.**

Answering Questions

With a favorable first impression established, it is time to reveal the substance of your product—you.

> **Decisions are made on the total interview.**

Preparing to Respond

Be ready and eager to answer questions effectively. Concentrate on answering confidently and thoroughly, and be prepared to address frequently asked questions.

- Tell me about yourself.
- Why do you want to work for us?

Be ready to
handle
traditional
questions.

- What are your greatest strengths? Weaknesses?
- What are your short-range career goals? Long-range goals?
- Why did you leave your position with _____?
- What did you like best in your position at _____? Like least?
- Why should we select you over the other applicants for this position?
- What do you know about our organization?

These traditional questions play major roles in selection interviews, particularly in the opening minutes. Interviewers use them to get applicants talking and relaxed, and to learn about them as human beings and professionals.

The nature of questioning has changed with interviewers asking more challenging questions about your experiences in **joblike situations** to see how you might fit in and function as an employee. Employers believe they can determine best how applicants might operate in specific positions by placing them in these positions during the interview. Task-oriented questions assess thinking and communication abilities and reveal how well you can operate in stressful or surprise situations. Here are common on-the-job question strategies:

Welcome
on-the-job
questions to
show what you
can do.

- *Behavior-based questions:*

  Tell me about a time when you led a team assigned to design a new software program.

- *Current critical incident questions:*

  We are facing a situation in which a client wants an immediate design change of a product we have recently started producing. If you were on our team, how would you recommend we address this?

- *Historical critical incident questions:*

  Last year we experienced a conflict between union and non-union members in our warehouse in Omaha. If you had been assigned the task of resolving this conflict, what would you have done?

- *Hypothetical questions:*

  Suppose you had a customer who claimed his SUV had been damaged while it was in our shop for an engine repair. How would you handle this?

- *Task-oriented questions:*

  Here's a ballpoint pen. Sell it to me.

Employers frequently require would-be teachers to teach, salespersons to sell, engineers to engineer, managers to manage, and designers to design. Job simulations, role-playing, presentations, and day-long case studies challenge applicants to demonstrate their knowledge, skills, experiences, maturity, and integrity on the job.

Structuring Answers

Questions that place applicants in job like situations typically require them to tell narratives about experiences or would-be experiences. Good stories are internally consistent, consistent with the facts employers hold to be true, relevant to questions asked and the applicant's claims, provide details that support claims, and reflect the applicant's beliefs and values.[23] Try one or more of these patterns to structure your answers in a way that tell your stories effectively.

Structure answers strategically.

Mini-speech method: Approach questions, particularly ones that require you to tell stories, as if you were giving a brief speech. This method is a good way to approach critical incident and hypothetical questions that *do not focus* specifically on your *past experiences.* Your speech would be in three traditional parts.

Introduction: Tell recruiters what you are going to tell them.

Body: Tell them.

Conclusion: Tell them what you told them.

STAR Method: The S.T.A.R. method is highly recommended for answering behavior-based questions because it zeroes in on behaviors and skills exhibited in *past experiences* that are highly relevant to the specific position being sought. It has four parts adding up to the word "star."

Situation: Describe the setting or background including when, where, and with whom.

Task: What needed to be done, why, and with what expectations?

Action: What action did you take and how did you do it?

Results: What were the results, accomplishments, consequences?

PAR Method: The P.A.R. method is a variation of the STAR approach and is recommended for behavioral-based questions. The goal is to focus on your past performance while emphasizing experiences, skills, leadership, and ability to get a job done. It has three parts.

P: The problem or task you were assigned

A: The actions you took solving the task or problem

R: The results or consequences of your actions

Responding Successfully

Listen and think, then respond.

Listen carefully to the **whole** question; **think** before opening your mouth; **structure** your answer clearly; provide **substance**; **phrase** your answer with good grammar and choice of words; aim your answer precisely at the **point** of the question; and show **enthusiasm** and a **positive attitude.** If you are answering a behavior-based, critical incident, hypothetical, or task question, do not hesitate to ask for additional clarification or seek more information on background or organizational policies that may be important to your response. Answer questions thoroughly but know when to stop. Knowing when to stop may be a problem in telephone interviews because you do not have the advantage of nonverbal cues from the recruiter to signal that you have answered the question and it is time to move on.

Do not underestimate the importance of words. For instance, when answering a question about working in teams, the recruiter may be focusing on your use of **pronouns.** If you use *us, we,* and *our,* you indicate that you work well in teams. If you use *I, me,* and *mine,* you indicate you work better alone. Use **action verbs** to show you are a **doer** and

technical jargon to show experience and familiarity with your field and the position for which you are interviewing. **Qualifiers** such as "maybe," "perhaps," and "sort of" communicate hesitancy and that you are unsure of yourself. Avoid **meaningless slang** such as "you know," "know what I'm sayin'," "know what I mean," "and stuff like that," and "that sort of thing." A Marist College poll identified words such as "actually," "whatever," "awesome," and "literally" and phrases such as "twenty-four seven," "It is what it is," and "At the end of the day" to be among the most annoying.[24] I would add "ton of" as in "I have a ton of experience."

Be **honest** and **authentic** in your answers. If you appear evasive or hesitant in responding, the recruiter may interpret this as evidence of dishonesty or fear of revealing something the recruiter has a right to know. Do not create and rehearse answers that merely sound good or provide what you think the recruiter wants to hear. Beware of sources, particularly the Internet, that offer sure-fire answers to a variety of common interview questions. There is rarely a single correct answer to any question. Five recruiters from the same organization may be seeking different answers to the same question.

Your **attitudes** can make or break an interview. Be positive and realistic about yourself and your future but not arrogant or cocky. Speak positively about your education, training, experiences, and former employers. Show sincere interest in this position with this organization. Be flexible in the position you are seeking and willing to bend a little to fit a position and organizational needs. You are not going to start at the top.

Use your **head** instead of your mouth. The author remembers too well answering this question during one of his first interviews, "Tell me about yourself" with "Well, there's not much to tell." Recruiters tell similar stories. When one recruiter asked "Why should I hire you?" one applicant replied that he would be a great asset to the company softball team while another said he was bored with watching television. In another instance, an applicant defended his resume by declaring, "My resume might look like I am a job hopper. But I want you to know that I never left any of those jobs voluntarily." Unthinking applicants often reveal fatal symptoms of the "foot-in-mouth disease."

Responding to Unlawful Questions

Although EEO laws and guidelines pertaining to lawful and unlawful questions recruiters may ask during employment interviews have been widely disseminated for decades and most employers inform their employees involved in recruiting about what they can and cannot ask applicants, a survey revealed one in five employers admit they have unknowingly asked unlawful questions. At least one in three employers admit they are unsure of the lawfulness of certain questions.[25] These figures do not include employers who knowingly and intentionally ask unlawful questions. Applicants, particularly women, are likely to encounter a variety of unlawful questions.

Unlawful questions pose serious dilemmas for applicants. On one hand, if you reply honestly and directly, you may not be hired. On the other hand, if you refuse to answer an unlawful question (nearly impossible to do graciously), you may be seen as uncooperative, evasive, or to be "one of those" and not be hired. You must be prepared to respond to unlawful questions tactfully and effectively.

Do not be evasive in answers.

Do not be surprised if you are asked unlawful questions.

Be prepared to reply effectively to unlawful questions.

First, review the EEO laws and the question exercise in Chapter 7. In the vast majority of interviews, these areas of inquiry are **unlawful** because they do not pertain to **bona fide occupational qualifications (BFOQs):** gender, race, ethnic group or origin, age, religion, marital status, parental status, sexual orientation, physical appearance, disabilities, citizenship, place of birth, military discharge, and arrest records. All questions must pertain to an applicant's ability to perform a particular job.

Second, be familiar with tricks employers may play to obtain unlawful and irrelevant information without asking a direct question. For example, a benefits person

> Beware of recruiter tricks to get unlawful information.

may ask you which health insurance plan you would choose if hired; your answer may reveal that you are married and have children, that you are a single parent, or that you have a serious medical problem. During lunch or dinner or a tour of the organization's facilities when you are least expecting serious questions, an employer, perhaps a female, may probe into child care under the guise of talking about her own problems: "What a day! My daughter Emily woke up this morning with a fever, my husband is out of town, and I had an eight o'clock conference downtown. Do you ever have days like this?" You may begin to tell problems you have had with your children or family members and, in the process, reveal a great deal of irrelevant, unlawful, and perhaps damaging information without knowing it. Employers have learned how to get unlawful information through lawful questions. Instead of asking, "Do you have children?" an employer asks, "Is there any limit on your ability to work overtime (evenings, weekends, holidays)?" They may use coded questions and comments.

- "Our employees put a lot into their work" means "Older workers like you don't have much energy."
- "We have a very young staff" means "You won't fit in."
- "I'm sure your former company had its own corporate culture, just as we do here" means "Hispanics need not apply."
- "We are a very traditional company" means "We don't hire women beyond clerical staff."

Third, know how important this position with this organization is for you and your career. If it is highly important, you may decide to take the chance. After all, you may be

> Weigh your needs and desires when answering.

able to change this organization's attitudes, atmosphere, and recruiting practices from the inside when you have a position.

Fourth, learn and practice a variety of tactics for responding to unlawful questions. The following tactics will help you handle difficult situations while supporting your candidacy for a position.

Refuse to answer the question. This is the most commonly suggested tactic, but it is also the most difficult to use **tactfully.**

1. **Recruiter:** How old are you?

    Applicant: Is age a requirement for this position?

2. **Recruiter:** Do you plan to have children?

    Applicant: My plans to have a family will not interfere if I am hired for this position.

Provide a brief, direct answer in hopes the recruiter will move on to lawful, relevant questions.

1. **Recruiter:** What does your wife do?

   Applicant: She's a pharmacist.
2. **Recruiter:** Do you attend church often?

   Applicant: Yes.

Combine a brief answer with a tactful inquiry that skirts the question and attempts to guide the employer away from an unlawful inquiry with a job-related question.

1. **Recruiter:** What does your husband do?

   Applicant: He's in construction. Why do you ask?
2. **Recruiter:** I see you use a wheelchair; how might this affect your work?

   Applicant: How is this a concern for a position in industrial design?

Neutralize an employer's concern.

1. **Recruiter:** Do you plan on having a family?

   Applicant: Yes. I'm looking forward to the challenges of both family and career. I've observed professors and staff during internships handling both quite successfully.
2. **Recruiter:** What will happen if your husband were to get transferred?

   Applicant: The same that would happen if I were to get transferred.

Take advantage of the question.

1. **Recruiter:** Where were you born?

   Applicant: I am quite proud that I grew up in the Dominican Republic because it has helped me work with people of highly diverse backgrounds.
2. **Recruiter:** I see you're married.

   Applicant: Yes, I am, and I believe that is a plus. Studies show that married employees are more stable and dependable than unmarried employees.

A tongue in cheek response sends an unmistakable signal to the employer that a question is unlawful. Bernice Sandler, an authority on discrimination in hiring, cautions that this response must be accompanied by appropriate nonverbal signals (smile, facial expression, tone of voice) to avoid offending the recruiter.

1. **Recruiter:** Who will take care of your children?

   Applicant: (smiling, pleasant tone of voice) Are you trying to see if I can recognize an unlawful question?

2. **Recruiter:** How long do you expect to work for us?

   Applicant: (smiling, pleasant tone of voice) Is this a test to see how I might reply to an unlawful question?

Exercise #1—Which Questions Are Unlawful, Why, and How Might You Reply to Each.

If you were a Hispanic, female, soon-to-be college graduate applying for a management position with an automobile manufacturer located in Missouri, which of these questions are unlawful? Why do you think this question is unlawful? If it is, how would you reply to it?

1. How well do you speak Spanish?

   _____

2. Any marriage plans?

   _____

3. What do you do when you're not working?

   _____

4. Is your family from the Midwest?

   _____

5. I see you wear hearing aids. Any problem with working in a factory?

   _____

6. Tell me about your internship with GE Aviation.

   _____

7. How long would you plan to work for us?

   _____

8. Which religious holidays do you observe?

   _____

9. I see you were in Army ROTC in college. How was that for a woman?

   _____

10. Do you have a significant other?

    _____

Asking Questions

The majority of applicants review common recruiter questions they discover from their network, on the Internet, and in publications and plan how they might reply to each. On the other hand, a relatively small percentage of applicants give much thought to the questions they will ask during interviews even though most recruiters will provide time for them to do so. It is critical that you take full advantage of this opportunity to ask questions that reveal your preparation, professionalism, interests, motivations, and maturity and obtain information about the organization and the position for which you are interviewing.

Guidelines for Asking Questions

Prepare a moderate schedule of carefully phrased, open-ended questions. Review the question guidelines and question pitfalls discussed in Chapter 3 and the specific applicant question guidelines listed below before preparing your questions.

- Always come to an interview with more questions than you are likely to have time to ask. Recruiters identify having too few questions or none at all as a major mistake, and successful applicants ask more questions than unsuccessful applicants. However, if a recruiter answers all of your questions when giving information, simply reply, "You have answered all of my questions." Do not create a question "off the top of your head" because if it were important, it would be on your list. It may do more harm than good.

- Do not waste time asking for information that is readily available on the organization's Web site, publications, and the Internet. Asking such questions also indicates that you have expended little effort researching the position and organization. The recruiter may assume that you have little interest in the position or are lazy.

- Never ask about salary until you are negotiating an employment offer. Before then, a recruiter may reply, "We are competitive," or toss it back to you with, "What salary do you expect?" If you have done your homework, you should be aware of the salary ranges for positions in your field and how they will be higher when the cost of living is higher. If salary appears to be your primary concern for choosing a position, the employer will turn to others.

- Avoid the "me . . . me . . . me . . . complex" in which your questions focus on what **you** will get, how much **you** will get, and when **you** will get it. These questions establish an impression that you are **self-centered** with little interest in what you can give to the organization and others. Employers are looking for employees who will be team-oriented and organization-centered. They want you to be interested in rising to higher levels within their organizations, but they also expect you to be interested in and dedicated to the position for which you are interviewing.

- Phrase each question carefully to avoid the following pitfalls.

  1. *The yes/no question* is likely to gain little if any information.

     Bad: Do you like working for this company?

     Good: What do you like most about working for this company?

  2. *The Have to question* may give the impression that you will be an unhappy and uncooperative employee.

     Bad: Would I have to travel much?

     Good: How much travel would this position entail?

  3. *The typology question* focuses on type rather than an explanation.

     Bad: What type of team training program do you employ?

     Good: Tell me about your team training program.

How you ask may be more important than what you ask.

4. *The pleading question* (often in a series) seems to beg for answers.

   Bad: Could you please tell me about your expansion plans?

   Good: Tell me about your expansion plans.

5. *The little bitty question* may signal lack of interest in detailed information, perhaps asking a question merely to ask a question.

   Bad: Tell me a little bit about your new office in Atlanta.

   Good: Tell me about your new office in Atlanta.

6. *The uninformed question* exhibits lack of knowledge about a position and field.

   Bad: Does your sales staff work on commission or what?

   Good: How is commission determined by sales area?

Ask your most important question first.

Rank order your questions according to their importance for you because you never know how much time the employer will give you to question. Make sure the most important ones get asked. Open-ended questions with lengthy answers limit the number you can ask. Recruiters assume you will ask the most important questions first and will be turned off if they are about salary and benefits, let alone retirement plan.

Sample Applicant Questions

The following sample applicant questions show interest in the position and the organization, are not overly self-centered, and meet question guidelines:

Adapt your questions to each position and organization.

- What is the rate of turnover in this position?
- Describe your ideal employee for me.
- Tell me about the culture of your organization.
- How does your organization encourage employees to come up with new ideas?
- How much choice would I have in selecting geographical location?
- What is a typical workday for this position?
- What is the possibility of flexible working hours?
- How does your organization evaluate employees?
- What characteristics are you looking for in applicants for this position?
- How might your organization support me if I wanted to pursue an MBA?
- How often would I be working as part of a team?
- What, in your estimation, is the most unique characteristic of your organization?
- How might an advanced degree affect my position in your organization?
- Tell me about where other persons who have held this position have advanced within the organization.
- What do you like most about working for this organization?
- Tell me about the merger with TelEx.
- I noticed in *The Wall Street Journal* last week that your stock has risen almost 4 percent during this economic recession. What explains this increase?

- Tell me about the people I would be working with.
- Tell me about your training program.
- What major departmental changes do you anticipate during the next five years?
- What is the most important criterion for selecting a person for this position?

The following questions may help with a variety of positions in new and startup organizations:

- Which of your products are most in demand?
- Who are your major competitors?
- How much collective experience do your top officers have in the field?
- What are your plans for going public?
- Who are the major regulators of your business?

The Closing

Be aware of everything you say and do.

The closing stage of the employment interview is usually brief. Play an active role in the closing but avoid saying or doing anything that may harm what has been a strong interview. Express your interest in the position and organization. And discover what will happen next, when, and whom you should contact and how if you need to get in touch about the position. Ask for the position tactfully.

The interview "Is not over 'til it's over." When a member of the organization walks you to the outer office, the elevator, or the parking lot, the interview is not over. When a person takes you on a tour of the organization or the area, it is not over. When a person takes you to lunch or dinner, it is not over. The employer will note everything you do and say. Positions are lost because of the way applicants react during a tour, converse informally, meet other people, eat dinner, or handle alcoholic beverages.

Evaluation and Follow-Up

Debrief yourself immediately following each interview. Jot down your answers to tough questions, information the recruiter provided, and the recruiter's answers to your questions. Make a list of pros and cons of the position and organization and what you don't know that would be critical in making a decision. How well did you do? Do not over-react. Your positive or negative reactions may be exaggerated. So, jot down the highs and lows with the following checklist and then decide how to prepare better and interact more effectively during your next interview.

- How adequate was my preparation?
- How effective was I during the opening?
- How appropriate were my dress and appearance?
- What opportunities to sell myself did I hit and miss?
- How thorough and to the point were my answers?

- How well did I adapt my questions to this organization and position?

- How effectively did I show interest in this organization and position?

- How much information on this position and organization did I obtain to make a good career decision?

Be thorough in your debriefing.

Follow up the interview with a brief, professional letter thanking the interviewer for the time given you. Promptness is less important than content. Avoid firing off letters with little thought. Lisa Ryan, managing director for recruiting at Heyman Associates of New York, tells the story about walking a person to the elevator and finding an e-mail thank-you note waiting for her when she returned to her office moments later. The candidate had e-mailed her from the elevator. She recommends that you "put some substance into your thank-you note."[26] Emphasize your interest in this position and organization. Not only is the thank-you letter the polite thing to do but it provides an excuse to contact the interviewer, keeps your name alive, and includes additional information that might help the organization decide in your favor.

Quality applicants write thank-you notes.

Handling Rejection

All applicants face rejection, even when they feel interviews went well. Potential employers reject applicants for a variety of reasons, often because of fit or because another applicant has a valued experience or skill. They may interview dozens of people for a single position and must make difficult choices. You will never hear from some recruiters.

How you handle rejections influences your attitudes, attitudes that may lead to further rejections. One writer warns: "**Don't be a victim.** The worst thing tired and frustrated job seekers can do is to conclude that employer reps and hiring managers are out to get them, that the job search process is out of their control, and that they're the victims of some evil, monolithic power."[27] Do not take rejection personally.

Learn from rejections.

Use each interview as a learning process. Ask what you might do differently in the next interview. How did you handle behavioral-based and critical incident questions? How effective were your questions? How thorough was your preparation? How qualified were you for this position? What might you have done or not done to turn off for the recruiter?

Summary

Technology enables you to communicate instantly and to send and check information immediately. The scanning of resumes and the use of the Internet as sources for positions and resume storage are changing the face of job searching. Personality, integrity, and drug tests are adding a new dimension to the process.

We have become a part of the global community and economy and are undergoing a second industrial revolution moving from a manufacturing to a service- and information-oriented society. Technology enables us to locate positions, attain information, send letters and resumes, and communicate quickly with employers around the world. The best positions in the future will go to those who understand and are prepared for the selection process. You must know yourself, the position, and the organization to persuade an employer to select you from hundreds of other applicants. The job search must be extensive and rely more on network-ing and hard work than merely appearing at your college career center for an interview. Your resumes and cover letters must be thorough, professional, attractive, adapted to specific posi-tions with specific organizations, and persuasive.

Interviewing skills are increasingly important because employers are looking for employees with communication, interpersonal, and people skills. You can exhibit these best during the interview. Take an active part in the opening, answer questions thoroughly and to the point, and ask carefully phrased questions about the position and the organiza-tion. Take an active part in the closing, and be sure the interviewer knows you want this position. Close on a high note.

Follow up the interview with a carefully crafted thank-you letter that expresses again your interest in this position and organization. Do an insightful evaluation that addresses strengths and weaknesses and with future interviews in mind.

Key Terms and Concepts

Appearance	First impression	Portfolio
Arrival	Follow-up	Relationship
Attitudes	Functional format resume	Research
Behavior-based	Honesty tests	Resume
Branding	Integrity interview	Screening interview
Career/job fair	Joblike situations	Self-analysis
Career objective	Mini-speech method	Social media
Chronological format resume	Network tree	STAR method
Cover letter	Networking	Successful applicants
Determinate interview	Nonverbal communication	Talent-based
Dress	PAR method	Trait-based
Electronically scanned	Percentage agencies	Unsuccessful applicants
Fee-paid positions	Placement agency	

Review Questions

1. Why is it important to develop a personal brand before applying for positions?
2. How do you develop a network tree?
3. How can you make the most of job fairs you attend?
4. How can you use social media to your advantage when seeking employment oppor-tunities?
5. What should you learn about a position and organization prior to the interview?
6. How can you make your resume most impressive for a position in your field?
7. What should you include in a cover letter?
8. What advice would you give an applicant concerning dress and appearance in an interview?
9. What advice would you give an applicant concerning interview etiquette?

10. Compare and contrast the STAR and PAR methods in structuring answers.
11. Illustrate three tactics you might use if a recruiter were to ask you an unlawful question such as "Do you have a significant other?"
12. Identify three applicant question pitfalls and how you can avoid each?
13. What guidelines should you follow when constructing a list of questions to ask during an interview in your field?
14. What are five follow-up questions you might ask yourself during a postinterview evaluation?
15. What does it mean to say "An interview is not over until it's over?"

Student Activities

1. Contact recruiters of several companies or organizations and discover if they currently employ a behavior-based, talent-based, or trait-based question system. If they do, discover why they use a specific system, how they have modified it over time, and how they train interviewers to use it.
2. Interview a staff member at your college career center to discover how the center might help you locate positions. You are a history major with the ultimate goal of owning and operating a used bookstore with specialties in U.S. history in general and military history in particular. Discover how the center can help you prepare for, locate, and take part in interviews for positions that will give you experiences relevant to financing and operating a book store.
3. Take the Myers-Briggs Personality Indicator. How do the results compare to your self-perceptions? How might these results help determine career paths and positions?
4. Interview five recent college graduates with your major. How large were their networks, and how did they use these networks to locate positions? Who on their networks proved most helpful? How many interviews were involved in the hiring process for their current positions? Did they experience panel interviews as well as traditional one-on-one interviews? How did screening interviews differ from determinate interviews? What were the most critical questions they were asked? What were the most critical questions they asked?

Notes

1. Lois J. Einhorn, *Interviewing . . . A Job in Itself* (Bloomington, IN: The Career Center, 1977), pp. 3–5.
2. Monsterstaff, "5 for Friday: Personal Branding for Job Seekers Edition," https://www.monster.com/career-advice/article/5-for-friday-personal-branding-for-job-seekers-edition, accessed July 24, 2019.

3. Brand Yourself, "Personal Brand Statement Examples and Tips," May 24, 2018, https://brandyourself.com/blog/how-tos/personal-brand-statement-7-winning-steps-to-creating-one, accessed July 24, 2019; Joyce Lain Kennedy, "How to Create a Personal Brand for Your Job Search," https://www.dummies.com/careers/find-a-job/how-to-create-a-personal-brand-for-your-job-search, accessed July 24, 2019.

4. Lilly Mathis, "10 Industries that Need More Workers," https://monster.com/career-advice/article/shrm-industries-need-more-workers-1216, accessed July 4, 2019; Sam Becker, "10 Jobs that Still Can't Find Enough Qualified Employees," https://www.cheatsheet.com/money-careers/jobs-qualified-employees.html, accessed July 4, 2019.

5. Lou Adler, "New Survey Reveals 85% of All Jobs Are filled Via Networking," https://ww.linkedin.com/pulse/new-survey-reveals-85-all-jobs-filled-via-networking-lou,adler, accessed July 5, 2019; "How Many Jobs Are Found Through Networking, Really? April 6, 2017, https://www.payscale.com/career-news/2017/04/many-jobs-found-networking, accessed July 5, 2019.; Jeff Gillis, "Top 5 Networking Tips for Job Seekers," https://the interviewguys.com/top-5-tips-for-job-seekers, accessed July 5, 2019.

6. Susan P. Joyce, "Guide to Social Media and Job Search," https://www.job-hunt.org/social/networking,social-media.shtml, accessed July 8, 2019; Erin Greenwald, "45 Things to Do on Social Media to Find Jobs," https://www.themuse.com/advice/45-things-to-do-on-social-media-to-find-jobs, accessed July 14, 2019; "How to Effectively Use Social Media in Your Job Search," mgt.buffalo.edu/career-resource-center/students/networking/social-media/using.html, accessed July 14, 2019.

7. Barbara Safini, "Hot Job Site: Brand-Yourself.com," http://jobs.aol.com/articles/2011/01//10/hot-job-site-brand-yourself-com, accessed July 30, 2012.

8. Robert Half, "Find Me a Job! How a Recruiting Agency Can Help You," August 23, 2018, https://www.roberthalf.com/blog/job-market/find-me-a-job-how-a-recruiting-agency-can-help, accessed July 15, 2019; Jake Butler and updated by Jess Aszkenasy, "How to Find a Job Using Recruitment Agencies," https://www. Save the student.org/student-jobs/how-to-find-a-job using-recruitment-agencies.html, accessed July 15, 2019.

9. Carole Martin, "Ten Interview Fashion Blunders," http://career advice monster.monster.com, accessed August 10, 2012.

10. Richard N. Bolles, *What Color Is Your Parachute? 2016* (Berkeley, CA: Ten Speed Press, 2016), p. 53.

11. Morgan Greenwald, "27 Lies Everyone Puts on a Resume," July 11, 2019, https://bestlifeonline.com/lying-on-resume, accessed July 30, 2019; Monica Torres, "Nearly Half of Us Are Lying on Our Resumes, Survey Finds," August 22, 2017, https://www.theladders.com/career-advice/nearly-half-of-us-are-lying-on-our-resumes-survey-finds, accessed March 14, 2019.

12. Dawn Papandrea, "The Biggest Resume Lies to Avoid," https://www.monster.com/career-advice/article/the-truth-about-resume-lies-hot-jobs, accessed July 31, 2019; Catherine Conlan, "What Really Happens When You Lie on Your Resume," https://www.monster.com/career-advice/article/when-you-lie-on-your-resume, accessed July 31, 2019.

13. Wes Weller, "5 Tips for Turning Your Resume into an Interview," http://blog.hiredmy-way.com/5-tips-for-turning-your-resume-into-an-interview, accessed August 3, 2012; Fleur Bradley, "10 Phrases to Ban from Your Resume," http://www.msnbc.com/id 37219334/ns/business-careers/t/phrases-ban-your-resume, accessed August 3, 2012.

14. Anne Fisher, "Wd u rite a resume like this?" June 4, 2014, fortune.com/2014/06/04 /resume-errors-snafus, accessed January 14, 2016.

15. Lisa McGrimmon, "Scannable Resume Formatting Guidelines," https://www .careerchoiceguide.com/scannable-resume.html, accessed August 1, 2019.

16. "The New Electronic Job Search Phenomenon," an Interview with Joyce Lain Kennedy, Wiley, http://archives.obs-us.com/obs/german/books/kennedy/JLKInterview .html, accessed December 2, 2008.

17. https://owl.purdue.edu/owl/jopb_search_writing_/rsumes_and_vitas/scannable _resumes_presentation.html, accessed August 5, 2019.

18. Annette Bruzzeze, "Online Resumes Can Trigger Identity Theft," usatoday.30.usatoday .com, accessed January 14, 2016.

19. Allison Doyle, "The Difference Between a Resume and a Curriculum Vitae," July 30, 2019, https://www.thebalancecareers/cv-vs-resume-2058495, accessed August 7, 2019; Eric Titner, "When Do You Need a Resume versus a CV?" thejobnetwork, Lafayette, Indiana, *Journal & Courier*, June 24, 2018, C14.

20. Monster staff, "Smart Tips to Help You Format and Write a Cover Letter," https://www.monster.com/career-advice/article/sample-cover-letter," accessed August 8, 2019.

21. Carole Martin, "The 2-Minute Drill," http://career-advice.monster.com/job-interview /interview-appearance/the 2-minute-drill/article.aspzx, accessed August 10, 2012; Carole Martin, "10 Interview Fashion Blunders," http://career-advicemonster.com/job -interview/interview-appearance/10-interview-fasion-blunders/article.aspx, accessed August 10, 2012.

22. Reeves, "Is Your Body Betraying You in Job Interviews?" http://forbes.com, accessed October 20, 2006.

23. Esther Choy, "5 Storytelling Tips to Help You Ace Your Job Interview," May 24, 2019, forbes.com/site/estherchoy/2019/03/24/5-storytelling-tips-help-you-ace-your-job -interview/#6d3fbb584b1, accessed August 29, 2019.

24. "12/18: 'Whatever' Loses Ground but Retains Annoying Word Title," maristpoll.marist .edu/1218-whatever-loses-ground-but-retains-annoying-word-title/tag/annoying -word/#sthash.PuqpwD7N.dpbs, accessed August 29, 2019.

25. Career Builder, "1 in 5 Employers Has Unknowingly Asked an Illegal Interview Question," April 9, 2015, CareerBuilder.com, accessed August 30, 2019.

26. Kris Maher, "The Jungle: Focus on Recruitment, Pay and Getting Ahead," *The Wall Street Journal,* January 14, 2003, p. B10.

27. "Job Seekers, Take Heart—and Control," *BusinessWeek Online,* http://www .businessweek.com, accessed September 11, 2006.

Resources

Bolles, Richard N. *What Color Is Your Parachute 2019. A Practical Manual for Job-Hunters and Career-Changers.* Berkeley, CA: Ten Speed Press, 2019.

DeCarlo, Laura. *Resumes for Dummies.* Indianapolis, IN: Wiley, 2015.

Enelow, Wendy S., and Shelly Goldman. *Insider's Guide to Finding a Job.* Indianapolis, IN: JIST Works, 2005.

Martin, Carole. *What to Say in Every Job Interview.* New York: McGraw-Hill, 2013.

O'Donnell, Neil. *Job Interview Essentials: Strategies for Excelling During a Job Interview.* Amazon Digital Services, 2018.

The Performance Review Interview

A s soon as an organization makes an offer of employment to an applicant it believes to be an ideal fit for the position and organization and an applicant accepts this offer that appears to be an ideal career and life choice, both parties enter into a professional relationship. The employer's goals should be to develop, empower, and retain the best talent they have attracted. And the employee's goals should be to achieve a high level of performance, learn and grow, set future performance targets, and work toward long-range career objectives. Frequent performance reviews, formal and informal, are essential toward achieving the goals of both parties.

The performance review is critical to the goals of employer and employee.

Not long ago, performance reviews were called "appraisals" and were typically annual or semiannual, top-down, judgmental processes with little or no input from the employee. The emphasis was typically on what the employee was doing wrong and had to change, or else. Following an extensive review of the literature and research on the "appraisal process," Michael Gordon and Vernon Miller drew two conclusions: that the process is the "source of widespread dissatisfaction" and "is an indispensable management responsibility."[1] Those of us who have been intimately involved in performance reviews can relate to these findings. In place of the traditional judgmental process, Gordon and Miller advocate an interview that is "a conversation about performance" that serves as the "defining moment in the appraisal process."[2] It takes both parties to make this conversation a success, but Gordon and Miller also discovered that few interview parties have training in conducting and taking part in performance interviews.

The nature of the review process is undergoing change at the right time.

Fortunately, the performance review philosophy Gordon and Miller advocate appears to be taking hold at the right time because it is ideally suited to the millennial population that will soon dominate the workforce from which employers must seek and retain employees. This generation places high value on collaboration, mentoring, development, professional and personal growth, and opportunities to make a difference.

The objectives of this chapter are to introduce you to the notion of the performance review interview as a *coaching process*, to ways of preparing effectively for these critical *organizational conversations*, to a variety of *review models*, to the principles of *conducting* and *taking part* in performance interviews, and to the performance *problem* interview. Let us begin by approaching the performance interview as a coaching event.

The Interview as a Coaching Opportunity

Management consultant Garold L. Markle advocates what he calls "catalytic coaching" designed to "energize and engage the human spirit at work." He claims this approach "spells the end of the performance review" as we have known it. Markle describes catalytic coaching as:

> A comprehensive, integrated performance management system built on a paradigm of development. Its purpose is to enable individuals to improve their production capabilities and rise to their potential, ultimately causing organizations to generate better business results. It features clearly defined infrastructure, methodology and skill sets. It assigns responsibility for career development to employees and establishes the boss as developmental coach.[3]

Coaching is the centerpiece of effective performance reviews.

Catalytic coaching is *future* rather than *past* centered, places responsibility on the employee rather than the supervisor, and deals with salary indirectly. The supervisor is a coach rather than evaluator.

When the author reviewed several performance review models designed to develop employees and enhance performance, the notion of coaching—effective communication in a nonjudgmental atmosphere—was the cornerstone of each.

This philosophy heightens the need for frequent contacts, discussions, and interviews between employers and employees that result in more favorable job-related performance ratings.[4] Conversations about performance become reviews of prior discussions connected closely to developmental and coaching plans. Employees know what to expect and are not confronted with surprises.

Create a supportive climate that involves the interviewee.

A relaxed and supportive climate based on mutual trust is critical for performance review interviews because employees must see the process as fair. Gordon and Miller claim "the nature of the communication that takes place" is "critical in creating" this sense of fairness.[5] Employees want to be treated sensitively without being judged and to get credit and rewarded for what they have done. Trust encourages employees to participate actively and equally in all aspects of the review and makes them feel free to express feelings and ideas.

"Too seldom" is a common complaint.

Employers play a major role in creating a positive and supportive climate by continually monitoring the employee's progress, offering psychological support in the forms of praise and encouragement, helping correct mistakes, and offering substantial feedback. They base their reviews on performance, not on the individual, by providing performance-related information, measuring performance against specific standards agreed upon during previous reviews, and giving feedback on a regular basis to avoid formal, once-a-year "tooth-pulling" reviews both parties dread. They identify poor performance immediately before damage to the organization and the employee is irreparable, and avoid surprises during the interview caused by withholding criticisms until a formal review session.

Preparing for the Performance Interview

Training and preparation are essential because both parties must create a genuine dialogue by listening to what the other is saying and not interrupting to get in your "two cents worth." Be patient. Encourage the other to speak freely and openly. Ask appropriate and tactful questions. Be careful of "Why" questions and how you ask them because they may place the other party on the defensive and signal disapproval, disbelief, or mistrust. The employer should provide guidance and support while minimizing the role of evaluator that may reduce the two-way communication process and damage the relationship. Address performance-related information, assign goals, and provide feedback that is equitable, accurate, and clear.

Reviewing Rules, Laws, and Regulations

While no EEO laws address the performance review specifically, the EEO laws and guidelines reviewed in Chapter 7 on the recruiting interview pertain to all aspects of employer-employee relations, including hiring, training, compensating, performance reviewing, promoting, transferring, and discharging. The employer must ensure that no employee is "held to higher standards or given negative evaluations because of race, color, religion, sex (including pregnancy, sexual orientation, or gender identity), national origin, disability, age (40 or older), or genetic information (including family medical history."[6]

Performance reviews must be standardized in form and administration, measure work performance, and be applied equally to all employees. "Using unreliable and unvalidated performance review" systems may cause serious legal problems because personal preferences, prejudices, and first impressions may lead to intentionally inflating or deflating performance ratings.[7] Communication between "superiors" and "subordinates"—so-called upward and downward communication—may lead to ritual forms of address "that guided by commonly understood cultural and social stereotypes, traditional etiquette, and gender-specific rules" may violate EEO laws and regulations.[8] As the American workforce continues to grow older and become more diverse, discrimination in performance reviews will become a prominent area of litigation. Employers must be particularly cautious when assessing traits such as honesty, integrity, appearance, initiative, leadership, attitude, and loyalty that are difficult to rate objectively.

Diane Chinn and Maurice Baskin, authorities on performance reviews and EEO laws, offer suggestions to make all reviews conform to the law and avoid lawsuits.[9] Supervisors who conduct performance reviews must receive detailed written guidelines and instructions and be trained

■ *Supervisors at all levels have found it useful to talk periodically with each subordinate about personal and work-related issues.*

Chabruken/The Image Bank/Getty Images

in conducting all aspects of reviews, particularly the interview. They must follow these guidelines to the letter. Have two or more staff review employees separately as cross-checks on accuracy and avoidance of bias. Be sure performance appraisals are reviewed with employees, making sure employees have the opportunity to offer suggestions and raise concerns before signing them. Employees should have full access to all records pertaining to their work.

Selecting Review Model

Theorists and organizations have developed performance review models that meet EEO laws and conduct fair and objective performance-centered interviews applicable to different types of positions and organizations. Their goals are to establish competencies, set goals and expectations, monitor performance, and provide meaningful feedback.

Behaviorally Anchored Rating Scales (BARS) Model

In the **behaviorally anchored rating scales** (BARS) model, employers identify skills essential to a specific position through a position analysis and then set standards with the aid of industrial engineers. Typical jobs with behaviors identified and standards set include telephone survey takers (at so many telephone calls per hour), meter readers for utility companies (at so many meters per hour), and data entry staff or programmers (at so many lines of entry per hour). Job analysts identify specific skills and weigh their relative worth and usage. Each job has specific measurable skills that eliminate game-playing and subjective interpretation by employers.

Employees report high levels of review satisfaction with the BARS model because they feel they have greater impact upon the process and see employers as supportive. They know what skills they are expected to have, their relative worth to the organization, and how their performance will be measured. However, not every job has measurable or easily identifiable skills, and arguments often arise over when, how, and by whom specific standards are set. Gordon and Miller discovered that "Raters distort the evaluations they make on subjective instruments in order to achieve goals other than providing an accurate assessment of the employee's performance (e.g., maintaining interpersonal relationships and group harmony)."[10]

Management by Objectives (MBO) Model

The **management by objectives** model involves a supervisor and an employee in a mutual (50-50) setting of results-oriented goals rather than activities to be performed. Advocates of the MBO model contend that behaviorally based measures can account for more job complexity, be rated directly to what an employee does, and minimize factors the employee cannot control. This model is designed to be less role ambiguous and subjective than person-based measures by making clear which behaviors are required for a specific job. It facilitates performance feedback and goal setting by encouraging employer-employee discussions regarding strengths and weaknesses.

The MBO model classifies all work in terms of four major elements: inputs, activities, outputs, and feedback. Inputs include equipment, tools, materials, money, and staff needed to do the work. Activities refer to the actual work performed: typing, writing, drawing, calculating, selling, writing, shipping. Outputs are results, end products, dollars, reports prepared, or services rendered. Feedback refers to subsequent supervisor reaction (or lack of it) to the output. When you act as a performance review interviewer using an MBO model, keep several principles in mind.

1. Always consider quality, quantity, time, and cost. The more criteria you use, the greater the chances that the measurement will be accurate.

> **Do not consider too many objectives.**

2. State results in terms of ranges rather than absolutes. Allow for freedom of movement and adjustment.

3. Keep the number of measurable objectives critical to performance to no more than six or eight, and set a mutual environment.

4. Try for trade-offs between mutually exclusive aims and measures. An objective that is too complex may be self-defeating. For example, attempts to reduce labor and decrease cost at the same time may create more problems than you can solve.

5. When the value of the performance is abstract, initiate practices that make it measurable.

6. If you cannot predict conditions on which performance success depends, use a floating or gliding goal that enables you to adapt to changing circumstances. Unfortunately the strengths of the MBO model, including its interactive nature and adaptability to complex positions, have led many organizations to abandon it because of "the large number of meetings required and the amount of documentation necessitated." Gordon and Miller write that unlike other models, it cannot be standardized to facilitate comparisons "across individuals or organizational units."[11]

Universal Performance Interviewing (UPI) Model

William B. Cash developed the **universal performance interviewing model** and tested it in more than 40 organizations.[12] This model begins with four basic questions that can serve as guidelines for fairness and comparisons among employees. Interviewers must be able to specify what is missing or not being done well so they can provide feedback to institute change.

> **The UPI model focuses on performance and work requirements.**

1. What is not being done that should be?

2. What expectations are not being met at what standard?

3. Could the person do it if motivated?

4. Does the individual have the skills to perform as needed?

Narrow each problem to a coachable answer. For example, maybe no one has emphasized that getting 100 percent of customers' numbers at the beginning of calls is critical because the customer number drives the system and makes it easier to access billing and other information under that number. An employee may know a customer's number by heart and intend to place it in the correct position on the screen after the customer hangs up. The observation-judgment dilemma has always been a problem for performance reviewers.

> **Understand why performance is lagging.**

The four questions in conjunction with six key words shown in Figure 9.1 enable employers to make several observations about performance. This model can be employed with others (such as the popular 360-degree review process) or with separate observations by supervisors, peers, and customers (internal and external) that can be compared to one another for consistency, trends, and rater reliability.

A sheet of paper with the four questions in columns can provide the bases for coaching sessions that take place weekly for production workers and monthly for professionals. A summary session may be done quarterly with an annual review to set goals for the coming year, review progress, and look at developmental needs.

> **Reviews must recognize excellence as well as problems.**

Once you have answers to the four basic questions, start on the model with *keep*. When an employee is doing something well, make sure the person knows you appreciate a job well done. Then go to *stop,* followed by *start, less, more,* and finishing with a time frame for improving performance. The word *now* emphasizes the importance of making appropriate changes immediately. Define *now* specifically in terms of weeks or perhaps months.

> **Play the role of coach rather than evaluator or disciplinarian.**

The universal performance interviewing model enables the coach to start with positive behavior for the employee to maintain, followed by behaviors to be corrected now. This begins the interview on a positive note. The *stop* list should be the shortest and reserved for behaviors that are qualitatively and procedurally incorrect, place an employee at risk, or are destructive to others in the workplace.

Present each of the four questions and the six words at different verbal and nonverbal levels, including hints, suggestions, and corrections. For example, you might say:

I want you to stop doing . . .   You must do more of . . .

I want you to start doing . . . now   You must do less of . . .

Figure 9.1   *Six key words in the universal performance interviewing model*

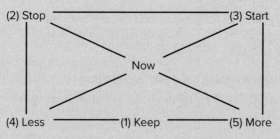

Interviewers may spend too much time on the analytical end and too little time on a specific behavior to be altered and how. If there is no specific alternative behavior, do not discuss it.

Use the customer service representative mentioned earlier as an example. Assume that the representative knows many customer numbers because of the frequency of calls from them and has the numbers memorized. She thinks it is unnecessary to log each number into the system until she has finished discussing specific problems with customers. One of the following styles may present the problem without making it worse.

- *Hint:* (smiling pleasantly) I noticed you were busy this morning when I stopped by to observe you. I just thought it might be easier for you to record each customer's number at the beginning of your conversation.

- *Suggestion:* (neutral facial expression and matter-of-fact vocal inflections) Just one idea came to mind from my observation this morning. I'd like to see you record each customer's number early so it doesn't get lost in the shuffle of answers to other callers.

- *Correction:* (stern voice and face) Based on my observation this morning, you must be sure to record each customer's number before you do anything else on the system for that number. This number drives our entire system, and problems result when it is not recorded immediately.

> **Hint and suggest before correcting.**

A major purpose of every performance interview is to provide accurate feedback to the employee about what must be altered, changed, or eliminated and when. Most employees want to do a good job, and the performance mentor or coach must provide direction for resolving problems.

> **Vague comments and suggestions may harm relationships and fail to improve performance.**

Another part of the model, crucial in performance interviews, are the two Ss—*specific* and *several*. Performance interviews are not guessing games. The two Ss enable interviewers to provide specific examples to show the problem is not a one-time incident.

Figure 9.2 includes all parts of the universal performance interviewing model. It enables you to measure or observe on-the-job behavior and either compare it to goals or quickly correct the smallest error.

Figure 9.2 *The universal performance interviewing model*

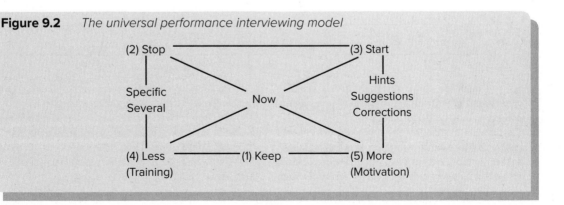

The 360-Degree Approach

The **360-degree** approach, while controversial, has gained acceptance in many large organizations. It enables them to receive input on employee performance from major constituents such as clients, customers, subcontractors, supervisors, and peers.

Although firms employ different 360-degree processes, an employee typically meets with a mentor or coach to select a review team that may include a direct supervisor, staff at the same level as the employee, colleagues, and staff from other departments within the organization. The process requires a review team with interpersonal and coaching skills. Each member of the review team fills out a questionnaire covering the employee's skills, knowledge, and style. When the completed questionnaires are summarized, scored, and displayed on a spreadsheet, the facilitator takes the raw data and interviews each team member. The employee receives the data prior to an interview with the team. The purpose of the review interview is to provide objective, behavior-based feedback, and suggestions for improvement. Compliments are integral to the process.

The facilitator may ask the employee to start with reactions to the data and then ask open questions with neutral probes. For example:

- Tell me about your responsibilities in R&D.

    Tell me more.

    Explain it to me.

    Describe your frustrations with the consultants' training manual.

- If you were going to take on a similar project, what would you do more or less of?

- When you identified people in accounting as "bean-counters," what did you mean?

    How did they behave?

    What did they say?

    What did they do?

Once the feedback session is completed, both parties formulate a plan for improvement.

> The 360-degree approach involves multiple observers.

> The 360-approach uses a team feedback interview.

> Employ open questions and probe into answers.

ON THE WEB

As you begin to think seriously about specific careers and organizations, investigate how organizations assess the performance of employees. Use the Internet to discover the types of performance review models used by employers in which you have a career interest. Access two types of resources. First, research employers through general resources such as CareerBuilder (http://www.careerbuilder.com), MonsterTrak (http://www.monstertrak.com/), and Monster (http://www.monster.com/). Second, check the Web sites of specific organizations such as Pricewaterhousecoopers (http://www.pwc.com), Ford (http://www.ford.com/), and Electronic Data Systems (http://www.eds.com).

The use of **multisource feedback** for employee development works best in organizations that use a goal-setting process from the top down. The 360-degree approach has a number of pluses. The questionnaires and interview provide objective data and feedback necessary for employee improvement and development because this feedback emanates from multiple sources: supervisors, peers, subordinates, and clients. The employee controls who gives feedback but is able to read, hear, and discuss the data that provide documentation for dealing with the performance review.

Be aware of pluses and minuses of each review model.

Although the 360-degree approach is used widely as a performance review model, its critics raise serious questions that organizations need to address to make it reliable and effective.[13] Some critics see the 360-degree approach as too similar to the old appraisal system in which superiors placed undue emphasis on what the employee was not doing well. They also cite untrained staff with little experience in important areas leading to deficient data on performance. Careful selection of the review team with strong employee input can reduce the influence of superiors, and training can resolve lack of experience and expertise of team members. Another criticism is that anonymous input from the team may be inaccurate, incompetent, and biased. Organizations must build transparency into the system that provides quality input while protecting the employee and members of the team. Critics also attack the underlying assumption that more people involved necessarily make for better performance reviews. Limiting the number of team members can resolve this concern. Garold Markle criticizes the 360-degree approach as too time-consuming on the parts of employee and staff. It may take weeks or months to complete. Organizations selecting this approach must develop tight time-lines for conducting and completing performance reviews using this system so they do not consume too many resources and drag on too long. Timely feedback and improvements in performance are essential to all review models.

Select a model best suited to your organization and employees.

Choosing from among these models, modifying one of them, or creating a model that seems best for your organization and employees is critical to the review process. Unfortunately, studies reveal that many organizations try one model or system after another and often adopt one that other organizations are abandoning.[14]

The Interviewer in the Performance Review Interview

Select and understand the perspective of the interview.

Selecting a performance review model (or modifying one) is critical for developing, empowering, and maintaining the best talent. The model the employer selects will succeed in achieving these goals, however, only when both parties are prepared for the performance interview and conduct it skillfully and openly.

Preparing for the Interview

The interviewer must understand and appreciate the nature of the employee's position and work and then design forms and questionnaires that focus on relevant and measurable goals. Pay particular attention to the fit between the employee, the position, and the work performed. What is the primary purpose of this interview, particularly if it is one among several interviews? Study the employee's past record, recent performance reviews, and reports from the person's mentor or coach. Review the employee's self-evaluation if one is part of the process.

Know yourself. Do you have potential biases that may affect the interaction or the results of the review? For example, the **halo effect error** occurs when you give favorable ratings to all duties, even when an employee excels in only one or two? The **pitchfork error** happens when you provide negative ratings to all facets of performance because of a particular characteristic, trait, or habit you dislike in others. The **central tendency error** results when you avoid assigning extreme ratings to certain aspects of performance. The **recency error** occurs when you rely too heavily on the most recent events or performance levels. The **length of service error** leads you to assume that present performance is high because past performance has been high. The **loose rater error** occurs when you are reluctant to point out weak or problem areas and focus on the average or better areas of performance. The **tight rater error** occurs when you believe that no employee can perform at the necessary standards. The **competitive rater error** occurs when you believe no one can perform higher than your level of performance. Work on eliminating each of these errors. How comfortable are you with a developmental perspective that is employee-directed, bottom-up, skill-based, now- and future-oriented, and collaborative in nature? If a performance review team is involved, how comfortable and effective are you as a facilitator or as a team member?

Relationship influences both parties and the nature of the interview.

What is the nature of your past and current relationship with the employee? If you are serving as the employee's mentor or coach, how amicable and collaborative is this relationship? What is the level of trust between you and the employee and between each member of the review team and the employee? Effective communication and cooperation suffers whenever an employee has serious concerns about the fairness of any part of the review process and any member of the review team. Research indicates, for instance, that reviewers evaluate employees differently when their relationships differ.

Gordon and Miller discovered that "All employees (i.e., both newcomers and incumbents) in high-quality relationships with their manager (i.e., marked by trust, exchange, and favoritism) received high performance ratings regardless of their level of performance."[15]

Conducting the Performance Review Interview

The interviewer must choose a location that provides privacy because the interview addresses personal and sensitive matters. Seating should be comfortable and arranged to enhance communication while avoiding any semblance of superior and subordinate positions.

Opening the Interview

Greet the employee in a warm and friendly manner and begin with some small talk. Do not prolong the opening, however, because this may enhance apprehension of what may be coming. Fear of performance reviews often comes from a history of unpleasant and nonproductive encounters with interviewers and teams, and this history may interfere with the communication between the employer and the employee in this interview. As a result, the review process may fail to achieve its full potential unless the employer can defuse such concerns and fears at the outset.

Be prepared but flexible in opening the interview.

Begin orientation by noting that this is a routine part of the review process and not the result of some major problem or concern. Emphasize that it is a collaborative effort to develop and empower each employee to grow professionally and personally and to make a difference within the organization and community. Provide a brief outline of how the interview will proceed with the employee's input. If the employee wants to address a relevant topic or issue first, do it. No interview plan should be set in stone if it is to be a professional conversation about performance. Encourage the employee to ask questions, provide input, introduce topics, and participate freely.

Discussing Performance

Use all of your listening skills.

Communication skills are essential when discussing performance. Be aware of nonverbal cues you and the interviewee may be exchanging. It is often not **what is said** but **how it is said.** Avoid words and actions that either party may perceive as accusatory or threatening or to insinuate criticism, skepticism, or blame. Be an active listener, and adapt your listening approach to the changing needs of the interview, listening for comprehension when you need to understand, for evaluation when you must judge, with empathy when you must show sensitivity and understanding, and for resolution when developing courses of action to enhance performance.

Maintain an atmosphere that ensures two-way communication beyond Level 1 by being sensitive, providing feedback and positive reinforcement, reflecting feelings, and exchanging information. Feedback may be your most important skill. Consider using more than one interviewer because research indicates that the team approach produces higher judgment validation, better developmental action planning, greater compliance with EEO laws, more realistic promotion expectations, and reduced perception of favoritism.

Develop a true dialogue with the interviewee.

Make the discussion full and open between both parties with the goal of improving individual and organizational performance. Keys to success are your abilities to communicate information effectively and encourage open dialogue. Strive to be a coach in career management and development.

Discuss the interviewee's total performance, not just one event. Begin with areas of excellence so you can focus on the person's strengths. Strive for an objective, positive integration of work and results. Cover standards that are met and encourage the interviewee to identify strengths. Communicate factual, performance-related information and give specific examples.

Strive for a balance between praise and criticism.

Excessive praise or criticism may create anxiety and distrust. Employees expect and desire to discuss performance weaknesses. An employee who receives no negative feedback or suggestions of ways to improve will not know which behavior to change. Discuss needed improvements in terms of specific behaviors in a constructive, nondirective, problem-solving manner. Employees are likely to know what they are not doing, but unlikely to know what they should be doing. Let the employee provide input. Probe tactfully and sensitively for causes of problems. On the other hand, do not heap criticism upon the employee. The more you point out shortcomings, the more threatened, anxious, and defensive the employee will become. As a perceived threat grows, so will the person's negative attitude toward you and the review process. It is often not what is intended that counts but what the other party believes is intended.

Summarize the performance discussion and make sure the employee has had ample opportunity to ask questions and make comments before establishing goals.

Use reflective probes and mirror questions to verify information received and feedback given. Use clearinghouse questions to be sure the employee has no further concerns or comments.

Setting New Goals and a Plan of Action

Focus on the future and not the past.

Although you are likely to focus on past and current performance early in the interview, it is vitally important that you look toward future goals, growth, and paths for the employee. The millennial generation is heavily interested in professional and personal growth and opportunities to make a difference.

Review previous goals before setting new ones because both parties must be able to determine when goals have been met and why. Make goals few in number, specific and well-defined rather than ambiguous, practical, neither too easy nor too difficult, and measurable. Avoid either-or statements, demands, and ultimatums. Combining feedback and employee suggestions with clear goal setting—while avoiding intentional or unintentional imposition of goals—produces the highest employee satisfaction. Decide upon follow-up procedures with the employee and how goals will be implemented.

Closing the Interview

Close with the perception that the interview has been valuable for both parties.

Do not rush the closing. Be sure the interviewee understands all that has transpired. Conclude on a note of trust and open communication and with the feeling that this has been an important session for interviewee, interviewer, and the organization. If you have filled out a required form, sign off on all agreements. If organizational policy allows, permit interviewees to put notes by items they feel strongly about. Provide a copy of the signed form as a record of the plan for the coming performance period.

The Employee in the Performance Review Interview

Do a self-evaluation before the interview.

The interviewee must be thoroughly prepared for the performance review interview. Preparation includes:

- Maintaining complete, detailed, accurate, and verifiable records of career achievements, initiatives, accomplishments, successes, and problem areas.
- Making a list of goals set during the previous review interview.
- Keeping letters, e-mails, and texts that contain positive and unsolicited comments from supervisors, co-workers, clients, customers, and management.
- Analyzing strengths and weaknesses and being prepared for corrective actions with ideas about how to improve performance.

At least half of the responsibility for making the performance interview a success rests with the employee. Attitude is critical. Self-evaluation prior to the interview may soften criticism during the performance interview. The interviewee should approach the interview as an opportunity to obtain meaningful feedback on performance, display strengths and accomplishments, and discover prospects for advancement. Prepare concrete examples of how expectations have been met or exceeded. Prepare intelligent, well-thought-out and carefully phrased questions. Be ready to discuss career goals and interests.

> **Avoid unnecessary defensiveness.**

Maintain a productive, positive relationship with the interviewer and avoid defensiveness unless there is something to become defensive about. If placed on the defense, maintain direct eye contact and clarify the facts before answering charges. Ask, "How did this information come to your attention?" or "What are the exact production figures for the third quarter?" This provides time to formulate thorough and reasonable responses based on complete understanding of the situation. Answer all questions thoroughly. Ask for clarification of questions you do not understand. Offer explanations, not excuses. Assess your performance and abilities reasonably, while being honest with yourself and your supervisor. Realize that what you are, what you think you are, what others think you are, and what you would like to be may describe different people.

> **A good offense is better than a good defense.**

The performance review interview is not a time to be shy or self-effacing. Mention achievements such as special or extra projects, help given to other employees, and community involvement. Be honest about challenges or problems you expect to encounter in the future. Correct any of the interviewer's false impressions or mistaken assumptions. Do not be afraid to ask for help.

> **Leave your temper at the door.**

When confronting a serious problem, discover how much time is available to solve it. Suggest or request ways to solve differences as soon as possible. The interviewer is not out to humiliate you, but to help you grow for your own sake and that of the organization. Keep your cool. Telling off a supervisor may give you a brief sense of satisfaction, but the person will still be your supervisor and the problem will be worse. Do not try to improve everything at once. Set priorities with manageable short- and long-range goals.

During the closing, summarize or restate problems, solutions, and new goals in your own words. Be sure you understand all that has taken place and agreements for the next review period. Close on a positive note with a determination to meet the new goals.

The Performance Problem Interview

Employee problems range from excessive absences, simple theft, failure to follow rules and procedures, and insubordination with supervisors to actions that threaten the well-being of fellow employees and supervisors, the organization, or customers and clients. The current practice is to handle all but extreme cases as a performance problem that requires coaching and to avoid the use of the term *discipline* that *implies guilt*. In many states, employers must show *just cause* for disciplining or terminating an employee.

Determine Just Cause

When "just cause" pertains to employment, it means that an employer must have sufficient justification for disciplining an employee to improve performance (rather than as punishment) or to terminate employment because of "misconduct irreconcilable or inconsistent with the contract of employment."[16] The opposite of just cause is *at will* which means that "either party may terminate the employment relationship at any time for any reason."[17]

Seven tests are standard criteria employed in both union and nonunion discipline and termination actions.[18] They can serve as guides when conducting performance problem interviews.

- *Was the employee given clear and unambiguous warning of possible disciplinary consequences for failure to follow a rule or directive?*

  Follow an oral warning with a written warning within a short time.

- *Was the rule or directive reasonably related to the orderly, efficient, and safe operation of the organization?*

  This rule or directive must be applied routinely and equally to all similar employees.

Treat all employees fairly and equally.

- *Before taking action, was the alleged incident investigated timely to determine if the employee had in fact disobeyed a rule or directive?*

  Timely usually means that an investigation occurred within one to three days.

- *Was the investigation conducted fairly, objectively, and in an impartial manner?*

  Did the employer interview all parties involved and obtain all necessary proof and documentation?

- *Was adequate evidence and documentation gathered to prove that a violation of a rule or directive had occurred?*

  Write down the problem in detail and obtain necessary proof and records before arranging for a performance problem interview.

The punishment must fit the infraction.

- *Were all employees determined to be in violation of a rule or directive given equal treatment?*

  Each organizational investigation of a performance problem must be conducted in exactly the same manner with no evidence of discrimination.

- *Is the penalty applied reasonably related to the seriousness of the problem and the employee's total performance record?*

  Penalties must be appropriate for the performance problem and progressive rather than regressive in nature.

Preparing for the Interview

Practice before conducting the real thing.

Prepare for performance problem interviews by taking part in realistic role-playing cases. These rehearsals can lessen anxiety and help you anticipate employee reactions, questions, and rebuttals. The variety of situations and interviewees encountered can help you refine your case-making, questioning, and responding.

Prepare for common employee responses that occur in the majority of performance problem interviews.

Be prepared for common reactions and responses.

1. *Apparent compliance:* overpoliteness and deference, apologies, promises, or statements of good intentions.

2. *Relational leverage:* statements that they have been with the organization longer than the interviewer and therefore know best, that they are the best and you can't

fire or discipline them, reference to friends or relatives within the organization, or reference to your close relationship to them.

3. *Alibis:* claims of tiredness, sickness, being overworked, budget cuts, family problems, it's someone else's fault, or poor instructions or information.

4. *Avoidance:* disappearing on sick leave or vacation, failure to respond to memos or phone calls, or failure to make an appointment.

What
evidence do
you have
of the
infraction?

Review *how* you know the employee has committed an infraction that warrants an interview. Did you see the infraction directly, as in the case of absenteeism, poor workmanship, intoxication, harassing another employee, or insubordination? Did you find out indirectly through a third party or by observing the results (such as lateness of a report, poor quality products, or goals unmet)? Were you anticipating an infraction because of a previous incident, behavior, or stereotype? For example, African-Americans and other minorities are often watched more closely than others because supervisors believe they are more likely to violate rules. On the other hand, supervisors tend to be lenient with persons they perceive as likable, similar to themselves, or possessing high status or exceptional talent. Supervisors may avoid confronting persons they know will "explode" if confronted. Avoid the practice of **gunnysacking** (a word based on the old burlap bag) in which you store up several grievances before dumping them on an employee all at once. While evading confrontation for a time, gunnysacking merely delays the inevitable, significantly worsens your relationship with the employee, and clouds the issue that has finally brought the employee's behavior to this point. The interviewee is likely to be hostile with attention diverted to prior behaviors instead of the current and probably most important one. Delay is not the easy way out.

**Distinguish
between the
severity of
infractions.**

Decide whether the perceived problem warrants a review. Absenteeism and low performance are generally considered more serious than tardiness and horseplay. Determine the cause of the infraction because it will affect how you conduct the interview and determine what action to take.

Review the employee's past performance and history. Two basic reasons for action are poor performance and a troubled employee. When a person's performance gradually declines, the cause may be motivational, work-related, or lack of mentoring. Drops in performance are indicated by swings in the employee's behavior or mood. Keep an eye on indicators such as attendance, quality or quantity of work, willingness to take instructions, cooperation with supervisors, and interactions with colleagues and clients.

**Relational
dimensions
are critical in
performance
problem
interviews.**

When an employee's performance declines suddenly, causes may be a marital problem, a breakup with a girlfriend or boyfriend, problem with a child, money problems, a gambling habit, alcohol or drug dependency, or a physical or mental health problem. Clinical depression is common. These employees may need medical help or professional counseling. Know your limits. Coaching and mentoring may do more harm than good. Know that EEO laws restrict actions of employers in some of these situations. Review Chapter 11 on the counseling interview to see which problems lay counselors can and cannot address.

What is your relationship with the employee at this time? Often neither party may want to take part, and you may have delayed the interview until there is no recourse and multiple problems have piled up. As problems come to a head, you and the employee may come to dislike and mistrust one another, even to the point of verbal and nonverbal abuse.

Keep Self and the Situation under Control

Uncontrolled anger can destroy an interaction.

While you want to head off a problem before it becomes critical, do not conduct a performance problem interview when you are angry. You will be unable to control the interview if you are unable to control yourself. Trust, cooperation, and disclosure are difficult to attain in a threatening environment.

When one party has difficulty containing anger or animosity, follow these suggestions.

*   *Hold the interview in a private location.* Meet where you and the employee can discuss the problem freely and openly.

*   *When severe problems arise, consider delaying a confrontation and obtaining assistance.* Let tempers cool down. You may want to consult a counselor or call security before acting.

*   *Include a witness.* The witness should be another supervisor because using one employee as a witness against another employee is dangerous for all parties involved. Follow to the letter all procedures spelled out in the union contract and organizational policies.

Focus on the Problem

Deal with facts rather than impressions and opinions.

Deal in *facts,* such as absences, witnesses, departmental records, and previous disciplinary actions. Do not allow the situation to become a trading contest: "Well, look at all the times I have been on time" or "How come others get away with it?"

*   *Record all available facts.* Unions, EEOC, and attorneys often require complete and accurate records. Take detailed notes, record the time and date on all material that might be used later, and obtain the interviewee's signature or initials for legal protection. Establish a **paper trail.**

*   *Do not be accusatory.* Avoid words and statements such as troublemaker, drunk, thief, and liar. You cannot make medical diagnoses so avoid medical terms.

Ask questions that draw out the interviewee.

*   *Preface remarks carefully.* Begin comments with phrases such as "According to your attendance report . . . ," "As I understand it . . . ," and "I have observed . . ." These force you to be factual and avoid accusing an employee of being guilty until proven innocent.

*   *Ask questions that enable the employee to express feelings and explain behavior.* Begin questions with "Tell me what happened . . . ," "When he said that, what did you . . . ," "Why do you feel that . . . ?"
    Open-ended questions allow you to get facts, feelings, and explanations from the employee.

■ *Never conduct a performance review interview when you are angry and conduct the interview in a private location.*

praetorianphoto/E+/Getty Images

Avoid Conclusions during the Interview

A hastily drawn conclusion may create more problems than it solves. Some organizations train supervisors to use standard statements under particular circumstances. If you are sending an employee off the job, you may say:

"I do not believe you are in a condition to work, so I am sending you home. Report to me tomorrow at . . ."

"I want you to go to medical services and have a test made; bring me a slip from the physician when you return to my office."

"I'm sending you off the job. Call me tomorrow morning at nine, and we can discuss what action I will take."

Such statements give you time to talk to others, think about possible actions, and cool-off.

Closing the Interview

Be slow to draw conclusions.

Conclude the interview in neutral. If discipline is appropriate, do it. Realize, however, that delaying action may enable you to think more clearly about the incident. Be consistent with organizational policies, the union contract, and all employees. Refer to your organization's prescribed disciplinary actions for specific offenses.

Summary

Performance reviews play critical roles in developing, empowering, and motivating employees. They should occur frequently and be collaborative efforts between employer and employee in which the employer plays the role of coach and mentor. The performance review interview must be a professional conversation rather than a top-down appraisal and focus primarily on the future rather than the past. The employer must select a performance model, or modify one, that is best suited to the organization's philosophy and the employee's position and duties and assesses performance accurately and positively. Both parties must be well-informed and prepared for the performance review interview. Avoid surprises.

A performance problem interview takes place when an employer discovers an employee has problems in performance or on-the-job behavior. Do not delay in addressing problems or let them accumulate. Dropping several concerns at once on an employee, often called gunnysacking, is likely to result in a confrontation rather than a professional conversation seeking to resolve past problems and prevent future ones for the mutual benefit of employer and employee. Avoid interviews when you are angry. Strive to help the employee see how specific performance and behavior problems are affecting them, fellow employees, clients, and the organization. At the same time, strive to understand why the employee is having performance or behavioral issues.

Key Terms and Concepts

360-degree approach
At will
Behavior-based feedback
Behaviorally anchored
   rating scales
Catalytic coaching
Central tendency

Competitive rater
Gunnysacking
Halo effect
Just cause
Loose rater
Management by objectives
Multisource feedback

Pitchfork effect
Recency error
Supportive climate
Tight rater
Universal performance
   interviewing model

Review Questions

1. Explain what Gordon and Miller mean when they advocate a "conversation about performance" as a replacement for the traditional appraisal interview.

2. Explain the basics of Markle's "catalytic coaching" approach to the performance review.

3. How can the employer create a positive and supportive climate for the performance review interview?

4. While EEO laws do not address the performance review specifically, what must the employer do to avoid violating EEO laws during the interview?

5. Compare and contrast the behaviorally anchored rating scale (BARS) review model with management by objectives (MBO) model.

6. Explain how the universal performance interviewing (UPI) model is designed with the coaching perspective as its cornerstone.

7. What are common criticisms of the 360-degree approach to performance reviews?

8. Compare and contrast the halo effect error with the tight rater error.

9. How might the relational history of the interviewer and interviewee affect the performance review interview?

10. What are possible negative results of excessive praise or criticism during the interview?

11. How can the interviewee be thoroughly prepared for a performance review interview?

12. How does the performance problem interview differ from the performance review interview?

13. Compare and contrast "just cause" with "at will" situations when considering termination of employment.

14. Identify four standard criteria that may serve as guides with conducting problem performance interviews.

15. Why should employers avoid the practice called "gunnysacking?"

Student Activities

1. Interview a human resources director of a large retail store such as Target, Walmart, Meijer, or COSCO. Discover which performance review model(s) or systems they employ. Do they use different models or systems for different types of employees: sales associates, cashiers, stockroom employees, supervisors, part-time versus full-time employees? Have they adapted popular models to suit their organization? How do they train performance review interviewers? How do they try to eliminate bias in performance reviews?

2. Compare and contrast Garold Markle's "catalytic coaching" approach to performance review with the behaviorally anchored rating scales model, the management by objectives model, and the universal performance interviewing model. How might the catalytic coaching approach alter each and improve each?

3. Interview a supervisor at two different types of organizations such as medical, educational, retail, production, or warehouse. Discover the types and severity of disciplinary problems they encounter among employees in a typical year. Who were involved in these problems? What caused these problems? How do interviewers address these problems to avoid confrontations while resolving them?

4. Terminating employees is always a difficult decision for organizations to make and is fraught with problems ranging from an angry employee, to lawsuits for unfair and unjustified termination, to violence following termination. Interview three people who have experience in terminating employees to discover how they prepare cases for termination, conduct performance problem interviews that will result in termination, and how they attempt to safeguard against lawsuits and potential violence.

Notes

1. Michael E. Gordon and Vernon D. Miller, *Conversations About Job Performance: A Communication Perspective on the Appraisal Process* (New York: Business Expert Press, 2012), p. 7.

2. Gordon and Miller, p. x.

3. Garold L. Markle, *Catalytic Coaching: The End of the Performance Review* (Westport, CT: Quorum Books, 2000), p. 4.

4. K. Michele Kacmar, L. A. Witt, Suzanne Zivnuska, and Stanley M. Gully, "The Interactive Effect of Leader-Member Exchange and Communication Frequency on Performance Ratings," *Journal of Applied Psychology* 88 (2003), pp. 764–772.

5. Gordon and Miller, pp. 25–26.

6. "Making an Employment Decision," U.S. Equal Employment Opportunity Commission, https://www1.eeoc.gov//employers/small business/checklists/conducting_performance _evaluations.cfm, accessed September 20, 2019.

7. "Performance Appraisal," Answer.com, http://www.answers.com/topic/performance -appraisal?&print=true, accessed October 9, 2009.

8. H. Lloyd Goodall, Jr., Gerald L. Wilson, and Christopher F. Waagen, "The Performance Appraisal Interview: An Interpretive Reassessment," *Quarterly Journal of Speech* 72 (1986), pp. 74–75.

9. Diane Chinn, "Legal Implications Associated With a Performance Appraisal," http://www.eHow.com/info_8038194_legal-implications-associated-performance-appraisal .htm, accessed September 28, 2012; Maurice Baskin, "Legal Guidelines for Associations for Conducting Employee Evaluations and Performance Appraisals," http://www.asaecenter.org/Resources/whitepaperdetail.cfm?itemnumber=12208, accessed September 28, 2012.

10. Gordon and Miller, pp. 21 and 23.

11. Gordon and Miller, p. 25.

12. This explanation comes from a booklet prepared by Baxter/Travenol Laboratories titled *Performance Measurement Guide*. The model and system were developed by William B. Cash, Jr., Chris Janiak, and Sandy Mauch.

13. Vernon D. Miller and Fredric M. Jablin, "Maximizing Employees' Performance Appraisal Interviews: A Research and Training Agenda," paper presented at the 2003 annual meeting of the National Communication Association at Miami Beach; correspondence with Vernon Miller, December 12, 2008; Markle, pp. 76, 78.

14. Gordon and Miller, pp. ix and 17.

15. Gordon and Miller, p. 26.

16. "Just Cause Definition," http://www.duhaime.org/LegalDictionary/J/JustCause.aspx, accessed October 4, 2012; Diane Chinn, "Standard of Proof in an Employee's Discipline Case," http://smallbusiness.chron.com/standard-proof-employees-discipline -case-14236.html, accessed October 4, 2012.

17. Kirk A. Johnson and Elizabeth Moser, "Improvement #4: Limit 'Just Cause' Discipline and Discharge Clauses," http://www.mackinac.org/4915, accessed October 4, 2012.

18. "What Is Just Cause?" http://www.hr.ucdavis.edu/supervisor/Er/copy_of-Justcause, accessed October 4, 2012; "Seven Tests of Just Cause," http://hrweb.berkeley.edu /guides/managing-hr/er-labor/disciplinary/just-cause, accessed October 4, 2012; Diane Chinn, "Standard of Proof in an Employee's Discipline Case"; Improvement #4.

Resources

Cappelli, Peter and Anna Travis. *The Performance Management Revolution.* Cambridge, MA: Harvard Business School Press, 2016.

Fletcher, Clive. *Appraisal, Feedback, and Development: Making Performance Work.* New York: Routledge, 2008.

Gordon, Michael E., and Vernon D. Miller. *Conversations About Job Performance: A Communication Perspective on the Appraisal Process*. New York: Business Expert Press, 2012.

Markle, Garold L. *Catalytic Coaching: The End of the Performance Review*. Westport, CT: Quorum Books, 2000.

Winter, Graham. *The Man Who Cured the Performance Review*. New York: John Wiley, 2009.

The Persuasive Interview

A persuasive interview occurs whenever an interviewer attempts to influence how the interviewee **thinks, feels, and/or acts.** While sales interviews come readily to mind, you take part in persuasive interviews when assuming the interactive role of professor or student, attorney or client, candidate or voter, believer or nonbeliever, parent or child. Many interviews contain elements of persuasion such as investigations, surveys, recruiting, employment, performance reviews, counseling sessions, and health care. The pervasiveness of persuasion in our lives led Roderick Hart to claim that "one must only breathe to need to know something about persuasion."[1] Persuasive interviews range from everyday interactions such as an attempt to persuade a roommate how to be safe when walking on campus late at night to an attempt to persuade a member of Congress to change positions on complex issues such as global warming, immigration, or gun control. The persuasive interview, like all interviews, is a **mutual interaction** in which both parties must play active and critical roles. It is not something **done to** but **with** another party.

> Persuasion is pervasive in our society.

The objectives of this chapter are to introduce you to the ethical standards, responsibilities, and skill set essential for effective participation in persuasive interviews. These include knowing, understanding, and respecting the other party; being an active, critical, and open-minded participant; being informed on the issue and situation; and learning how to structure, develop, and support well-reasoned and ethical positions on issues and courses of action.

The Ethics of Persuasion

Since the fundamental intent of the persuasive interview is to **alter** or **sustain** an interviewee's ways of thinking, feeling, and/or acting, both parties "have the responsibility to uphold appropriate ethical standards of persuasion."[2] This is often easier said than done because it may be difficult to determine which ethical standards are most appropriate in specific situations and with diverse parties. Richard Johannesen writes that "**Ethical issues** focus on value judgments concerning degrees of right and wrong, virtue and vice, and ethical obligations in human conduct."[3] The words you choose tend to indicate how specific actions, situations, and relationships influence your judgments of degrees of right and wrong, goodness or badness in interactions. For example, if you believe the other party is making an untrue statement or claim, how do you decide if it is **lying** or merely misleading, fibbing, exaggerating, stretching, or spinning? If a party takes something that does not belong to them, what makes it **stealing** or merely misappropriating, taking, sampling, borrowing, or making a bad decision?

> Ethics and persuasion are intertwined.

Every tactic and strategy discussed in this chapter, including careful analysis of and adaptation to the other party, may be manipulated and become unethical. Although ethical standards vary widely in our society, you take on the responsibility of developing and adhering to an acceptable code of ethics whenever you attempt to alter or sustain the way another thinks, feels, and/or acts. Start from the position that you are responsible for what you do and the judgments you make during persuasive interviews. This is not far from the ancient golden rule, "Do unto others as you would have them do unto you." Gary Woodward and Robert Denton provide a starting point that is close to both the golden rule and the physician's Hippocratic Oath that contains the phrase, "First, do no harm." They write that "ethical communication should be fair, honest, and designed not to hurt people."[4]

> The golden rule is a starting point.

Be Honest: You are probably an honest person who tries to avoid hurting or offending others. At the same time, however, you may have "fibbed a bit" about why you missed a meeting, "exaggerated a bit" about your income, or "fudged a bit" about a promise? Herbert Simons suggests that you ask yourself, "Could I justify my act publicly if called on to do so?"[5] If you are truly honest, for instance, you will not conceal true motives and beliefs, compromise ideas and ideals, fail to divulge disbelief in the perceived effect of a proposal you are making, or camouflage commitments and pledges.

Be Fair: How vulnerable is the other party because of health, age, gender, income, status difference, or expertise? How serious are the potential consequences? How accurate and fair are your arguments, facts, language, tactics, and claims? Are you guilty of stockpiling objections and grievances until late in the interview? Strong and emotional disagreements are common in persuasive interviews, so be aware of the potential harm to your relationship and future interactions with this party.

> Honestly and fairness are the basis of ethical persuasion.

Be Skeptical: Trust in others is an admirable trait, but do not be gullible. The old adage "If it seems too good to be true, it probably isn't" is based on centuries of experience. Balance your trust with healthy skepticism. No con artist can be successful without your help and gullibility. Be wary of simplistic assertions, claims, promises, and solutions. Quick fixes that cost little are rarely quick or free. Listen, think, and question as an active participant in every persuasive interview.

Be Thoughtful and Deliberate: The notion of "buyer beware" is alive and well in our society and places the burden of proof solely on the interviewee. **Both parties** in persuasive interviews must listen, think, question, and conduct research before deciding to change the ways they think, feel, or act. Unfortunately, research indicates that we are often more interested in appearance than substance. If the other party looks like us, sounds like us, talks like us, acts like us, appears to have the right connections (social, political, business, religious, financial), we are likely to see claims and proposals as logical, substantive, and acceptable. In fact, the mere appearance or reasoning may be more persuasive than substance.

> Appearance often outweighs substance.

Be Open-Minded: Being open-minded does not mean you lack strong beliefs, attitudes, values, or commitments. It does mean that you are willing to change when situations, events, or substantive interactions warrant modifications or exceptions. Be careful

Be open to change when it is warranted.

of **profiling** the other party because or profession, political affiliation, religious prefer-ence, race, gender, age, or culture and then automatically assuming the party is trustwor-thy/untrustworthy, competent/incompetent, caring/uncaring. Do not reject an idea or proposal merely because it requires change.

Be Responsive: Be active throughout the interview. Make the other party aware of your concerns, needs, limitations, thoughts, and feelings as the interview progresses, rather than near or during the closing. Richard Johannesen writes that "persuasion can be seen as a transaction in which both persuaders and persuadees bear mutual respon-sibility to participate actively in the process."[6] With this statement clearly in mind, let us focus on the roles of interviewer and interviewee and how each must prepare for and participate in persuasive interviews.

Part 1: The Interviewer in the Persuasive Interview

The ability to **tailor** your persuasive effort to a **specific party** is perhaps the interview's most significant advantage over other forms of persuasion. Learn everything that is rel-evant concerning the other party and design your interview upon what you discover. A generic effort based on little personal information produces little success. The "cold call," for instance, generates only a 1 to 3 percent chance of gaining an appointment or follow-up, neither of which guarantees success.[7] There are no simple formulas for suc-cessful persuasive interviews, but your likelihood of success depends on how well you can satisfy five interrelated criteria.

1. Your proposal creates or addresses **this interviewee's** needs, desires, or motives.
2. Your proposal and you (including your profession and organization) are consistent with **this interviewee's** beliefs, attitudes, and values.
3. Your proposal is feasible, practical, or affordable for **this interviewee**.
4. Your proposal's advantages outweigh its disadvantages for **this interviewee**.
5. There is not better alternative course of action for **this interviewee**.

Study the Interviewee

Tailoring requires knowing.

Learn everything you can about the interviewee prior to the persuasive interview so you can tailor the interview to this party and prepare to establish a relationship that is essen-tial in interpersonal interactions.

Personal Characteristics

Identify relevant personal characteristics such as age, gender, race, size, disabilities, health, appearance, and intelligence. One or more of these may determine what a person can do or want to do. Beware of social stereotypes such as women are nurturing but winey, men are mechanically inclined but arrogant, gay men are creative but effeminate, elderly are trustworthy but gullible, college students are smart but partiers, Hispan-ics are hard workers but illegal aliens, professors are highly intelligent but have little common sense, and politicians are public servants but out for personal gain. In reality, each person is a composite of personal characteristics that challenges easy stereotyping. Research indicates, however, that level of intelligence tends to make interviewees less receptive to persuasion. Highly intelligent interviewees are more influenced by evidence and logical arguments and tend to be highly critical. Both factors make them more difficult to persuade.[8]

Educational, Social, and Economic Backgrounds

The level of educational attainment may affect interviewees in significant ways. For example, college graduates tend to be more involved in public affairs, the sciences, and cultural activities, to have good jobs with good incomes and to like them, to hold fewer stereotypes and prejudices, and to be more critical in thinking, flexible, and independent in attitudes.[9] Socioeconomic background and memberships are important because attitudes are strongly influenced by the groups to which we belong. The more committed an interviewee is to groups, the less likely you are to persuade with an effort that conflicts with group norms. Charles Larson writes that a major determinant of behavior intention is **Normative influence,** "a person's belief that important individuals or groups think it is advisable to perform or not to perform certain behaviors."[10] An interviewee's occupation, income, avocations and hobbies, superior/subordinate relationships, marital status, dependents, work experiences, and geographical background affect frames of reference—the persuadee's way of viewing people, places, things, events, and issues.[11]

> Group memberships influence attitudes and behaviors.

Culture

Cultural differences may affect persuasive interviews in a variety of ways. For example, those in individualistic Western cultures such as the United States, tend to be "**me centered**" and place importance on **individual** accomplishment, status, leadership, and accumulation of awards, wealth, large homes, luxury cars, and expensive clothing. Other cultures, particularly in Asia, are "**we centered**" and place importance on **group** or **team** accomplishment, status, leadership, and accumulation and judge emphasis on the individual as distasteful and offensive. They "place less importance on the opinions and preferences of the individual." In individualistic cultures "personal goals take precedence over the goals of one's group, and attitudes and perceptions link rather closely to behavior."[12] Some cultures consider bribery a normal part of business. Others feel it is necessary to give gifts as part of the process. Bargaining is an essential part of persuasion in many cultures, often preceded by a relationship-building period over dinner or tea. In the United States, "time is money," so Americans expect others to be on time. In Great Britain it is considered "correct" to be 5 to 15 minutes late, and in Italy a person may arrive two hours late and not understand why you are upset.

> Each culture has norms that affect values, beliefs, and attitudes.

Values/Beliefs/Attitudes

Each culture has a set of generally accepted **values**—fundamental beliefs about ideal states of existence and modes of behavior that motivate people to think, feel, or act in particular ways.[13] Values, often referred to as "hot buttons," are the foundations of beliefs and attitudes. The following scheme of values includes those central to the American value system, the hot buttons that motivate interviewees to think, feel, or act. As you review the schema of values below, determine which ones would be most **relevant** and **appropriate** for the interviewee in each of these scenarios: (1) You want to persuade a fellow student to take part in the Christmas stocking fund drive sponsored by the student government; (2) You want to persuade a member of your church, temple, or mosque to contribute time to a Habitat for Humanity home it is building; (3) You want to persuade an acquaintance to help clean up a neighborhood that was severely damaged by a recent flood; (4) You want to persuade a member of the ROTC at your university to contribute to the Wounded Warriors Fund.

Survival Values

Peace and tranquility	Preservation of health
Personal attractiveness	Safety and security

> Values are the "hot buttons" in persuasive interviews.

Social Values

Affection and popularity	Generosity
Cleanliness	Patriotism and loyalty
Conformity and imitation	Sociality and belonging

Success Values

Accumulation and ownership	Material comfort
Ambition	Pride, prestige, and social recognition
Competition	Sense of accomplishment
Happiness	

Independence Values

Equity and value of the individual	Freedom from restraint
Freedom from authority	Power and authority

Progress Values

Change and advancement	Quantification
Education and knowledge	Science and secular rationality
Efficiency and practicality	

Now that you studied this schema of values, which ones did you identify as relevant and appropriate for each of the four scenarios? Why these?

Because an interviewee's historical, social, religious, political, and economic **beliefs** are derived from values, the interviewer must determine which beliefs are relevant to the topic, issue, or proposal. For instance, if equity and value of the individual are significant values to an interviewee, he or she is likely to espouse equal rights and opportunities for women, LBGTs, African-Americans, and Hispanics. If education and knowledge

> Values are the foundations of our belief systems.

are significant values, a party is likely to support school funding referendums and college fund-raising campaigns and have strong interests in books, libraries, and databases.

Attitudes are relatively enduring combinations of beliefs that predispose people to respond in particular ways to persons, organizations, places, ideas, and issues. If you are a conservative, you are likely to react predictably to things you consider to be liberal. The reverse is true if you are a liberal. Attitudes come from beliefs that come from cherished values. Determine the interviewee's probable attitude toward the need or desire you will develop and the proposal you will make.

> **Attitudes tend to predict actions.**

Consider the other party's probable attitudes along an imaginary scale from 1 to 9 with 1, 2, and 3 indicating strongly positive; 4, 5, and 6 indicating neutrality or ambivalence; and 7, 8, and 9 indicating strongly negative.

Strongly for			**Undecided/neutral**				**Strongly against**	
1	2	3	4	5	6	7	8	9

From what you know about this interviewee, where along this scale is this person's attitude likely to rest? If on positions 1 or 2, little persuasive effort may be required. If on positions 8 or 9, persuasion may be impossible beyond a small shift in feeling or thinking. If the attitude is on positions 4, 5, or 6, theoretically you should be able to alter ways of thinking, feeling, or acting with a good persuasive effort. This may not be the case, however, if an interviewee is strongly committed to remaining neutral, undecided, or noncommitted.

> **Know what is possible, likely, and impossible.**

The interviewee's attitude toward the interviewer (credibility, image) is often the most important determinant of success. You must assess the interviewee's attitudes toward you, your profession, and the organization you represent. Several dimensions determine your credibility, including *trustworthy/safe* (honest, sincere, reliable, fair), *competent/expert* (intelligent, knowledgeable, good judgment, experienced), *goodwill* (caring, other-centered, sensitive, understanding), *composure* (poised, relaxed, calm, composed), and *dynamic/energetic* (decisive, strong, industrious, active). Think of your previous experiences with this party. If an interviewee dislikes you, distrusts your organization, or sees your profession as dishonest or untrustworthy, you must attempt to alter these attitudes during the interview or you will fail. Creating and maintaining high credibility relies on how your appearance, manner, reputation, attainments, personality, and character communicate trustworthiness, competence, caring, composure, and dynamism. On one hand, people react favorably to highly credible interviewers who are similar to them in important ways and appear to share their values, beliefs, and attitudes. On the other hand, they expect them to be wiser, braver, more knowledgeable, more experienced, and more insightful.

> **Low credibility may undermine the best effort.**

Emotions

Emotions (feelings, or passions) influence how we think, feel, and act. Some sources categorize them as **survival emotions** (hate, hear, anger, love, and sexual attraction) and **social emotions** (pride, shame, guilt, sympathy, pity, humor, joy, and sadness). Others categorize them as **positive** (happiness, joy, pride, relief, hope, compassion) or **negative** (fear, guilt, anger, sadness, disgust, and envy).[14] Regardless of how we categorize them, emotions and values are the "hot buttons" essential in persuasive interviews. You must

> **How we feel affects what we believe and do.**

Figure 10.1   *The relationship of values, beliefs, attitudes, and emotions*

```
                              E
                        V     m
                        a     o                          Persons
                        l     t                          Places
      Values } Beliefs } Attitudes } u     i   } Judgment/Action }   Things
                        e     o                          Ideas
                        s     n                          Acts
                              s
```

become aware of how the interviewee **feels** about a person, event, issue, problem, or solution at a given time and in a given situation so you can determine which emotions to appeal to in this interview.

Altering or reinforcing an interviewee's ways of thinking, feeling, or acting is a complex process. Figure 10.1 shows the relationship of values, beliefs, attitudes, and emotional appeals to judgment or action toward persons, places, things, ideas, and acts. The persuasion process starts with **values** (our fundamental beliefs about existence and behavior), that lead to **specific beliefs** (judgments about what is probably believable or true), that form **attitudes** (organizations of relevant beliefs and predispose an interviewee to respond in particular ways, that result in **judgments** or **actions**, triggered by **value** and **emotional appeals.**

Study the Situation

The interview situation is a total context of persons, relationships, motives, events, time, place, and objects. Study each element of the situation carefully, including atmosphere, timing, physical setting, and outside forces. These elements influence how an interview party interacts, acts, and reacts.

Atmosphere

What Is the **prevailing mood** in which this interview will take place: positive or negative, confident or fearful, friendly or hostile, accepting or rejecting, trusting or suspicious, caring or indifferent? What **triggers** an interview may affect the interaction in significant ways. Is it a regularly scheduled event or one without warning or notice, a scheduled event or one brought about by an emergency or crisis, a routine event or a unique event, a moment of opportunity or one fraught with dangers?

Interview parties may see the atmosphere quite differently.

Timing

Timing may be everything.

Philosophers, scientists, sales representatives, and even song writers have long proclaimed and illustrated that "Timing is everything." Although timing is not always "everything" in persuasive interviews, it is often critical. Some of us are morning people and some of us are afternoon or night people, meaning that this period is when we are at our peak abilities to think, feel, and act—and perhaps to persuade. It may be too early or too late in the day or time of year for some interviews. If you are contacting people about

■ *The persuasive situation is a total context of persons, relationships, events, time, place, and objects.*

praetorianphoto/E+/Getty Images

giving to a "Toys for Tots" campaign, you want to make contacts when the holiday season is most on their minds and they are in the mood for giving. College representatives contact alumni for donations when they are thinking of income tax deductions and not close to April 15 when they are thinking about tax payment. Asking for a raise on the same day your organization releases a bleak financial report is not good timing.

Physical Setting

> On whose turf will the interview take place?

Select a location that is comfortable, private, and free of interruptions, particularly telephone calls and people coming and going. If you know the interview may be lengthy, make an appointment and reserve a setting. Review the seating arrangements discussed in Chapter 2, and choose one that is most appropriate for this interview. Furnishings, objects, pictures, licenses, and awards may enhance the atmosphere of the interview and your credibility with the interviewee. Always be aware of **whose turf** you are on. Respect the location and understand the role you are playing in this setting. Interviewees may feel more comfortable and in control during interviews that take place in their homes, offices, or places of business. A specific location may enhance the persuasiveness of your interview. For instance, if you want to persuade a person to donate to the local civic theatre, the theatre itself would be an ideal setting. On the other hand, one or both parties may prefer a neutral location such as a restaurant, hotel or conference room, club, or park.

Outside Forces

> Outside forces may wage counter-persuasive efforts.

Outside forces (professional, organizational, legal, social, family) may have considerable influence on what you can and cannot do, need and need not do, and will or will not accomplish in a persuasive interview. Family members or friends, for example, may influence how an interviewee prepares for and interacts during an interview and follows up on agreements or commitments after the interview. Be aware of specific outside forces that may affect you as interviewer and the interviewee and determine which values, beliefs, and attitudes you must incorporate in an interview to alter a party's way of thinking, feeling, or acting.

Research the Issue

Strive to be the best informed and most authoritative person in each interview. Investigate all aspects of the issue, including events that have contributed to the problem, reasons for and against change, evidence on both sides of an issue, and possible solutions.

Search for up-to-date information. Remember that you are preparing to take part in a persuasive interview—an interactive process—and not a persuasive presentation to an audience of one. Determine ahead of time what an interviewee knows about and attitudes held toward an issue and possible solutions.[15] The interviewee can demand proof, ask for clarification of language or arguments, challenge assumptions, generalizations, and claims, and request documentation for evidence or identification of alleged authorities or experts. Interviewees are impressed with interviewers who do not become defensive or irritated but appear to be helpful and understanding by offering clear explanations and clarifications, satisfactory proof and documentation, and showing respect for their concerns and positions.

> **Have the facts and know how to use them.**

Sources

Do not overlook any potentially valuable source of information: the Internet, e-mail, interviews, letters, pamphlets, questionnaires, surveys, unpublished studies, reports, newspapers, periodicals, professional journals, and government documents. Use your own experiences and research. Know which sources are available to and respected by the interviewee.

Evidence

Search for a variety of evidence to support your need and proposal. Collect *examples,* both factual and hypothetical, to illustrate your points. People like good *stories* that make problems real. Gather *statistics* on relevant areas such as inflation, growth rates, expenses, benefits, insurance coverages, profits and losses, causes and effects. Collect *statements* from acknowledged *authorities* on the topic as well as *testimonials* from those who have joined, attended, purchased, signed, or believed. Look for *comparisons and contrasts* between situations, proposals, products, and services. Locate clear and supportable *definitions* for key terms and concepts.

Distinguish *opinion* (something that is assumed, usually cannot be observed, can be made at any time, and either is or should be believed tentatively) from *fact* (something that can be or has been observed, is verifiable, and is thought of as securely established). Present your evidence effectively, including thorough documentation of your sources. The substance of your persuasive interview enhances the long-term effect of your interview and is particularly important if a decision will not be made for weeks or months.

> **The effect of a well-supported interview lasts longer.**

Plan the Interview

After analyzing the interviewee, studying the situation, and researching the topic, tailor the interview to this interviewee.

Determine Your Purpose

If you know the interviewee will be a "hard sell" because of a value, belief, and attitude system, then your purpose may be merely to influence thinking or feeling in a minor way. Getting the interviewee to think about an action or to admit there is a problem may be a major success for a first interview. Later you might move the interviewee toward a more significant change or action. On the other hand, if the interviewee contacts you and says

Be realistic and patient.

he or she is considering a change in auto insurance providers, is interested in contributing to the United Way fund, or is thinking of taking a tour of the Rocky Mountains, you may move quickly through need and desire to solutions with a good chance of success.

Set a realistic goal for each interview. Significant changes come in increments after a series of interviews. Do not assume after one interview that an interviewee is not interested or will not change. Authorities on sales interviews claim that it typically takes five contacts before a sale is made. Be patient.

Select Main Points

Do not overload the interviewee.

Select points or reasons to establish a need or desire. If you rely on a **single point,** the interviewee may perceive little urgency in a situation that is so simple and find it easy to attack or reject the only point on which your persuasive effort rests. Research indicates that **more points** developed thoroughly enhance the effectiveness of persuasion immediately and over time, but more means three to four points or reasons, not six to eight. Too many points may consume a lot of time and overload the interviewee with too much information to process meaningfully. On the other hand, the interviewer may try to shorten the interview by developing each point superficially and produce little if any change in the interviewee's ways of thinking, feeling, or acting.

Know the strength of each point.

After developing three to four points thoroughly, weigh the strength of each with this interviewee in mind to determine **the order** in which you will present them. For example, college recruiters have discovered that prospective students tend to make their decisions with three criteria in mind and in this order: available majors, academic reputation, and financial aid. Starting with your strongest point first or last is about equal in effect but, if there is a real possibility that you may not get to the last point because of time or other commitments, begin with your strongest point.

Develop Main Points

Develop each point into what the interviewee will see as a valid and acceptable logical pattern. Effective interviews are carefully crafted blends of the logical and the psychological. You have choices to make.

Arguing from accepted belief, assumption, or proposition involves three explicitly stated or implied assertions (statements you believe and clearly want others to believe). For instance, a fire inspector might argue this way:

Your assertions must lead to your conclusion.

Assertion #1: All residents in apartments should have renter's insurance to replace their belongings in case of fire or theft.
Assertion #2: You reside in an apartment.
Point: You should have renter's insurance.

You need not state all three parts of this pattern if the interviewee is likely to provide the missing assertion or conclusion. Regardless, your argument rests on the first assertion that is the critical belief, assumption, or proposition. For instance, you might leave the second assertion unstated and let the interviewee provide it. This involves the interviewee in the process and encourages self-persuasion. This strategy is possible with all patterns of argument.

> *Assertion #1:* All residents in apartments should have renter's insurance to replace their belongings in case of fire or theft.
> *Assertion #2:* (left unstated)
> *Point:* You should have renter's insurance.

You might state your assertions and let the interviewee draw the conclusion.

> *Assertion #1:* All residents in apartments should have renter's insurance to replace their belongings in case of fire or theft.
> *Assertion #2:* You reside in an apartment.
> *Point:* (left unstated)

Arguing from condition is based on the assertion that if something does or does not happen, something else will or will not happen. You might reason this way with a friend.

> *Assertion #1:* If you continue vaping, you are likely to develop a long-term respiratory disease.
> *Assertion #2:* You seem intent on continuing vaping.
> *Point:* You are going to develop a long-term respiratory disease.

Weigh conditions carefully and support them effectively. As with arguing from accepted belief, you may invite the interviewee to fill in a missing part or parts.

Arguing from two choices is based on the assertion that there are only two possible proposals or courses of action. You remove one by showing it will not work or resolve a problem, and conclude the obvious.

> *Assertion #1:* You have two choices in purchasing a text for this course, traditional printed version or an e-book.
> *Assertion #2:* The printed version can be carried anywhere, highlighted, and used during class.
> *Point:* So, I recommend the traditional printed edition for my class.

> **Your evidence must warrant your conclusion.**

You must be able to limit the choices to two and then convince the interviewee that one is unacceptable so yours is the only option.

Arguing from example leads to a generalization about a whole class of people, places, things, or ideas from a sample of this class.

> *Sample:* In a recent survey of female members of the U.S. Navy, 56 percent reported having been sexually assaulted while on active duty.
> *Point:* The majority of female members of the U.S. Navy have been sexually assaulted while on active duty.

The quality of the sample, as in the survey interview, is critical in argument from example.

Arguing from cause-effect is related to example because interviewers often use a sample as proof of a causal relationship. Unlike the argument from example that leads to a generalization, this argument attempts to establish what caused a specific effect.

Beware of hasty
cause-effect
arguments.

Evidence: In a study of 1000 auto fatalities last year, 81 percent were not wearing
seatbelts.

Point: Not wearing seatbelts is the leading cause of fatalities in auto accidents.

Your evidence must convince the other party that this is the only or major cause
of an effect.

Arguing from facts, unlike arguing from example, does not rely on a **sample of a class**
of people, places, things, or ideas to prove a point but on a **body of facts** to prove a point
that best explains a phenomenon.

Facts: When investigating the robbery at The Burger Barn on IL 204, we discovered
no signs of a break-in, doors always locked after hours were opened, the safe
was apparently opened without force of any type, and only cash was taken from
the safe.

Point: This robbery was an inside job by a current or past employee.

Arguing from analogy occurs when you point out that two things (people, places,
objects, proposals, ideas) have important characteristics in common and draw a conclusion based on these similarities.

How similar are
the similarities?

Similarities: You say you would like to replace your current truck with one just
like it. The Utah, like your Type 20, seats five comfortably and has a hefty V-6
engine for hauling a quarter-ton load and maintaining Interstate speeds and
acceleration. It has a towing package that will handle a 24-foot travel trailer.
The Utah's fuel mileage is equal to or better than your current truck.

Point: The Utah is an ideal replacement for your current truck.

The number of significant similarities are critical in developing this argument.

Select Strategies

When you think
theories, think
strategies.

Researchers over the past half-century have developed a variety of theories from observation and experiment to explain how we become convinced to alter or sustain our ways
of thinking, feeling, and/or acting. Let's review five of these as **Persuasive Strategies**.

Identification Theory

Kenneth Burke claims that you persuade others by **identifying** with them, that is, by
establishing **consubstantiality** (substantial similarity) with them. The overlapping circles
in the interviewing model developed in Chapter 2 are based on Burke's theory that you
must literally talk the other's language through "speech, gesture, tonality, order, image,
attitude, *identifying* your ways with theirs."[16] There are several ways to establish this
common ground.

- *Associating* with groups to which you both belong, shared cultural heritage or
regional identification, programs you both support.
- *Disassociating* from groups, cultures, regions, or programs the interviewee
opposes or is distant from.

- Developing *appearance and visual symbols* that establish identification such as dress, hairstyle, makeup, jewelry, political buttons, or religious symbols.

> Appearance is important in perceiving common ground.

- Sharing *language* such as jargon, slang, colloquialisms, and in-group words and phrases.

- Employing *content and values* important to the interviewee.

Balance or Consistency Theory

According to **balance and consistency theories,** human beings strive for a harmonious existence with self (values, beliefs, and attitudes) and experience psychological discomfort (dissonance) when aspects of existence seem inconsistent or unbalanced.[17] Interviewees may experience **source-proposition conflict** when they strongly like a person but strongly dislike the person's position on an issue or strongly dislike a person but strongly support the position's position on an issue. Interviewees may experience **attitude-attitude conflict** when they strongly oppose government involvement in their lives but strongly favor laws outlawing abortion and allowing prayer in the public schools. Interviewees may experience **perception-perception conflict** when they see Mexico as a very beautiful but very dangerous place to visit. Interviewees may experience **behavior-attitude conflict** when they strongly believe in law and order but use fake ID cards to enter bars and do not report all of their income at tax time. Be aware that some people can tolerate considerable disharmony in their lives.

> An inter-viewer may create or resolve dissonance.

You may create psychological discomfort (dissonance) by attacking a source or pointing out attitude, perception, and behavioral conflicts. Then you show how the interviewee can bring these inconsistencies into balance by providing changes in sources, attitudes, perceptions, and behaviors. If you detect an interviewee is experiencing psychological discomfort, you may bring about balance or consistency by helping the interviewee see no inconsistency, perceive the inconsistency to be insignificant, or tolerate inconsistency.

Inoculation Theory

According to **inoculation theory** it is more effective to prevent undesired persuasive effects from occurring than using damage control afterward.[18] For example, a few years ago a colleague warned the author about a telephone scam that warned people their Microsoft license was about to run out and they needed to call a specific number immediately. A few days later he received such a call and simply ignored it. The colleague as interviewer prepared the interviewee to resist a persuasive effort by exposing him to small "doses" of a potential persuader's language, emotional appeals, arguments, claims, and evidence. You might provide arguments and evidence the interviewee may use when confronting an interviewer.

> An inoculation strategy immunizes an interviewee from future persuasion.

Psychological Reactance Theory

According to **psychological reactance theory,** people react negatively when someone threatens to restrict a behavior they want to engage in.[19] They may value the restricted behavior more and want to engage in it more frequently, or devalue alternatives they feel "stuck with" and resent the restricting agent. Limited editions of stamps and coins, tickets for the World Series, and seats for a Broadway hit play may enhance demand and increase their value. On the other hand, an interviewee may react negatively to apparent threats to join an athletic booster club or lose their prized seats. Avoid real or perceived pressure on the other party to think, feel, or act differently. Make your proposal attractive, make scarcity or a deadline known without appearing to threaten, develop a serious need without excessive appeals to fear, and offer choices.

> Restricting behavior may lead to persuasion or resentment.

Conducting the Interview

Strive to involve the interviewee as an active participant in the persuasive process from the opening through the closing. Make the interview a collaborative effort, not a speech to a party of one. Be flexible and adaptive.

Opening

> Avoid routine openings even for seemingly routine interviews.

Tailor your opening to this party, at this time, and in this situation. Employ what you know about this interviewee and your relational history to gain attention, create interest, establish rapport, and provide orientation to motivate the interviewee to play an active role in a collaborative effort. Do not rely on a standard opening such as those used in cold calls. Most of us are turned off by "one size fits all" openings designed for everyone and no one. Your interview may be short-lived.

If you have had little or no opportunity to study the interviewee ahead of time, use the first few minutes of the interview to discover how you can best adapt to this party. *Take note of* the interviewee's dress, appearance, and manner. *Ask a few questions* designed to discover background, interests, and attitudes critical to this interview. *Listen* to what the interviewee "says" verbally and nonverbally. If the party consists of more than one person, *detect* who is the leader or spokesperson.

> The opening sets the stage for all that follows.

Review the opening techniques and principles discussed in Chapter 4 and select the techniques suitable for this party and situation. Begin with a warm greeting and use the interviewee's name. If the person is a stranger, do not make your greeting sound like a question. This suggests you are unsure of the person's name or identity, unsure of yourself, or not prepared. If you know the interviewee well and both the situation and your relationship warrant it, use the person's first name or nickname.

It may be necessary to introduce yourself (name, position, title, background), your organization (name, location, nature, history, products, services), and state the purpose of the interview. Orientation is essential when you have not made an appointment or arrangements ahead of time. Each party must understand the purpose of the interview, how it will proceed, and how the parties will share control. Be brief.

You may begin with a sincere inquiry about family or mutual friends or small talk about the weather, sports, highway construction, or campus facilities. Do not prolong this stage. Be conscious of the interviewee's situation and preferences. If a person replies "What can I do for you?" immediately after the greeting, the person wants to get down to business.

Cultures differ in amount of acceptable small talk and socializing. Most Americans want to "get to the point" and "get the job done." Japanese and other cultures desire to

Reduce reticence by involving the interviewee immediately and often.

get acquainted, to follow "interaction rituals," and to go slower in making commitments and decisions.[20] Do not prolong this stage. Involve all members of the other party from the start so each plays an active role throughout the interaction. Americans, particularly males, take turns unevenly during interactions and speak at length during each turn. Japanese and others take turns evenly and make shorter statements.

Need or Desire

Create a need or desire by developing in detail the three or four points you selected in the preparation stage. Introduce them in the order you believe will be most effective, strongest point first or last with weaker points in the middle.

Develop One Point at a Time

Explain each point thoroughly. Provide sufficient evidence that is factually based, authoritative, recent, and well documented. Use a variety of evidence so the interviewee is neither buried under an avalanche of figures nor bored with one story after another. Incorporate the values, beliefs, and attitudes important to this interviewee.

Encourage Interaction

Don't lecture; interact.

You are more likely to persuade when the interviewee is actively involved. Stress how each point affects this interviewee's needs and desires. Try to get some sort of agreement before going to your next point, but do not ask for an agreement until you have **established something** upon which you both can agree.

With one point developed and agreed upon, move to point two, then three, and so on. Do not rush through a point or jump to the next one if the interviewee raises an objection or poses a question. Move on when the interviewee seems ready. Be patient and persistent.

Questions

You cannot rely on a schedule of questions, particularly when an interviewee sees no need, has no desire, or is unaware of options. Questions do play important functions, however, because they involve the interviewee as an active participant, discover information you do not have, reveal feelings and attitudes, and bring potential objections to the table.

Information-Gathering Questions

Use questions to analyze the interviewee.

Ask questions to determine knowledge level and to draw out concerns and objections. Listen carefully to responses and probe for accuracy and details.

- How often do you use MARTA?
- What concerns do you have about changing to a new software package?
- What do you know about the city's moratorium on new high-rise apartments?

Verification Questions

Use reflective, mirror, and clearinghouse questions to check the accuracy of assumptions, impressions, and information obtained before and during an interview. You may assume you have answered an objection or gotten an agreement when you have not. Be certain an interviewee understands the significance of your evidence and points. An interviewee's silence may indicate uncertainty, confusion, or disagreement as well as understanding and agreement.

- Do you agree, then, that we should hold the line on bonuses until the new fiscal year?
- Does this answer your questions about consolidating your student loans?
- You appear to be hesitant about transferring to New York City from Dayton.

Encouraging Interaction Questions

Employ questions to encourage the other party to play an active role in the interview. When a party knows what to expect in an interview and feels free to ask questions, you are more likely to receive meaningful feedback and draw out noncommittal interviewees.

- How effective was our demonstration for using the new Adobe Acrobat editing tools?
- What do you like best about e-textbooks?
- What are your reactions to the year-round school system proposal?

Attention and Interest Questions

Use questions to keep interviewees tuned in to what you are saying. They may be busy or preoccupied with other concerns, and interesting, challenging, and thought-provoking questions will maintain interest and attention and encourage participation.

- How are you feeling at this moment?
- What are your plans if the company announces layoffs that include you?
- What did you do first when ordered to evacuate your home because of the forest fire in 2020?

Agreement Questions

Use questions to obtain small agreements that lead to bigger agreements. Getting agreement after each point is likely to lead to agreement at the end. Ask for agreement or commitment only after you have developed a point thoroughly. Generalizations and claims seldom establish a need. Use a yes-response question (often in the form of a statement) to control the interview and lead to an agreement.

- Don't you see the risk of not having carbon dioxide detectors in your apartment?
- This is a good time to increase your 401k, isn't it?
- I'm sure you don't want to damage your lungs through vaping, right?

Objection Questions

Use questions to respond tactfully to objections and draw out unstated questions and objections. Get these on the table at the proper time.

Do not substitute questions for substance.

- You say you are afraid to travel to Mexico at this time; why is that?
- How important is this concern about an out-of-state internship?
- What will it take to convince you that this is not the time to start your own business?

Use leading and loaded questions sparingly because high-pressure tactics turn off interviewees.

Adapting to the Interviewee

Use what you have learned about the interviewee to determine the interviewee's probable predisposition toward you, the issue, and your proposal. Then select strategies most appropriate for this party at this time.

Indecisive, Uninterested Interviewees

The interviewee may see no personal need or relevance.

If an interviewee is indecisive, uninterested, or uncertain, use opening techniques to get the interviewee's attention and generate interest in the issue. Lead off with your strongest point and provide a variety of evidence that informs and persuades. Use questions to draw out feelings and perceptions and involve the interviewee.

Emphasize the urgency of the problem and the necessity of acting *now*. Use moderate fear appeals to awaken the interviewee to dangers to self, family, or friends. Appeal to values such as preservation of health, safety and security, freedom from restraint, ownership, and value of the individual. Show *how* this interviewee can make a difference.

Hostile Interviewees

Do not assume there will be hostility.

If you believe an interviewee may be hostile, be sure your impression is accurate. Do not mistake legitimate concerns or objections or a gruff demeanor for hostility. If a person is truly hostile, determine why; then consider a common ground approach.

- A **yes-but approach** begins with areas of agreement and similarity and gradually leads into points of disagreement. It lessens hostility and disagreement later by establishing common ground early on.
- A **yes-yes approach** gets an interviewee in the habit of agreeing, so when you reach apparent disagreements, the person may be less likely to disagree.
- An **implicative approach** withholds an explicit statement of purpose or intent to avoid a knee-jerk negative reaction from the interviewee. You want the interviewee to see the implications of what you are saying, perhaps feeling they came up with the concerns and solution.

You must get to the point in a reasonable amount of time.

Regardless of the common ground approach, listen, be polite, and avoid defensiveness or anger when working with hostile interviewees. Hostility may result from lack of information, misinformation, or rumors. Respond with facts, expert testimony, examples, stories, and comparisons that clarify, prove, and resolve issues between parties. Be willing to accept minor points of disagreement and to admit your proposal is not perfect; no proposal is. Employ **shock-absorber** phrases that reduce the sting of critical questions: "Many residents I talk to feel that way, however . . ." "That's an excellent question, but when you consider . . ." "I'm glad you brought that up because. . . ."

Closed-Minded and Authoritarian Interviewees

> Select evidence most appropriate for each party.

A **closed-minded or authoritarian interviewee** relies on trusted authorities and is most concerned about **who** supports a proposal. Facts alone, particularly statistics, will not do the job. Show that the interviewee's accepted authorities support your persuasive efforts. The closed-minded and authoritarian interviewee has strong, unchangeable central values and beliefs. Identify yourself and your proposal with these values and beliefs only when you truly share them. Do not bypass hierarchical channels or alter prescribed methods. Authoritarians react negatively to interviewers who do not belong or appear to be out of line, and may demand censure or punishment for appearing to violate accepted and valued norms.

Skeptical Interviewees

If the interviewee is skeptical, begin the interview by expressing some views the interviewee holds—a yes-but or yes-yes approach. Maintain positive nonverbal cues such as a firm handshake, good eye contact, a warm and friendly manner, and appropriate appearance and dress. If the interviewee feels you are young and inexperienced, allude tactfully to your qualifications, experiences, and training and provide substantial and authoritative evidence. Be well prepared and experienced without bragging. Avoid undue informality and a cocky attitude. If the interviewee sees you as argumentative, avoid confrontations, attacks on the person's position, and demands. If the interviewee thinks you are a know-it-all, be careful when referring to your qualifications, experiences, and achievements.

> Poor image or lack of credibility often leads to failure.

If the interviewee has concerns about your organization, try to withhold its name until you have created personal credibility with the interviewee. If the name must come out early in the interview, try to improve its image by countering common misperceptions, relating how it has changed, or identifying its strengths. You may have to distance yourself from some elements or past practices of your organization.

Shopping-Around Interviewees

> Prepare interviewees for counterpersuasion.

Interviewees may shop around before making a major purchase or decision and will face **counterpersuasion** from other interviewers. When meeting with a shopper or an undecided interviewee, forewarn and prepare the interviewee. Provide the interviewee with supportive arguments, evidence, and responses to questions or points others are likely to raise. Give small doses of the opposition's case (inoculation theory) to show the strengths and weaknesses of both sides. Develop a positive, factual, nonemotional approach that addresses the competition when necessary but dwells primarily on the strengths of *your* position and proposal.

Intelligent, Educated Interviewees

> A two-sided approach addresses but does not advocate each side.

The highly **intelligent or educated interviewee** tends to be less persuasible because of knowledge level, critical ability, and faculty for seeing the implications behind arguments and proposals. Such interviewees "are more likely to attend to and comprehend the message position but are less likely to yield to it."[21] For example, they are likely to see through the good guy–bad guy approach used in many situations.

When working with highly intelligent and educated interviewees, support your ideas thoroughly, develop arguments logically, and present a two-sided approach that weighs both sides of the issue. Minimize emotional appeals, particularly if the interviewee is neutral or initially disagrees with your position and proposal. Encourage the interviewee to ask questions, raise objections, and be an active participant.

If an interviewee is of low intelligence or education, develop a simple, one-sided approach to minimize confusion and maximize comprehension. A complex, two-sided approach and intricate arguments supported by a variety of evidence may confuse the interviewee. Use examples, stories, and comparisons rather than expert testimony and statistics.

The Solution

When you have presented the need, summarized your main points, and gotten important agreements, move to solutions.

Establishing Criteria

Establishing criteria is natural but often unconscious.

Begin the solution phase by establishing criteria (requirements, standards, rules, norms, principles) that any solution should meet. If the interviewee is obviously ready to move into this phase of the interview before you have presented all of your points, move on.

Establish a set of criteria *with the interviewee* for evaluating possible solutions. This process is natural to you. For example, when selecting a college major, you may have considered courses, core requirements, specialties, careers, faculty, availability of internships, and marketability when you graduate. In simple decisions such as selecting a place to eat, you may have criteria in mind such as type of food and beverage, cost, distance, location, atmosphere, music, availability of large screen television for watching a football game, and preferences of others. Use this natural process in persuasive interviews.

As you think of criteria prior to the interview and develop them with the interviewee during the interview, realize that not all criteria are of equal importance. For example, admissions directors at state universities have found that quality of school is the most important criterion for out-of-state applicants while cost is number 1 and quality is number 2 for in-state students. The situation can influence criteria. For instance, cost may override all other criteria during economic recessions.

Criteria are designed to evaluate and to persuade.

Establishing a set of criteria involves the interviewee in the process; shows that you are attempting to tailor your proposal to this party's needs, desires, and capabilities; provides a smooth transition from the need to the solution; and reduces the impression that you are overly eager to sell your point. Agreed-upon criteria enable you to build on a foundation of agreements, provide an effective means of comparing and assessing solutions, and deal with objections.

Considering the Solution

Seeing is believing.

If you consider more than one solution, deal with one at a time. Explain your solution in detail and use whatever visual aids might be available and appropriate: booklets and brochures, drawings and diagrams, graphs, letters, pictures, slides, computer printouts, sketch pads, swatches of materials, objects, and models. Interviewees may remember only about 10 percent of *what they hear* but 50 percent of *what they do* and 90 percent of *what they both see and do.*[22]

Approach the solution positively, constructively, and enthusiastically. Believe in what you are presenting and show it. Emphasize the strengths and benefits of your proposal rather than the weaknesses of the competition. Avoid **negative selling** unless the competition forces you to do so as a matter of self-defense. The interviewee is likely to be more interested in the advantages of your proposal than the disadvantages of another.

Help interviewees make decisions that are best for them. Encourage questions and active involvement. Do not assume the interviewee knows or understands the details of your solution. If you are considering more than one solution, deal with one at a time. Use repetition to enhance understanding, aid memory, gain and maintain attention, and make the interviewee aware of what is most important. Educate interviewees about options, requirements, time constraints, and new features.

Meeting Objections

> You cannot address an objection you do not know.

Perhaps nothing seems more threatening than the thought of an interviewee raising unexpected or difficult objections. Encourage the interviewee to voice objections to reveal the interviewee's concerns, fears, misunderstandings, and misinformation. Do not assume agreement because the interviewee raises no questions or objections. Watch for nonverbal clues such as restlessness, fidgeting, poor eye contact, raised eyebrows, confused expressions, signs of boredom, or silences. Find out what is happening within.

Objections are numerous and often issue, goal, situation, or interviewee specific.

> Anticipate common objections.

- *Procrastination: Never do today what you can put off until tomorrow.*
  Let me think about it.
  I've still got three weeks before the report is due.
  My old truck is doing fine, so I'll wait awhile.

- *Cost: That's a lot of money.*
  That iPhone is too expensive for me.
  I didn't expect remodeling to cost that much.
  That's pretty expensive for a two-day conference.

- *Tradition: We've always done it this way.*
  That's how we've always done business.
  We've always had our reunions in Savannah.
  My grandfather chose that line of clothing when he opened the business in 1972.

- *Uncertain future: Who knows what tomorrow will bring.*
  My job is rather iffy right now.
  The economy is struggling, so I'm reluctant to hire new staff.
  At my age, I don't buy green bananas.

> Meeting objections requires thought, understanding, tact, and substance.

- *Need: What's the problem?*
  We've got good investments, so we don't need life insurance.
  The current file system is working just fine.
  We don't have much crime around here, so we don't need an alarm system.

How to Approach Objections

Anticipate objections to eliminate surprises. Think about handling each objection as a series of steps.

Plan how to respond to reduce surprises.

Listen carefully, completely, and objectively, never assuming you understand the other person's point or concern until you have heard it.

Clarify the objection, making sure you understand exactly what it is and its importance before you respond.

Respond appropriately, tactfully, and seriously. *If an objection is serious to the interviewee, it is serious.* There are four common strategies for meeting objections.

Minimize the Objection

Minimize an objection by restating it to make it less important or by comparing it to other weightier matters. Provide evidence to reduce its importance.

> Reduce the significance of the objection.

1. **Interviewee:** I've thought about doing a couple of internships, but they would add at least a semester or two and to my student loans.

2. **Interviewer:** That's probably true on both counts, but weigh the two. Both time and cost will be minimal for a semester or two while you will learn critical skills you cannot learn in a classroom and make you highly marketable when you graduate. The construction management firms I have contacted in the last few years report that they hire nearly all new employees from students who have interned with them and they pay them more. They know them personally and professionally.

Capitalize on the Objection

Capitalize on an objection to *clarify* your point, *review* the proposal's advantages, *offer* more evidence, or *isolate* the motive behind the objection. Convert a perceived disadvantage into an advantage.

> Take advantage of the objection.

1. **Interviewee:** I would like to study abroad for a semester, probably in England or Scotland, but alums I talk to say it is very expensive to study in either country.

2. **Interviewer:** That was the case a few years ago, but since Great Britain left the EU, it has become much cheaper because English and Scottish universities are now competing with the EU for top American students. Now is a great time to study in either country.

Deny an Objection

Deny an objection *directly* or *indirectly* by offering new or more accurate information or by introducing new features of a proposal. You cannot deny an objection by merely denying it; *prove it.*

> If you deny it, you must prove it isn't so.

1. **Interviewee:** I'm afraid the bill you are sponsoring on gun control will lead to outlawing hunting, skeet shooting, and even target shooting.

2. **Interviewer:** The bill I am proposing would ban only the purchase of large clips and magazines that hold more than ten rounds and enable killers to shoot numerous kids, shoppers, and fellow workers without taking time to reload. I have enjoyed skeet and competitive shooting for years and own a number of shotguns and target rifles.

Confirm an Objection

Confirm an objection by agreeing with the interviewee. It is better to be honest and admit problems than to offer weak defenses.

1. **Interviewee:** I would love to take a tour of Japan, but I'm afraid it would be way too expensive.

2. **Interviewer:** Your fear is justified. Air fares to Japan are very high and so are expenditures while in Japan. The total cost would be in the range of $12,000 a person, but the tour is worth every dollar.

Closing

Approach the closing positively and confidently. Do not pressure the interviewee or appear too eager. Interviewers may hesitate to close, fearing they may fail to persuade, while interviewees fear they will make a wrong decision. Hesitation to ask for a sale is the major cause of failure to sell.

The closing consists of three stages: (1) trial closing, (2) contract or agreement, and (3) leave-taking.

Trial Closing

As you enter the closing phase of the interview, pay close attention to verbal and nonverbal clues that the interviewee is ready to consider or make a decision. Verbal clues may include questions such as "How soon might you start construction?" or "When might this new model be available?" Statements may include "This may be a good time for considering a new investment." or "I don't think we can ignore this problem much longer." Common nonverbal clues are vocal emphasis, head nods, smiles or frowns, glances between members of the interviewee party, or leafing through a report, pictures, or a brochure. Do not prolong the need phase if an interviewee is ready to move on. You may talk yourself out of a solution.

Ask a yes-response or leading question to verify your impression that the interviewee is ready to close: "Do you want to wait until there's a serious accident?" or "This is the time to act, isn't it?" After you ask a trial closing question, *be quiet!* Give the interviewee time to think and self-persuade. Silence communicates confidence and gives the interviewee an opportunity to raise unanswered questions and objections.

If you get a no to your trial closing question, ask why. You may need to review the criteria, compare advantages and disadvantages of acting now, or provide more information. An interviewee may not be ready to act. Fear of possible consequences and how others may react (outside forces) may overcome a need or desire.

If you get a yes to your trial closing question, lead into the contract or agreement stage: "We can sign off on this today." "We can have this equipment installed within two weeks." "It would be a relief to have this decision made."

Contract or Agreement

After a successful trial closing, move to the contract or agreement stage. This is a critical time because the interviewee knows the closing and a commitment are coming. Be natural and pleasant. Maintain good communication. Consider closing techniques appropriate for this stage.

■ *The contract or agreement stage is critical because the interviewee knows a commitment is imminent.*

- An *assumptive close* addresses part of the agreement with a phrase, such as "I assume that you prefer . . ."
- A *summary close* summarizes agreements made as a basis for decisions.
- An *elimination of a single objection close* responds to the single objection that stands in the way of an agreement.
- An *either-or close* limits the interviewee's choices, then shows that the solution you advocate has the most advantages and the fewest disadvantages.

> **Select closing techniques most appropriate for this interview and interviewee.**

- An *I'll think it over close* acknowledges the interviewee's desire to think about a decision. Try to discover the level of interest and why the interviewee is hesitating.
- A *sense of urgency close* stresses why an interviewee should act now.
- A *price close* emphasizes the savings possible or the bottom line of the offer.

Leave-Taking

> **Leave-taking should reinforce all you have accomplished.**

When the contract or agreement is completed, no agreement or contract is reached, or another interview is necessary, conclude pleasantly and positively. An **abrupt** or **curt leave-taking** may undo the rapport, trust, and relationship you have established and preclude future interviews with this party. Adapt verbal and nonverbal leave-taking techniques or combine them to suit each interviewee. Be sincere and honest in this final closing phase, and make no promises you cannot or will not keep because of personal or authority limitations, organizational policies, laws, or time constraints.

Summary Outline

This outline summarizes the elements in the structure of a persuasive interview that covers need/desire and solution.

I. Opening the interview
    A. Select the most appropriate techniques from Chapter 4.
    B. Establish rapport according to relationship and situation.
    C. Provide appropriate orientation.

II. Creating a need or desire
    A. Provide an appropriate statement of purpose.
    B. Develop a need point-by-point with maximum involvement of and careful adaptation to the other party.
        1. Use appropriate argument patterns.
        2. Provide a variety of evidence.

3. Employ effective strategies.
4. Appeal to important values and emotions.
5. Obtain overt agreements as you proceed, being sure to point out how the interviewee party is involved or must be concerned.

    C. Summarize the need or problem and attain overt agreements from the interviewee.

III. Establishing criteria
    A. Present the criteria you have in mind, explaining briefly the rationale and importance of each criterion.
    B. Encourage the interviewee to add criteria.
    C. Involve the interviewee in the discussion of criteria.
    D. Summarize and get agreement on all criteria.

IV. Presenting the solution
    A. Present one solution at a time.
       1. Explain the solution in detail using visual aids when possible.
       2. Evaluate the solution using agreed-upon criteria.
    B. Respond to anticipated and vocalized objections.
    C. Get agreement on the appropriateness, quality, and feasibility of the preferred solution.

V. Closing the interview
    A. Begin a trial closing as soon as it seems appropriate to do so.
    B. When the trial closing is successful, move to a contract or agreement with the interviewee.
    C. Use appropriate leave-taking techniques discussed in this chapter and Chapter 4.

> **There is no set pattern for all persuasive interviews.**

You will not develop all parts of this plan in every interview. If an interviewee agrees with the need or problem prior to the interview, merely summarize the need in the opening and move directly to criteria. An interviewee may see the need but not agree with your proposed solution. Or an interviewee may feel constraints making any move impossible at this time. Feasibility is the central concern in this interview, not need or a specific proposal. The interviewee may like your proposal but see no personal need.

Part 2: The Interviewee in the Persuasive Interview

Keep two principles in mind as you focus on the interviewee in the persuasive interview: (1) persuasion is done **with** and not **to another** and (2) **both parties** are responsible for the **success** or **failure** of persuasive interviews.

Be an Informed Participant

Unlike interviewers who may have taken courses and training in how to persuade others, few interviewees have had similar preparation in how to play the role of receivers. Part 2 of this chapter introduces you to the **tricks of the trade**, so to speak, to level the persuasive playing field.

Psychological Strategies

Learned principles may lead to automatic actions.

Part 1 introduced you to strategies (theories) interviewers use in efforts to change the way you think, feel, and/or act. Let's review several from the perspective of the interviewee. For instance, **standard-learned principles** may guide our beliefs, decisions, and actions. We learn from an early age what it means, for example, to be a good Methodist, Democrat, citizen, student, parent, worker, or care giver.[23] Widely accepted truisms may serve as **self-persuaders:**

If an expert says so, it must be true.	Hard work pays off.
If it's in print, it must be so.	We control our destiny.
If it meets industry standards, it's safe.	My word is my bond.
The world is a dangerous place.	You get what you pay for.
Time is money.	If it's expensive, it's good.

Upscale retailers, for example, depend on these standard/learned principles to move expensive, high-quality items ranging from jewelry to automobiles.

Seek significant differences.

In the **contrast principle,** interviewers know that if a second item is fairly different from the first in attractiveness, cost, or size, it seems *more different* than it actually is. If I want to rent you an apartment, I may show you a rundown one first and then a somewhat better apartment. You may see the second apartment as substantially rather than moderately better. If a tour agent can persuade you to go on an expensive cruise down the Danube River in Europe, the optional excursions may appear quite reasonable in comparison.

We feel obligated to return favors.

The **rule of reciprocation** instills in you a sense of obligation to repay in kind what another provides.[24] For instance, if a person gives you a free soft drink and then asks you to buy a raffle ticket, you feel obligated to buy the ticket even though it may cost more than the soft drink. This process is at work every time you open your mail and discover yet another packet of personalized address labels. You are likely to send in a donation or not use the labels even though you did not request them. If you use the labels and do not send in a donation, you may experience psychological discomfort and fear shame if someone discovers your action.

One concession deserves another, or not.

In a **reciprocal concessions** strategy, you feel a sense of obligation to make a concession in response to a concession. Parties employ this psychological strategy in employment-management negotiations when an employee concedes on health care and the other then feels obligated to concede on retirement benefits. This strategy occurs in everyday interactions such as when a roommate agrees to provide the car for spring break and you feel obligated to pay for the gas.

Persuaders may ask for a lot and settle for less.

A **rejection then retreat** strategy begins with one proposal that makes a second more acceptable. If you reject the first you may feel both obligated or relieved to agree to the second. One study discovered that if Boy Scouts asked persons to purchase $5 circus tickets and were turned down, the same persons were likely to say yes to a second proposal of a $1 chocolate bar. The Boy Scouts gained either way, and the persuadees felt good about helping out for a lesser amount. Salespersons often start with the top of the line and then retreat to a fallback position *if* necessary.

In **undercover** or **stealth marketing,** an interviewer party of two or more persons pretends to be a friendly, disinterested party, and not a sales representative. For example, two people appearing to be tourists or visitors ask a person passing by if she will take their picture. The cooperative passerby agrees and just happens to notice that the couple has a very interesting and attractive digital camera, and asks about it. The party, who just happen to be undercover sales reps for this camera company, gladly comply. The persuadee has no idea that a sales interview is taking place.

Be a Critical Participant

Language Strategies

| Seek the meanings of symbols. |

Woodward and Denton write that language "is far more than a collection of words and rules for proper usage. Language is the instrument and vehicle of human action and expression."[25] Skilled interviewers are keenly aware of the power and manipulation of verbal symbols, but too many of us see these symbols as merely words and rules. Larson warns that "as receivers, we need to get to the bottom of persuasive meanings; carefully analyzing the symbols used or misused by persuaders can help us get there."[26] The following are common language strategies.

Framing and Reframing

| Jargon is not harmless. |

Persuaders use language to frame or construct the way you see people, places, things, and objects. For instance, **jargon** substitutes peculiar words for common words. While some jargon seems harmless enough (schedule irregularity for airline flight delay), others can hide the truth (terminological inexactitude for lie), make something sound more technical than it is (emergency exit light for a flashlight), more valuable than it is (garment management system for one hook and two hangers), or less severe (collateral damage for the killing of civilians during military actions).

| Ambiguities say little but sound like a lot. |

Strategic ambiguities are words with multiple or vague meanings. Persuaders want you to interpret the words according to their specific needs or perceptions without asking embarrassing, negative, or insightful questions. If a politician claims to be a conservative or moderate, what exactly is this person? What is a lifetime guarantee or a limited warranty? What is an affordable apartment or a top salary? What is free-range poultry or poultry raised the old-fashioned way? We pay premium prices for lite, diet, natural, and low-carb products without knowing how these differ from ones that are not.

| Imagery substitutes for experiences. |

Imagery—word pictures—contains multisensory words to color what you have experienced, will experience, may experience, or experience indirectly. A representative of a travel agency, with the aid of leaflets, posters, and Web sites, will help you visualize skiing in Switzerland, visiting the Aztec ruins in Mexico, surfing in Hawaii, or seeing the wildlife of Kenya. On the other hand, an interviewer might employ the same tactics to paint a negative picture complete with apocalyptic images and dire predictions if you vote for a political opponent, purchase a competing product, join a different religious group, accept a scholarship with another school, or travel to Kenya, instead of South Africa.

Euphemisms substitute *better sounding* words for common words. Cadillac was the first to substitute preowned for used cars to emphasize ownership rather than use. Real estate agencies are now substituting the word "bought" for "sold" to emphasize purchasing rather than selling. You might find an inexpensive interview suit but not a cheap one and purchase it from a sales associate rather than a clerk. A lifelike Christmas tree sounds better than an artificial one. When you walk into a women's department for clothing, you may see signs for "women's sizes" that sound better than "large sizes." On the other hand, when you walk into a men's department, you may see signs for "large men's sizes" but not "petite men's sizes." Words make a difference. Would you go into a favorite campus hangout and order a "diet Beer?" You might well order a "lite beer."

Differentiation is not an attempt to find a better-sounding word but to alter how you see *reality*. For example, when an animal rights advocate wants you to become an animal guardian instead of an animal owner, this person wants to change how you see your relationship with your pet. Calling female members of an organization, women, is not "political correctness"—a euphemism—but an effort to change perceptions of the abilities, capabilities, and maturity of women compared to girls. The purposes of euphemisms and differentiation are very different; the first wants to make something *sound better* while the second seeks to change your *visions of reality*.

Appealing to the People

Interviewers appeal to your faith in the rule and wisdom of "the people," following Lincoln's adage that "you can fool all of the people some of the time and some of the people all of the time, but you can't fool all of the people all of the time." The *ad populum* tactic claims to speak on behalf of the people—the alleged majority—such as voters, students, employees, college athletes, consumers, and small business owners. It is the "common folk," of course, not the elite, the government, the administration, or the executives. When, for instance, an attorney claims that he is "here for the people," who are these people?

The **bandwagon** tactic urges you to follow the crowd, to do what everyone else is allegedly doing, buying, wearing, attending, or voting. It appeals to your desire to belong and conform, often accompanied by a note of urgency: "Everyone's going," "Football tickets are really going fast," and "The party is behind Jim in this election." Listen for qualifiers such as nearly, probably, almost, and majority. Ask for numbers or names of those who have signed a petition, agreed to a change, or joined an organization. Be cautious of phrases such as, "people in the know" and "those who are on the move" that are designed to pressure and flatter.

Simplifying the Complex

Interviewers attempt to reduce complex problems, issues, controversies, and situations to their simplest elements. The **thin entering wedge,** also known as the **domino effect** or the **slippery slope,** claims that one decision, action, or law after another is leading toward disastrous consequences. Talk to a person who is against censorship, gun control, or same-sex marriages and you are likely to hear how censorship of books in public schools is one more step toward censoring all reading materials, how the registration of handguns is yet another step toward outlawing and confiscating all guns, and how same-sex marriage is a slippery slope toward the destruction of the home and the family. Look for evidence of a related, intentional string of actions that are tipping dominos, producing wedges, or sliding down a dangerous slope.

Euphemisms replace substance with sound.

Words may alter reality.

For many of us, the majority rules.

Have an inquiring mind.

Fear of chain reactions may stifle any action.

> Slogans are clever phrases and more.

Slogans are clever words or phrases that encapsulate positions, stands, or goals. They are a vague but powerful means to alter the way you think, feel, or act because they are catchy and entice you to fill in the meaning—to self-persuade. Interviewers rely on slogans to attract customers, recruits, contributors, and loyalty and may change them to communicate different messages. For instance, when Purdue University changed its slogan from "Touching tomorrow today" and then "Discover Purdue" with "Purdue: It's Happening Here," the president explained that "there is a tremendous amount of excitement around campus. . . . I think this theme is just trying to capture that sense of energy, momentum and pride that we have at Purdue."[27] Ask what slogans mean and if they truly represent a person, organization, campaign, or solution.

> Polarizing limits our choices and our thinking.

An interviewer may **polarize** people, organizations, positions, or courses of action by claiming that you have only a choice of two: conservative or liberal, friend or foe, Chevy or Ford, wind power or nuclear power, for gun control or against gun control. It is a simplistic but persuasive view of the world. Are you either a conservative or liberal, a mixture of each, or something else?

Dodging the Issue

> Attacking a source does not address the issue.

Interviewers may attempt to dodge critical issues, questions, or objections. **Ad hominem** (getting personal) dodges undesired challenges by discrediting a source because of age, culture, gender, race, affiliation, or past positions, statements, or claims. A parent may tell a child to "just consider the source" when the child is called a name or has a belief challenged. An acquaintance may urge you to ignore research conducted by a known conservative or liberal, government agency or corporate association, religious or secular organization. Insist that the interviewer address the issue, point, or substance of the research.

> Sharing guilt misses the point.

You have used the *tu quoque* tactic since childhood to dodge an issue or objection by revolving it upon the challenger or questioner: Classic *tu quoque* responses include "You're one too," "It takes one to know one," "So do you," "I suppose you never cheated on your taxes?"

> Blaming others merely dodges responsibility.

Interviewers may dodge issues by **transferring guilt** to others, making the accuser, victim, or questioner the guilty party. Cheating on an exam is the professor's fault; failing to report all income on a tax report is the IRS's fault; parking illegally is the college's fault for not providing enough parking places. Defense attorneys turn victims of crimes into the guilty parties, particularly in rape and abuse cases.

Logical Strategies

As discussed earlier, persuaders develop arguments into what appear to be valid and logical patterns. Recognize and challenge these patterns.

> What is the sample from which a generalization is based?

Argument from example is a statement, based on a sample, about the distribution of some characteristic among the members of a whole class of people, places, or things. If you recognize this pattern, ask

- What is the total amount of this sample?
- What is the nature of this sample?
- When was the sample taken?
- What is the interviewer asserting from this sample?

Beware of the *hasty generalization* in which the persuader generalizes to a whole group from one or a few examples. For instance, a friend may warn you against dining at a particular restaurant because he had a bad meal there once.

Argument from cause-to-effect addresses what caused an effect. Ask questions such as

> **Be careful of coincidences seen as causes.**

- Was this cause able to generate this effect?
- Was this cause the only possible cause?
- Was this cause the major cause?
- What evidence is offered to establish this causal link?
- Is a coincidence mistaken for the cause?

> **Just because B followed A does not mean A caused B.**

Beware of the *post hoc* or **scrambling cause–effect** fallacy that argues simply because B followed A, A must have caused B. For instance, I got the flu the day after I got that flu shot, so the shot gave me the flu.

Arguing from fact or hypothesis offers the best explanation for a body of facts and is the type of reasoning investigators use when trying to explain murders, disasters, accidents, and teams losing in the NCAA's March madness.

> **Be a super-sleuth when encountering hypotheses.**

- How frequently is this hypothesis accurate with these facts?
- Is the body of facts sufficient?
- What facts would make the claim more or less convincing?
- How simple or complex is the hypothesis?

> **A sign may have many meanings or no meanings.**

Arguing from sign is a claim that two or more variables are related in such a way that the presence or absence of one may be taken as an indication of the presence or absence of the other. For example, if the flag on the post office is at half-mast, you may reason that someone of importance has died. Ask these questions when hearing an argument from the sign:

- What is the relationship between the variables?
- Is the presence or absence verifiable?
- What is the believability or reliability of the sign?

> **Look for important differences as well as important similarities.**

Arguing from analogy compares two people, places, things, or proposals that have several important characteristics and then claims they share other important characteristics.

- How similar are the similarities?
- Are enough similarities provided?
- Are important **dissimilarities** ignored?
- Are the similarities critical to the claim?

> **Identify the major assertion upon which the argument rests.**

Arguing from accepted belief, assumption, or proposition is based on a statement that is thought to be accepted or proven. The remainder of the argument follows from this assertion, such as: Using marijuana leads to use of hard drugs such as heroin and coke. John is using marijuana, so he will eventually turn to hard drugs. Ask these questions:

- Do you accept the foundational assertion?
- Do the other assertions follow logically from this assertion?
- Does the claim necessarily follow from these assertions?

"If" arguments may ignore obvious or unpredictable conditions.

Beware of arguments based on alleged self-evident truths that cannot be questioned or disputed because they are "fact."

In argument from condition, an interviewer asserts that if something does or does not happen, something else will or will not happen. "If you stop smoking, you will not get lung cancer." The central focus is the word *if.* Ask these questions:

- Is the condition acceptable?
- Is this the only condition?
- Is this the major condition?

Evidence

Look closely at the evidence an interviewer offers (or does not offer) to gain attention and interest, establish credibility and legitimacy, support arguments, develop a need, and present a solution. Evidence includes examples, stories, authorities or witnesses, comparisons and contrasts, statistics, and key definitions. Question the acceptability of the interviewer's evidence.

Assess the reliability and expertise of sources.

- *Is the evidence trustworthy?* Are the persuader and the persons and organizations being cited unbiased and reliable? Are the sources of the evidence (newspapers, reports, Internet, publications) unbiased and reliable?
- *Is the evidence authoritative?* What are the training, experience, and reputation of the authorities or witnesses being cited? Were they in positions to have observed the facts, events, or data?
- *Is the evidence recent?* Is it the most recent available? Are newer statistics or findings available? Have authorities changed their minds?
- *Is the evidence documented sufficiently?* Do you know where and how the statistics or results were determined? Who determined them? Where and when were they reported?
- *Is the evidence communicated accurately?* Can you detect alterations or deletions in quotations, statistics, or documentation? Is the evidence cited in context?

Insist on both quantity and quality of evidence.

- *Is the evidence sufficient in quantity?* Are enough authorities cited? Enough examples given? Enough points of comparison made? Adequate facts revealed?
- *Is the evidence sufficient in quality?* Are opinions stated as facts? How satisfactory is the sample used for generalizations and causal arguments? Does proof evidence (factual illustrations, statistics, authority, detailed comparisons) outweigh clarifying evidence (hypothetical illustrations, paid testimonials, figurative analogies, and metaphors)?

Be an active participant. Each interview has the potential of altering or reinforcing the way you think, feel, or act, including the money you spend, the votes you cast, the relationships you establish or maintain, the possessions you protect, the work you do, and the life you lead. Ask questions to obtain information and explanations, probe into vague and ambiguous words and comments, and reveal feelings and attitudes that may lie hidden or merely suggested. There are no foolish questions, only questions you fail to ask.

The Opening

Play an active role in the opening because it initiates the persuasive process.

Be alert and active from the first moments of the interview. If it is a "cold call" in which you have had no time to prepare, use carefully phrased questions to discover the identity, position, and qualifications of the interviewer. Discover the real purpose and intent of the interview.

Too many persuadees play passive roles during openings. Here is an example from an interview in one of the author's classes. The persuadee is head of surgery at this hospital, believes in following strict hierarchies with surgeons at the top, feels physicians rather than nurses should detect and address real problems, and is all business.

Persuader: Dr. Smalley, I'm Lilly McDowell, one of the surgical nurse supervisors.

Persuadee: Hi Lilly, have a seat.

Persuader: I'd like to talk to you about the problems we are having with surgical patients after they leave the hospital and a solution to this problem.

Persuadee: Okay.

Persuader: Well, we have discovered that . . .

The interviewee does not exhibit his personality or attitudes and learns little about the purpose of this interview, how long it will take, or the nature of the problem. He allows the interviewer to launch into the need without question even though the interviewer appears to be encroaching on his authority and status, his area of expertise and responsibility, and does not explain the nature of the problem or how it was determined.

Need or Desire

Ask questions, challenge arguments, and demand proof.

If an interviewer attempts to conduct an interview without a clear purpose and in which the need is a collection of generalizations and ambiguous claims, insist on a point-by-point development with each point crafted carefully and logically, supported with adequate evidence, and adapted to *your* values, beliefs, and attitudes. Beware of fallacies and tactics that dodge your questions and objections. If an interviewer attempts to introduce another point rather than address your concerns, insist on answers to your questions and objections and get agreements before proceeding to another point.

Weigh evidence carefully. Be on guard against psychological strategies designed to manipulate your reactions and make you feel obligated to reply in kind. Do not tolerate negative selling or mudslinging. Insist on getting agreements before going into criteria or a solution.

Criteria

Employ criteria to weigh solutions.

Establish criteria with the interviewer that any solution should meet. Appropriate criteria enable both parties to assess how well a solution meets a need and is feasible for this interviewee. An interviewer may come to an interview with a list of criteria, and this helps the process and shows planning. Take an active part in establishing criteria. Are the criteria clear? Do you wish to modify some criteria? Which are the most important criteria? Are there criteria you wish to add?

Solution

Be sure the solution meets the need and is the best available.

An interviewer may claim there is only *one* obvious solution to the need or desire agreed upon when there is rarely only one solution to a problem. Insist upon a detailed presentation of each possible solution. Ask questions and raise objections. Be sure the criteria are applied equally to each solution to determine which is best for you in this situation. If possible, insist on seeing, feeling, hearing, or experiencing the product or proposal.

When you have agreed upon a solution or course of action, beware of qualifiers or "add-ons" such as guarantees, rebates, accessories, processing fees, and commitments. What exactly is a "lifetime" warranty or guarantee? The persuader may hope that once you have made the *big* decision, you will agree to *small* decisions—the contrast principle discussed earlier. What are you getting for "free"?

The Closing

Take your time when making a final decision.

Do not rush into making a decision or commitment. You have little to gain and much to lose. A common tactic is to create a psychological reaction by claiming the possibility of censorship or the scarcity of a product. An organization may produce a limited number of books, coins, cars, or positions to make them more in demand, to urge you to act quickly before it is too late.

Take time to think about a decision; sleep on it. Be sure your questions and objections are answered satisfactorily. Understand the possible ramifications of your decision. Consider getting a second or third opinion. Talk to persons who have relevant expertise or experiences. Check out competing products, candidates, offers, and programs. For instance, visit several universities before deciding where to pursue a graduate or professional degree; try out several laptops before deciding which to purchase; listen or talk to different political candidates before voting.

ON THE WEB

Assume you are going to purchase a new car upon graduation. You want to be thoroughly informed and prepared when you contact sales representatives so you can make an intelligent decision and get a good deal. Use the World Wide Web to access information on brands, models, features, comparative prices, and assessments by automotive experts. Sample manufacturer sites are Toyota (http://www.toyota.com), Acura (http://www.acura.com), Mazda (http://mazdausa.com), Buick (http://www.parkavenue.com), and Chrysler (http://www.chryslercars.com). What information is readily available on the Internet, and why is this so? What information is not included on the Internet, and why is this so? What are common persuasive tactics used on the Internet? What questions does your research suggest you pursue during interviews?

Summary

Good persuasive interviews are ones in which both parties are actively involved in interpersonal interactions in which both parties speak and listen effectively. Persuasion should be *done with* not *to* another party.

Good persuasive interviews are honest endeavors conducted according to fundamental ethical guidelines. They are not games in which the end justifies the means or *buyer beware* is a guiding principle. The appeal should be to the head and the heart rather than relying on emotional hot buttons that may override critical thought and decision making.

Good persuasive interviews are carefully researched, planned, and structured, yet they remain flexible enough to meet unforeseen reactions, objections, and arguments. The interviewer adapts the effort to *this persuadee*; develops, supports, and documents important reasons for a change in thinking, feeling, or acting; and presents a detailed solution that meets criteria agreed upon by both parties. Persuasion often entails several contacts in which the persuader and persuadee reach incremental agreements.

Good persuasive interviews involve the interviewee as a responsible, informed, critical, and active participant who plays a central role. The interviewee acts ethically, listens carefully, asks insightful and challenging questions, raises important objections, challenges evidence and arguments, recognizes common persuasive tactics for what they are, and weighs solutions according to agreed-upon criteria.

Key Terms and Concepts

Ad hominem
Ad populum
Agreement questions
Analyzing the interviewee
Arguing from accepted belief
Arguing from analogy
Arguing from cause–effect
Arguing from condition
Arguing from example
Arguing from facts
Arguing from two choices
Argument from sign
Attention and interest questions
Attitude–attitude conflict
Attitudes
Balance or consistency theory

Bandwagon tactic
Behavior–attitude conflict
Beliefs
Buyer beware
Closed-minded or authoritarian interviewee
Cold calls
Consubstantiality
Contract or agreement closing
Contrast principle
Criteria
Culture
Differentiation
Domino effect
Dissonance
Encouraging interaction questions
Ethics
Evidence

False dichotomy
Framing
Hasty generalization
Hostile interviewee
Identification theory
Implicative approach
Indecisive interviewee
Intelligent interviewee
Interrelated conditions
Motives
Name-calling
Normative influence
Objection questions
Objections
One-sided approach
Open-minded
Polarization
Post hoc fallacy
Prospecting
Psychological discomfort

Psychological reactance
  theory
Psychological strategies
Reciprocal concessions
Rejection then retreat
Rule of reciprocation
Scrambling cause–effect
Self-evident truths
Shock-absorber phrases
Shopping-around
  interviewee

Skeptical interviewee
Slippery slope
Slogans
Socioeconomic
  background
Solution
Source-perception
  conflict
Standard/learned
  principles
Stealth marketing

Strategic ambiguities
Thin entering wedge
Transferring guilt
Tu quoque
Trial closing
Two-sided approach
Undercover marketing
Values
Verification questions
Yes-but approach
Yes-yes approach

Review Questions

1. What is the fundamental intent of the persuasive interview?

2. Identify and explain four guidelines essential for a personal code of ethics for taking part in persuasive interviews.

3. What is the interview's most significant advantage over other forms of persuasion?

4. How might cultural differences affect persuasive interviews?

5. How are values, beliefs, attitudes, and emotions connected in persuasive interviews?

6. When developing an argument during a persuasive interview, how and why might you leave an assertion on the point itself unstated?

7. Why is identification theory considered so important in persuasive interviews?

8. How might you use inoculation theory in a persuasive interview?

9. Why is the role of questions limited in persuasive interviews?

10. What should you do and not do when interviewing a closed-minded or authoritarian interviewee?

11. How might you approach objections during a persuasive interview?

12. What is a trial closing?

13. Identify and explain how you might react to three common psychological strategies the interview might employ.

14. What are the differences between euphemisms and differentiations persuaders use in interviews?

15. Explain how persuaders use the "thin entering wedge," also known as the "domino effect" or "slippery slope effect," during interviews.

Student Activities

1. Locate a professional (sales representative, recruiter, fund-raiser) who conducts persuasive interviews on a regular basis and spend a day on the job with this person. Observe how this person prepares for each interview, selects strategies, opens interviews, develops needs and solutions, closes interviews, and adapts to interviewees.

2. Select three persons in different career fields (e.g., sales, medicine, athletics, lobbying, recruiting, advocacy) who have extensive experience in persuasive interviewing. Probe into how they prepare for and try to persuade three of the following types of interviewees: indecisive, hostile, closed-minded, skeptical, shopping around, highly educated. Which do they find most difficult? What are their most effective strategies for each? Which value and emotional appeals do they use most often and why?

3. Identify an acquaintance or family member who is known for driving hard bargains. Go with this person to a persuasive interview; it need not be a sales situation. Observe the role this person plays in the opening, how this person handles the need or desire, the information this person obtains, objections and questions raised about the solution, and how this person negotiates a final decision. If this interviewee threatens to go to a competitor or a person higher up in an organization, how does the interviewer react?

4. Keep a log over a two-week period of the telephone and e-mail solicitations you receive. How well are these adapted to you as a person and to your needs, desires, and motives? Which values and emotions do they use as triggering devices? How ethical are their tactics? Which types of evidence do they employ? How do they react when you raise questions or objections? How do they close the interviews?

Notes

1. Roderick P. Hart, "Teaching Persuasion," in *Teaching Communication: Theory, Research, and Methods,* John A. Daly, Gustav W. Friedrich, and Anita L. Vangelisti, eds. (Hillsdale, NJ: Lawrence Erlbaum, 1999), p. 133.

2. Richard L. Johannesen, "Perspectives on Ethics in Persuasion," in *Persuasion: Reception and Responsibility*, Charles U. Larson, ed. (Belmont, CA: Wadsworth/Cengage Learning, 2013), p. 41.

3. Johannesen, p. 41.

4. Gary C. Woodward and Robert E. Denton, Jr., *Persuasion and Influence in American Life* (Long Grove, IL: Waveland Press, 2009), p. 350.

5. Herbert W. Simons, *Persuasion in Society* (Thousand Oaks, CA: Sage, 2001), p. 374.

6. Johannesen, p. 46.

7. John Jantsch, "The Abusive Math of Cold Calling," ducttapemarketing/the-abusive-math-of-cold-calling, accessed November 5, 2019; Kosti Lepojarvi, "Cold Calling Is Dead? Not So Fast," leadfeeder.com/blog/cold-calling-is-dead/#gref, accessed November 25, 2019.

8. Deirdre Johnston, *The Art and Science of Persuasion* (Madison, WI: Brown & Benchmark, 1994), p. 185; Sharon Shavitt and Timothy Brock, *Persuasion: Psychological Insights and Perspectives* (Boston, MA: Allyn and Bacon, 1994), pp. 152–153.

9. "College and Its Effect on Students: Early Work on the Impact of College, Nine Generalizations, Later Studies, Pascrella and Terenzini," http://education.stateuniversity.com/pages1844/College-its-Effect-on-Students.html, accessed September 10, 2012.

10. Larson, p. 91.

11. Franklin J. Boster and Michael G. Cruz, "Persuading in the Small Group Context," in *The Persuasion Handbook: Developments in Theory and Practice,* James Price Dillard and Michael Pfau, eds. (Thousand Oaks, CA: Sage Publications, 2002), pp. 477–494.

12. Saron Shavitt and Michelle R. Nelson, "The Role of Attitude Functions in Persuasion and Judgment," in *The Persuasion Handbook: Developments in Theory and Practice,* James Price Dillard and Michael Pfau, eds. (Thousand Oaks, CA: Sage Publications, 2002), pp. 149–150.

13. Milton Rokeach, *Beliefs, Attitudes, and Values* (San Francisco, CA: Jossey-Bass, 1968), p. 124.

14. Robin L. Nabi, "Discrete Emotions and Persuasion," in *The Persuasion Handbook: Developments in Theory and Practice,* James Price Dillard and Michael Pfau, eds. (Thousand Oaks, CA: Sage Publications, 2002), pp. 291–298.

15. Rodney A. Reynolds and J. Lynn Reynolds, "Evidence," in *The Persuasion Handbook: Developments in Theory and Practice*, James Price Dillard and Michael Pfau, eds. (Thousand Oaks, CA: Sage Publications, 2002), pp. 427–434.

16. Kenneth Burke, *A Rhetoric of Motives* (Berkeley, CA: University of California Press, 1969), p. 55 and pp. 21–45; Charles J. Stewart, Craig Allen Smith, and Robert E. Denton, Jr., *Persuasion and Social Movements* (Prospects Heights, IL: Waveland Press, 2012), pp. 144–148.

17. Eddie Harmon-Jones, "A Cognitive Dissonance Theory Perspective on Persuasion," in *The Persuasion Handbook: Developments in Theory and Practice,* James Price Dillard and Michael Pfau, eds. (Thousand Oaks, CA: Sage Publications, 2002), pp. 99–116.

18. Erin Allison Szabo and Michael Pfau, "Nuances in Inoculation: Theory and Applications," in *The Persuasion Handbook: Developments in Theory and Practice,* James Price Dillard and Michael Pfau, eds. (Thousand Oaks, CA: Sage Publications, 2002), pp. 233–237.

19. Michael Burgoon, Eusebio Alvaro, Joseph Grandpre, and Michael Voulodakis, "Revisiting the Theory of Psychological Reactance," in *The Persuasion Handbook: Developments in Theory and Practice,* James Price Dillard and Michael Pfau, eds. (Thousand Oaks, CA: Sage Publications, 2002), pp. 213–218.

20. Judith N. Martin and Thomas K. Nakayama, *Experiencing Intercultural Communication* (New York: McGraw-Hill, 2011), pp. 261–262 and 321–322.

21. Shavitt and Brock, pp. 152–153.

22. Larson, p. 295.

23. Gerald L. Miller, "On Being Persuaded: Some Basic Distinctions," in *The Persuasion Handbook: Developments in Theory and Practice,* James Price Dillard and Michael Pfau, eds. (Thousand, Oaks, CA: Sage Publications, 2002), pp. 7–8.

24. Kelton V.L. Rhoads and Robert B. Cialdini, "The Business of Influence: Principles That Lead to Success In Commercial Settings," in *The Persuasion Handbook: Developments in Theory and Practice,* James Price Dillard and Michael Pfau, eds. (Thousand Oaks, CA: Sage Publications, 2002), pp. 513–520.

25. Woodward and Denton, p. 50.

26. Larson (2004), pp. 103–104.

27. West Lafayette, IN, *The Exponent*, August 22, 2003, p. B1.

Resources

Cialdini, Robert B. *Influence: Science and Practice*. Boston, MA: Allyn and Bacon, 2013.

Dillard, James Price, and Michael Pfau, eds. *The Persuasion Handbook: Developments in Theory and Practice*. Thousand Oaks, CA: Sage, 2002.

Johannesen, Richard L., Kathleen Valde, and Karen Whedbee. *Ethics in Human Communication*. Long Grove, IL: Waveland Press, 2008.

Larson, Charles U. *Persuasion: Reception and Responsibility*. Belmont, CA: Thomson/Wadsworth, 2013.

Woodward, Gary C., and Robert E. Denton. *Persuasion and Influence in American Life*. Long Grove, IL: Waveland Press, 2018.

The Counseling Interview

When you think of **counseling**, a highly trained psychiatrist or psychologist may come to mind or ones you have encountered such as academic, career, family, grief, financial, legal, marriage, religious, and investment counselors. All of these professionals have trained and developed expertise in specific areas. While few people in our society have these counseling credentials, **all of us** counsel others on a regular basis. Family members, friends, neighbors, co-workers, students, and team members want us to **listen** to problems and concerns, to show **interest** or **compassion**, and to offer a bit of **advice** or **assistance**. You are likely to comply because that is what we do as human beings. Experts in crisis management claim that in a time of crisis "everyone is a resource."[1] So-called "lay counselors" like you with minimum training and experience have proven to be quite successful in counseling situations because we tend to seek help from people we know, trust, are similar to us, are open and caring, and are good listeners.[2]

> The counselor is a helper, not a problem solver.

The counseling or "helping" interview, whether conducted by a highly trained professional or a lay counselor, has the same purpose: to **assist** another party to **gain insights** into and **ways of coping** with a **personal problem**. The **interviewee's task** is to **resolve** the **problem** such as a fractured relationship, inadequate performance at work, poor grades, loss of family member, or low motivation. Counseling interviews are among the most sensitive because they occur when another party feels **unsure** of or **not capable** of resolving a problem and may have been persuaded or compelled to participate.

The objectives of this chapter are to introduce you to the basic principles of counseling including ethical responsibilities when helping another person, important steps in preparing for a counseling interview, nondirective and directive interviewing approaches, structuring the interview, and the critical ingredients of a successful counseling interview. This chapter prepares you to help those who turn to you for assistance with day-to-day problems in their personal and work lives. **It does not prepare you to be a psychotherapist or to handle critical problems such as drug or alcohol abuse, severe psychological problems, or legal issues.**

Ethics and the Counseling Interview

Whenever you agree to listen to another's problem, help weigh its ramifications, and suggest possible courses of action, you are likely to influence that person's life in significant ways. Everything you say and do in these interactions must adhere to a strong code of ethics and "bear public scrutiny of its application."[3] The American Counseling Association (ACA) states that "Through a chosen ethical decision-making process and evaluation of the context of the situation, counselors work collaboratively with clients to make decisions that promote clients' growth and development." Be aware of seven ethical principles inherent in every counseling interview in which you participate as interviewer or interviewee.

| Know when to say no. |

Establish and Maintain Trust

The American Counseling Association identifies **trust** as "the cornerstone of the counseling relationship,"[4] and as Sherry Cormier and her colleagues write, the "values of a sound relationship base cannot be overlooked." When communicating "interest in and acceptance of the client as a unique and worthwhile person," the interviewer "builds sufficient trust for eventual self-disclosure and self-revelation to occur."[5] A person thinking of change, engaging in change, or trying to maintain change is most likely to **accept** an interviewer's help when it is believed to be **genuine** and **trustworthy**.[6] In addition, disclosure of innermost thoughts and concerns depends upon a person's **trust** in the interviewer to keep interactions **strictly confidential**.

| Trust is essential for effective counseling. |

Act in the Interviewee's Best Interests

You act in the interviewee's best interests when you respect the person's dignity, are aware of the person's ability to make sound choices and decisions, and offer choices and decisions that are within the person's beliefs, attitudes, and values. Interviewees may gain insights and perspectives for making changes when they perceive important similarities with interviewers that indicate equal and favorable relationships with persons who can understand their problems and situations.[7]

| Beware of preconceptions. |

Be well-informed about relevant information on the interviewee's socioeconomic status, education, work history, family background, group memberships, medical and psychological histories, test results, and past problems and courses of action. Talk to people who know the interviewee well to gain insights into the interviewee that will guide you when conducting the counseling interview. Assess information from others carefully. Do they have reasons to lie or exaggerate? Have they formed negative, defensive, or wary attitudes toward a person because of secondhand information? You may discover the opposite is true when you interact directly with them. Beware of preconceptions that may lead you to prejudge an interviewee or anticipate a defensive or antagonistic interaction. Be especially cautious when working with children.

Understand Your Limitations

Be aware of your counseling experiences, skills, and limitations so you can avoid interactions for which you are not adequately prepared. "Self-awareness is an important aspect of competence and involves a balanced assessment of our strengths and limitations."[8] You must know when to refer an interviewee to a counselor with more appropriate skills and expertise. For instance, a professor may be highly skilled in educational counseling but have little or no ability to deal with the psychological or medical needs of a student. A financial counselor may be able to help a widow or widower with investing insurance benefits but not with handling grief.

| Mutual respect is critical to self-disclosure. |

| Know your limits. |

Skilled counselors are open-minded, optimistic, self-assured, relaxed, flexible, and patient. They are people-centered rather than problem-centered, sensitive to others' needs, able to communicate understanding, warmth, comfort, and reassurance, and give interviewees undivided and focused attention. They provide appropriate verbal and nonverbal responses, and they are excellent listeners. Jeffrey Kottler, author of *A Brief Primer of Helping Skills,* claims, "*Listening is the most crucial helping skill.*"[9]

> Listening is your critical skill.

How comfortable are you when a person reveals an embarrassing problem or incident or expresses intense feelings of sorrow, anxiety, fear, or anger? How comfortable are you with using proper terms and names for conditions, actions, and body parts? Your unease may become apparent to the interviewee and stifle disclosure and communication.

Do Not Impose Your Values, Beliefs, and Attitudes

You bring who you are to every counseling interview, including your values, beliefs, attitudes, personality, and experiences. Be acutely aware of the important values you hold and how you communicate these to others through eye contact, voice, manner, words, dress, and appearance. Helen Cameron cautions, "Anyone who feels they can operate from a *value neutral* perspective is deeply mistaken."[10] How do your values compare and contrast with those of the interviewee? It is not enough to tolerate differences in values and the beliefs and attitudes that emanate from them; you must understand and respect value differences. You must suspend judgment and avoid becoming argumentative and defensive. Guide the direction and flow of the interview without ordering, prescribing, or persuading.

> Can you reveal your motives and agenda?

Respect Diversity

Be **culturally aware** in today's global village because "Culture controls our lives and defines reality for us, with or without our permission and/or intentional awareness."[11] **Understand** and **appreciate** the interviewee's culture and how it is similar to and different from yours. Cormier, Nurius, Na-Yeun Choi, and Osborn claim that you must "regard *all* conversations as 'cross-cultural.'"[12] Culture includes not only gender, race, ethnicity, and national origin but also sexual orientation, socioeconomic class, geographical area, religion or spirituality, physical and mental abilities, and family form. Do not assume cultural differences are greater than all other considerations in counseling interviews. Qualities intrinsic to personalities, values, attitudes, and nonverbal behavior often account for counseling effectiveness.

> Strive to be more than "culturally aware."

If you feel inadequately prepared for cross-cultural counseling situations, seek training and assistance from those with expertise and skill in interacting with others in culturally appropriate ways.[13] Learn to recognize and avoid common cultural generalizations and stereotypes such as people on welfare are lazy, Hispanics are illegal immigrants, women are nurturing, young workers are superior to old workers, Muslims are terrorists, and Asian students are high academic achievers. Research indicates that when a match of world views is present in interactions, parties establish good working relationships because interviewees feel more understood and appreciated as individuals.

> We all value our values.

Maintain Relational Boundaries

Be aware of relational boundaries.

Maintain appropriate relational boundaries with interviewees, particularly when you have an administrative, supervisory, professional, or evaluative role as a teacher, employer, counselor, coach, or physician. Avoid nonverbal actions and words that might be interpreted as authoritative harassment. Maintain an emotional and relational distance to avoid any form of unintentional or intentional intimacy with an interviewee. Sources warn that it is an easy step across the line to sexual involvement. News reports of male and female teachers having affairs with their students are distressingly common. Thousands of men and women helped families, friends, and co-workers following the tragedy of September 11, 2001. In some cases, the helpers became emotionally and sexually involved to the extent that they destroyed their own families while trying to help others.

Do No Harm

Helping others may be dangerous to both parties.

This code encompasses all others. Be aware of dangers in trying to help others. Always act within the boundaries of your competence to avoid giving bad or ill-informed advice. Regardless of the advice you give, you may be blamed for outcomes or lack of them. Behave legally, morally, and ethically at all times. Know when to refer the interviewee to a professional with greater counseling and specialized skills. Reports of suicides, sexual molestation and assault, and violent attacks in homes, schools, businesses, theaters, and shopping centers by disturbed individuals often reveal that the perpetrators had sought help or revealed their intentions to others. When a person's "condition indicates that there is a clear and imminent danger" to self or others, you must refer this person to a more qualified counselor, inform possible victims, and notify authorities immediately.[14]

Prepare Thoroughly for the Counseling Interview

An interviewee may reject your offer to help in a counseling situation for a variety of reasons. When you know an interviewee thoroughly, you are better able to understand why the interviewee may be both asking for and rejecting your offer to help. What is the history, nature, and status of your relationship? What do you know about the problem? A rejection may not be as real and final as it sounds. How might you reply to **apparent** rejections such as the following?

Be prepared to reply to apparent rejections.

1. Now is not a good time.
2. If I need your help, I'll ask for it.
3. You've never been married, so you wouldn't understand.
4. I can take care of myself.
5. No one knows how I feel.
6. Don't tell mom and dad.
7. You don't know what it's like being a college student today.
8. Get off my back.
9. I have to get back to work.
10. I'm not the problem.

SDI Productions/E+/Getty Images

■ *Provide a climate conducive to effective counseling, which is a quiet, comfortable, private location, free of interruptions.*

If you cannot reply effectively to simple rejections such as these, there will be no counseling interview.

Select an Approach

This chapter emphasizes a **client-centered approach** to the counseling interview during which the interviewer focuses on what the interviewee is feeling and saying verbally and nonverbally.[15] The interviewee typically determines topics, decides when and how each is discussed, and sets the pace and length of the interview. The interviewer assists the interviewee in obtaining accurate information, gaining insights, defining and analyzing a problem, and discovering and evaluating solutions by engaging, listening, observing, understanding, encouraging, reassuring, validating, and reaffirming. The client-centered approach is based on the theory that the interviewee is more capable of analyzing problems, assessing solutions, and making correct decisions than the interviewer.

> The interviewer assists rather than directs.

While we recommend a client-centered approach for most counseling interviews, your knowledge of an interviewee may indicate the need for a more directive, highly structured approach. For instance, the interviewee may know or understand little about a problem and solutions (or be misinformed about both) and be unable to visualize a current or future problem and making sound decisions. Some interviewees prefer a directive approach. For instance, a study of Asian-American students discovered that when career counselors used a directive approach, students saw them as more empathetic, culturally competent, and providing concrete guidance that produced immediate benefits.[16]

Combination of Approaches

You may select a **combination** of approaches for specific purposes during an interview. For example, you might begin an interview with a client-centered approach to encourage the interviewee to talk, reveal feelings, and address a problem and its causes. Then you might switch to a directive approach to provide information the interviewee does not have, to eliminate misunderstandings, or to discuss possible courses of action.

Select a Structure

> Be flexible and adaptable.

There are many ways to structure counseling interviews, and both theorists and practitioners advocate a variety of different stages. Hartsough, Echterling, and Zarle developed a "sequential phase model" that the author is applicable in a wide variety of counseling situations.[17] They developed this structure originally for handling calls to campus and community crisis centers. Figure 11.1 illustrates their sequential phase model.

Figure 11.1 *Phases of counseling interviews*

Affective	Cognitive
1. Establishment of a helpful climate	**2.** Assessment of crisis
a. Making contact	*a.* Accepting information
b. Defining roles	*b.* Encouraging information
c. Developing a relationship	*c.* Restating information
	d. Questioning for information
3. Affect integration	**4.** Problem solving
a. Accepting feelings	*a.* Offering information or explanations
b. Encouraging feelings	*b.* Generating alternatives
c. Reflecting feelings	*c.* Decision making
d. Questioning for feelings	*d.* Mobilizing resources
e. Relating feelings to consequences or precedents	

The affective or emotional phases, boxes 1 and 3, involve the interviewee's feelings of trust in the counselor, feelings about self, and feelings about the problem. A nondirective approach is usually best for the affective phases of the interview. The cognitive or thinking phases, boxes 2 and 4, involve thinking about the problem and taking action. A directive or combination of approaches is usually best for the cognitive phases.

The typical counseling interview begins with establishing rapport and a feeling of trust (phase 1), proceeds to discovering the nature of the interviewee's problem (phase 2), probes more deeply into the interviewee's feelings (phase 3), and comes to a decision about a course of action (phase 4). Except in emergencies, you should not move from phase 1 to phase 4, or omit phase 3 without careful thought. If you do not discover the depth of the interviewee's feelings, you are unlikely to understand the problem or solutions.

Do not expect to move through all four phases in every counseling interview or to proceed uninterrupted in numerical order. You may go back and forth between phases 2 and 3, or between phases 3 and 4, as different aspects of the problem are revealed or disclosed, feelings increase or decrease in intensity, and solutions are introduced and weighed. Unless the interviewee wants specific information (where to get medical or housing assistance, how to drop or add a course, how to get an emergency monetary loan), you may not get to phase 4 until a second, third, or fourth interview. Be patient.

Select the Setting

Select a setting that is quiet, comfortable, free of interruptions, and private. If other employees, students, workers, or clients can overhear the interview, the interviewee is unlikely to be open and honest about a personal problem. An office or conference room with a closed-door and no interior windows may be ideal. Consider a neutral location such as a lounge area, restaurant, or park where privacy is possible and the interviewee may feel less threatened and more relaxed. Some interviewees may feel safe and comfortable only on their **own turf** such as their home, room, office, or place of business.

> Setting and seating may be critical when counseling.

When possible, arrange the seating so that both parties can communicate freely. You may sit on the floor with a child, perhaps playing a game, drawing pictures, or looking at a book. An optimal interpersonal distance is 3.5 feet. Students comment that an interviewer behind a desk makes them ill at ease, as though the "mighty one" is sitting in judgment. They prefer a chair at the end of the desk—at a right angle to the interviewer—or in chairs facing one another with no desk in between.

A round table is a traditional arrangement for problem solving. An interviewee may prefer something similar, like a dining room or kitchen table, because it includes no power or leader position and they often handle personal matters around the dining or kitchen table.

Conducting the Interview

As you approach the interview, remember that you are "investing in people" and that people can change, grow, and improve. Accept the person as the person is. Do not approach the interview as an opportunity to remodel an individual to your liking. The interview is a learning process for both parties and is unlikely to be a one-shot effort.

The Opening

> Desire to help and show it.

The first few minutes set the verbal and psychological tone for the counseling interview. Express your interest in helping and avoid being, or appear to be, condescending or patronizing. Your frustration from past contacts or lack of interviewee performance may lead you to blurt out, "It's about time you came in!" or "What's wrong now?" Stifle your irritation and attempt to understand "the client's world from inside the client's frame of reference."[18]

Initial Comments and Reactions

Do not second-guess the interviewee's reason for making an appointment or dropping by. Avoid statements such as:

I think I know why you're here.

Is this about the grade report from your math professor?

Are you still sending nasty text messages to your supervisor?

What's the problem now?

A person may not have initiated this interview for any of these reasons but feel threatened or angry by your comment and attitude. Your interruption may ruin an opening the interviewee has prepared that would have revealed why the interviewee has turned to you for help.

> **Be tactful and neutral but not indifferent.**

Avoid tactless and leading reactions common in interactions with family members, children, friends, and associates. All of us have been on the receiving end of such statements as:

Where did you get that tattoo?

I see you have pink hair today.

You've been doing what we agreed to last time, haven't you?

You look like you just got out of bed.

> **Prepare the interviewee for what comes next.**

Such tactless comments and reactions are likely to set a negative tone for the interview and lessen the interviewee's self-confidence and self-esteem when both are needed.

If you have initiated the counseling session, state clearly and honestly what you want to talk about and why. An interviewee may not know what to expect or why the interview is taking place. Anxiety may be high and seriously affect interactions throughout the interview. If there is a time constraint for the interview, make this known so both parties can work within it and avoid an awkward closing when time is up. Take time to get acquainted or reacquainted and to commence a working relationship, even when you have a relational history.

An interviewee may begin by talking about the building, books on the shelves, pictures on the walls, the view out the window, or the weather. Be patient. The person is sizing up you, the situation, and the setting and building up nerve to introduce an issue.

The **rapport** stage is your opportunity to show attention, interest, fairness, willingness to listen, and ability to maintain confidences. Both parties are establishing trust. Discover the interviewee's expectations and apprehensions about the interview and attitudes toward you, your position, your organization, and counseling sessions.

The Body

During this stage of the interview, focus attention on what is most important and of greatest concern to the interviewee and how the interviewee might best resolve this problem or issue.

Self-Disclosure

> **Climate is critical to self-disclosure.**

Self-disclosure is essential to the success of counseling interviews, but "self-disclosing is a very complex process that involves intricate decision making."[19] The **climate** initiated in the opening minutes may be the most important determinate of the level of self-disclosure throughout the interview. A positive climate creates trust and engenders "feelings of safety, pride, and authenticity." The ability and willingness to **disclose** beliefs, attitudes, concerns, and feelings typically determine the interviewee's decision to seek help and the degree to which the interview will be successful. The interviewee must believe that keeping secrets and hiding the truth will inhibit the helping process "whereas disclosing produces a sense of relief from physical as well as emotional tension."[20]

Enhance self-disclosure through appropriate reactions and responses. Prepare for surprises so you will not be shocked by what you see and hear. Tasteful humor may reduce tensions but must not appear to minimize the interviewee's problem or feelings. Listen empathically and allow your voice, facial expressions, eye contact, gestures, and posture to communicate a confident, warm, and caring image. As a rule, minimize highly directive responses. Focus on strengths and achievements rather than weaknesses and failures and that which most needs attention. This approach tends to build confidence and a feeling that it is safe to disclose beliefs, attitudes, and feelings. The way you play your role as interviewer may affect the interviewee's perceptions of your attractiveness and level of expertise and determine the level of self-disclosure. Research indicates that **interviewer self-disclosure** of experiences and background at times may have a favorable impact on the interviewee's willingness to self-disclose important insights and information.[21] Limit your self-disclosure, however, because your goal is to enhance **interviewee self-disclosure**.[22]

Culture and gender may determine self-disclosure in counseling interviews. A study of African-Americans engaging in counseling at a community health agency discovered that African-Americans in this setting "engaged in an ongoing assessing process." Initially, they assessed client-therapist match [white or black], which was influenced by three factors: salience of Black identity, court involvement, and ideology similarity between client and therapist. These clients then assessed their safety in therapy and their counselor's effectiveness simultaneously. They used this information to monitor and manage their degree of self-disclosing along a continuum.[23] Counselor self-disclosure in cross-cultural counseling—particularly their reactions to and experiences of racism or oppression may improve the counseling relationship and make clients feel more understood.[24] Gender may determine self-disclosure. Females disclose significantly more about themselves and their problems than do males, especially on intimate topics such as sex, and a person's self-disclosure history often affects disclosure in other interviews. Males often have psychological defenses to protect themselves from feelings of weakness and to restrict emotional reactions.

Listening

Focus on the interviewee's problem and concerns.

Master the skill of listening for **empathy** to reassure, comfort, show warmth, and understand the interviewee's world and problem. Listen for **comprehension** to receive, understand, and recall interactions accurately and completely. Be patient and give your undivided attention to the interviewee's verbal and nonverbal communication to detect meanings and implications and to what is intentionally or unintentionally omitted. Do not interrupt, take over the conversation, or interject personal opinions, problems, or experiences. Remain focused on the interviewee. Avoid criticizing, judging, moralizing, or blaming.

Use nonverbal communication such as remaining silent when the interviewee pauses to encourage the interviewee to continue talking and elaborating. Show attention by leaning forward, facing the interviewee squarely, and maintaining eye contact. Facial expressions such as smiles, attentive body postures, and gestures communicate warmth and enthusiasm.

Observing

Observe nonverbal signals but interpret them cautiously.

Observe how the interviewee sits, gestures, fidgets, and maintains eye contact. Pay attention to the voice for loudness, timidity, evidence of tenseness, and changes. These observations provide clues about the seriousness of the problem and the interviewee's state of mind. Deceptive answers may be lengthier, more hesitant, and with long pauses. People maintain eye contact longer when they lie.

If you are going to take notes or record the interview, explain why, and stop if you detect that either activity is affecting the interview adversely. People may be hesitant to leave a recording that others might hear. They are willing to confide in you, but not others.

Questioning

Keep questions open ended.

Questions may play important roles in counseling interviews, but asking too many questions may be detrimental to the helping process. They may interrupt the interviewee, change topics, break the extent of self-disclosure, stifle the interviewee's questions, or reduce the interviewee's role to respondent. Do not interject a question into every moment of silence or hesitation. **Be patient!** Ask carefully phrased questions at strategic times during the interview. For example:

Nudging probes encourage interviewees to keep talking.
Informational probes seek clarification, understanding, explanation, and self-disclosure.
Reflective probes assure that you understand the interviewee correctly.
Clearinghouse probes ensure that you have obtained all important information concerning an issue or problem.

Steele and Echterling recommend two types of questions, the first is to *find meanings* in situations:[25]

What worries you most right now?

What do you think you can learn from that?

What scares you most now?

The second is to focus on the interviewee's effort to *get through* an emotional situation:

How did you get through that?

How are you finding it possible to get through this family crisis?

What did you do to feel better about this?

Avoid **curious probes** into feelings and embarrassing incidents, especially if the interviewee seems hesitant to elaborate. Beware of questions that communicate disapproval, displeasure, or mistrust that make the interviewee less open and trusting. Avoid leading questions except under *unusual* circumstances. Counselors working with children may go through intensive training in programs such as "Finding Words" that stress the use of nonleading questions. Avoid *why* questions that appear to demand explanations and justifications and put the interviewee on the defensive. Imagine how an interviewee might react to questions such as, *Why* weren't you on time? *Why* did you do that? *Why* confront Doug? *Why* do you think that?

Responding

This chapter has focused on a client-centered approach to the counseling interview in which the interviewer's role is to assist the interviewee in gaining insights into a problem and ways of coping with it. The interviewee's role is to resolve the problem. That said,

Understand your role in the client-centered interview.

however, the interviewer cannot avoid the role of respondent, often because the interviewee will not let you.

Highly nondirective responses and reactions encourage interviewees to be self-reliant by continuing to talk, analyze a problem, and assess a solution. One tactic is to reply with **silence** to encourage the interviewee to continue.

> **Interviewee:** I'm thinking of dropping out of school for a year.
>
> **Interviewer:** (silence)

A second tactic, similar to silence, is to employ a **semi-verbal phrase**.

> **Interviewee:** My supervisor thinks I can't do anything right.
>
> **Interviewer:** Uh huh.

Enable the interviewee to maintain control of the interview.

The danger of these tactics is that a prolonged silence may become awkward for both parties. If the interviewee appears to be unable to continue, choose another tactic.

A third tactic is to **return a question** to the interviewee rather than answer it.

> **Interviewer:** Should I file a sexual harassment complaint against my team leader who continues to tell sexually explicit jokes at our training sessions?
>
> **Interviewee:** What do you think?

■ *Review the interviewee's file prior to the interview so you can devote full attention during the interview.*

Purestock/SuperStock

Do not continue to return the question if the interviewee appears to have lack of information or is misinformed, genuinely undecided, or unable to make a choice.

A fourth tactic is to **invite** the interviewee to discuss a problem or idea.

> **Interviewee:** I don't think I can handle the stress of air traffic controller much longer.
>
> **Interviewer:** Would you like to talk about it?

An invitation tactic is most appropriate when an interviewee is willing and able to discuss, explain, and disclose feelings and information.

A fifth tactic is a **reflective question** to clarify or verify the interviewee's statement or response.

> **Interviewee:** I can't seem to manage my work schedule and classes this year like I've done in the past.
>
> **Interviewer:** Are you saying your junior year is somehow different from previous years?

Listen carefully and make a concerted effort verbally and nonverbally not to lead the interviewee.

Nondirective responses and reactions are appropriate when the interviewer is a good source of advice and encouragement because of position, experiences, or reputation as a "listening ear."

> **Interviewee:** I'm really struggling in my writing assignments because I've never had to do much writing.
>
> **Interviewer:** I hear this from a lot of students. Why don't you go to the Writing Lab in the English department? They can be very helpful.

An interviewee may only need a bit of information you can provide. Be specific and only as thorough as necessary in the information and recommendations you provide.

> **Interviewee:** If I switch majors from building construction to civil engineering, will all of the courses I have taken transfer to the new major?
>
> **Interviewer:** Your general education requirements will transfer, but you will need to take higher level math and science classes.

If you do not have the information or realize the problem is beyond your expertise, suggest resources or refer the interviewee to a better qualified counselor. Avoid unrealistic and unsatisfactory responses such as, "There's nothing to worry about." "You will do just fine." "Everything will work out for the best." "Just say no." "All parents go through this with their first child." "You'll look back at this and have a good laugh."

Do not fall into the *we* trap. Think of when you experienced common *we'isms* from counselors, teachers, health care providers, parents, and others.

How are *we* doing this afternoon?

We can handle it.

Let's take it one day at a time.

Are *we* ready for the exam?

Have you felt like shouting, "What do you mean *we*? I'm the one taking the test (getting the shot, undergoing therapy, overcoming grief)!"

> **Directive responses advise and evaluate but do not dictate.**

Directive reactions and responses go beyond encouragement and information to mild advice and evaluations or judgments. In the following interchange, the interviewer supports the interviewee's ideas and urges action:

> **Interviewee:** I've never been good at English, so I'm struggling with writing assignments this semester.
>
> **Interviewer:** Lots of students relate these concerns. Go to the English Writing Lab to get some help with your writing assignments.

A directive response may mildly question the interviewee's comments or ideas. Be tactful and cautious.

> **Interviewee:** My supervisor is talking about scheduling me to work on Sundays, and that would make it impossible for me to attend worship services.

Interviewee: All employers are required to make reasonable accommodations for people to practice their religious beliefs. Talk to your supervisor about your concerns.

The interviewer may provide information and personal preference when asked.

Interviewee: If you were me, what would you do?

Interviewer: I would get my GED first and then consider taking courses at the community college.

Mild directive reactions and responses may challenge an interviewee's actions, ideas, or judgments, or urge the person to pursue a specific course or to accept information or ideas. Employ directive responses only when nondirective responses do not work.

Beware of **highly directive responses** such as leading and loaded questions, judgments, orders, and ultimatums. You will be crossing the line from helper to persuader, advisor, judge, or dictator. The change in behavior, attitude, and resolution of a problem must come from the interviewee, not from the top down. Interviewees who receive helpful information and positive feedback comply more with the interviewer's recommendations and return more for counseling. They are more likely to implement recommendations when there is a good match between the recommendation and the problem, the recommendation is not too difficult to implement, and when it is built on the interviewee's strengths.

> Strive to be a helpful resource.

Nonverbal behaviors are critical when responding in counseling interviews. Your tone of voice, speaking rate, gestures, and facial expressions must communicate interest and empathy. Holding an interviewee's hand or a simple touch when appropriate may reassure and express caring and understanding. On the other hand, rolling your eyes, raising an eyebrow, crossing your arms, and sitting forward may signal disapproval or disbelief. Ruth Purtilo identifies five kinds of smiles, each of which may send a negative message: I know something you don't know; poor, poor you; don't tell me that; I'm smarter than you are; and I don't like you either.[26]

The Closing

Review the verbal and nonverbal leave-taking actions discussed in Chapter 4. Determine which techniques are most appropriate for each interaction. Avoid making interviewees feel they have imposed on you or they are at the end of an assembly line. Progress made during interviews may be lost along with the relationships you have tried to foster. Be sure interviewees know when and why the closing is commencing. Do not ask new questions or address new topics. Leave the door open for future contacts.

Evaluate the Interview

> Review all you did and did not do and accomplish.

Think carefully and critically about each counseling interview. Perceptive analysis will improve your helping interactions with others. Be realistic. They are interactions between complex human beings, at least one of whom has a problem and may not know it, want to admit it, or desire to do what it takes to resolve it. Do not expect to have met all expectations or complete an interview with a neat solution. Be content with having stirred thought and enabled the interviewee to discuss a problem and express feelings.

As you review the counseling interview, ask yourself: How adequately did I review the interviewee and the interviewee's problem beforehand? How conducive were the location and climate to openness and disclosure beyond Level 1? How appropriate were my directive and nondirective responses? How skillful were my questions in quality and quantity? How insightfully did I listen? How effectively did I help the interviewee gain insights into problems and make decisions? Did I agree or disagree too readily? What did I do to enhance the likelihood of interviewee compliance with suggested actions?

> How prepared were you for this interaction?

Your perceptions of how the interview went and how the interviewee reacted may be exaggerated or incorrect. You may be surprised by your successes and your failures in attempts to help others. Some of each are short-lived.

The Telephone and Online Interview

Telephone and online counseling interviews are growing in popularity because they can take place at times and places convenient for both interviewer and interviewee. They are inexpensive and can take place globally and in different time zones. The hectic pace of today's world has made it increasingly difficult to balance family life and work life and to schedule appointments. Crisis centers and professional counselors have used the telephone and online interview effectively for years. A study of interviewees discovered they were satisfied with the counseling they received and rated the counseling relationship and level of interpersonal influence similar to face-to-face counseling.[27]

Interviewees not only find the electronic interview convenient, but they like its anonymity and degree of confidentiality. They relax more in the privacy, familiarity, and comfort of their own surroundings and disclose more to the interviewer.[28] Interviewers report, however, that they miss the visual contact with interviewees and must overcome this by using their voices as substitutes for nonverbal cues, eye contact, gestures, physical appearance, clothes, and place. They warn that it is easier to sound facetious on the telephone than when facing the interviewee physically.

ON THE WEB

Selecting counseling approaches and responses most appropriate for a particular interviewee and problem may be critical to the outcome of the interview. Philosophies and practices differ among counselors and counseling agencies. Use the Internet to explore the interviewing approaches currently advocated and illustrated by researchers, practitioners, and agencies when dealing with a variety of clients and problems. Useful sources are the Pamphlet Page (http://uhs.uchicago.edu/scrs/vpc/virtulets.html), the Counseling Center Village (http://ub-counseling.buffalo.edu/ccv.html), and Counseling and Psychological Services at Purdue University (http://www.purdue.edu/caps).

Summary

You take part in a counseling interview each time you try to help a person gain insight into a physical, career, emotional, or social problem and discover ways to cope. The counseling interview is a highly sensitive interview because it usually occurs when a person feels incapable of handling a problem or a counselor decides that a helping session is needed.

Preparation enables you to determine how to listen, question, inform, explain, respond, and relate to each interviewee. It is essential for the interviewer to provide a climate in which the interviewee feels free to disclose information critical to the success of the interview. No two interviews are identical because no two interviewees and situations are identical. Thus, there are many suggestions but few rules for selecting interview approaches, responses, questions, and structures. Above all, know when to recommend a professional counselor because a person's problem is beyond your expertise to address. Do no harm.

Key Terms and Concepts

Client-centered approach	Directive reactions	Lay counselor
Cognitive phase	Expressed feelings	Make meaning questions
Compliance	Getting through questions	Sequential phase model
Curious probes	Highly directive reactions	
Directive approach	Nondirective approach	

Review Questions

1. What is a common name for the counseling interview that identifies its central purpose?
2. What is the central purpose of all counseling interviews?
3. What is a lay counselor?
4. According to the American Counseling Association, what is the cornerstone of the counseling relationship?
5. Why is the interviewer's "self-awareness" critical to the counseling interview?
6. What are the basics of a "client-centered approach" to the counseling interview?
7. Of the seven ethical principles discussed in this chapter, which is the most fundamental?
8. What are the phases in Hartsough, Echterline, and Zarle's "sequential phase model?"
9. Why is interviewee self-disclosure so important in the counseling interview?
10. What is the most important determinate of the level of interviewee self-disclosure throughout the interview?
11. When is the verbal and psychological tone set for the interview?
12. As a general rule, why should you minimize directive responses?
13. Explain which form of listening the interviewer should master.
14. When may questions become detrimental to the counseling interview?
15. Why are telephone and online counseling interviews growing in popularity with both interviewers and interviewees?

Student Activities

1. Visit a crisis center in your community or on your campus. Talk with counselors about their training techniques and self-evaluations. Ask about the code of ethics they are expected to follow and what ethical issues they have encountered when taking crisis calls. Which approach, directive or nondirective, do they find most useful? What roles do questions play in the counseling interview? How do they maintain focus on the interviewee and the interviewee's problems? Observe how volunteer counselors handle telephone counseling. How does telephone counseling differ from face-to-face counseling?

2. Interview three different types of counselors, such as a marriage counselor, a student counselor, a financial counselor, or a legal counselor. How are their approaches and techniques similar and different? What kinds of training have they had? How much training do they consider essential? In their estimation, what makes a "successful" counselor?

3. Create in detail a counseling situation in which you might be involved in your future profession or field. Develop a complete approach to the case, beginning with setting and furniture arrangement. How would you begin the interview? What questions would you ask? How much would you disclose about yourself—training, background, experiences, and so on? What kinds of reactions and responses would you use? What solution would you suggest? What would you do and not do to aid interviewee compliance? How would you close the interview?

4. Interview an experienced CASA/GAL (Court Appointed Special Advocate for children or Guardian Ad Litum). Explore the training that is required to become a CASA. What kinds of cases has this volunteer handled? Which have proven to be the most difficult? How do CASAs attempt to establish relationships with their assigned children? What may threaten the relationships they establish? How do they communicate with different-age children? How do they adapt to children from cultures very different from their own? What is the most important skill they have learned about counseling?

Notes

1. William Steele, "Crisis Intervention: The First Few Days—Summary of Dr. Lennis Echterling's Presentation," reprinted from *Trauma And Loss: Research and Interventions* V4 N2 2004, http://www.tlcinst.org/crisisint.html, accessed July 5, 2010.

2. Anna Martin, "What Is Lay Counseling?" www.thecounsellorsguide.co.uk/wgat-lay-counseling.html, accessed November 3, 2019.

3. "2014 ACA Code of Ethics" (American Counseling Association, 2005).

4. "2014 ACA Code of Ethics," p. 4.

5. Sherry Cormier, Paula S. Nurius, and Cynthia J. Osborn, *Interviewing and Change Strategies for Helpers: Fundamental Skills and Cognitive Behavioral Interventions* (Belmont, CA: Brooks/Cole, 2009), p. 5.

6. William A. Satterfield, Sidne A. Buelow, William J. Lyddon, and J. T. Johnson, "Client Stages of Change and Expectations about Counseling," *Journal of Counseling Psychology* 42 (1995), pp. 476–478.

7. Jennifer R. Henretty, Joseph M. Currier, Jefferey S. Berman, and Heidi M. Levitt, "The Impact of Counselor Self-Disclosure on Clients: A Meta-Analytic Review of Experimental and Quasi-Experimental Research," *Journal of Counseling Psychology* 61 (2, April 2014), pp. 191–207.

8. Cormier, Nurius, and Osborn, p. 17.

9. Jeffrey A. Kotter, *A Brief Primer of Helping Skills* (Thousand Oaks, CA: Sage, 2008), p. 73.

10. Helen Cameron, *Counseling Interviewing: A Guide for the Helping Professions* (New York: Palgrave Macmillan, 2008), p. 14.

11. Paul B. Pedersen, "Ethics, Competence, and Professional Issues in Cross-Cultural Counseling," in *Counseling Across Cultures*, Paul B. Pedersen, Juris G. Draguns, Walter J. Lonner, and Joseph E. Trimble, eds. (Thousand Oaks, CA: Sage), p. 5.

12. Cormier, Nurius, Na-Yeun Choi, and Osborn, p. 25. Na-Yeun Choi, Helen Youngju Kim, Elisabeth Gruber, "Mexican American Women College Students' Willingness to seek Counseling: The Role of Religious Cultural Values, Eitology Beliefs, and Stigma," *Journal of Counseling Psychology* 66 (2019), pp. 577–587.

13. Madonna G. Constantine, Anika K. Warren, and Marie L. Miville, "White Racial Identity Dyadic Interactions in Supervision: Implications for Supervisees' Multicultural Counseling Competence," *Journal of Counseling Psychology* 52 (2005), p. 495.

14. "Code of Ethics," National Board for Certified Counselors, June 8, 2012.

15. Kendra Cherry, "How Client-Centered Therapy Works," December 11, 2019, verywellmind.com/client-centered-therapy-2795999, accessed January 22, 2020.

16. Lisa C. Li and Bryan S. K. Kim, "Effects of Counseling Style and Client Adherence to Asian Cultural Values on Counseling Process with Asian American College Students," *Journal of Counseling Psychology* 51 (2004), pp. 158–167.

17. Lennis G. Echterling, Don M. Hartsough, and H. Zarle, "Testing a Model for the Process of Telephone Crisis Intervention," *American Journal of Community Psychiatrists* 8 (1980), pp. 715–725.

18. Cameron, p. 23.

19. Earlise C. Ward, "Keeping It Real: A Grounded Theory Study of African American Clients Engaging in Counseling at a Community Mental Health Agency," *Journal of Counseling Psychology* 52 (2005), p. 479.

20. Barry A. Farber, Kathryn C. Berano, and Joseph A. Capobianco, "Client's Perceptions of the Process and Consequences of Self-Disclosure in Psychotherapy," *Journal of Counseling Psychology* 51 (2004), pp. 340–346.

21. Jennifer R. Henretty, Joseph M. Currier, Jefferey S. Berman, and Heidi M. Levitt, "The Impact of Counselor Self-Disclosure on Clients: A Meta-Analytic Review of Experimental and Quasi-Experimental Research," *Journal of Counseling Psychology* 61 (2, April 2014), pp. 191–207.

22. Kevin J. Drab, "The Ten Basic Counseling Skills," www.people.vcu/krahall/resources /cnslskills, accessed January 20, 2020.

23. Ward, p. 471.

24. Alan W. Burkard, Sarah Knox, Michael Groen, Maria Perez, and Shirley A. Hess, "European American Therapist Self-Disclosure in Cross-Cultural Counseling," *Journal of Counseling Psychology* 53 (2006), p. 15.

25. Steele and Echterling.

26. Ruth Purtilo, *The Allied Health Professional and the Patient: Techniques of Effective Interaction* (Philadelphia, PA: Saunders, 1973), pp. 96–97.

27. Robert J. Reese, Collie W. Conoley, and Daniel F. Brossart, "Effectiveness of Telephone Counseling: A Field-Based Investigation," *Journal of Counseling Psychology* 49 (2002), pp. 233–242.

28. "Telephone Counseling," European Association for Counseling, 2020, eac.eu.com/accredited-counselors/telephone-counseling, accessed January 31, 2020.

Resources

Cameron, Helen. *The Counseling Interview: A Guide for the Helping Professions*. New York: Palgrave Macmillan, 2008.

Cormier, Sherry, Paula S. Nurius, and Cynthia J. Osborn. *Interviewing and Change Strategies for Helpers: Fundamental Skills and Cognitive Behavioral Interventions*. Belmont, CA: Brooks/Cole, 2009.

Hill, Clara E. *Helping Skills: Facilitating Exploration, Insight, and Action*. Washington, DC: American Psychological Association, 2017.

McAuliffe, Garrett J. and Associates, eds. *Culturally Alert Counseling: A Comprehensive Introduction.* Thousand Oaks, CA: Sage, 2019.

Nelson-Jones, Richard. *Basic Counseling Skills: A Helper's Manual.* Thousand Oaks, CA: Sage, 2015.

The Health Care Interview

The growing emphasis on preventive medicine, health education, dissemination of information through electronic media, and health insurance coverage has greatly increased the frequency of health care interviews in our society. They involve a wide variety of health care professionals and often result in long-term relationships with nurses, nurse practitioners, physicians, surgeons, and therapists. The degree of seriousness ranges from routine checkups and treatment of minor diseases to life-threatening illnesses and accidents. The health care interview is arguably the most complex and threatening interaction because a medical professional (1) must obtain insightful, accurate, and sometimes embarrassing information from a patient who may be reluctant to provide it; (2) make accurate diagnoses of physical and mental problems, (3) help the patient understand and process the complicated and intricate information often phrased in what appears to be a foreign language; and (4) persuade the patient to take medications and follow regimens exactly as prescribed.

> Health care interviews often serve a variety of purposes.

For those of you reading this chapter who are preparing for careers in health care, its relevancy will be obvious. Those of you with no interest in a health care career may struggle to see its relevancy to your life and career. **All of you,** whether professional or patient, will take part in health care interviews on a routine and non-routine basis throughout your lives. These interviews may consider simple assessments such as general health, eye sight, hearing, blood pressure, and heart rate. Others such as the flu, common cold, sinus infection, or virus may take you to an urgent care. Injuries from sports, workouts, falls, and car accidents may take you to the ER. And serious, life-threatening ailments such as cancer or heart disease may involve you and your family in serious long-term care. The more you know about what **does** and **should** take place in the health care interview the better able you will be to communicate with patients and health care professionals and to improve the care given and received.

The objectives of this chapter are to introduce you to the ethical responsibilities of both parties in the health care interview, the growing emphasis on patient-centered care (PCC), ways to create a collaborative relationship in the health care interview, the critical role of patient perceptions of the interviewer's communication and competence, the principles of gathering and giving information, and ways to counsel and persuade to reach agreements and motivate the interviewee to comply with prescribed courses of action, and the critical role the patient plays throughout this process.

Ethics and the Health Care Interview

Both parties involved in health care interviews must be aware that "Ethical issues are involved in most, if not all, decisions that relate to the goals, design, implementation, and evaluation of any health care intervention." And "these ethical issues are often implicit and embedded in subtle decision-making processes, and their delineation requires an assessment of unintended impacts."[1] As with all human interactions, it is often difficult to create and apply a single code of ethics to complex health care interventions and assessments that pertain to specific individuals with specific needs, problems, and abilities in specific situations, and with specific health care providers who may range from licensed practical nurses and emergency medical technicians, to highly trained specialists in practices such as neurology, oncology, and psychiatry. Fortunately, health care associations provide a core of ethical standards appropriate for health care interviews.[2]

The centuries old adage of *do good* and do *no harm* is the "foremost ethical maxim for health care providers and includes physiological, psychological, social, and cultural aspects of harm" and good.[3] Unfortunately, the intention to do good may do harm. For example, recommended physical activities or medications may result in injuries or complications. To do good while avoiding harm, includes being competent as a health care provider, remaining within your area of expertise, communicating truthfully, assuming responsibility for individual and professional actions, and reporting health care professionals who appear to be deficient in character or competence. "Truthful communication also requires that all relevant information should be provided, as indicated by the ethical standard of *completeness*" and accuracy.[4]

Health care providers must *respect the rights* and *dignity* of each patient. The U.S. public policy and medical ethics recognize that "access to quality emergency care is an individual right that should be available to all who seek it."[5] The vulnerability of patients must be a fundamental concern. Vicki Lachman, a clinical professor and director in Advanced Practice Nursing writes, "The nurse attends to the vulnerability of the patient, principally because the patient's needs have the potential to create dependency."[6] Health care providers must safeguard the patient's rights of *confidences* and *privacy*, and "disclose confidential information only with the consent of the patient or when required by an overriding duty such as the duty to protect others or to obey the law."[7]

Health care providers must *respect diversity* of patients and avoid any act that excludes, segregates, or demeans the dignity of the patient. They must provide "services based on human need, with respect for human dignity, unrestricted by consideration of nationality, race, creed, color, ethnic origin, gender, age, sexual orientation, or socioeconomic status."[8] There may be inherent problems with meeting this standard. For instance, "the obligations to promote people's health by encouraging them to adopt health promoting behaviors may conflict with the obligation to respect their autonomy."[9] People "have an intrinsic right to make decisions for themselves," and "health care providers may come from different ethnic groups, whose values and life circumstances differ from those" of their patients.[10] The solution may be a "culturally centered" approach that provides "marginalized groups with opportunities to engage in critical dialogues and have their voices heard by their own community."[11]

Health care providers must maintain *appropriate boundaries* in the provider-patient relationship. For instance, "The Principles of Medical Ethics" of the American Psychiatric Association state that "the provider must be ever vigilant about the impact that his or her conduct has upon the boundaries of the doctor-patient relationship."[12] "The inherent inequality in the doctor-patient relationship may lead to exploitation of the patient."

Patient-Centered Care (PCC)

> **Patient-centered care is both new and very old.**

The relationship between health care provider and patient is critical in every health care interview in which health care providers and patients prefer a collaborative partnership and a mutual participation in health care. The emphasis in twenty-first century health care commonly called patient-centered care (PCC) is on patients and providers as "co-agents in a problem-solving context."[13] The American Medical Association claims that "The patient-physician relationship is of greatest benefit to patients when they bring medical problems to the attention of their physicians in a timely fashion, provide information about their medical condition to the best of their ability, and work with their physician in a mutually respectful alliance."[14]

Advocates of co-agency contend that when patients are more actively involved as partners, rather than passive bystanders, they are more satisfied with their care, receive more information and support, are more committed to treatment regimens and managing health issues, have a stronger sense of control over their health, and experience better health.[15]

> **A reciprocal relationship is key.**

Patient-centered health care will continue to advance in the United States when both parties share control and actively seek to reduce *relational distance*. While both parties in health care interviews are unique in some ways, they share perceptions, needs, values, beliefs, attitudes, and experiences. Both must strive to maintain dignity, privacy, self-respect, and comfort. The goal of each health care interaction is to "develop a reciprocal relationship, where the exchange of information, identification of problems, and development of solutions is an interactive process."[16] Establishing a collaborative relationship ensures "that health decisions respect patient's wants, needs, and preferences" and that patients have the information and support to make effective decisions to take part in their health care.[17] How patients perceive their relationships with providers influence the roles they play in interviews.

> **Both parties must strive to reduce relational distance.**

Reducing relational distance between interview parties is central to patient-centered care, but neither party should rush this relationship too quickly. Each party must strive to know and understand one another because mutual understanding reduces relational distance. Parties enhance the relationship by being relaxed and confident, showing interest in one another as unique persons, maintaining objectivity, being sincere and honest, treating one another with respect, paying attention to verbal and nonverbal messages, remaining flexible, and maintaining appropriate degrees of control. Affectionate communication is basic in human relationships across cultures when it is seen by both parties as appropriate and within acceptable ranges.[18]

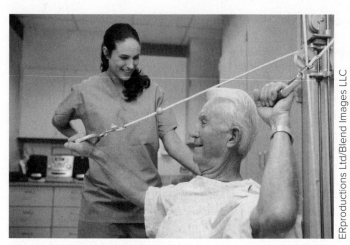

ERproductions Ltd/Blend Images LLC

■ *The development of positive relationships between health care providers and receivers is essential for effective communication and health care.*

Although the PCC relationship is ideal, providers and patients continue to believe the burden to make this relationship work rests on providers.[19] Studies also indicate that a significant percentage of patients expect providers to be in charge, to use controlling language, and to make final decisions. If providers do not meet these expectations, patients are dissatisfied with interactions, frustrated, confused, and even angry because the providers did not behave as expected. They are less likely to follow the provider's recommendations.[20] The health care provider's "ability to be flexible and adaptable is extremely important in medical encounters."[21]

Sharing Control

> **Both parties must share control.**

Although sharing control is essential in patient-centered interviews, tradition tilts control toward the health care provider who is highly trained, speaks in scientific terms and acronyms, is clothed in a suit or uniform, selects the timing and setting, structures the interview, and is taught to be emotionally uninvolved. It is not surprising, then, that providers often reassert their authority when patients challenge their knowledge or diagnosis. For instance, a study discovered that when patients (particularly males) present findings from Internet searches, providers may dismiss this research because they feel "loss of control" and see this challenge as "face threatening."[22]

> **Patients must be active and responsive.**

The tilting of control in the health care interview is not solely the fault of the provider. The patient may see every health problem as a crisis, have little medical knowledge of or be misinformed about health problems, see the environment as threatening, and prefer a "paternalistic model of health care."[23] It is difficult to see one's self as a true collaborator when in pain, highly medicated, and sitting nude on a cold table. A patient may appear to be compliant while employing subtle control strategies, such as changing topics, asking numerous questions, giving short, unrevealing answers, withholding vital information, or talking incessantly. Some patients demonstrate relational power through silence or agree with a provider during the interview and then ignore prescriptions, regimens, and advice afterward.

Both parties must negotiate and share control "as partners striving for a common goal."[24] Providers must develop positive relational climates by showing interest in the patient's lifestyle, nonmedical concerns, and overall well-being. Supportive talk that includes statements of reassurance, support, and empathy demonstrates interpersonal sensitivity and sincere interest in the patient as a person. Empathy is "an essential element of the physician-patient relationship," and a showing of empathy increases patient satisfaction and reduces time and expense. "Empathy is not just something that is 'given' from physician to patient. Instead, a transactional communication perspective informs us that the physician and patient mutually influence each other during the interaction."[25] Some patients provide repeated opportunities for empathic responses while others provide little or none. When patients do so, physicians have "a clear tendency for acknowledging, pursuing, and confirming patients' empathic opportunities."

> It takes two to form an effective relationship.

The provider must encourage the patient to express ideas, expectations, fears, and feelings about the medical problem and value the patient's expertise. Treat one another as equals. The patient must come to the interview well informed about the health problem and ready to provide detailed information as honestly and accurately as possible, express concerns, respond effectively to the provider's questions, and state opinions, suggestions, and preferences.

Appreciating Diversity

While we understand intuitively that patients from other cultures experience and react differently in health care interviews, few of us acknowledge that health care providers also experience stress and anxiety when interacting with patients of different cultures. Research indicates that provider's perceptions of patients are influenced significantly by cultural and ethnic differences.[26]

Gender

> Age and sex influence communication and treatment.

Women are more concerned about health than men and more verbal during interactions. This may be a learned difference because more health care information in the media is aimed at women than men. Women spend more communication time with providers and are more active communicators during these visits, but their providers take their concerns less seriously. On the other hand, male patients tend to be more domineering than females regardless of the gender of the provider.[27] As more females have entered the fields of obstetrics and gynecology, a significant percentage of women patients have chosen female physicians. This has led male physicians to improve their interpersonal communication skills.[28] Greater patient-centeredness by both male and female physicians has led to a "stronger positive effect on satisfaction and evaluations for male than for female physicians."[29] Patients do not see this as evidence of clinical competence for female physicians but merely as "expected female behavior."

Age

Age is a growing factor as life expectancy increases and the baby boomer generation reaches retirement age. Older patients are more reluctant to "challenge the physician's authority" than younger patients, often with good reason. Providers who are mostly under 55 are "significantly less egalitarian, less patient, and less respectful with older patients," perhaps reflecting society's attitudes toward "aging" and the wisdom of our elders. Providers are "less likely to raise psychological issues with" older patients.[30] When a patient is incapacitated, often because of age, it is wise to involve a surrogate (spouse or child) or a health care proxy who may have important information to share with the physician and be able to collaborate about the patient's care.[31] Young patients are more comfortable with "bothering" health care providers with questions and challenges because they are less awed by authorities and credentials.

Culture

Cultural differences may affect health care interviews in a variety of ways and require providers to adapt their approaches and communication styles. African-American and Puerto Rican patients have indicated that their race, ethnicity, and lower economic status impacted negatively on their information seeking (particularly HIV-related information) and health care.[32] Patients of a lower social class may be openly reluctant to challenge physicians so they attempt to control the relationship.[33] Arab cultures practice close proximity and kissing among men; both actions may be seen as offensive in American or European health care interactions. Native American and Asian cultures prize nonverbal communication, while American and German cultures prize verbal communication. Hispanics value interpersonal behaviors such as smiling, eye contact, patience, and "formal greetings, introductions, and farewells. These friendly behaviors lead them to feel better understood and to view information as more believable and accurate."[34] Medical philosophies differ among countries, and these differences might pose problems for nonnative health care providers and patients[35]:

- French physicians tend to discount statistics and emphasize logic.
- German physicians tend to be authoritarian romantics.
- English physicians tend to be paternalistic.
- American physicians tend to be aggressive and want to "do something."

These differences affect communication roles and control sharing in health care interviews. Providers must be culturally sensitive to differences in reporting pain, understanding informed consent, using appropriate language, and disclosing information that may rely on cultural knowledge, modesty, and comfort. Alice Chen relates an instance when she was treating a Muslim woman and ordered an X-ray to assess for arthritis. A male X-ray technician wanted to lift up the horrified woman's hijab so he could position the equipment properly. Chen referred her to a different facility with a notation that the patient needed a female technician.[36]

Stereotypes

The perception of patients as childlike is revealed in condescending attitudes and baby talk with adults. Twenty percent of staff interactions in nursing homes may qualify as *baby talk,* a speech style common when speaking to infants that has a "slower rate, exaggerated intonation, elevated pitch and volume, greater repetition, and simpler vocabulary and grammar." [37] Health care providers use *elderspeak* when addressing older adults. Examples include "Hi *sweetie*. It's time for *our* exercise," "Good girl. You ate all of your dinner," and "Good morning *big guy*. Are *we* ready for *our* bath?" The results of such "inappropriately intimate and childish" baby talk and elderspeak are "decreased self-esteem, depression, withdrawal, and the assumption of dependent behaviors congruent with stereotypes of frail elders."

> **Health communication differs in the global village.**

> **"Good" patients get better health care.**

The stereotypical *good patient* is cooperative, quiet, obedient, grateful, unaggressive, considerate, and dispassionate. *Good patients* tend to get better treatment than *bad patients*. Patients seen as lower class get more pessimistic diagnoses and prognoses. Overweight patients are deemed *less* likable, seductive, well educated, in need of help, or likely to benefit from help and *more* emotional, defensive, warm, and likely to have continuing problems.

Creating and Maintaining Trust

> Confidentiality and trust go hand in hand.

Trust is essential in health care interactions that deal with intimate and sensitive personal information and must maximize self-disclosure. Trust comes about when both parties "see one another as legitimate agents of knowledge and perception."[38] Breaches of confidentiality may lead to discrimination, economic devastation, social stigma, and destroyed trust, and any hope of building or maintaining a productive relationship. They may be intentional or unintentional and occur in many places: elevators, hallways, cafeterias, providers' offices, hospital rooms, cocktail parties, or over the telephone, particularly the ubiquitous cell phone. Maria Brann and Marifran Mattson relate an instance in which a patient tried to keep the reason for her appointment confidential by handing the provider a written note; the provider insisted that the patient read the note aloud. In another situation, a patient tried to answer confidential questions quietly, but the provider proceeded to ask questions about her situation in a loud voice.[39] Common sense solutions are talking and answering questions in soft tones, exchanging information only with providers who have a need to know, and conducting interactions in private, audibly secure locations.

> Providers and patients co-create trust.

Trust is established in the early minutes of interviews when both parties are determining if they can trust one another. It is further negotiated as both parties "enact behaviors" that construct "shared expectations of a trusting relationship."[40] Spontaneous humor, for instance, can "facilitate positive patient–provider interactions" and "create a patient-centered environment" that affects "patients' positive attitude and happiness."[41] The results are positive perceptions of caregivers that enhance trustworthiness and lead to better health outcomes, increased compliance with providers' advice, and fewer malpractice suits. Providers can enhance trust through supportive talk that increases patient participation in interviews and by eliciting full disclosure of information, clarifying information, and assessing social and psychological factors involved in illness.[42]

Communication is central to patient-centered care and to establishing a productive relationship between health care provider and patient. Observable communication skills, however, may not be sufficient to achieve either. Moira Stewart and her colleagues discovered that "The differences in interviewing skills may not be associated with patient responses. Physicians may learn to go through the motions of patient-centered interviewing without understanding what it means to be truly attentive and a responsive listener."[43] "Education about communication should go beyond skills training to a deeper understanding of what it means to be a responsive partner for the patient." Patients expect health care providers to listen, ask questions to understand and clarify their problems and concerns, reply to their questions, and provide information that is clear and relatively free of technical jargon, and offer recommendations they can remember and follow correctly.[44]

> Skills training is the first step.

Opening the Interview

The opening of the health care interview has significant impact on the remainder of the interview. Neither party should approach it as routine.

Enhancing the Climate

Both parties rely heavily on interviews to get and give information, but the start of the process is often taken for granted. The interviewer must establish an atmosphere conducive to open communication about feelings, concerns, and attitudes.

> **Location and setting promote collaborative interactions.**

Select a comfortable, attractive, quiet, nonthreatening, and private location free of interruptions in which interactions will remain confidential. Check out a typical pediatrics area and one for adults of all ages and conditions. The first is designed thoughtfully in every detail (pictures, aquarium, toys, plants, books) for the young patient and parents to minimize fear and anxiety and maximize cooperation and communication. The second is likely to be a stark waiting room with a television and a few medical magazines. The adult patient is then typically called to a treatment room, given a few perfunctory tests, asked to put on a hospital gown (open in the back and drafty), and then left alone for several minutes with an examining table, a variety of medical gadgets, and a few charts of the human's insides. This setting does little to relieve anxiety and tension.

Creating a Positive First Impression

The patient's impression of the health care interviewer in the first few minutes of the interview is critical in creating a positive, stable, and lasting relationship that will significantly influence this and future interactions. Michela Rimondini and her colleagues warn that "You only have one chance for a first impression!"[45] Adapt the opening to each patient. In a study of provider–patient satisfaction, Mohan Dutta discovered that "open physician-patient communicative style is not the universal solution to patient needs. Instead, the fundamental message that emerges from this research is the need for tailoring the health care providers' communicative styles depending on the needs of the patient."[46]

> **The opening should relax and inform the patient while building trust.**

Begin with a pleasant greeting and **introduce yourself and position if unacquainted.** A little small talk, humor, or self-disclosure may relax the patient, encourage interaction, and enrich the relationship. Review the patient's file before entering the room so you can start on a personal and knowledgeable level. If the patient has been waiting for a significant amount of time, apologize for the inconvenience and explain why. Urgent care and emergency rooms are notorious for hours-long waits that frustrate and anger patients. Make arrangements for staff to explain the reasons for delays, educate patients about health issues that should get primary rather than emergency care, inform patients about how health problems are prioritized, make them feel occupied, move patients to different locations so they do not feel forgotten, and **show empathy and concern.**[47]

Simple politeness and courtesy—treating people the way you would want to be treated—can defuse an angry or impatient interviewee and show you value the person's time and are sensitive to perceptions and needs. Judith Spiers addresses the relevance of *politeness theory* and how it can improve communication in the health care interaction.

Politeness
breeds
politeness.

Politeness is used primarily to ease social interaction by providing a ritualistic form of verbal interaction that cushions the stark nature of many interactions such as requests, commands, or questioning. Politeness provides a means for covering embarrassment, anger, or fear in situations in which it would not be to one's advantage to show these emotions either as a reflection of one's self or because of the reaction of the other.[48]

This advice helps health care receivers "save face" in a threatening situation over which they have little control.

Perceptions of "time pressures and medical terminology influence patient participation and the development of rapport in medical encounters."[49] When a provider consults more and uses little medical terminology, patients seek more information and believe they have established a good relationship with the health care provider.

The Body of the Interview

The opening questions health care providers ask and how quickly they ask them after an interview starts establish a good relationship, build and maintain rapport, and get adequate and insightful information.

Opening questions discover the patient's needs.

When a patient initiates the medical interview without explanation, the provider may ask a **general inquiry** question such as, "What brings you in this afternoon?" "What seems to be the problem?" or "How can I help you today?" When a patient has given a reason when making an appointment or informed the provider's nurse, the provider may ask a **confirmatory** question such as, "I understand you are having a severe migraine this morning?" "You're having a problem with your right shoulder?" "Tell me about your pain you are experiencing today." A second type of confirmatory question focuses on specific symptoms, such as, "Is the pain mainly on your left side?" "Does the dizziness usually occur when you bend over?" **General inquiry** questions elicit longer explanations of problems, including the most common or current symptoms. **Restrictive closed questions** initiate problem presentations and distinctively communicate "physicians' readiness to initiate and enforce the initiation, of the next phase of the visit: information gathering."[50]

Some health care providers conduct electronic interviews with patients prior to face-to-face visits. Patients select from a list of medical complaints and then reply to a series of questions phrased in language they understand. When providers enter the treatment rooms for face-to-face interactions, both patient and provider are ready to begin the interview. One provider relates, "My total focus is on the patient, and it's unusual for me to need to look at the computer."[51]

When providers initiate interviews, the opening questions may be open-ended such as, "How has your health been since we last met in June?" or closed such as, "Have you experienced any side-effects from the medication for your cholesterol?" What takes place after the opening questions depends on the specific reasons for the visit. If it is a routine checkup, the provider may orient the patient as to what will take place during the interview. If it is follow-up session, the provider may move to the body of the interview with a series of questions aimed at a specific problem or results of a previous treatment.

Getting Information

Seeking information consumes significant portions of most health care interviews, but it is not a simple or easy task to perform. The health care interviewer must understand the barriers to patient disclosure of information and ways to elicit honest, accurate, relevant, and complete information essential to successful interviews.

Barriers to Getting Information

Patients may be psychologically, physically, or emotionally unable to recall and articulate information accurately and completely. For example, patients may have poor memories because of psychological problems, health issues, accidents, or age. They may tell "little white lies" or try to camouflage real problems by making allegorical statements such as "It's probably just growing pains." "You know how teenagers are." "That's what happens when you get old."[52] Frightened and anxious patients leave out significant parts of medical histories, and this may explain why mothers recall only about half of their children's major illnesses.

> **Self-disclosure is central in the health care interview.**

Patients may resist giving information to avoid criticism or lectures on weight gain, smoking, drinking too much alcohol, eating too many sweets, taking too many over the counter drugs, or not working out enough. Patients may feel uncomfortable or embarrassed during interactions dealing with sexual organs, sexual activities, and sexually transmitted diseases. They may withhold information to avoid receiving bad news regardless of the consequences, such as getting skin cancer for not using sun screen. They may fear that giving depressing information to others may negatively impact the support they will receive.[53] Some patients try to assess the possible reactions of health care providers or outcomes to their sharing or disclosing of information prior to interviews. The more they are uncertain, the less information they will disclose.[54] A constructive way for the patient to reduce anxiety about provider reaction is "to share a small piece of information to assess the receiver's response," sort of testing the waters before fully disclosing.[55]

The means health care providers employ to get information often add to the barriers patients raise in exchanging information. The traditional history-taking portion of interviews is often longer than discussions of diagnostic and prognostic issues. The manner tends to be impersonal with many questions having little or nothing to do with the patient's current problem or concern. Patients in great pain or psychological discomfort may become angry or numbed by endless, closed questions, what one researcher calls "negative weakening." The author witnessed this wearing down process while visiting a family member in a nursing home in Florida. An elderly, ill, confused, and angry patient had just been admitted to the same room as the author's mother-in-law. Two medical personnel entered soon thereafter and began to ask a lengthy list of questions. Many would have taxed a medically fit person, and it did not take long before the patient was exhausted and obviously confused. The interview droned on, even though one of the questioners remarked to the other, "I don't know why we don't do this over two or three days. It's not like she's going anywhere." The interview continued with diminishing returns.

> **Provider dominance deadens interactions.**

A series of rapid-fire closed questions clearly sets the tone for the relationship: the provider is in charge, wants short answers, is in a hurry, and is not interested in explanations. One study revealed that 87 percent of questions were closed or moderately closed and that 80 percent of answers provided only solicited information with no volunteering.[56] Providers control interactions through closed questions, content selection, and changing of topics. They routinely ask questions such as: Do you have regular bowel movements? Do you feel tired? Are you ever short of breath? Any chest pains? Providers should stop and think what answers to these routine questions really mean. What does *regular* mean? Who doesn't feel *tired*? Who hasn't been *short of breath* from time to time or experienced an occasional *chest pain*? What does a yes or no answer to any of these questions tell the health care provider?

> **Explain medical terms and procedures.**

Do not assume familiarity with medical *jargon* and *acronyms* that are useful for interactions with other medical professionals. One study discovered that 20 percent or more of respondents did not know the meaning of such common terms as abscess, sutures, tumor, and cervix, and the percentages escalated with more uncommon words such as edema and triglyceride. Persons over 65 are less knowledgeable than ones between 45 and 64, and more educated respondents are most familiar with medical terms.[57] Patients seldom ask for clarification or repetition of questions or terminology because they feel it is the provider's responsibility to know and explain terms.

Researchers are focusing on "health literacy" and its potentially adverse effects on information giving and processing. One study used structured interviews with patients and discovered that "lower health literacy predicted lower self-efficacy, which predicted feeling less well informed and less prepared, being more confused about the procedure and its hazards, and wanting more information about risks."[58] Similarly, Maria Dahm's research revealed that patients' impressions about medical terms in interviews aligned with guidelines that promoted use of lay language and more detailed explanations.[59] She discovered that, contrary to these guidelines, "physicians often sought to clarify (semi-technical) terms by adopting topic controlling strategies such as using closed questions or taking extended histories." These tactics limit "patients' opportunity to speak and therefore can have effects on partnership building and, in turn, on the patient-physician relationship."

Improving Information Getting

> **Encourage turn-taking.**

The key to improving information getting in health care interviews is to find ways to foster exchanges that create a collaborative effort. Providers can improve patient disclosure and honesty by using their first names during openings, being friendly, not appearing to be in a hurry, and promoting turn-taking so patients feel freer to ask questions, provide details, and react to information they receive. Nonverbal cues such as pauses, eye contact, and head nods and verbal signals invite interactions rather than monologues. Be careful of verbal routines such as "Okay?" "Right?" and "Uh-huh" that patients interpret as inviting agreement rather than questions or competing notions.

Patients who play active roles provide more details about their symptoms and medical history, get more thorough answers to their questions, and prompt health care providers to volunteer more information and use "supportive utterances." Donald Cegala and his colleagues believe that high patient participation "helps the physician to understand more accurately the patient's goals, interests, and concerns, thus allowing the physician to better align his or her communication with the patient's agenda."[60]

Ask and Answer Questions

Use a funnel sequence that begins with open questions to communicate interest, encourage lengthy, revealing responses, and show trust in the patient as a collaborator to provide important information, including information you might not think to ask for. Ask open questions that are free of interviewer bias and invite rather than demand answers, give patients a greater feeling of control, and demonstrate the provider's listening skills.

The funnel sequence gives a sense of sharing control.

Use an inverted funnel sequence cautiously because closed questions asked early in an interview may set a superior-to-subordinate tone and communicate the provider's desire for brief answers and control. A patient's short answers reveal little and hide fears, feelings, and symptoms. Patients may be unable or unwilling to respond appropriately to open-ended questions that come later.

Listen carefully for hidden as well as obvious requests and responses. Is there evidence of confusion, hesitation, apprehension, or uncertainty? Patients should prepare lists of questions prior to interviews so they can think about concerns without the pressure of interactions with providers. Do not hesitate to ask the other party to repeat or rephrase an unclear question. You cannot reply sufficiently if you do not understand what is being asked. Dr. Nancy Jasper, a clinical professor at Columbia University illustrates the need to probe into answers, particularly when patients are "fudging with the truth."

> I always ask my patients whether they smoke. . . . A lot of women will say, "No but I am a social smoker." And I say, "You'll have to define that for me because I have no idea what that means." They'll say they only smoke on the weekends. But you start to uncover more when you ask: "How many cigarettes do you smoke in a week?"[61]

Both parties must listen carefully to understand what one another is really saying before proceeding.

Tell Stories

Encourage storytelling and listen.

What patients want most is an opportunity to tell their stories, and these narratives are "essential to the diagnostic process" and the most efficient approach to eliciting necessary information.[62] Gary Kreps and Barbara Thornton write,

> Stories are used by consumers of health care to explain to their doctors or nurses what their ailments are and how they feel about these health problems. . . . By listening to the stories a person tells about his or her health condition, the provider can learn a great deal about the person's cultural orientation, health belief system, and psychological orientation toward the condition.[63]

Susan Eggly writes that both parties must co-create the illness narrative so they can influence one another and shape the narrative as it is told.[64] She identifies three types of stories: "narratives that emerge through the co-constructed chronology of key events, the co-constructed repetition and elaboration of key events, and the co-constructed interpretation of the meaning of key events." Collaboration in storytelling is important because patients routinely omit valuable information from narratives they think is unimportant, do not feel safe in revealing, or assume the provider would not be interested.

Roter and Hall write, "From the patient perspective . . . the opportunity to relate the illness narrative and reflect on experience, perspective, and interpretation of symptoms and circumstances may hold therapeutic value, and, consequently, patients' disclosure, especially in the psychological realm, can be viewed as an indicator of the visit's patient-centered focus."[65]

Avoid interruptions during narratives, especially when patients become overwhelmed with emotion. The success of the interview may be due to the number of words the provider does *not say* or the number of questions *not asked*. Some researchers use the phrase "empathic opportunity terminator" to identify interactions that redirect interviews and cut off further revelations of patients' emotional concerns.[66] In the first interaction below, the physician changes the subject.

> **The less you talk, the more you may say.**

Patient: I'm in the process of retiring . . .

Physician: You are?

Patient: Yeah. I'll be 73 in February.

Physician: How's your back?

In this interaction, the physician retreats to an earlier, less emotional concern.

Patient: And right now I'm real nauseous and sick. I lost 10 pounds in six days.

Physician: Okay. You lost 10 pounds.

Patient: And I'm getting, and I'm getting worse. I'm not getting any better.

Physician: Okay . . . and right now you are not able to eat anything, you said?

Older patients give significantly longer presentations and narratives than younger patients, but they do not reveal more current symptoms. They do offer more information about a symptom, "engage in more painful self-disclosure," and disclose more about seemingly irrelevant matters such as family finances.[67] Be patient and probe for relevant specifics and explanations. "It is particularly critical to understand how communication processes change and how older adults communicate their concerns and feelings."[68] When older patients discuss a loss in later life, they shift "from a primarily factual mode (what the loss was, how the loss occurred, etc.) to a focus on the impact of this loss on their lives (e.g., handling new tasks and expressions of emotions)."

Listen, Observe, and Talk

> **Be patient and persistent.**

Be patient and use nudging probes to encourage patients to continue with narratives or answers. Avoid irritating interjections such as *right, fine, okay,* and *good*. Avoid guessing games. Ask, "When does your back hurt?" not "Does it hurt when you first get up? When you stand a lot? When you sit for a while?" Avoid double-barreled questions such as "And in your family, has there been high blood pressure or strokes? Diabetes or cancer?" Employ reflective and mirror questions to check for accuracy and understanding. Listen for important clues in answers, what patients are suggesting or implying verbally and nonverbally. Make it clear to parents, spouses, relatives, or friends present that the patient must answer questions if physically and mentally able to do so.

Use leading
questions
with caution.

Leading questions such as "You're staying on your diet, aren't you?" signal you want agreement, a yes answer, and that is likely what you will get even if it is false. Annette Harres discusses the importance of "tag questions" to elicit information, summarize and confirm information, express empathy, and provide positive feedback.[69] "You can bend your knee, can't you?" "You've been here before, haven't you?" "I'm sure it's been a very difficult adjustment since your husband Paul died."

Addressing the Language Barrier

Health care professionals have long recognized that **communication** breakdowns are the most common cause of **health errors**, and this problem is exacerbated by an estimated "95 million people" who "do not have the fundamental literacy skills in English to understand even the most basic" health information such as how and when to take medication.[70] Nearly half of this number have little or no command of the English language. The misinterpretation of a single word, such as "irritate," may lead to delayed care and medical errors. Latino patients who prefer to speak Spanish rather than English "experience higher levels of decision dissatisfaction and decision regret than those from other cultural and ethnic groups."[71]

Providers have tried a variety of solutions. For example, family and friends may speak the patient's native language or be more fluent in English, but they may not repeat all of a provider's questions or explanations or be able to translate or explain medical terms accurately into the patient's native language or at the patient's level of understanding.[72] Children as interpreters pose problems because their command of the parents' native language may be minimal, "their understanding of medical concepts tends to be simplistic at best," and "parents can be embarrassed or reluctant to disclose important symptoms and details to their child."[73] Providers have used professional interpreters "to encourage provider–patient rapport, to read patients' nonverbal behaviors, and to help patients seek or express information," but the provider's medical specialty such as mental health, gynecology, and oncology may require translators with specialized knowledge and training. "It is a common practice to avoid repeated use of the same interpreter to avoid patient–interpreter bonding," but some providers prefer the same interpreter to "increase interpreters' familiarity with patients' medical history and their ability to anticipate and facilitate the provider's agenda."[74]

Successful programs have included comprehensive interpreter services in a language such as Spanish, creation of a course to teach Spanish to health care professionals, and use of specific phrases in Spanish to assess acute pain. They are limited, of course, to a single language. Some large medical facilities include a number of interpreters who are fluent in languages they encounter most often. A national system of interpreters fluent in many languages and trained in health care, similar to the one operated by the Australian government on a 24/7 basis, would be ideal.

Giving Information

Patients
remember
little and
follow less.

Giving sufficient information that is insightful, accurate, and memorable is a critical part of nearly every health care interview, but the failure rate as indicated in Chapter 5 continues to be very high. A recent study indicated that only 36 percent of patients recalled information without a prompt by the provider. A more positive study indicated that while 85 percent of patients recalled information correctly, the lost 15 percent might be the most consequential.[75]

A Shared Problem

The health care interview, like all interviews, is a collaborative effort, so the failure to give and recall information and follow instructions is shared by provider and patient.

The Provider's Role

Health care providers place greater emphasis on information getting than giving even though the strongest predictor of patient satisfaction is how much information is given for a condition and treatment. In a typical 20-minute interview, less than 2 minutes is devoted to information giving. Providers may be reluctant to provide information because they do not want to get involved, fear patients' reactions, feel they (particularly nonphysicians) are not allowed to give information, or fear giving incorrect information. Nurses, for instance, are often uncertain about what a physician wants the patient to know or has told the patient.

> Beware of faulty assumptions.

Providers underestimate the patient's need or desire for information and overestimate the amount of information they give. On the other hand, patients cite insufficient information as a major failure of health care and are turning to the Internet in rapidly increasing numbers. A study of cancer patients revealed that barely over 50 percent of those who wanted a *quantitative* prognosis got one and over 60 percent of those who did not want a *qualitative* prognosis got one.[76] Providers often assume patients understand what they tell them, including subtle recommendations and information laced with medical jargon and acronyms. Metaphors such as "We're turning a corner," "There's light at the end of the tunnel," and "The Central Hospital family is here to help" require patients to complete the implied comparison, and the result may be confusion and anxiety rather than comfort and reassurance. Providers give more information and elaborate explanations to educated, older, and female patients.

As patients turn increasingly to the Internet for information, health care professionals are disturbed that 72 percent of patients believe all or most of what they read on the Internet, regardless of source. This is particularly true for so-called seeker patients with higher educations and incomes, who are younger, and who are actively involved in interpersonal networks. They are "health conscious" and like the active "involvement in the processing of information."[77] It is less true for nonseeker patients who are older, have less education, and come from low income groups. They "intentionally avoid information that may cause them anxiety or stress."[78]

The Patient's Role

> Patients may hear what they want to hear.

Patients often exaggerate their abilities to recall information accurately and completely without taking notes or using aids and, if they cannot recall information they assume is a simple task, they may be too embarrassed to admit it. On the other hand, they may protect themselves from unpleasant experiences by refusing to listen or interpreting information and instructions according to their personalities. For instance, if a provider says, "You have six months to a year to live," a pessimist may tell friends, "I have less than six months to live," while an optimist may relate cheerfully, "The doctor says I might live for years."

> Use acronyms cautiously.

Patients may not understand or comprehend information because they are untrained or inexperienced in medical situations. They can be confused by conflicting reports, studies, and the media. For instance, in the fall of 2009, the U.S. Preventive Services Task Force recommended that women over 40 should undergo screening mammography only every two years instead of the traditional every-year testing. This created a major controversy among health professionals and organizations with many stating their conflicting opinions through the media. Such controversies pose particular problems for older patients who have less knowledge and understanding of medical situations and greater difficulties in giving information.[79] Patients are bombarded with unfamiliar acronyms (IV, EKG, D & C) and jargon (adhesions, contusions, nodules, cysts, benign tumors). The names of many pharmaceuticals are nearly impossible to pronounce, let alone understand. Hagihara, Tarumi, and Nobutomo investigated the common phenomenon in which physicians' and patients' understanding and evaluation of medical test results and diagnoses differ markedly. They recommend "To avoid either a failure on the part of the patient to understand the explanation, or a patient misunderstanding the physician's explanation, physicians should pay more attention both to the topic under discussion and to their patients' questions and attitudes."[80]

The aura of authority may inhibit patients from seeking clarification or explanation. A woman who did not understand what *nodule* meant did not ask questions "because they all seem so busy, I really did not want to be a nuisance . . . and anyway she [nurse] behaved as though she expected me to know and I did not want to upset her."[81] The desire for a favorable prognosis leads patients to oversimplify complex situations or misinterpret information. Others are afraid they will appear stupid if they ask questions about words, explanations, problems, or procedures. For a variety of reasons, "patients routinely pass up, or actively 'withhold,' an opportunity to" ask about "the nature of the illness, its relative seriousness or the course it is likely to follow."[82]

Many of us rely on **lay theories** to communicate and interpret health problems. Common "theories" include: All *natural* products are healthful. If I no longer feel bad, I do not need to take my medicine. If a little of this medicine helps, a lot will do more good. If this medication helped me, it will help you. Radiation and chemicals are bad for you. Katherine Rowan and Michele Hoover write that "scientific notions that contradict these and other powerful lay theories are often difficult for patients to understand because patients' own lay alternatives seem irrefutably commonsensical."[83]

> A little knowledge can be dangerous.

Information may be lost or distorted because of how it is given and how it is received. Providers may rely on a single medium, such as oral information giving, but research reveals that about one-third of patients remember oral diagnoses while 70 percent recall written diagnoses. Oral exchanges are often so brief and ambiguous that they are confusing or meaningless. A provider made this comment: "Now, Mr. Brown, you will find that for some weeks you will tire easily, but you must get plenty of exercise." How long is "some weeks"; what does "tire easily" mean; and how much is "plenty of exercise"? Health care professionals routinely prescribe medications to be taken four times a day without telling the patient what that means: every six hours, every four hours with a maximum of four doses within 24 hours, or as needed, not to exceed four a day. Health care providers *overload* patients with data, details, and explanations far beyond their abilities to comprehend and recall.

Giving Information Effectively

Part 2 of Chapter 5 offers a variety of ways to give information more effectively. Review these carefully, including do not overload the interviewee with information and details, provide only essential information, know how this interviewee processes and retains information, structure the way you give information, preview the information before giving it, and use nonverbal communication to call attention to critical pieces of information. This chapter focuses on the patient in the health care interview.

Perhaps the most effective means of helping patients to recall information and treatment recommendations is to develop relationships in which they play an active role in the health care interview. Remember that "medical decision making is much more than a cognitive process. It is also a social event, one defined by the nature of the communication and the relationship between the clinician and the patient/family."[84]

> An inquisitive patient is an informed patient.

If you detect patients are adhering to one of the lay theories mentioned earlier, help them recognize this theory and its apparent reasonableness and show its fallacies and potentially dangerous results. Encourage patients to ask questions by building in pauses and inviting inquiries throughout the presentation. A silent patient may feel intimidated, hopelessly confused, or believe it is the provider's responsibility to provide adequate and clear information. Ask patients to repeat or explain what you have said and look for distortions, missing pieces, and misunderstandings.

Do not overload patients with information. Discover what they know and proceed. Reduce explanations and information to common and simple terms. Define technical terms and procedures or translate them into words and experiences patients understand. Present information in two or more interviews instead of one lengthy interview. As a rule, provide only enough clearly relevant information to satisfy the patient and the situation.

Present important instructions first so they do not get lost in reactions to a diagnosis. Repeat important items strategically two or more times during the interaction so they are highlighted and easy to recall. Repetition may involve other health care professionals. For example, it is common practice for a physician to order a prescription and explain what it is, what it is for, how it should be taken, and its possible effects. A nurse may repeat this information before the patient leaves the facility. Then the pharmacist who fills the prescription may repeat this same information and note that it is printed on the label. The more repetitions the better.

Giving bad news is one of the most difficult tasks health care providers face in interviews. There is no simple formula for giving bad news because what works for one patient may not work with another. A common recommendation is to precede bad news with a "warning shot" such as "I'm afraid I have some bad news." Morgan Pantuck asks, "Does it work?" and concludes, "It depends on who you ask."[85] Steven Pantilat advises, "You can't make it somehow OK for the patient, but it's important not to make it worse."[86]

Prepare ahead of time by determining to the best of your knowledge what the patient knows and expects about the bad news. What do others likely to take part in the interview know and expect: parents, spouse, significant other, children, and friends. Think carefully about how you will phrase and deliver the bad news. What resources can you offer the patient? Do you want to begin with a "warning shot?"

Practitioners recommend that you tell the truth with empathy and in simple, clear words that avoid jargon, technical terms, and euphemisms. Then be quiet. After a moment of silence, it is okay to say "I'm sorry." You might ask, "What questions do you have?" Do not interrupt the patient. Avoid unrealistic comments such as, "I know how you feel?" You cannot know this unless you have gone through an identical situation recently. Even then, you are focusing attention on you rather than the patient. When the patient is ready, provide a full explanation, be sure they have understood what you said, and offer realistic hope. It may be best to delay planning and questions until the shock has worn off.[87]

Use media, such as pamphlets, leaflets, charts, pictures, slides, DVDs, the Internet, models, and recordings. Dentists, for example, use models of teeth and jaws to explain dental problems and DVDs to show the benefits of flossing and brushing frequently. Emergency medical technicians use mannequins to teach CPR. Never hand a pamphlet or leaflet to a patient and say, "This will answer all of your questions." Patients say they are helpful but admit they seldom read them.

Involve others in the process such as interpreters, family members, and friends to provide social support for the patient and prepare others to assist the patient in recalling information more thoroughly and accurately. Be aware, however, that you may be creating a **triadic** instead of a **dyadic** interaction in which the third party might interfere with and contradict the information and recommendations you are giving to the patient. In the worst case scenario, family members may use the patient to acquire pain killers for their use or to sell.[88]

Land line telephones and cell phones, account for nearly 25 percent of all patient–provider interactions. Nurse call centers that integrate assessment, advice, and appointment systems are increasing rapidly and have transitioned from "nurse advice" to "telephone risk assessment." If nurses and other practitioners can satisfy patients and physicians that they are effective information conduits as part of a health care triad, the result will be timeliness, accuracy, quantity, and usefulness of information. Perceptions of accuracy and reliability—trust—are best when the telephone provider is seen as a reinforcer. The telephone provider must note time, date, information, and recommendations for the file and pass on information to other providers.

Videoconference technology, including the use of Skype, enables providers and patients to interact visually over long distances, faster, and with less expense and to involve specialists in other locations. For instance, physicians in New Jersey are using "telepsychiatry" to treat patients more quickly and to counter the national shortage of psychiatrists, particularly child psychiatrists. Patients and providers must be prepared to deal with the differences from face-to-face encounters. There are fewer nonverbal cues to signal when a question or piece of information is clearly understood or an answer or explanation is sufficient so the interviewer can proceed to other matters. Answers and explanations tend to be longer and the result is less turn-taking and meaningful interaction between parties.

Counseling and Persuading

Health care providers tend to be *task oriented* and expect patients to follow their recommendations because they have the authority, expertise, and training. Unfortunately, patient compliance has been notoriously low, as low as 20 percent for prescribed drugs and as high as 50 percent for long-term treatment plans. With these compliance problems and the ever-greater emphasis on treating the whole person, providers must also act as **counselors** to help patients understand and deal with problems and **persuaders** to convince patients to follow recommendations accurately and faithfully.

Tell the truth, show empathy, use simple words.

Employ a variety of resources.

The telephone accounts for one-fourth of health care interviews.

Information giving does not ensure compliance.

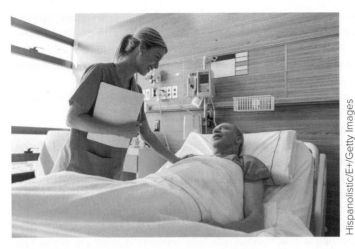

Hispanolistic/E+/Getty Images

Health care professionals may spend little time talking with patients because they are task oriented rather than people oriented.

Watch for hints and clues about real problems.

Barriers to Effective Counseling and Persuading

Patients may make the health care interaction difficult by remaining silent, withdrawing, or complaining about a physical problem rather than admitting a psychological one. One of my students reported that she had missed an examination and several class sessions because she had cancer. Only later did I learn through a third party that the student had long suffered from severe depression and suicidal tendencies. She felt it was more acceptable to have a physical than a mental problem. A provider may dismiss a patient with a diagnosis of stress, nerves, or overactive imagination.

Health care providers may spend little time talking with patients because there are many tasks to perform and talking is thought to be a social rather than a medical activity. Predictably, providers fail to detect subtle clues and hints that a patient wants to talk about a different and more serious medical issue.

Providers may employ a variety of **blocking tactics** to avoid counseling and persuading. Researchers and practitioners have identified several common tactics. Providers may attempt to dodge an issue by using humor, pursuing a less threatening line of conversation, providing minimal encouragement, denying the severity of the problem, pretending to have a lack of information, or rejecting the patient's source of information such as the Internet or popular magazines. On the other hand, providers may try to avoid an issue entirely by pretending not to hear a question or comment, ignoring a question or comment, changing the subject, becoming engrossed in a physical task, hiding behind hospital rules, passing the buck to another provider, or leaving the room. The nurse in the following exchange exhibits common blocking tactics.

Nurse: There you are, dear. Okay? (gives a tablet to the patient)

Patient: Thank you. Do you know, I can't feel anything at all with my fingers nowadays?

Nurse: Can't you? (minimal encouragement)

Patient: No, I go to pick up a knife and take my hand away and it's not there anymore.

Nurse: Oh, I broke my pencil! (walks away)

The patient desperately wants to talk to the nurse about a frightening and worsening condition, but the nurse is determined not to get involved or discuss the problem.

Effective Counseling and Persuading

Review the principles and guidelines presented in Chapters 10 and 11 that are relevant to the health care setting. Parties should plan for each interview with five relational factors in mind: empathy, trust, honesty, mutual respect, and caring. Source credibility has long been recognized as a key ingredient in the counseling and persuasion process. Paulsel, McCroskey, and Richmond discovered that "perceptions of physician, nurse, and support staff competence and caring were positively correlated with patients' satisfaction with the care they received and their physician."[89]

Select an Appropriate Interviewing Approach

Tradition is not always best.

Providers have traditionally tried two approaches. The first is a paternalistic approach in which the provider assumes the patient will see the wisdom of advice provided and alter attitudes and behavior accordingly. The second is an advise and educate approach that explains the medical reasons why and hopes for the best. Neither approach has produced results beyond 50 percent compliance. Telling patients what to do when they do not want to do it does not motivate them to act, and repeating unwanted advice may alienate them and produce resistance. Deborah Grandinetti advises, "change isn't an event; it's a process."[90]

Select an approach that is collaborative and best suited to this patient at this time. Barbara Sharf and Suzanne Poirier use a theoretical framework that psychiatrists Szasz and Hollender developed to teach medical students how to select appropriate interview approaches.[91]

- An active (directive approach) is recommended when a patient is passive and unable to participate.

- An advisory (nondirective) approach is recommended when a patient is compliant because of acute illness and thus not at full capacity.

- A mutual participation (combination directive–nondirective) is recommended when gathering data, solving problems, and managing an illness of a patient who can participate fully.

Develop a collaborative effort.

Above all, health care providers must approach interviews as **collaborative efforts** in which they show mutual sensitivity and respect for patients' concerns, reasons, and arguments. Lisa Mahler recommends that providers should "have patients voice their own reasons for change." The patient—not the physician—must articulate reasons for making or not making—a change.[92] A collaborative effort promotes **self**-persuasion. When patients see their providers as participatory decision-makers and credible experts, they are more likely to seek advice and adhere to their providers' recommendations.[93] Credibility is the key to agreement with medical advice. Patients usually have logical reasons for resisting recommendations and eventually for not complying with them. They perceive them to be time-consuming, embarrassing, painful, costly, ineffective, or have potentially dangerous side effects. Providers must rely on their credibility as participatory decision-makers and provide carefully supported arguments that show respect while effectively countering those of their patients.

Be Realistic in Expectations

Let patients set the pace of interactions because significant changes come about over time and in a series of stages. Do not try to rush the process or skip stages before the patient is ready to move ahead. Smokers, drinkers, drug users, and those overweight cannot and will not change in one giant step. The failure rate is steep for those who try.

Shock tactics based on intense fear appeals may backfire. For instance, when a physician emphasized the danger of swallowing medication for a canker sore in a direct and dire manner, the patient did not get the medication filled. Another physician employed self-deprecating humor and a lighter tone when prescribing acne medication, and the patient filled it.[94] Intense fear appeals may lead to patient denial or avoidance of regimens, medications, and checkups. These appeals "mainly scare those who are already scared" and do not produce "desired protective practices or norms."[95] Low or moderate fear appeals in conjunction with humor facilitates an open, personal, and caring interview climate; aids patients in losing their patient role; and enables both parties to convey thoughts and feelings in a nonthreatening and collaborative manner. Avoid insensitive humor that may embarrass, hurt, or mock the other party.

> Humor is an effective facilitator.

Encourage Interaction

Encourage patients to talk. If you share your experiences and feelings, the patient is more likely to confide in you. This promotes self-disclosure. Employ nonverbal communication to show that you care and want to listen. Listen with comprehension so that you understand what the patient is saying and implying. Listen with empathy so you can see the situation as the patient sees it. Do not ask too many questions. Question sequences such as the following encourage interviewees to talk about a problem and its seriousness.[96]

> Sharing and caring are essential.

Interviewer: If you developed a complication from smoking, say lung disease, do you think you would quit smoking?

Interviewee: Yes, I think so.

Interviewer: Do you want to wait until you get a complication to decide to change?

Interviewee: No, I don't think so.

Interviewer: Why wait?

Use a range of responses and reactions (from highly nondirective to highly directive). Give advice only when the patient lacks information, is misinformed, does not react to less directive means, or challenges information and recommendations. Avoid blaming or judging that may create an adversarial relationship.

Consider Recommendations

Introduce recommendations when the patient is ready to listen and comply. Compliance with recommendations is low when patients have no symptoms (such as skin cancer), recommendations are preventive in nature (such as diabetes), or recommended regimens will last a long time (such as regular workouts).[97] Only 10 percent of providers report they are successful in "helping patients change any health-related" behavior.[98] Work collaboratively to create plans of action—and alternative options—in the context of each patient's life by acknowledging the patient's social, psychological, and financial constraints. Share the logic (good reasons) behind your recommendations. Encourage patients to create their own health narratives—to tell their own stories—so they assume accountability for the decisions being made during the interview. Identify short-term goals so long-term goals do not appear so daunting.

> Collaborate to achieve incremental changes.

Present specific instructions and demonstrate how easy they are to follow. Express hope and recall challenges the patient has met in the past. The goals are to encourage patients, give them hope, and provide good reasons for complying with *mutually* agreed upon recommendations. Persuade the patient they will work, are doable, and are effective. You cannot resolve the patient's problem; only the patient can do that.

Closing the Interview

Make the closing a collaborative effort.

Be sure both parties are ready to close the health care interview. Research indicates that providers are most likely to initiate premature closings when they become **certain of their assumptions** about patients' symptoms, particularly when assessing the cause of pain. They are less likely to do so when they take time to explore patients' experiences and stories.[99] Listen to what patients may or may not be saying. Use clearinghouse probing questions to be sure you have discussed everything of importance. Patients may hold back information or concerns until the closing minutes of the interview. They may ask questions or make seemingly off-hand comments when providers are busy and paying less attention while writing out regimens, ordering prescriptions, and entering information into a computer. A significant patient health concern or problem may get lost in the closing process.

Important questions and revelations occur during the closing.

Provide a thorough but not overwhelming summary. Be sure both parties "are on the same page" and understand completely and accurately what was discussed, the information they have exchanged, and agreements reached together. Patients must leave with a clear and accurate understanding of everything that has transpired during the interview and realistic expectations of what providers can and cannot do. Assess successful information exchange by asking patients to explain important items in their own words. They may reveal confusions, misunderstandings, and counterproductive intentions.

Close interactions positively and productively while communicating empathy, trust, and care. The roles both parties play will enhance or detract from their relationship and influence their next interactions, or whether there will be next interactions. Researchers have discovered that "Patients' post-visit satisfaction with physicians' communication is important because it is positively associated with objective measures of physicians' task proficiency, patients' adherence to medical recommendations, and patients' continuity of care."[100]

Summary

The health care interview is common, difficult, and complex. Situations vary from routine to life-threatening and the perceptions of both parties influence the nature and success of interviews. For a health care interview to succeed, it must be a collaborative effort between provider and patient, and this requires a relationship based on high ethical standards, trust, respect, sharing of control, equality of treatment, and understanding. A collaborative and productive relationship will reduce the anxiety, fear, hostility, and reticence that often accompany health care interviews. Provider and patient must strive to be effective information getters, information givers, and counselor–persuaders.

Providers (from receptionist to physician) and patients (including families and friends) must believe good communication is essential in health care interviews and that communication skills do not come naturally or with experience. Skills require training and practice. Each party must learn how to listen as well as speak, understand as well as inform, commit to as well as seek resolutions to problems. Communication without commitment is fruitless. Both parties must follow through with agreements and prescribed regimens and medications.

Key Terms and Concepts

Assumptions	Elderspeak	Politeness theory
Baby talk	Face threatening	Relational distance
Blocking tactics	General inquiry questions	Self-persuasion
Climate	Information overload	Stereotypes
Co-agency	Jargon	Stories/narratives
Collaboration	Lay theories	Task oriented
Confirmatory questions	Patient-centered care	Trust
Counselors	Persuaders	

Review Questions

1. Why is the health care interview arguably the most complex and threatening interaction between parties?

2. What is the foremost ethical maxim for health care providers?

3. What are the *appropriate boundaries* in the provider–patient relationship?

4. What is meant by the term "patient-centered care" (PCC)?

5. Explain why creating a first impression is so critical in health care interviews.

6. How can the interviewer show empathy in the health care interview?

7. Why is it so difficult for the health care interviewer to share control with the patient?

8. How do patients of different cultures make it necessary for health care providers to adapt their approaches and communication styles?

9. When and how is trust established in health care interviews?

10. What is "politeness theory" and how does it pertain to health care interviews?

11. Why do patients resist giving information in the health care interview?

12. What should the interviewer do and not do when preparing for and giving bad news in the health care interview?

13. Why are patient stories or narratives essential to the diagnostic process?

14. Why do health care providers underestimate the patient's need and desire for information?

15. What are "lay theories," and how can interviewers overcome them?

Student Activities

1. Nurse practitioners are becoming common in health care, often seeing patients instead of physicians. Interview experienced nurse practitioners and discuss how they establishe and maintain relationships with patients and other members of their health care organization: receptionists, technicians, nurses, and physicians. How do the nurse practitioners deal with patients who clearly expect to see a physician rather than a "nurse"? How do they deal with physicians who see them as encroaching on their turf?

2. Interview three different health care providers (e.g., an EMT, a nurse, a nurse practitioner, a physician, a surgeon, an optometrist) about the problems they encounter when giving information to patients. Which techniques have worked well and which have failed? How do they approach giving information to patients of different cultures, ages, genders, levels of education, and health status? What kinds of information tend to get lost or misinterpreted most often? Why does this happen?

3. Visit a pediatric ward of a hospital. Observe how child-life specialists address and interact with young patients. Talk with them about their training in communication with small children. What communication problems do they experience that are unique to different ages of children?

4. Your campus, like most in the United States, is likely to have students and families from many different countries. Visit the campus health center or a local hospital and discuss how they interact effectively with patients who speak little or no English. What types of interpreters have they used: family, hospital, volunteer, or telephone interpreters? Which do they use most often? What problems have they encountered with interpreters?

Notes

1. Nurit Guttman, "Ethics in Communication for Health Promotion in Clinical Settings and Campaigns," in *The Routledge Handbook of Health Communication*, Teresa L. Thompson, Roxanne Parrott, and Jon F. Nussbaum, eds. (New York: Routledge, 2011), p. 632.

2. "AAMA Medical Assistant Code of Ethics," http://www.aama-ntl.org/about/code_creed .aspx?print=true, accessed October 31, 2012; "Principles of Medical Ethics," AMA, http://www/ama.assn.org/ama/pub/physician-resources/medical-ethics/code-medical -ethics, accessed October 31, 2012.

3. Guttman, p. 633; "*The Principles of Medical Ethics*" (Arlington, VA: American Psychiatric Association, 2009), p. 3.

4. Guttman, p. 634.

5. "Code of Ethics for Emergency Physicians," http://www.acep.org/Content. aspx?id=29144, accessed October 31, 2012.

6. Vicki D. Lachman, "Applying the Ethics of Care to Your Nursing Practice," *MDSURG Nursing* 21 (March–April 2012), p. 113.

7. "Code of Ethics for Emergency Physicians."

8. *"The Principles of Medical Ethics."*

9. Guttman, p. 633.

10. Guttman, pp. 633–635.

11. Mohan J. Dutta, "Communicating about Culture and Health: Theorizing Culture-Centered and Cultural Sensitivity Approaches," *Communication Theory* 17 (August, 2007), pp. 304–328.

12. *"The Principles of Medical Ethics."*

13. Amanda Young and Linda Flower, "Patients as Partners, Patients as Problem-Solvers," *Health Communication* 14 (2001), p. 76.

14. "Opinion 10.01—Fundamental Elements of the Patient-Physician Relationship," http://www.ama-assn.org/ama/pub/physician-resources/medical-ethics/code-medical-ethics.page.

15. Richard L. Street, Jr., and Bradford Millay, "Analyzing Patient Participation in Medical Encounters," *Health Communication* 13 (2001), p. 61; Christina M. Sabee, Carma L. Bylund, Rebecca S. Imes, Amy A. Sanford, and Ian S. Rice, "Patients' Attributions for Health-Care Provider Responses to Patients' Presentation of Internet Health Research," *Southern Communication Journal* 72 (July–September 2007), pp. 265–266.

16. Young and Flower, p. 71.

17. Kami J. Silk, Catherine Kingsley Westerman, Renee Strom, and Kyle R. Andrews, "The Role of Patient-Centeredness in Predicting Compliance with Mammogram Recommendations: An Analysis of the Health Information National Trends Survey," *Communication Research Reports* 25 (May 2008), p. 132.

18. Colin Hesse and Emily A. Rauscher, "The Relationships Between Doctor-Patient Affectionate Communication and Patient Perceptions and Outcomes," *Health Communication* 34 (2019), pp. 881–891.

19. Diana Louise Carter, "Doctors, Patients Need to Communicate," Lafayette, IN *Journal & Courier*, February 22, 2004, p. E5.

20. Joshua M. Averbeck, "Patient-Provider Orientation as a Language Expectancy Origin for Controlling Language in Doctor-Patient Interactions," *Communication Reports* 28 (2015), pp. 65–79.

21. Hullman and Daily, p. 321.

22. Sabee, Bylund, Imes, Sanford, and Rice, pp. 268, 278–282.

23. Sabee, Bylund, Imes, Sanford, and Rice, p. 266; Silk, Westerman, Strom, and Andrews, p. 139.

24. Kandi L. Walker, Christa L. Arnold, Michelle Miller-Day, and Lynn M. Webb, "Investigating the Physician-Patient Relationship: Examining Emerging Themes," *Health Communication* 14 (2001), p. 56.

25. Carma L. Bylund and Gregory Makoul, "Examining Empathy in Medical Encounters: An Observational Study Using the Empathic Communication Coding System," *Health Communication* 18 (2005), pp. 123–140.

26. Donald J. Cegala, "An Exploration of Factors Promoting Patient Participation in Primary Care Medical Interviews," *Health Communication* 26 (2011), p. 432.

27. Marie R. Haug, "The Effects of Physician/Elder Patient Characteristics on Health Communication," *Health Communication* 8 (1996), pp. 253–254; Anne S. Gabbard-Alley, "Health Communication and Gender," *Health Communication* 7 (1995), pp. 35–54; von Friederichs-Fitzwater and Gilgun, p. 84.

28. Carma Bylund, "Mothers' Involvement in Decision Making During the Birthing Process: A Quantitative Analysis of Women's Online Birth Stories," *Health Communication* 18 (2005), p. 35.

29. Judith A. Hall, Debra L. Roter, Danielle Vlanch-Hartigan, Marianne Schmid Mast, and Curtis A. Pitegoff, "How Patient-Centered Do Female Physicians Need to Be? Analogue Patients' Satisfaction with Male and Female Physicians' Identical Behaviors," *Health Communication* 30 (9, 2015), pp. 894–900, DOI: 10.1080/10410236.2014.900892.

30. Haug, pp. 252–253; Connie J. Conlee, Jane Olvera, and Nancy N. Vagim, "The Relationship among Physician Nonverbal Immediacy and Measures of Patient Satisfaction with Physician Care," *Communication Reports* 6 (1993), p. 26.

31. G. Winzelberg, A. Meier, and L. Hanson, "Identifying Opportunities and Challenges to Improving Physician-Surrogate Communication," *The Gerontologist* 44 (October 2005), p. 1.

32. Karolynn Siegel and Victoria Raveis, "Perceptions of Access to HIV-Related Information, Care, and Services among Infected Minority Men," *Qualitative Health Care* 7 (1997), pp. 9–31.

33. Merlene M. von Friederichs-Fitzwater and John Gilgun, "Relational Control in Physician-Patient encounters," *Health Communication* 3 (2001), p. 84.

34. Alicia A. Bergman and Stacey L. Connaughton, "What Is Patient-Centered Care Really? Voices of Hispanic Prenatal Patients," *Health Communication* 28 (8, 2013), pp. 789–799, DOI: 10.1080/10410236.2012.725124.

35. Gary L. Kreps and Barbara C. Thornton, *Health Communication: Theory and Practice* (Prospects-Heights, IL: Waveland Press, 1992), pp. 157–178. See also Gary L. Kreps, *Effective Communication in Multicultural Health Care Settings* (Thousand Oaks, CA: Sage, 1994).

36. Alice Chen, "Doctoring Across the Language Divide," *Health Affairs*, May/June 2006, p. 810.

37. Kristine Williams, Susan Kemper, and Mary Lee Hummert, "Improving Nursing Home Communication: An Intervention to Reduce Elderspeak," *The Gerontologist*, April 2003, pp. 242–247.

38. Young and Flower, p. 72.

39. Maria Brann and Marifran Mattson, "Toward a Typology of Confidentiality Breaches in Health Care Communication: An Ethic of Care Analysis of Provider Practices and Patient Perceptions," *Health Communication* 16 (2004), pp. 230 and 241.

40. Walker, Arnold, Miller-Day, and Webb, p. 57.

41. Juliann Scholl and Sandra L. Ragan, "The Use of Humor in Promoting Positive Provider–Patient Interaction in a Hospital Rehabilitation Unit," *Health Communication* 15 (2003), pp. 319 and 321. Wayne A. Beach and Erin Prickett "Laughter, Humor, and Cancer: Delicate Moments and Poignant Interactional Circumstances," *Health Communication* 32 (2017), pp. 791–802.

42. Taya Flores, "Humanistic Medicine: Compassion and Communication Vital to Patients," Lafayette, IN *Journal & Courier*, March 31, 2009, p. D1.

43. Moira Stewart, Judith Belle Brown, Anna Donner, Ian R. McWhinney, Julian Oates, Wayne Weston, and John Jordan, "The Impact of Patient-Centered Care on Outcomes," *The Journal of Family Practice* 49 (September 2000), pp. 796–804.

44. J.B. Christianson, H. Warrick, M. Finch, and W. Jonas, *Physician Communication with Patients: Research Findings and Challenges* (Ann Arbor, MI: University of Michigan Press, 2012), p. 1.

45. Michela Rimondini, Maria Angela Mazzi, Isolde Martina Busch, and Jozien Bensing, "You have only one chance for a first impression! Impact of Patients' First Impression on the Global Quality Assessment of Doctors' Communication Approach," *Health Communication* 34 (2019), pp. 1413–1422.

46. Mohan J. Dutta, "The Relation Between Health Orientation, Provider–Patient Communication, and Satisfaction: An Individual-Difference Approach," *Health Communication* 18 (2005), p. 300.

47. Elizabeth L. Cohen, Holly A. Wilkin, Michael Tannenbaum, Melissa S. Plew, and Leon L. Haley, Jr., "When Patients Are Impatient: The Communication Strategies Utilized by Emergency Department Employees to Manage Patients Frustrated by Wait Times," *Health Communication* 28 (3, 2013), pp. 275–285, DOI: 10.1080/10410236.2012.680948.

48. Judith Ann Spiers, "The Use of Face Work and Politeness Theory," *Qualitative Health Research* 8 (1998), pp. 25–47.

49. Maria R. Dahm, "Tales of Time, Terms, and Patient Information-Seeking Behavior—An Exploratory Qualitative Study," *Health Communication* 27 (2012), pp. 682 and 688.

50. John Heritage and Jeffrey D. Robinson, "The Structure of Patients' Presenting Concerns: Physicians' Opening Questions," *Health Communication* 19 (2006), p. 100.

51. "Improving Care with an Automated Patient History," Online CME from Medscape, *Family Practice Medicine* (2007), pp. 39–43, http://www.medscape.com/viewarticle/561574 + 3, accessed December 2, 2008.

52. Delthia Ricks, "Study: Women Fudge the Truth with Doctors," *Indianapolis Star*, April 1, 2007, p. A21.

53. Kathryn Greene, Kate Magsamen-Conrad, Maria K. Venetis, Maria G. Checton, Zhanna Bagdasarov, and Smita C. Banerjee, "Assessing Health Diagnosis Disclosure Decisions in Relationships: Testing the Disclosure Decision-Making Model," *Health Communication* 27 (2012), p. 365.

54. Maria G. Checton and Kathryn Greene, "Beyond Initial Disclosure: The Role of Prognosis and Symptom Uncertainty in Patterns of Disclosure in Relationships," *Health Communication* 27 (2012), p. 152.

55. Greene, Magsamen-Conrad, Venetis, Checton, Bagdasarov, and Banerjee, p. 366.

56. Kelly S. McNellis, "Assessing Communication Competence in the Primary Care Interview," *Communication Studies* 53 (2002), p. 412.

57. Carol Lynn Thompson and Linda M. Pledger, "Doctor–Patient Communication: Is Patient Knowledge of Medical Terminology Improving?" *Health Communication* 5 (1993), pp. 89–97.

58. Erin Donovan-Kicken, Michael Mackert, Trey D. Guinn, Andrew C. Tollison, Barbara Breckinridge, and Stephen J. Pot, "Health Literacy, Self-Efficacy, and Patients' Assessment of Medical Disclosure and Consent Documentation," *Health Communication* 27 (2012), p. 581.

59. Dahm, pp. 686–687.

60. Donald J. Cegala, Richard L. Street, Jr., and C. Randall Clinch, "The Impact of Patient Participation on Physician's Information Provision during a Primary Care Interview," *Health Communication* 21 (2007), pp. 177 and 181.

61. Ricks, p. A21.

62. Susan Eggly, "Physician–Patient Co-Construction of Illness Narratives in the Medical Interview," *Health Communication* 14 (2002), pp. 340 and 358.

63. Kreps and Thornton, p. 37.

64. Eggly, p. 343.

65. Debra L. Roter and Judith A. Hall, "How Medical Interaction Shapes and Reflects the Physician-Patient Relationship," in *The Routledge Handbook of Health Communication* (New York: Routledge, 2011), p. 57.

66. Marlene von Friederichs-Fitzwater, Edward D. Callahan, and John Williams, "Relational Control in Physician–Patient Encounters," *Health Communication* 3 (1991), pp. 17–36.

67. Heritage and Robinson, p. 100.

68. Scott E. Caplan, Beth J. Haslett, and Brant R. Burleson, "Telling It Like It Is: The Adaptive Function of Narratives in Coping with Loss in Later Life," *Health Communication* 17 (2005), pp. 233–252.

69. Annette Harres, "'But Basically You're Feeling Well, Are You?': Tag Questions in Medical Consultations," *Health Communication* 10 (1998), pp. 111–123.

70. "American Medical Association Report Provides Guidelines for Improved Patient Communication," *U.S. Newswire*, June 19, 2006, accessed October 25, 2006.

71. Mary Politi and Richard L. Street, Jr., "Patient-Centered Communication during Collaborative Decision Making," in *The Routledge Handbook of Health Communication* (New York: Routledge, 2011), p. 410.

72. Michael Greenbaum and Glenn Flores, "Lost in Translation," *Modern Healthcare*, May 3, 2004, p. 21.

73. Chen, p. 812.

74. Elaine Hsieh, Dyah Pitaloka, and Amy J. Johnson, "Bilingual Health Communication: Distinctive Needs of Providers from Five Specialties," *Health Communication* 28 (6, 2013), pp. 557–567, DOI: 10.1080/10410236.2012.702644.

75. Sara Heath, "Patient Recall Suffers as Patients Remember Half of Health Info," Patient Engagement Hit, March 26, 2018, xtelligent Healthcare Media, https://patientengagementhit.com.

76. Stan A. Kaplowitz, Shelly Campo, and Wai Tat Chiu, "Cancer Patients' Desires for Communication of Prognosis Information," *Health Communication* 14 (2002), p. 237.

77. Mohan J. Dutta, "Primary Sources of Health Information: Comparisons in the Domain of Health Attitudes, Health Cognitions, and Health Behaviors," *Health Communication* 16 (2004), p. 285.

78. Shoba Ramanadhan and K. Viswanath, "Health and the Information Seeker: A Profile," *Health Communication* 20 (2006), pp. 131–139.

79. S. Deborah Majerovitz, Michele G. Greene, Ronald A. Adelman, George M. Brody, Kathleen Leber, and Susan W. Healy, "Older Patients' Understanding of Medical Information in the Emergency Department," *Health Communication* 9 (1997), pp. 237–251.

80. Akihito Hagihara, Kimio Tarumi, and Koichi Nobutomo, "Physicians' and Patients' Recognition of the Level of the Physician's Explanation in Medical Encounters," *Health Communication* 20 (2006), p. 104.

81. Patricia MacMillan, "What's in a Word?" *Nursing Times*, February 26, 1981, p. 354.

82. Jeffrey D. Robinson, "An Interactional Structure of Medical Activities during Acute Visits and Its Implications for Patients' Participation," *Health Communication* 15 (2003), p. 49.

83. Katherine E. Rowan and D. Michele Hoover, "Communicating Risk to Patients: Diagnosing and Overcoming Lay Theories," in *Communicating Risk to Patients* (Rockville, MD: The U.S. Pharmacopeial Convention, 1995), p. 74.

84. Politi and Street, p. 400.

85. Morgan Pantuck, "The Bad News About Delivering Bad News," *UNDARK* https:// undark.org/2019/05/02/bad-news-in-medicine, accessed June 27, 2019.

86. Larry Beresford, "How Can Doctors Share Bad News with Patients?" *Medical News Today,* July 24, 2017, https://www.medicalnewstoday.com/articles/318067.php, accessed June 27, 2019.

87. Beresford; Kimberley R. Monden, Lonnie Gentry, and Thomas R. Cox, "Delivering Bad News to Patients," *Baylor University Medical Center Proceedings* 29 (2016), pp. 101–102; Rose Raymond, "How to Break Bad News to Patients: Experts Offer Best Practices," *The Do*, February 28, 2017, https://the do.osteopathic.org/2017/02 /how-to-break-bad-news-to-patients-experts-offer-best-practices/, accessed June 27, 2019.

88. Scott A. Eldredge, Elizabeth D. Dalton, and Laura E. Miller, "Pain Management as Triadic Interaction: Shifting Alliances in Nurse-Patient-Family-Member Communication," *Southern Communication Journal* 79 (November–December 2014), pp. 448–467.

89. Michelle L. Paulsel, James C. McCroskey, and Virginia P. Richmond, "Perceptions of Health Care Professionals' Credibility as a Predictor of Patients' Satisfaction with Their Health Care and Physician," *Communication Research Reports* 23 (2006), p. 74.

90. Deborah Grandinetti, "Turning No to Yes: How to Motivate the Reluctant Patient," *Medical Economics*, June 15, 1998, pp. 97–111.

91. Barbara F. Sharf and Suzanne Poirier, "Exploring (UN)Common Ground: Communication and Literature in a Health Care Setting," *Communication Education* 37 (1988), pp. 227–229.

92. Lisa Mahler, "Motivational Interviewing: What, When, Why," *Patient Care*, September 15, 1998, pp. 55–60.

93. Nanon H.M. Labrie and Peter J. Schulz, "The Effects of General Practitioners' Use of Argumentation to Support Their Treatment Advice: Results of an Experimental Study Using Video-Vignettes," *Health Communication* 30 (10, 2015), pp. 951–961, DOI: 10.1080/10410236.2014.909276.

94. Roxanne Parrott, "Exploring Family Practitioners' and Patients' Information Exchange about Prescribed Medications: Implications for Practitioners' Interviewing and Patients' Understanding," *Health Communication* 6 (1994), pp. 267–280.

95. Guttman, p. 637.

96. Grandinetti, pp. 97–111.

97. Shelley D. Lane, "Communication and Patient Compliance," in *Explorations in Provider and Patient Interaction*, Loyd F. Pettegrew, ed. (Louisville, KY: Humana, 1982), pp. 59–69.

98. Mahler, pp. 55–60.

99. Cleveland G. Shields, Miclelle A. Finley, Cezanne M. Elias, Casey J. Coker, Jennifer J. Griggs, Kevin Fiscella, and Ronald M. Epstein, "Pain Assessment: The Roles of Physician Certainty and Curiosity," *Health Communication* 28 (7, 2013), pp. 740–746, DOI: 10.1080/10410236.2012.715380.

100. Jeffrey D. Robinson, Janice L. Raup-Krieger, Greg Burke, Valerie Weber, and Brett Oesterling, "The Relative Influence of Patients' Pre-Visit Global Satisfaction with Medical Care on Patients' Post-Visit Satisfaction with Physicians' Communication," *Communication Research Reports* 25 (February 2008), p. 2.

Resources

Christianson, Jon B., Louise H. Warrick, Michael Finch, and Wayne Jonas. *Physician Communication with Patients: Research Findings and Challenges*. Ann Arbor, MI: University of Michigan Press, 2012.

Kar, Snehendu B. *Health Communication: A Multicultural Perspective*. Thousand Oaks, CA: Sage, 2001.

Murero, Monica, and Ronald E. Rice. *The Internet and Health Care: Theory, Research and Practice*. Mahwah, NJ: Lawrence Erlbaum, 2006.

Ray, Eileen Berlin, and Gary L. Kreps, eds. *Health Communication in Practice: A Case Study Approach*. Mahwah, NJ: Lawrence Erlbaum, 2005.

Thompson, Teresa L., Roxanne Parrott, and Jon F. Nussbaum. *The Routledge Handbook of Health Communication*. New York: Routledge, 2011.

Wright, Kevin B., Lisa Sparks, and H. Dan O'Hair. *Health Communication in the 21st Century*. Hoboken, NJ: Wiley-Blackwell Publishing, 2012.

GLOSSARY

Abrupt or curt: short and often rude responses or curtailing of interactions.

Accidental bias: when an interviewer unintentionally leads respondents to give answers they feel the interviewer wants them to give rather than their true feelings, attitudes, or beliefs.

Ad hominem: an effort to dodge an issue or challenge by discrediting the source that raised it.

Ad populum: an appeal to or on behalf of the majority.

Ambiguity: words to which interview parties may assign very different meanings.

Analysis: a careful examination of the nature and content of answers and impressions noted during an interview.

Appearance: how you look to the other party in the interview, including dress and physical appearance.

Applicant profile: the required knowledge, experiences, skills, and personal traits necessary to perform a job satisfactorily.

Application form: a form created by an organization to gather basic information about applicants, including their backgrounds, experiences, education, and career interests.

Appraisal perspective: the performance interview is seen as required, scheduled, superior-conducted and directed, adversarial, evaluative, and past-oriented.

Aptitude tests: tests that identify the abilities of a potential employee to predict how well and quickly the person will learn the tasks required of a position.

Arguing from accepted belief: argument based on an accepted belief, assumption, or proposition.

Arguing from analogy: argument based on common characteristics of two people, places, objects, proposals, or ideas shared.

Arguing from cause-effect: an argument that attempts to establish a causal relationship.

Arguing from condition: an argument based on the assertion that if something does or does not happen, something else will or will not happen.

Arguing from example: an argument based on a sampling of a given class of people, places, or things.

Arguing from facts: an argument based on a conclusion that best explains a body of facts.

Arguing from two choices: arguing that there are only two possible proposals or courses of action and then eliminating one of the choices.

Arrival: the point at which one interview party encounters the other to initiate an interview.

Assumptions: assuming that something is true or false, is intended or unintended, exists or does not exist, is desired or undesired, will or will not happen.

Atmosphere and setting: the environment in which an interview is taking place and whether it is conducive to effective communication between the two parties in the interview.

Attitude: relatively enduring combinations of beliefs that predispose people to respond in particular ways to persons, organizations, places, ideas, and issues.

At will: an employment situation in which either party may terminate the employment relationship at any time and for any reason.

Baby talk: speaking to elder patients as if they were infants, including slower rate, exaggerated intonation, and simpler vocabulary.

Balance or consistency theory: a theory based on the belief that human beings strive for a harmonious existence with self and others and experience psychological discomfort (dissonance) when they do not.

Bandwagon tactic: a tactic that urges a person to follow the crowd, to do what everyone else is doing.

Basic skills tests: tests that measure mathematics, measurement, reading, and spelling skills.

Behavior-based selection: selection based upon the behaviors desired in a position and behaviors exhibited by applicants.

Behavior-based selection technique: a selection technique that begins with a needs and position analysis to determine which behaviors are essential for performing a particular job and proceeds to match applicants with this analysis.

Behaviorally anchored rating scale (BARS) model: a performance review model that identifies essential skills for a specific job and sets standards through a job analysis.

Belief: the trust or confidence placed in social, political, historic, economic, and religious claims.

Bipolar question: a question that limits the respondent to two polar choices such as yes or no, agree or disagree.

Birds of a feather syndrome: the selection of employees most similar to interviewers.

Blocking tactics: efforts of interviewers to avoid counseling or getting involved with interviewees, particularly in the health care setting.

Board interview: when two to five persons representing an organization may interview an applicant at the same time.

Bogardus Social Distance scales: questions that determine how respondents feel about social relationships and distances from them.

Bona fide occupational qualifications (BFOQ): requirements essential for performing a particular job.

Branding: when an applicant presents a carefully crafted image to potential employers through social media.

Broadcast interview: an interview that takes place live over radio or television or will be played all or in part at a later time.

Built-in bias: interviewer bias that is intentionally or unintentionally built into a schedule of questions.

Career/Job fairs: gatherings of organizations and companies, often at malls or on college campuses, during which job seekers may make contacts with representatives and gather information about employment opportunities.

Career objective: a brief, concise statement of a targeted career goal.

Case approach: when an applicant is placed into a carefully crafted situation that takes hours to study and resolve.

Catalytic coaching: a comprehensive, integrated performance management system based on a paradigm of development.

Cause-to-effect sequence: interview sequence that addresses causes and effects separately but relationally.

Central tendency: when interviewers refrain from assigning extreme ratings to facets of performance.

Chain or contingency strategy: a strategy that allows for preplanned secondary questions in survey interviews.

Chain format: when one recruiter for an organization converses with an applicant for several minutes and then passes the applicant along to another recruiter for the organization who probes into job skills, technical knowledge, or another area.

Chronological format résumé: a résumé that lists education, training, and experiences in chronological order.

Clearinghouse probe: a question designed to discover whether previous questions have uncovered everything of importance on a topic or issue.

Client-centered approach: a counseling approach that focuses on the client rather than content or situation.

Climate: The atmosphere in which interview parties feel free to express opinions, feelings, and attitudes.

Closed-minded or authoritarian interviewees: parties with unchangeable central beliefs who rely on trusted authorities when making decisions.

Closed question: a question that is narrow in focus and restricts the respondent's freedom to determine the amount and kind of information to offer.

Closing: the portion of an interview that brings it to an end.

Coaching: helping to improve performance rather than judging or criticizing performance.

Cognitive phase: the thinking and assessing phase of a counseling interview.

Cold calls: persuasive interview contacts made without an appointment or prior notice.

Collaborative: a mutual effort by both parties to inform, analyze, and resolve problems.

Collectivist culture: a culture that places high value on group image, group esteem, group reliance, group awareness, and group achievement.

Combination schedule: a question schedule that combines two schedules, such as highly scheduled and highly scheduled standardized.

Common ground: shared similarities that enable parties to communicate effectively.

Communication interactions: verbal and nonverbal exchanges that take place during interviews.

Comparison tactic: a person points out a few similarities between two places, people, or things and then draws conclusions from this superficial comparison.

Competitive rater: an interviewer who believes that no one can perform higher than his or her level of performance.

Complement: to complete, support, or repeat.

Complex interpersonal communication process: the assumption that one-to-one communication is simple is belied by the many variables that interact in this process.

Compliance: when an interviewee follows assessments and courses of action agreed to during a counseling interview.

Confirmatory questions: questions designed to verify understanding of an interviewee's (typically medical patients) concerns, problems, or statements.

Connotations: positive and negative meanings of words.

Consubstantiality: the effort to establish a substantial sameness or similarity between interviewer and interviewee.

Contrast principle: if a second item or choice is fairly different from the first, it seems more different than it actually is.

Control: the extent to which one or both interview parties directs an interview.

Convenience sample: a sample taken when and where it is most convenient for the interviewee.

Conversation: an unstructured interaction between two or more people with no predetermined purpose other than enjoyment of the process.

Counselors: those who help interviewees to gain insights into and to cope with problems.

Counter persuasion: persuasion aimed at an interviewee by a persuader's competitor or antagonist following a persuasive interview.

Cover letter: a letter an applicant sends to a prospective employer that expresses interest in and qualifications for a position.

Coverage bias: occurs when cell phone only users who are often younger or of low economic status are excluded from a survey sample.

Critical incident question: a question that asks applicants how they might resolve a current problem the recruiter's organization is facing.

Cross-sectional study: a study that determines what is known, thought, or felt during a narrow time span.

Culture: shared customs, norms, knowledge, attitudes, values, and traits of a racial, religious, social, or corporate group.

Curious question pitfall: a question that is irrelevant to the interview and satisfies only the interviewer's curiosity.

Defensive climate: a climate that appears threatening to one or both parties in an interview.

Determinate interviews: an interview designed to determine whether or not to make a job offer to an applicant.

Dialectical tensions: the result of conflicts over opposing needs and desires or between contrasting "voices" in an interview.

Dialogic listening: a means of focusing on ours rather than mine or yours to resolve a problem or task.

Diamond sequence: a question sequence that places two funnel sequences top to top.

Differentiation: an attempt through language to alter how a person sees reality by renaming it.

Directive approach: an interview in which the interviewer controls subject matter, length of answers, climate, and formality.

Directive reactions: when an interviewer reacts to a client with specific evaluations and advice.

Disclosure: the willingness and ability to reveal feelings, beliefs, attitudes, and information to another party.

Dishonesty: lying to or deceiving another interview party.

Don't ask, don't tell question pitfall: a question that delves into information or an emotional area that a respondent may be incapable of addressing because of social, psychological, or situational constraints.

Double-barreled question pitfall: a question that contains two or more questions.

Downward communication: an interview in which a superior in the organizational hierarchy is attempting to interact as an interviewer with a subordinate in the hierarchy.

Dyadic: an interaction that involves two distinct parties.

EEO laws: state and federal laws that pertain to recruiting and reviewing the performance of employees.

EEO violation question pitfall: when an interviewer asks an unlawful question during a recruiting interview.

Elderspeak: speaking to elder patients as if they were children, including addressing them as sweeties, girl or boy, and honey and employing the collective pronoun our (e.g., "it's time for our bath").

Electronic interviews: interviews conducted over the telephone, through conference calls, by video talk-back, or over the Internet.

Electronically scanned résumé: a résumé designed in format and wording to be scanned electronically by recruiters.

E-mail interviews: interviews conducted through electronic e-mail rather than face-to-face.

Equal Employment Opportunity Commission: the agency assigned the task of overseeing and carrying out EEO laws.

Equal Employment Opportunity (EEO) laws: laws that pertain to employment and performance review interviews.

Ethical issues: issues that focus on value judgments concerning degrees of right and wrong, goodness and badness, in human conduct.

Euphemism: the substitution of a better sounding word for a common one.

Evaluative interval scales: questions that ask respondents to make judgments about persons, places, things, or ideas.

Evaluative response question pitfall: when an interviewer expresses judgmental feelings about an answer that may bias or skew the next answer.

Evasive interviewee: an interviewee who evades questions and gives indirect answers.

Evidence: examples, stories, comparisons, testimony, and statistics that support a claim.

Exchanging: a sharing of roles, responsibilities, feelings, beliefs, motives, and information during an interview.

Expressed feelings: feelings an interviewee expresses overtly and openly during a counseling interaction.

Face-to-face interview: an interview in which both parties are present physically in the same space during an interview.

Face threatening: interview interactions in which questions and answers may threaten the power or credibility of the interviewer or the interviewee.

Failed departure: when an interview has come to a close and parties have taken leave of one another only to come in contact accidentally later, often with a degree of communicative awkwardness.

False assumptions: assuming incorrectly that something is true or false, intended or unintended, exists or does not exist, desired or undesired, will or will not happen.

False closing: when verbal and nonverbal messages signal the closing of the interview is commencing but a party introduces a new topic or issue.

Feedback: verbal and nonverbal reactions of an interview party.

Feelings: emotions such as pride, fear, love, anger, and sympathy.

Fee-paid positions: when an organization retains a placement agency to locate qualified applicants and pays fees the agency would normally charge applicants.

Filter strategy: a question strategy that enables the interviewer to determine an interviewee's knowledge of a topic.

First impression: the initial impression one makes on another as a result of appearance, dress, manner, and quality of communication.

Flexibility: the ability to adapt during interviews to unexpected exchanges, answers, information, or attitudes.

Focus group interviews: a small group of people (6 to 12) act as an interviewee party with a highly skilled interviewer who asks a carefully selected set of questions that focus on a specific topic.

Framing: how we use language to construct the way we see people, places, things, and objects.

Frequency interval scales: questions that ask respondents to select a number that most accurately reflects how often they do or don't use or do something.

Functional résumé format: a résumé in which an applicant places experiences under headings that highlight qualifications for a position.

Funnel sequence: a question sequence that begins with a broad, open-ended question and proceeds with ever-more restricted questions.

Gender: how interview parties being female or male affects interview interactions.

General inquiry questions: an opening question that determines why an interviewee (often a medical patient) has initiated an interview.

Generic message: a persuasive message designed for a variety of audiences rather than a specific targeted audience.

Getting through questions: questions in counseling interviews designed to enable interviewees to manage their emotions.

Global relationships: relationships between parties from different countries and cultures.

Goal oriented: an interaction in which the interviewer is goal or task oriented rather than people oriented.

Ground rules: rules governing an interview agreed to by both parties.

Group interview: an interview in which there are multiple interviewers, such as several journalists at a press conference.

Guessing question pitfall: when a questioner attempts to guess information instead of asking for it.

Gunnysacking: the practice of storing up grievances before dumping them on an interviewee (often an employee) all at once.

Halo effect: when an interviewer gives favorable ratings to all job duties when an interviewee excels in only one.

Hasty generalization tactic: a person generalizes to a whole group of people, places, or things from only one or a few examples.

Highly closed questions: questions that can be answered with a single word or short phrase, most often a yes or no.

Highly directed reactions and responses: when an interviewer offers ultimatums and strong advice.

Highly nondirective reactions and responses: when an interviewer offers no information, assistance, or evaluations but encourages the interviewee to communicate, analyze, and be self-reliant.

Highly scheduled interview: a schedule in which the interviewer prepares all questions and their exact wording prior to an interview.

Highly scheduled standardized interview: a schedule in which the interviewer prepares all questions and their exact wording as well as answer options prior to an interview.

Historical critical incident question: a question that asks applicants how they would have resolved a problem the recruiter's organization faced in the past.

Honesty tests: tests designed to assess the ethics, honesty, and integrity of job applicants.

Hourglass sequence: a question sequence that begins with open questions, proceeds to closed questions, and ends with open questions.

Hyperpersonal revelations: highly personal (perhaps intimate) revelations of a person during an interview that reveals too much information.

Hypothetical question: a hypothetical but realistic question that asks respondents how they would handle a situation or problem.

Identification theory: a theory that persons persuade others by identifying with them in a variety of ways.

Idioms: expressions unique to a culture or nation likely to be misunderstood by a person from a different culture or nation.

Imagery: creating pictures or images in a person's mind through highly descriptive language.

Implicative approach: an approach that withholds an explicit statement of purpose or intent until the interviewee sees the implications and suggests a course of action.

Individualist culture: a culture that places high value on self-image, self-esteem, self-reliance, self-awareness, and individual achievement.

Induced compliance theory: a theory designed to change thinking, feeling, or acting by inducing others to engage in activities counter to their values, beliefs, or attitudes.

Inform: to provide information or knowledge to another party.

Information: stories, illustrations, comparisons, experiences, quotations, statistics, definitions, and explanations that apprise interview parties of problems, solutions, situations, and events.

Information-gathering interviews: interviews designed to obtain facts, opinions, data, feelings, attitudes, beliefs, reactions, advice, or feedback.

Information-giving interview: interviews designed to exchange data, knowledge, direction, instructions, orientation, clarification, or warnings.

Information overload: when interviewees are provided with more information than they can process or recall.

Informational probe: a question designed to obtain additional information when an answer appears to be superficial, vague, or ambiguous or to suggest a feeling or attitude.

Initiating the interview: the process by which an interview is arranged and started.

Inoculation theory: a theory based on the belief that it is often more effective to prevent undesired persuasion from occurring than trying damage control afterward.

Integrity interviews: interviews designed to assess the honesty and integrity of prospective employees.

Intelligent or educated interviewee: an interviewee with high levels of intelligence or informal and formal education.

Interactional: the exchanging or sharing of roles, responsibilities, feelings, beliefs, motives, and information.

Internet interview: an interview that takes place solely through the Internet.

Interpersonal communication process: a complex and often puzzling communication interaction with another party.

Interval scales: survey question scales that provide distances between measures.

Interview: an interactional communication process between two parties, at least one of whom has a predetermined and serious purpose, and involves the asking and answering of questions.

Interview evaluation: the formal or informal process of evaluating applicants following recruiting interviews.

Interview guide: a carefully structured outline of topics and subtopics to be covered during an interview.

Interview schedule: a list of questions an interviewer prepares prior to an interview.

Interviewee: the party who is not in basic control of the interaction, such as a respondent in a survey interview or an applicant in a recruiting interview.

Interviewer bias: when respondents give answers they feel questioners want them to give rather than express their true feelings, attitudes, or beliefs.

Inverted funnel sequence: a sequence that begins with closed questions and proceeds toward open questions.

Jargon: words that organizations or groups alter or create for specialized use.

Job/career fairs: gatherings of recruiters from a variety of organizations on college campuses or malls in which applicants can obtain information, make contacts, and take part in interviews.

Joblike situations: simulated job situations through questions or role playing that enable the recruiter to perceive how an applicant might act on the job.

Joint actions: when interview parties understand that what each does will impact the other and act in the other's party's interest.

Journalist's interview guide: a guide that focuses on who, what, when, where, how, and why.

Just cause: the fair and equitable treatment of each employee in a job class.

Key informant: a person who can supply information on situations, assist in selecting interviewees, and aid in securing interviewee cooperation.

Knowledge workers: workers that create and access information rather than manufacture products and are valued for their knowledge, ability to motivate others, and teamwork.

Language strategies: the strategic use of language in human interactions and expressions.

Law of recency: people tend to recall the last thing said or done in interviews.

Lay counselor: a person with little or no formal training in counseling.

Lay theories: commonsense theories patients hold about health care that often resist scientific notions and research findings.

Leading question: a question that suggests implicitly or explicitly the expected or desired answer.

Leaning question strategy: a question strategy that enables interviewers to reduce the number of undecided and don't know responses in surveys.

Learning organization: an organization that places high value on knowledge, skills, competencies, opportunities for learning, and employees as intellectual capital.

Leave-taking: the effort to bring an interview to a close.

Length of service error: when an interviewer assumes that present performance is high because past performance was high.

Letters of recommendation: letters sent by references to prospective employers on behalf of persons applying for specific positions.

Level 1 interactions: interactions that are relatively safe and nonthreatening.

Level 2 interactions: interactions that require a moderate degree of trust and may be moderately threatening because of exchange of beliefs, attitudes, values, and positions on issues.

Level 3 interactions: interactions that require a great deal of trust because parties disclose fully their feelings, beliefs, attitudes, and perceptions on intimate and controversial topics.

Level of confidence: the mathematical probability that the survey is within an accepted margin of error.

Level of information: the amount and sophistication of information an interviewee has to offer.

Likert scale: interval scale questions that ask respondents to make judgments about persons, places, things, or ideas.

Listening: the deliberate process of receiving, understanding, evaluating, and retaining what is seen and heard.

Listening for comprehension: receiving, understanding, and remembering messages as accurately as possible.

Listening for empathy: a method of communicating an attitude of genuine concern, understanding, and involvement.

Listening for evaluation: a means of judging what is heard and observed.

Listening for resolution: a means of mutually resolving a problem or task.

Loaded question: a question with strong direction or dictation of the answer desired through the use of name calling or emotionally charged words.

Logical strategies: the development of arguments into apparently valid and acceptable patterns.

Longitudinal study: a study to determine trends in what is known, thought, or felt over a period of time.

Loose rater: an interviewer who is reluctant to point out weak areas and dwells on the average or better areas of performance.

Make meaning questions: questions in counseling interviews designed to determine what an interviewee is most concerned about in an interview.

Management by objectives (MBO) model: a performance review model that involves a manager and a subordinate in a mutual (50-50) setting of results-oriented goals rather than activities to be performed.

Margin of error: the degree of similarity between sample results and the results from a 100 percent count obtained in an identical manner.

Marginalized respondent: a respondent who is unlikely to be surveyed because of culture, demographics, or lack of a telephone or easily accessed telephone number or residential address.

Matching process: the process of matching an applicant with a specific position and organization.

Meaning making: actions and questions designed to evoke meaning.

Metaphorical questions: questions that include metaphors, such as "establishing a level playing field" or addressing a company as a "family."

Millennial generation: the generation born from the early 1980s to around 2004.

Mirror probe: a question that summarizes a series of answers to ensure accurate understanding and retention.

Moderately scheduled interview: a schedule in which the interviewer prepares all major questions with possible probing questions under each prior to an interview.

Motives: values such as security, belonging, freedom, ambition, and preservation of health.

Multisource feedback: feedback from a number of sources.

Mutual product: when the results of interviews depend upon the contributions of both parties.

Naming: the labeling of people, places, or things to make them appear different, to alter perceptions of reality.

Negative face: the desire to be free of imposition or intrusion.

Negative politeness: an effort to protect another person when negative face needs are threatened.

Negative selling: the attempt to persuade by attacking another or another's proposal rather than supporting yourself or your proposal.

Network tree: a listing of names, addresses, and telephone numbers of primary contacts who can provide leads for job openings and additional contacts.

Networking: creating a list of contacts for possible employment positions.

Neutral question: a question that allows a respondent to determine an answer with no overt direction or pressure from the questioner.

Neutralize: any effort to remove an obstacle to making a favorable impression or attaining a position, including recruiter questions that violate EEO laws.

Nexting: verbal and nonverbal signals from one party that it is time for the other party to enter into the interaction or to become silent.

Noise: anything that may interfere with the communication process, such as machinery, ringing telephones, doors opening and closing, others talking, traffic, and music.

Nominal scales: questions that provide mutually exclusive variables and ask respondents to pick or name the most appropriate.

Nondirective approach: an interview in which the interviewee controls subject matter, length of answers, climate, and formality.

Nondirective reaction: when an interviewer reacts to a client without giving advice or specific direction.

Non-probability sampling: when a survey taker does not know the chance each member of a population has of being interviewed.

Nonscheduled interview: an interview guide of topic and subtopics with no prepared questions prior to an interview.

Nontraditional forms: newer forms of interviewing such as focus groups, videoconferences, e-mail interviews, and virtual interviews.

Nonverbal closing actions: nonverbal actions that signal a closing is commencing, such as leaning forward, uncrossing legs, breaking eye contact, and offering to shake hands.

Nonverbal communication: nonverbal signals such as physical appearance, dress, eye contact, voice, touches, head nods, hand shakes, and posture.

Nonverbal interactions: nonverbal signals such as physical appearance, dress, eye contact, voice, touches, head nods, hand shakes, and posture.

Normative competence: when an interview party understands the parts each party will play in a relationship and develops workable rules and norms.

Normative influence: a person's beliefs of which behaviors important individuals or groups think are advisable or inadvisable to perform.

Nudging probe: a word or brief phrase that urges a respondent to continue answering.

Numerical interview scales: questions that ask respondents to select a range or level that accurately reflects an age, income level, educational level, and so on.

Observing: paying close attention to surroundings, people, dress, appearance, and nonverbal communication.

Off the record: information that cannot be reported following an interview.

Open question: a question that allows the respondent considerable freedom in determining the amount and kind of information to offer.

Open-to-closed pitfall: when a questioner asks an open question but changes it to a closed question before a respondent can reply.

Opening: the first minutes of an interview in which the interviewer attempts to establish rapport and orient the interviewee.

Opening question: the initial question during the body of an interview.

Opening techniques: verbal and nonverbal signals that establish rapport and orient the interviewee.

Order bias: possible influence on how interviewees respond due to the order of answer options in survey questions.

Ordinal scales: questions that ask respondents to rate or rank options in their implied relationship to one another.

Orientation: the portion of the opening in which the interviewer explains the purpose, length, and nature of the interview.

Outside forces: influential others such as family, friends, employers, and agencies who are not part of the interview but may affect one or both parties before, during, or after an interview.

Overt identification: an attempt to establish a "we are one and the same" perception.

Panel interview: when two to five persons representing an organization may interview an applicant at the same time.

Paper trail: written materials that allow the tracing of an individual or organization's actions or opinions.

PAR method: when an applicant structures an answer by addressing an assigned problem or task, actions taken to solve the assigned problem or task, and the results or consequences of actions taken.

Party: the interviewer or interviewee side in an interview.

Patient-centered care (PCC): when a patient's needs, preferences, and beliefs are respected at all times.

Percentage agencies: placement agencies whose fee for finding positions for clients is a specific percentage of the first year's salary.

Perceptions: the ways people see and interpret themselves, other people, places, things, events, and nonverbal signals.

Personal interview: a survey interview that takes place face-to-face.

Personal space: an imaginary bubble around us that we consider almost as private as our body.

Personality tests: tests designed to assess the people skills of applicants.

Persuaders: interviewers who attempt to alter the ways interviewees think, feel, and/or act.

Persuasive interviews: an interview designed to change an interviewee's way of thinking, feeling, and/or acting.

Phases of counseling interviews: a structural format for counseling interviews such as the sequential phase model developed by Hartsough, Echterling, and Zarle.

Pitchfork effect: when an interviewer gives negative ratings to all facets of performance because of a particular trait the interviewer dislikes in others.

Placement agency: an agency that provides services such as career counseling, résumé preparation, employer contacts, and interview opportunities for those seeking positions.

Placement interviews: interviews designed to assign employees to positions or to move them from one position or location to another.

Polarizing: the attempt to limit choices or positions to polar opposites.

Politeness theory: a theory that claims all humans want to be appreciated, approved, liked, honored, and protected.

Population: all persons able and qualified to respond in a particular survey.

Portfolio: a small and varied collection of an applicant's best work.

Positive attention: attention that generates recruiter interest in an applicant.

Positive face: the desire to be appreciated, approved, liked, and honored.

Positive politeness: an effort to show concern by complimenting and using respectful forms of address.

Post hoc or scrambling cause-effect tactic: basing a cause-effect relationship on coincidence, a minor cause, or a single cause.

Power speech: words that express certainty, challenges, verbal aggression, and metaphors.

Powerless speech: words and nonfluencies that express apologies, disclaimers, excuses, and uncertainty.

Precision journalism: journalistic reports based on survey research data.

Predetermined: planned in advance of an interaction.

Press conference: a setting in which multiple interviewers interview one interviewee.

Pretest: the test of an interview schedule with a small sample of respondents prior to a survey to detect possible problems that might result during the survey.

Primary question: a question that introduces a topic or new area within a topic and can stand alone out of context.

Privacy: freedom from unwanted intrusion into or access to interview interactions.

Probability sampling: when a survey taker knows that each member of a population has a certain chance of being interviewed.

Probing: the attempt to discover additional information and understanding.

Probing question: a question that attempts to discover additional information following a primary or secondary question and cannot stand alone out of context.

Problems of the interviewee's behavior interviews: interviews designed to review, separate, correct, or counsel interviewees for their behavior.

Problems of the interviewer's behavior interviews: interviews designed to receive complaints, grievances, or suggestions concerning the interviewer's behavior.

Problem-solution sequence: an outline divided into problem and solution phases.

Problem-solving interviews: interviews designed to discuss mutually shared problems, receive suggestions for solutions, or implement solutions.

Process: a dynamic, continuing, ever-changing interaction of variables.

Prospecting: a systematic selection of interviewees who are good prospects for persuasive interviews.

Proximics: the study of how people perceive and use occupational, social, and personal space.

Proximity: the physical distance between interview parties.

Psychological reactance theory: a theory based on the claim that people react negatively when someone threatens to restrict or does restrict a behavior they want to engage in.

Psychological strategies: strategies designed to create psychological discomfort—dissonance—to alter ways of thinking, feeling, and acting.

Purpose: the reason or goal for a party conducting or taking part in an interview.

Qualitative survey: a survey in which findings are presented in textual form, usually words.

Quantitative survey: a survey in which findings are presented in numerical form, such as percentages and frequencies.

Question: any statement or nonverbal act that invites an answer.

Question pitfall: a slight alteration of questions, often unintentional, that changes them from open to closed, primary to secondary, and neutral to leading.

Question sequence: the strategic interconnection of questions.

Quintamensional design sequence: a five-step sequence designed to assess the intensity of a respondent's opinions and attitudes.

Random digit dialing: a system that randomly generates telephone numbers in target area codes and prefix areas for selecting a survey sample.

Random sampling: selecting respondents randomly from a container, a list, or group.

Ranking ordinal scale: questions that ask respondents to rank options in their implied relationship to one another.

Rapport: a process of establishing and sustaining a relationship by creating feelings of goodwill and trust.

Rating ordinal scale: questions that ask respondents to rate options in their implied relationship to one another.

Real setting: an interview setting with all of its defects and problems.

Reasoning from accepted belief, assumption, or proposition: reasoning based on the assertion that a belief, assumption, or proposition is true and without question.

Reasoning from analogy: reasoning based on points of similarity that two people, places, or things have in common.

Reasoning from cause-effect: reasoning based on a causal relationship.

Reasoning from condition: reasoning based on the assertion that if something does or does not happen, something else will or will not happen.

Reasoning from example: reasoning based on a generalization about a whole class of people, places, or things from a sampling of the class.

Reasoning from facts: reasoning that offers a conclusion as the best explanation for available evidence.

Reasoning from sign: a claim that two or more variables are related so the presence or absence of one indicates the presence or absence of the other.

Recall: the ability of an interview party to remember and report accurately what took place during an interview, including agreements, information exchanged, attitudes, and climate.

Recency error: when an interviewer relies too heavily on the most recent events or performance levels.

Reciprocal concessions: the effort to instill a sense of obligation in another to make a concession after the other party has made one.

Recording: taking mental or physical note of what is taking place during an interview.

References: names of persons applicants give to prospective employers who can provide assessments of their qualifications for positions.

Reflective probe: a question that reflects the answer received to verify or clarify what the respondent intended to say.

Reinforce: strengthening or making stronger.

Rejection then retreat: the persuader retreats to a second or fall back option if the interviewee rejects the preferred proposal.

Relational: an interpersonal connection between two parties or persons.

Relational dimensions: critical dimensions such as similarity, inclusion, affection, and trust that determine the nature of relationships.

Relational distance: the closeness of the relationship between interview parties.

Relational history: the past, present, and future connections between two parties or persons.

Relational memory: what interview parties remember from previous encounters with one another.

Relational uncertainty: when either party is unaware of the degree of warmth, sharing of control, or level of trust that will exist during an interview.

Relationship: an interpersonal connection between parties that influences their interest in the outcome of the interview.

Reliability: the assurance that the same information can be collected in repeated interviews.

Repeat question strategy: a question strategy that enables the interviewer to determine interviewee consistency in responses on a topic.

Replicability: the ability to duplicate interviews regardless of interviewers, interviewees, and situations.

Report: a formal or informal recording of the information attained during an interview.

Reproducibility: the ability to duplicate interviews regardless of interviewer, interviewee, and situation.

Research: a careful search for background materials, information, facts, and theories pertaining to a subject, person, or organization.

Restatement probe: a question that restates all or part of the original question that remains unanswered.

Résumé: a brief accounting of an applicant's career goal, education, training, and experiences.

Résumé or application form question pitfall: asking a question that is already answered on the résumé or application form.

Reticent interviewee: an interviewee who seems unwilling or unable to talk and respond freely.

Role competence: the ability of an interview party to play the roles of interviewer and interviewee effectively.

Rule of reciprocation: instills in an interviewee a sense of obligation to repay in kind what another provides.

Sample point or block sampling: preassigned numbers and types of respondents are chosen from assigned geographical areas.

Sample size: the number of persons interviewed during a survey when the whole population is too large to interview.

Sampling principles: principles that create a sample that accurately represents the population under study.

Scannable résumé: a résumé designed specifically to be scanned effectively by electronic software used by recruiters.

Scanning software: computer software that enables recruiters to scan résumés electronically to reduce the time required to select applicants to be interviewed.

Screening interviews: interviews designed to select applicants for additional interviews.

Selection interview: an interview in which the purpose is to select a person for employment or membership within an organization.

Self: focus of the interviewee on the interviewee during a counseling interview.

Self-analysis: a careful, thorough, and insightful analysis of self an applicant conducts prior to taking part in interviews.

Self-concept: how a person perceives self physically, socially, and psychologically.

Self-disclosure: the willingness and ability to disclose information pertaining to oneself.

Self-esteem: positive and negative feelings a person has of self.

Self-evident truth: a claim that a question or issue is not arguable because it is settled by rule or fact.

Self-fulfilling prophecy: a prediction that comes true because a person expects or predicts it will be so.

Self-identity: how, what, and with whom people identify themselves.

Self-persuasion: a situation in which a persuader encourages a person to persuade self rather than being persuaded by another.

Self-selection: when respondents alone determine if they will be included in a survey sample.

Seminar format: an interview format in which one or more recruiters interview several applicants at the same time.

Sequential phase model: a counseling model that cen-ters on four phases based on affective (emotional) and cognitive (thinking) functions.

Sex: the genders of interview parties.

Shock-absorber phrases: phrases that reduce the sting of critical questions.

Shuffle strategy: a question strategy that enables interviewers to avoid responses based on the order rather than the content of answer options.

Silence: the absence of vocal communication from one or both parties in an interview.

Silent probe: when an interviewer remains silent after an answer and may use nonverbal signals to encourage the respondent to continue answering.

Similarity: characteristics, experiences, interests, beliefs, attitudes, values, and expectations interview parties have in common.

Situation: a total interview context that includes events prior to and after, time, place, and surroundings.

Situational schema: a schema that includes all of the different types of interviews.

Skip interval or random digit sample: a sampling method in which every predetermined number on a list is selected, such as every 10th name in a directory.

Skype: a program that enables interviewers and interviewees to communicate instantly over the Internet by using a microphone and webcam.

Slang: unofficial jargon that groups use.

Slogan or tabloid thinking: a clever phrase that encapsulates a position, stand, or goal of a persuader.

Social media: blogs and Web sites such as My Space and Facebook that interviewers and interviewees use to interact socially with others.

Sound-alikes: words that sound alike but have different meanings.

Space sequence: an outline that arranges topics and subtopics according to spatial divisions such as left to right, north to south.

Standard/learned principle: principles people learn through life that automatically guide actions and decisions.

STAR method: when an applicant structures an answer in four parts by addressing the situation, the task, the action taken, and the results of this action.

Status difference: the difference in social or organizational hierarchy between interviewer and interviewee.

Stealth marketing: when a sales representative pretends to be a friendly, disinterested party rather than a sales representative.

Strategic ambiguities: the strategic use of words with multiple or vague meanings to avoid specific definitions or explanations.

Strategic answers: when interviewees answer questions to their advantage.

Stratified random sampling: a sampling method that selects the number of respondents according to their percentages in the target population.

Structure: a predetermined arrangement of parts or stages into a meaningful whole.

Supportive climate: a climate in which there is trust and respect between parties.

System: a degree of structure or organization that guides a planned interaction between two parties.

Table of random numbers: a sample of respondents selected by assigning each respondent a number and using a table of random numbers for picking a sample.

Talent or trait-based selection process: a recruiting interview in which all interviewer questions focus on specific talents or traits included in the applicant profile.

Talkative interviewee: an interviewee who gives overly long answers and talks too freely.

Task oriented: an interviewer who is more concerned with performing a task efficiently and effectively than in communicating effectively with an interviewee.

Team interview: when two to five persons representing an organization may interview an applicant at the same time.

Telephone interview: an interview that is conducted over the telephone rather than face-to-face.

Tell me everything question pitfall: an extremely open question with no restrictions or guidelines for the respondent.

Territorial markers: an imaginary bubble around us that we consider nearly as private as our body.

Territoriality: the physical and psychological space in which an interview takes place.

Test of job relatedness: effort to meet EEO laws by establishing legally defensible selection criteria, asking questions related to these criteria, asking the same questions of all applicants, being cautious when probing into answers, being cautious during informal chit-chat, focusing questions on what applicants can do, and steering applicants away from volunteering unlawful information.

The 360-degree approach: a performance review model that obtains as many views of a person's performance as possible from observers who interact with the person on a regular basis.

Thin entering wedge (domino effect or slippery slope) tactic: an argument that one decision, action, or law after another is leading inevitably toward some sort of danger.

Tight rater: an interviewer who believes that no one can perform at the necessary standards.

Time sequence: an outline that treats topics and subtopics in chronological order.

Timing: The strategic selection of time and date to maximize likelihood of success.

Too high, too low question pitfall: a question that asks for information that is beneath or above the interviewee's level of information or expertise.

Tongue-in-cheek test response: a pleasant, perhaps humorous response that sends a signal to a recruiter that he or she has asked an unlawful question.

Topical sequence: an outline sequence that follows the natural divisions of a topic or subtopic.

Traditional forms: standard types of interviews such as informational, survey, employment, performance review, counseling, and health care.

Traditional recruiter questions: common questions generations of recruiters have asked, such as where do you plan to be five years from now.

Transfer interviews: interviews designed to promote employees, to assign them to positions, or to move them from one position or location to another.

Transferring guilt: an effort to dodge an issue by turning the accuser, victim, or questioner into the guilty party.

Trial closing: the attempt to determine if an interviewee is ready to close an interview with an agreement of some sort.

Tunnel sequence: a series of similar questions that are either open or closed.

Tu quoque: an effort to dodge an issue or objection by revolving it upon the challenger or questioner.

Two parties: an interviewer and an interviewee party consisting of one or more persons with distinct roles and purposes such as getting and giving information, counseling and being counseled, persuading and being persuaded, recruiting and being recruited.

Undercover marketing: when a sales representative pretends to be a friendly, disinterested party rather than a sales representative. Also called stealth marketing.

Unintentional bipolar question pitfall: a question unintentionally designed to elicit a yes or no answer or a choice among two poles such as approve or disapprove when the interviewer desires a lengthy answer.

Unintentional leading question pitfall: a question unintentionally phrased to influence how an interviewee will answer a question.

Unipolar question: a question that has only one obvious or desired answer.

Universal performance interviewing model: a performance review that focuses on coaching by starting with positive behavior a manager wants the employee to maintain and then moving to behaviors that need to be corrected.

Unsanitized setting: a real-world interview setting with all of its problems, crises, interruptions, and unexpected happenings.

Upward communication: an interview in which a subordinate in an organizational hierarchy is attempting to interact as interviewer with a superior in the hierarchy.

Value judgments: each party must determine what is ethical according to personal and prevailing societal values in judging the degree of right and wrong, goodness or badness in diverse situations and actions.

Values: fundamental beliefs about ideal states of existence and modes of behavior.

Verbal interactions: words (arbitrary connections of letters) that serve as symbols for people, places, things, events, beliefs, and feelings.

Videoconference: technology that enables interview parties to see and hear one another and to interact in real time.

Virtual interview: an electronic interview employed most often for practice and simulation.

Web survey: a survey that is conducted over the Internet rather than face-to-face or over the telephone.

Webinar: a presentation to an audience on the Web that may become an interview if it is a collaborative exchange between two parties who ask questions and provide answers to one another.

Yes (no) question pitfall: a question that has only one obvious answer.

Yes-but approach: an approach that begins with areas of agreement and approaches points of disagreement after goodwill and a supportive climate are established.

Yes-yes approach: the attempt to get another party in the habit of saying yes so agreements may continue.

AUTHOR INDEX

SUBJECT INDEX